READING THE TALE OF GENJI

ITS PICTURE SCROLLS, TEXTS AND ROMANCE

Errata
Page 94, line 8   「は」 → 「君は」
Plate 6.1 Credit should read: From *Le Roman de la Rose*
The British Library Board (Harley 4425, f. 12v)
Plate 6.5 Credit should read: From the *Haft Paykar*, by Nizami.
The British Library Board (Or. 12208, f. 220)

Detail from *The Tale of Genji Illustrations, The Bell Cricket II*, Gotoh Museum, Tokyo. [See plate 2.4]

Reading
The Tale of Genji
Its Picture-Scrolls, Texts and Romance

☙

Edited By

Richard Stanley-Baker, Murakami Fuminobu
and Jeremy Tambling

GLOBAL
ORIENTAL

READING *THE TALE OF GENJI*
ITS PICTURE-SCROLLS, TEXTS AND ROMANCE

Edited by Richard Stanley-Baker, Murakami Fuminobu and Jeremy Tambling

First published 2009 by
GLOBAL ORIENTAL LTD
PO Box 219
Folkestone
Kent CT20 2WP
UK

www.globaloriental.co.uk

© Global Oriental 2009

ISBN 978-1-905246-75-5

All rights reserved. No part of this publication
may be reproduced or transmitted in any form or
by any electronic, mechanical, or other means,
now known or hereafter invented, or in any
information storage or retrieval system, without
prior permission in writing from the publishers.

British Library Cataloguing in Publication Data
A CIP catalogue entry for this book is available
from the British Library

Set in Plantin 10 on 12 point by Mark Heslington, Scarborough, North Yorkshire
Printed and bound in England by CPI Antony Rowe, Chippenham, Wiltshire

Contents

※

Plate section faces page 110

Preface	*vii*
A Note to the Reader	*ix*
List of Plates	*xi*
List of Contributors	*xiii*
Introduction: Reading *The Genji Scrolls* and *The Tale of Genji* RICHARD STANLEY-BAKER, MURAKAMI FUMINOBU AND JEREMY TAMBLING	*xv*

PART I: READING *THE GENJI SCROLLS*

1. Scripting the Moribund: *The Genji Scrolls*' Aesthetics of Decomposition
   REGINALD JACKSON 3

2. The Narration of Tales, The Narration of Paintings
   SANO MIDORI (TRANSLATED BY SINEAD KEHOE) 37

PART II: READING THE *GENJI* TEXTS

3. Displacements of Conquest, or Exile, *The Tale of Genji*, and Post-Cold War Learning
   RICHARD H. OKADA 63

4. Person, Honorifics and Tense in *The Tale of Genji*
   MURAKAMI FUMINOBU 80

PART III: READING THE *GENJI* ROMANCE

5. 'Kiritsubo': *Genji*, Spacing and Naming
   JEREMY TAMBLING 103

6. *Genji* and the Gardens of Medieval Romance 132
   RICHARD STANLEY-BAKER

Appendix: Key to *The Tale of Genji* chapter titles, with lists of
attributed teams 171

Bibliography of Japanese Sources 175

General Index 180

Author Index 186

Preface

☙

The genesis of this project took place initially among the three editors at the University of Hong Kong (though two of them are no longer in the university), coming from three departments in the Faculty of Arts – Fine Arts, Comparative Literature and Japanese Studies. For completing this project, we owe a debt for a support from a university grant at the University of Hong Kong which helped fund initial developments. Our thanks however, are due to scholars not only from the University of Hong Kong but from many other universities who have helped us: especially Richard Bowring at Cambridge and colleagues in Art and Architecture and in East Asian Studies at Princeton, particularly Shimizu Yoshiaki and Richard Okada, who invited one of the editors, Richard Stanley-Baker, as a visiting professor in 2000. Scholars in Japan were approached, and Egami Yasushi, formerly of the Tokyo National Research Institute of Cultural Properties, and Takahashi Tōru of Nagoya University provided us with material which we planned to include, but were unable to secure sufficient funding for illustrating a project which was initially quite heavily art and calligraphy oriented. Although in the end, to our regret, we were not able to include these materials, we wish to express our gratitude for their enthusiasm and support.

We thank our families and friends. We are especially grateful to Sally Stewart and Heather Stanley-Baker for so much invaluable time spent copy-editing. Also our thanks go to Pauline Tambling, Kiyama Tomoko and Nanako. To Annie Carver we owe a debt for constant inspiration and support. And not least we would like to thank the late Helen Stanley-Baker, mother of Richard, for her constant support and very kind contribution towards illustrations costs.

A Note to the Reader

☙

Japanese names appear in Japanese order (surname or family name followed by personal name, as in Egami Yasushi) in all cases except where the publication is in English and the name appears in the reversed English order, as in Haruo Shirane.

Genji monogatari emaki 源氏物語絵巻 (*The Tale of Genji Picture Scrolls*) are currently housed at the Tokugawa (Nagoya) and Gotō Museums (Tokyo), with the exception of one piece in the Tokyo National Museum. The textual excerpts are more widely distributed, with many of the fragments in Japanese private collections. In 1937, the scroll materials were, for preservation purposes, taken apart and single leaves of paintings and double leaves of text were placed in wooden boxes. Therefore, the work is no longer in the scroll format. But hereafter we call them *The Tale of Genji Picture Scrolls*, or *The Tale of Genji Scrolls* or just the *Genji Scrolls*, sometimes the *Genji Scrolls* (T/G). In contrast, Yamamoto Shunshō's 山本春正 *E-iri Genji monogatari* 絵入源氏物語 produced in the seventeenth century is called *The Illustrated Tale of Genji*.

The Japanese and English texts of *The Tale of Genji* we used are:

Yamagishi Tokuhei 山岸徳平 ed., *Genji monogatari* 源氏物語 (*The Tale of Genji*), *Iwanami nihon koten bungaku taikei* 岩波日本古典文学大系 (*Iwanami Compendium of Classical Japanese Literature*) (Tokyo: Iwanami Shoten, 1957–1968) (NKBT volume: page).

Yanai Shigeshi 柳井滋, et al. eds., *Genji monogatari* (*The Tale of Genji*), *Iwanami shin nihon koten bungaku taikei* 岩波新日本古典文学大系 (*New Compendium of Classical Literature*) (Tokyo: Iwanami Shoten, 1993–1997) (SNKBT volume: page).

Abe Akio 阿部秋生, Akiyama Ken 秋山虔 and Imai Gen'e 今井源衛 eds., *Genji monogatari* (*The Tale of Genji*), *Shōgakukan nihon koten bungaku zenshū* 小学館日本古典文学全集 (*Shōgakukan Compendium of Classical Japanese Literature*) (Tokyo: Shōgakukan, 1970–1976) (NKBZ volume: page).

Abe Akio, et al. eds., *Genji monogatari* (*The Tale of Genji*), *Shinpen Shōgakukan nihon koten bungaku zenshū* 新編小学館日本古典文学全集 (*New Shōgakukan Compendium of Classical Japanese Literature*) (Tokyo: Shōgakukan, 1994–1998) (SNKBZ volume: page).

The Tale of Genji translated by Edward G. Seidensticker (Harmondsworth, New York, Ringwood, Ontario, and Auckland: Penguin, 1981; New York: Alfred Knopf, 1976, 1985) ('Seidensticker' or 'S').

The Tale of Genji translated by Royall Tyler (New York: Viking, 2001) ('Tyler' or 'T').

The Tale of Genji translated by Helen Craig McCullough in *Selections from Genji and Heike* (Stanford: Stanford University Press, 1994) ('M').

Paintings and text excerpts from *The Tale of Genji Scrolls* are referred to in italics (as in *The Bell Cricket*), while the chapters of the text on *The Tale of Genji* are given as, for instance, 'The Bell Cricket' ('Suzumushi') (in quotation marks).

List of Plates

ರಿ

Plate section faces page 110

CHAPTER 1

1-1   *Sanjūrokunin kashū*, Honganji, Kyoto.
1-2   *Heike Nōkyō*: Preface, frontispiece (Illustrated Lotus Sutra scrolls, offered by Heike clan; Jō-bon:*mikaeshi*). Itsukushima Shrine.
1-3   *The Oak Tree II*. Painting. Tokugawa Museum, Nagoya.
1-4   *Katsura-bon Man'yōshū*. Yamato Bunkakan Museum, Nara.
1-5   *Kōya-gire 2 Kokin wakashū*. Mitsui Bunkō, Tokyo.
1-6   *The Oak Tree I*, sheet 2. Tokugawa Museum, Nagoya.
1-7   *The Oak Tree I*, sheet 3. Tokugawa Museum, Nagoya.
1-8a/b   *The Oak Tree I*, sheets 1 and 2. Tokugawa Museum, Nagoya.
1-9   *The Oak Tree I*, sheet 2, detail, columns 4–8.
1-10 *The Oak Tree I*, sheet 3, detail of column 13: '*kakaru kokoro susumuru ya*'.
1-11 *The Oak Tree 1*, sheet 1. Tokugawa Museum, Nagoya.
1-12 *The Oak Tree I*, sheet 2, detail columns 5–9, with willow tree.
1-13 *The Oak Tree I*, 'yami', first column of sheet 2.
1-14a/b *The Oak Tree II*, sheets 3 and 4. Tokugawa Museum, Nagoya.
1-15 *The Oak Tree II*, sheet 5. Tokugawa Museum, Nagoya.
1-16 *The Oak Tree II*, sheet 3. Tokugawa Museum, Nagoya.
1-17 *The Oak Tree II*, sheets 3 and 4. Tokugawa Museum, Nagoya.
1-18a, 18b, 18c *The Oak Tree II*, sheets 2, 3, 4. Tokugawa Museum, Nagoya.
1-19 *The Oak Tree II*, sheet 8. Tokugawa Museum, Nagoya.
1-20 *The Oak Tree II*, sheet 4. Tokugawa Museum, Nagoya.
1-21 *The Oak Tree II*, sheet 6. Tokugawa Museum, Nagoya.
1-22 *The Law*: painting. The Gotō Museum, Tokyo.
1-23 *The Law*, sheet 1. The Gotō Museum, Tokyo.
1-24 *The Law*, sheet 1. The Gotō Museum, Tokyo.
1-25 *The Law*, sheet 2. The Gotō Museum, Tokyo.
1-26 *The Law*, sheet 5: *midare-gaki*. The Gotō Museum, Tokyo.

xii LIST OF PLATES

CHAPTER 2

2-1   (A and B), from *The Tale of Genji, Asaki yume mishi* (*Passing Dreams*).
2–1   (C), from *The Tale of Genji, Asaki yume mishi* (*Passing Dreams*).
2-2   *Evening Mist*. Gotoh Museum, Tokyo.
2-3   *The Ivy I*. Tokugawa Museum, Nagoya.
2-4   *The Bell Cricket II*. Gotoh Museum, Tokyo.
2-5   From *The Illustrated Tale of Wakeful Sleep* (*Nezame monogatari emaki*). Yamato Bunkakan Museum, Nara.
2-6   *Bamboo River I*. Tokugawa Museum, Nagoya.

CHAPTER 6

6-1   From *The Roman de la Rose*. Harley 4425, British Library.
6-2   The Kajūji villa, Kyoto.
6-3   Hōjūji reconstructed; Kanagawa Prefectural Museum, Yokohama.
6-4   *The Lady at the Bridge*. Tokugawa Museum, Nagoya.
6-5   From the *Haft Paykar*, by Nizami. British Library
6-6   *Bamboo River II*. Tokugawa Museum, Nagoya.
6-7   *The Bell Cricket I*. Gotoh Museum, Tokyo.
6-8   From the *Annual Ceremonies* scrolls, Tanaka collection.
6-9   Mōtsuji temple, Hiraizumi.

List of Contributors

೫

Reginald JACKSON is an Assistant Professor of Theater Studies and East Asian Languages and Literatures at Yale University. Having earned his Ph.D. from the department of East Asian Studies at Princeton University in 2007, he is currently completing revisions for his book manuscript, '*Midare* Performance and the Ethics of Decomposition', which examines tropes of degenerescence in relation to conceptions of virtuosity and the ethics of representation in medieval Japanese dance-drama and calligraphy. From 2005–2006 he served as a Fulbright Research Fellow at the Nogami Memorial Institute for Noh Drama Research in Tokyo. His new project, 'Re-Orienting Intensities: Afro-Asian Performance and the Politics of Gesture', explores the ways in which intensity, as embodied through gesture, exerts pressure upon the representational politics that underpin modern Japanese and African-American cultural production.

Sinead KEHOE is a Assistant Curator, Department of Asian Art at the Metropolitan Museum of Art, N.Y., and is a doctoral candidate at Princeton. She has written articles on Japanese art, including: *Princeton University Art Museum: Handbook of the Collections*. (Princeton, N. J.: Princeton University Art Museum, 2007; contributing author); in *Awakenings: Zen Figure Painting in Medieval Japan*. (New Haven, CT: Yale University Press, 2007; contributing author); '*Nisomandara-zō wo megutte*', *Kajima bijutsu zaidan kenkyū hōkoku*, no.22, Tokyo, 2005; 'Even Ten, but Only Once: Pure Land Patriarchs at Sentaiji Temple', *Transactions of the International Conference of Eastern Studies*, No. XLVIII, 2003.

MURAKAMI Fuminobu is Associate Professor at the Department of Japanese Studies, School of Modern Languages and Cultures, University of Hong Kong. He teaches Japanese language, literature, film and culture. He is author of *Postmodern, Feminist and Postcolonial Currents in Contemporary Japanese Culture* (Routledge: hardcover 2005; paperback 2009), *Ideology and Narrative in Modern Japanese Literature* (Van Gorcum, 1996).

H. Richard OKADA teaches Japanese literature and culture at Princeton University. He has been writing on TV dramas, the interfaces between ecology and Japanese culture, contemporary music, *zainichi* Korean matters and the institutional parameters of Japan studies. He is also editing a three-volume set of essays published in English on *The Tale of Genji* to be published by

Routledge. Recent publications include, 'The Possibility and Impossibility of *Zainichi* in *Go*', dealing with both the novel *GO* by Kaneshiro Kazuki and the film *GO* directed by Yukisada Isao, 'Areas, Disciplines, and Ethnicity', analysing the relations between scholarly disciplines and ethnicity, and 'Translation, Cosmology, and Gender' (in Japanese) critiquing recent studies of *The Tale of Genji* by American scholars.

SANO Midori, presently Senior Professor at Gakushōin University, Tokyo, has published eight books, namely *Genji monogatari emaki* (Illustrated Handscroll of the Tale of Genji) (Tokyo: Shōgakukan, 1981); *Ōcho-emaki to Sōshoku-kyō* (Illustrated Handscrolls of the Imperial Court and Decorative Sutras), Volume 8 of the Complete Works of Japanese Art series (Tokyo: Kōdansha, 1990. Author and Editor); *Nihon bijutsukan* (Japanese Art Museum) (Tokyo: Shōgakukan, 1997. Author and Editor); *Fūryū, zōkei, monogatari (Elegance, Formation, and Narrative)* Doctoral thesis (Tokyo: Skydoor, 1997); *Asahi hyakka Nihon no kokuhō* (The Asahi Series on the National Treasures of Japan) (Tokyo: Asahi shinbunsya, 1998–1999. Author and Editor); *Jikkuri mitai Genji monogatari emaki* (A Close Look at the Genji Scrolls) (Tokyo: Shōgakukan, 2000); *Chūsei no bi to chikara* (Beauty and Power in the Medieval Era) (Tokyo: Chūkōronsha, 2004. Co-Author); *Chūsei Nihon no monogatari to kaiga* (Medieval Japanese Narrative and Painting) (Tokyo: Hōsō daigaku (The University of the Air Press), 2004. Co-Author); *Kokka* no. 1358 *Tokushū Genji-e* (Special Issue: *Genji-e*) (Tokyo: Kokkasha, 2008. Author and editor). She has also been a Visiting Professor at Princeton, and participated in the Genji seminars there with Profs. Shimizu and Okada, and has published some seventy scholarly articles.

Richard STANLEY-BAKER taught at Hong Kong University from 1985–2005; at National Taiwan University from 1980–85; Professor at The University of Tokyo (1995–96); Visiting Professor at Princeton University (1999–2000. He translated from Japanese Takahashi Sei'ichirō's *Traditional Woodblock Prints of Japan* (Tokyo: Weatherhill, 1972); major articles include 'Japanese ink painting of the Muromachi Period', Grove ed., *The Dictionary of Art* (1996); 'Marching in Time: Muromachi Ink Painting and the Zhe School', in Richard Barnhart, *Painters of the Great Ming: The Imperial Court and the Zhe School*, (Dallas: Dallas Art Museum, 1993); 'Mythic and Sacred Gardens in Medieval Japan: Sacral Mediation in the Rokuonji and Saihōji Gardens', in *Sacred Gardens and Landscapes: Ritual and Agency*, Studies in Landscape Architecture (Washington, D.C. : Dumbarton Oaks 2007).

Jeremy TAMBLING is Professor of Literature at the University of Manchester, and before that, Professor of Comparative Literature at the University of Hong Kong. He is author of several books, and two forthcoming: *Allegory* in the 'New Critical Idiom' series (Routledge, 2009) and *Dante in Purgatory: States of Affect* (Brepols 2010)), both of which relate to his interest in critical theory and medievalism East and West. His most recent book is *Going Astray: Dickens and London* (Longman, 2008).

INTRODUCTION

READING *THE GENJI SCROLLS* AND *THE TALE OF GENJI*

RICHARD STANLEY-BAKER, JEREMY TAMBLING AND MURAKAMI FUMINOBU

❧

READING A CLASSIC: *THE TALE OF GENJI*

This book is a collection of six individual studies of *The Tale of Genji Scrolls* and *The Tale of Genji* texts, and attempts to explore how these two works could be related to comparativist and other critical dimensions connected with new critical theory. All six writers approach the *Genji Scrolls* and the *Genji* texts from standpoints aligned with the newer developments in late-twentieth-century critical theories – cultural studies, narrative painting, narratology, comparative literature and a global view of medieval romance. What is unique in this volume is not only the adaptation of the new critical theory to medieval Japanese artistic and literary works, but also the attention given to multidisciplinary and interdisciplinary aspects. Important in this aspect is the background of interdisciplinary seminars held at Princeton in the past few years by the art historian Shimizu Yoshiaki and Heian literature specialist Richard Okada, which led to the studies included here by those who participated, namely Sano Midori, Reginald Jackson and Sinead Kehoe who examine the *Genji Scrolls*. Many now tend to consider 'reading' this elaborate product with several sheets of text 'excerpts' (*kotobagaki* 詞書) for each painting, as an inseparable part of 'reading' the *Genji*. Thus, to read the *Genji Scrolls* and *Genji* texts in one volume is what we aim at in this collection of papers. In this regard, the first two chapters by Reginald Jackson and Sano Midori on the *Genji Scrolls*, and the succeeding two chapters by Richard Okada and Murakami Fuminobu on the *Genji* texts are particularly welcome as far as achieving this aim is concerned. Besides the multidisciplinary and interdisciplinary aspects, the study of Japanese texts in the Heian period in comparison with Western medieval texts, though each in their different cultural contexts, has not yet been fully updated. In this regard, we hope that the last two essays in this volume, written by Jeremy Tambling and Richard Stanley-Baker respectively, may help to redress that balance.

Let us ask first in this introduction why do we read the classics such as *The Tale of Genji Scrolls* and *The Tale of Genji* now? Jorge Luis Borges commented in 1938 on Arthur Waley's 1925 to 1933 translations of *Genji* into English.[1] He found in Waley an:

> ... almost miraculous naturalness, and what interests us is ... the human passions of the novel. Such an interest is just: Murasaki's work is what one would quite precisely call a psychological novel ... In Europe it would have been inconceivable before the nineteenth century. This is not to say that Murasaki is more intense or more memorable or 'better' than Fielding or Cervantes; rather that she is more complex, and the civilization to which she belonged was more refined.[2]

Borges' optimistic praise, however, has recently encountered the scepticism on the classics in general. For instance, Haruo Shirane and Tomi Suzuki in their *Inventing the Classics: Modernity, National Identity and Japanese Literature* argue that 'classics' have been 'invented' for nationalist purposes.[3] How then should we avoid the nationalistic response in our approach to a classic? In this regard, the last two chapters in this volume written by two of the editors of this book, Jeremy Tambling and Richard Stanley-Baker, could be seen as an attempt to subvert its nationalistic confinement by locating the *Genji* in a different space of European medieval romance. We hope the kind of alternative reading which they attempt to present here could be, as Richard Okada mentions in his own chapter, one way of beginning to displace nation-state parameters by looking towards different worlds of analysis.

Concerning the reading of the classics from a different perspective, Italo Calvino defines the classics in his posthumously published essay: 'Why Read the Classics?' It demands the reader's attention because of the power it has to command fresh readings and re-readings. Calvino provides fourteen definitions of a classic, and concludes his essay by saying that he should rewrite it so that people do not believe that the classics must be read because they serve some purpose. Rather, he says: 'reading the classics is always better than not reading them'. This point concludes his last two definitions of the classic: 'A classic is a work which relegates the noise of the present to a background hum which at the same time the classics cannot exist without ... [and] ... a classic is a work which persists as background noise even when a present that is totally incompatible with it holds sway.'[4] On that basis, *Genji* is essential reading both because it points up the incompatibility of a past text – a past way of constructing the world – with the present, and because it also has, according to Ōba Minako, a continuity with her present Japan.[5]

CHAPTER OVERVIEW

Part I of this book, entitled 'Reading *The Genji Scrolls*', consists of two chapters: Chapter 1, 'Scripting the Moribund: *The Genji Scrolls*' Aesthetics of

Decomposition' by Reginald Jackson, represents the work of a younger scholar, also a member of the Princeton seminars. This is a close reading of the elements in the calligraphy and paper décor in the excerpted text sections of two chapters, *The Oak Tree*, and *The Law*. Jackson, focusing on sickness and the moribund, makes fruitful use of recent developments in contemporary Japanese and Western scholarship and criticism, which highlight the complexity, subtlety and mutual responsiveness of the interrelated texts, painting, calligraphy and the decorated papers used for presentation of calligraphy.

Chapter 2, by Sano Midori, who has been an occasional participant in the Princeton seminars, examines *The Tale of Genji Scrolls* to reveal 'the narration of tales and the narration of paintings'. She explores issues in narratology that are native to the text, including the staging of narrative time, intertextual time, the 'here and now', and the contrasting staging of the 'story'. Sano analyses the 'reader's glance' over the 'painted story', its interaction with the 'voice' of the *kotobagaki* 'excerpt' texts, the 'ladies-in-waiting' and their relationship to the implied omniscience of the 'narrator's voice', and goes on to look at other voices who 'did not see all the details ...'. In addition, with reference to both text and its illustrations, she constructs the 'reader beyond the plot', and his or her experience and expectations with regard to 'reading the text'.

Part II, 'Reading the *Genji* Texts', consists of chapters on the *Genji* texts. Chapter 3 by Richard Okada, a leading member of the Princeton art and literature seminars, reminds us that there is no 'reading' of the text that would establish a 'true meaning', and that all meanings are historically positioned. Okada examines the role of *Genji* in the 'national literature' of Japan; the aesthetic displacements placed upon the text by patriarchalist Western scholars, the social and other ironies surrounding the notion of 'exile', and 'transgression' in the text and the affective displacements imposed by the text of *Genji vis-à-vis* traditions of criticism in the late-twentieth century.

In Chapter 4, Murakami Fuminobu examines 'Person, Honorifics and Tense in *The Tale of Genji*' and explains how the use of honorific particles in the classical text serves to identify otherwise unspecified characters in the novel, in order to articulate the character of the narrative voice and point of view, to widen the distance between character and narrator and to differentiate in subtle ways the distinction between character and narrator. Further, the uses of temporal particles 'き' and 'けり' serve to disclose and differentiate 'time of narration' and 'time within narration'. He maps precisely how narrative discourse in *Genji* is subtly, almost invisibly, manipulated by means of particles and honorifics in the classical language – features which are lost but somehow realized in different ways in translation.

Part III, 'Reading the *Genji* Romance', also comprising two chapters, examines *Genji* and European medieval romance in comparative perspective. Chapter 5 by Jeremy Tambling, '"Kiritsubo": *Genji*, Spacing and Naming', subjects the very first chapter of the *Genji* to close analysis in terms of developments in narratology, notably the criticism of Mikhail Bakhtin and Roland

Barthes, with reference to Chrétien de Troyes' Arthurian romances of the twelfth century, such as *Cligés*; *Eric and Enide* and *Yvain*. By locating the *Genji* in comparison with twelfth-century European romances, this chapter challenges the specialists' confinement in their own space and subsequently attempts to avert the nationalist purposes.

Chapter 6, '*Genji* and the Gardens of Medieval Romance' by Richard Stanley-Baker, also aims to locate the *Genji* in a globalized view of medieval romance, unrestricted by nationalist culture or place. This examines the medieval garden in Japan as a literary phenomenon in romance literature comparable to the imagery and literary strategies found in twelfth-century French and Persian romance. The polyphonic strategies in European romance texts, which include 'narrator's' comments or interventions, and a variety of plays on voice and identity in love stories, such as is found in Chrétien de Troyes' *Tristan and Iseut* and others. The gardens of *Genji* are compared with traditions in Western medieval literature such as the 'enclosed garden' (*hortus conclusus*) of allegories like the *Roman de la Rose*, or the *Haft Paykar*; they are found to be gardens of love and myth, and enjoy a taut proximity to historic gardens and their rituals; they are examined as tropes of earthly paradise (the *locus amoenus*), no less than spiritual paradises of purity and perfection, often mediated by gnostic canons; and further as *mandalas* of universal rule by the gentleman-sage-ruler.

NOTES

1. *The Tale of Genji: A Novel in Six Parts*, translated by Arthur Waley (London: Allen and Unwin, 1925–1933).
2. Jorge Luis Borges, *Non-Fiction 1922–1986*, Eliot Weinberger ed. (Harmondsworth: Penguin, 1999), p. 187.
3. *Inventing the Classics: Modernity, National Identity and Japanese Literature*, edited by Haruo Shirane and Tomi Suzuki (Stanford: Stanford University Press, 1999), pp. 11–14.
4. Italo Calvino, *Why Read the Classics?*, translated by Martin McLaughlin (New York: Pantheon Books, 1991), pp. 8–9.
5. Ōba Minako, 'Special Address: Without Beginning, Without End', *The Woman's Hand: Gender and Theory in Japanese Women's Writing*, edited by Paul Gordon Schalow and Janet A. Walker (Stanford: Stanford University Press, 1996), pp. 19–40.

Part 1

Reading *The Genji Scrolls*

1

SCRIPTING THE MORIBUND: *THE GENJI SCROLLS'* AESTHETICS OF DECOMPOSITION

REGINALD JACKSON

☙

OVERTURE

The Intendant knows his days are numbered. Having been possessed by a spirit, he has become gravely ill, and no remedy exists.[1] He realizes what little time remains, and must write – now. The ailing noble bolsters his gaunt body upon an armrest, and, taking up a brush, he stumbles out a letter. 'His tears flowed faster now, and he wrote his reply lying down, between bouts of weeping. The words made no sense and resembled the tracks of strange birds.'[2] The letter's script has splintered, interrupting his effort to convey meaning in its loathsome refraction of his faltering body: '… he wrote, but his hand was trembling badly, and he gave up saying all he wished'.[3] The disease has taken its toll: Kashiwagi can now manage to produce only a withered script. Moreover, the scroll composed to reproduce his plight is also fraught with injured scribble.[4] Sobbing, he composes a desperate poem to his lover:

> When the end has come, and from my *smouldering pyre smoke rises at last*, I know this undying flame even then will burn for you.[5]

Like the pyre smoke from his poem, death looms dark and close: along the scroll's surface, clouds of swarthy silver prowl towards the bedridden Kashiwagi as he wastes away.[6] Disgusted by the sight of his broken strokes, the Oak Intendant abandons his brush forever.

> *Within a fortnight, Kashiwagi is dead.*

READING INFIRM DEPICTIONS: PORTRAYALS OF ILLNESS AND CALLIGRAPHIC DISTENSION IN THE GENJI SCROLLS' *KASHIWAGI* AND *MINORI*

I think that illness does violence to language, and, by extension, to written and pictorial representations. As a motif, it taints several sheets of the *Genji Scrolls*, distending the calligraphic script brushed upon its sheets and plaguing their lavish patterns. My aim here is to investigate the mechanics of that distension. Over the course of this section, I will argue that illness is not only linked to specific modes of writing, but, moreover, that in certain textual and pictorial contexts, illness also manifests itself within that writing. Two central questions to be posed along those lines are: 'what elements constitute textual and pictorial portrayals of illness in the *Genji Scrolls*?' and 'What is the nature of illness' relationship to certain calligraphic techniques?' These are both facets of the larger question I will be addressing in this section, which is: what and how does illness signify in the contexts of the *Genji Scrolls*? Specifically, the primary goals of this exploration are to illustrate what role illness plays in writing and to demonstrate how illness alters and compels calligraphic writing in the *Genji Scrolls*. I will demonstrate the extent to which illness as a motif informs, directs and even *infects* the composition and choreography of certain textual and pictorial portrayals.

Although my discussion will be based upon the *Genji monogatari emaki* 源氏物語絵巻 (*The Tale of Genji Picture Scrolls*),[7] I will also refer frequently to passages from *The Tale of Genji* in order to link my analysis of the calligraphy and paintings in the *Genji Scrolls* with their most immediate textual source.[8] My hope is that my analyses of picture, paper and calligraphy will create an assemblage that resists exclusive classification as solely 'art historical' or 'literary' to the extent that it performs a mode of reading that undermines the narrowed interpretive scope of such a bifurcation. Like the *tangled-script* explored herein, these critical manoeuvres will necessarily disorient somewhat, but, hopefully will have a worthwhile outcome.

Illness is suffused throughout *Genji*: it taints the text and shades the *Scrolls*. In the pictorial, calligraphic and textual representations for 'Kashiwagi', in particular, its pervasive presence is undeniable.[9] As such, that is where I will concentrate my diagnosis. We will begin at the start of the chapter:

> The Intendant of the Right Gate Watch remained as ill as before, and meanwhile the New Year came. He saw his parents' grief and knew that willing himself to go would not help, since that would be a grave sin, but where was he to find the desire to cling to life?[10]

These are the chapter's first two sentences, and they highlight Kashiwagi's distress as well as his sickly condition. That illness appears here at the very start speaks to the motif's importance in the chapter as well as in the *Genji Scrolls*; its mention sets the tone for the rest of the 'Kashiwagi' chapter. Kashiwagi's affliction mounts gradually, consuming his body and psyche as it unsettles the people in his sphere of influence. It is, in fact, this ability of illness to unsettle, disturb, disrupt and injure – to inflict both corporeal and representational injury – that has captivated me most, and so, that will be the focal point of my analysis.

We learn very early on in the chapter that Kashiwagi does not have long to live. He decides to write a letter to Onna San no Miya, one of Genji's wives, with whom he has had a secret liaison and fathered a child (and who, by the way, has also been struck with illness):

> You must have had occasion to hear that everything may well be over for me soon. The news means so little to you that you do not even ask how I am, and I understand that, but still, your silence is bitterly unkind!' *he wrote, but his hand was trembling badly, and he gave up trying to say all he wished.*
>
> When the end has come, and from my smouldering pyre smoke rises at last, I know this undying flame even then will burn for you.[11]

In addition to his keen anxiety over preceding his parents in death, Kashiwagi is also troubled by his love's callous response to his sickly condition. This depression heightens the fatigue wrought by Kashiwagi's ailment, kindling the deterioration of his script, in turn. In this moment, Kashiwagi becomes physically incapable of an inscription characterized by gentility because his hand has betrayed his frayed, moribund constitution. What we observe in Kashiwagi's trembling hand, then, is more than an instance of emotional agitation: it represents his illness' incipient threat to writing manifested in physical terms.

We get a sense from the above quoted passage about Kashiwagi that he is troubled. (He is, after all, upset that Onna San no Miya has not inquired after him.) But we also discover that Kashiwagi's illness, in addition to Onna San no Miya's cold-hearted response to it, has marred his writing into nearly indecipherable scrawl. In trying to compose another poem, his hand falters further:

> … いとど泣きまさりたまひて、御返り、臥しながらうち休みつつ書いたまふ。言の葉のつづきもなう、あやしき鳥の跡のやうにて[12]
>
> His tears flowed faster now, and he wrote his reply lying down, between bouts of weeping. *The words made no sense and resembled the tracks of strange birds …* He felt even worse after this confused effort at writing.[13]

Before, Kashiwagi's writing merely quavered; now, it has splintered completely. This failed inscriptive attempt occurs after the first-quoted composition, and time has elapsed since then. Kashiwagi's sickness has worsened accordingly, and, consequently, his ability to write has deteriorated further over the course of this temporal shift. Note in particular here that the words Kashiwagi writes, 'made no sense and resembled the tracks of strange birds' [*ayashiki tori no ato*]. This detail is interesting, in part, because it implies that Kashiwagi has become dehumanized by his illness, as his writing takes on animalistic traits (and 'strange' ones at that).[14]

In the *Shichiyō seishin betsugyōhō* (1204), we find a pictorial reference roughly contemporaneous with the *Genji Scrolls* that suggests that the 'bird foot' motif coded specifically for the mental and physical impairments caused by illness.[15] Locating in this volume pictures of 'The Ogre causing fear of darkness and loss of control of the limbs' and 'The Ogre causing paralysis and constipation', we see that both ogres have chicken feet. Specifically, the 'Ogre of Darkness' has bird legs, while the 'Ogre of Constipated Paralysis' is painted with both bird legs *and* arms: there is clearly something about bird traits (and their feet in particular) that denotes sickness. Along these lines, we should also consider that 'a further distinguishing feature [of the ogres] is an arrow which is shot into the forehead of practically every figure. Their repulsive subhuman appearances together with the arrow may be interpreted as symbolic of the disease they carry with them.'[16] These figures' penetrations provide a telling hint of the pejorative significance of bird-like characteristics when used in reference to humans, and help us grasp better the derogatory import of those pedal traits' mentioned in 'Kashiwagi'.

Furthermore, a glance at the polyvalent possibilities of '*ato*' yields several relevant resonant options: bird *tracks*, *stains* of silver on the sheet, the spirit that has *remained* in Kashiwagi's body the *mark* of disease that the possessing spirit deposits in Kashiwagi's body, and the corporeal *pain* (suggested by the homophonic variant 痕 'scar' or 'wound') Kashiwagi no doubt feels, as well as the inscriptive injury represented in the ragged calligraphic columns found in the *Genji Scrolls*.[17] I see all of these valences as circulating within the signifying field surrounding and suffusing the 'Kashiwagi' chapter, as well as the calligraphic and pictorial interpretations produced, by extension.

Turning to the *Scrolls*, we see that the sub-humanity implied by the bird-foot reference evinces itself *in writing*. In other words, the boundary between humanity and inhumanity is drawn – and crossed – with the ink of Kashiwagi's simulated brushwork.[18] Note, too, that just as the sickness has wounded Kashiwagi's writing, his subsequent perception of that wounded writing worsens his condition, harming him more as a result of his 'confused effort'. More significantly, the phrase tells us that the illness that has rent Kashiwagi's ability to write has in turn ruptured that writing's signifying capabilities: the ailment has annihilated the very meaning writing is meant to convey. His writing 'makes no sense', its mutated materiality having alienated both the implied reader and Kashiwagi himself. This fracturing of linguistic coherence is a telling consequence of illness' inscriptive injury. In order to understand better the nature of the disruption that occurs when Kashiwagi attempts to write his letter, we should pause to consider further the nature of illness' injurious effect on language's representational capacity.

In *The Body in Pain*, Elaine Scarry outlines a typology of pain based upon its violent effects on language. Although Scarry's analysis is based primarily on the economies of pain that circulate between torturers and their victims, some of her insights are still applicable to this exploration of illness – and to Kashiwagi's case, in particular. As Scarry explains: 'A fifth dimension of physical pain is its ability to destroy language, the power of verbal objectification, a major source of our self-extension, a vehicle through which the pain could be lifted out into the world and eliminated.'[19] I think it appropriate to consider illness, as an experience of prolonged agony or psycho-somatic hurt, in relation to Scarry's model; therefore, I would like to posit illness as a sub-category within her rubric of pain.[20] Although Scarry comments upon a violence done to verbal objectification here, her insight can apply aptly to a discussion of writing, and of Kashiwagi's fractured script in particular.[21] Examining the *kotobagaki* 詞書き ('narrative calligraphic prefaces') of the *Kashiwagi* sets will provide us a better sense of how this linguistic collapse manifests itself in calligraphic terms.

ART HISTORICAL BACKGROUND

Prior to the Meiji Period, *The Tale of Genji Scrolls* (源氏物語絵巻) were known as the *Takayoshi Genji* 隆能源氏, after a late-twelfth-century imperial court artist named Fujiwara Takayoshi 藤原隆能 who was believed to have been the sole creator of the scrolls. However, analysis of the painting and calligraphy styles used in the scrolls indicated that several different artists had produced them.[22] The *Genji Scrolls* were produced by painters, calligraphers and paper designers affiliated with the *e-dokoro* 絵所 (Imperial Painting Bureau) during the mid-twelfth century.

Although art historian Sano Midori suggests a date of circa 1140 for the *Scrolls*, Gotō Museum Curator Tagoya Akira lists their date of production at roughly 1160.[23] Depending, then, on when we posit the *Genji Scrolls'* making, we might understand them either as foreshadowing the political and social upheaval of aristocratic society caused by the Hogen and Heiji Insurrections (保元の乱, 1156; 平治の乱, 1160), or as having been wrought in their aftermath. Significantly, Sano contextualizes the production of the scrolls within an imperilled, deteriorating social milieu; as she explains it, 'the *ritsuryō* legislative framework had already lost its form and the system of *kampaku* governance, which attempted to effect a consolidation of the most powerful court families' wealth and influence, had encountered its demise'.[24] Over the course of this chapter I will explore the multiple ways in which this 'death is encountered' (終焉を迎え) in the context of the *Genji Scrolls*, and I will return to reconsider Sano's point at the chapter's close.

Most of the scroll sections have been lost, but it is thought that at one time, sections that corresponded to each of *The Tale of Genji's* fifty-four chapters existed. Each scroll section consists of a painted interpretation of one scene from a particular chapter from *Genji*. Each of these is preceded by a calligraphic excerpt of the Genji text that relates the scene depicted in the painting. These *kotobagaki* were done in five different hands, with the most skilled calligrapher writing for the most famous scenes.[25] Sponsored by competing aristocrats, groups of artists worked closely as an ensemble to produce the scrolls; a head artist, or *e-shi* 絵師 would see to the *shita-gaki* 下書き or 'undersketch' (basically an outline of characters and architectural shapes) for each scene and then other painters who proceeded to overlay the pigments (e.g. crushed-shell white, malachite green, ferrous red, etc.).[26] There were also craftsmen who designed various papers upon which the specific calligraphy for each scene would be choreographed.

These papers could involve special dying techniques with substances such as pomegranate juice, or indigo, and often included striking overlays of mica powder (*unmo* 雲母), or any number of sprinklings of placements of cut gold or silver foil (*kiri-haku* 切り箔), 'wild hairs' ('*noge*' 野毛 also made of silver), or silver dust ('*mijin*,' 微塵 which oxidizes quickly, turning a dark-grey colour). These materials were coordinated to suit the thematic and emotional tenor of the chapter (as decided amongst the artists), and could be likened to the visual equivalent of a movie soundtrack, non-diegetic, but still crucial for setting the visual mood of the calligraphy and conveying meaning in ways more diffuse and less linearly communicative than the calligraphic script itself.

Each painting in the *Genji Scrolls* was originally preceded by a *kotobagaki* (narrative prefaces of varying lengths introducing their subsequent pictorial scene) and each *kotobagaki* provided a framing narrative to contextualize and foreshadow the scene depicted in the painting.[27] In the case of the *Genji Scrolls*, the *kotobagaki* represent the earliest extant version of the text of the *Tale of Genji*. The textual portions were excerpted by the craftsmen's patrons for their emotional interest, entertainment value, poetic and aesthetic appeal, and then the principal artisan would decide on how best to depict the scene described in the writing in pictorial form.[28] The patron would also select a particular calligrapher to write the text. In terms of paper design and the use of metallic elements, the *Genji Scrolls* take their cue from works like the *Honganji-bon sanjūrokunin kashū* 本願寺本三十六人歌集 (ca. 1112; Fig. 1-1: *Sanjūrokunin kashū*), and the *Heike Nōkyō* 平家納経 (1164) (Fig. 1-2: *Heikenōkyō jōbon*).[29]

Five calligraphic hands have been identified and both *Minori* and the three *Kashiwagi* sections are categorized together as having been done by the same person – considered by scholars like Akiyama Terukazu to have been the most skilled calligrapher of the group.[30] The *Kashiwagi I kotobagaki* is comprised of three sheets of dyed paper, each with an average height of 22 centimetres, and with a total length of 68.1 centimetres.[31] *Kashiwagi I* and *Kashiwagi II* are both believed to have been done by the same calligrapher, Fujiwara Sadanaga 藤原定長 (1139?–1202, also known later as the monk Jakuren 寂蓮),[32] and have been grouped together accordingly.[33] This calligrapher's style has been classified as belonging to the *Sessonji* 世尊寺 school lineage, founded by master calligrapher Fujiwara no Yukinari 藤原行成 (972–1027),[34] whose calligraphy is generally taken to represent the most archetypal example of the 'classic Japanese-style' (上代和様) of Heian *kana* 仮名 script.[35]

The sections *Kashiwagi II* (Fig. 1-15, sheet five) and *Minori* (Fig. 1-26, *The Law*, sheet five) stand out for the *midare-gaki* 乱れ書き, or 'tangled-script' that occupies their final sheets. This special type of writing, characterized by extremely rapid brushwork in which the brush rarely leaves the paper to create long sequences of connected characters whose vertical columns overlap such that they seem to 'tangle', represents a distinctive feature of the *Genji Scrolls*. Although this particular mode of writing is most pronounced in these sections of the *Genji Scrolls*, it should be seen as fitting within a broader context of other late Heian calligraphic texts such as the *Sekido-bon wakanrōeishū*

関戸本和漢朗詠集 (ca. 1050); *Katsura-bon manyōshū* 桂本万葉集 (ca. 1050; Fig. 1-4); and *Tōshi-gire* 通切れ (ca. 1120) by Fujiwara Sadazane 藤原定実 (1077? – 1120?), with which it shares perhaps the closest resemblance.[36] Significantly, all of these examples derive from the calligraphy style of Kōya-gire 2 style (高野切れ二種: Fig. 1-5), which is marked by a heightened velocity, greater propensity toward consecutive linking of individual characters, and a strong diagonal inclination of characters within columns.[37]

Although scholars have tended overwhelmingly to emphasize the *midare-gaki*'s significance as a major component of characters' 'psychological portrayal' (心理描写),[38] insofar as this reading relies most readily upon problematic assumptions about the status of *The Tale of Genji* as a work of 'romanticist literature' (ロマン主義の文学) and other inapt characterizations,[39] I have resisted its pull here. Instead, I have sought to shift the interpretive stress from the characters' minds to their bodies as a means of focusing more on the dynamic production of representations rather than any simple 'expressions' of interior emotion by subjects already posited and known. In this vein, reading and writing will be featured as a practice of self-constitution conditioned by ideological forces that exert pressures upon corporeal beings.

One of the primary goals of this investigation will be to highlight the ways in which the materiality of texts and bodies is perpetually configured, disfigured and refigured through the operations of apprehending ideological subjects and objects. From this point of introduction, I will now move to discuss the actual *Genji Scrolls*' paper decoration and calligraphy.

PAPER DESIGN / CALLIGRAPHY

On the second sheet of the first 'Kashiwagi' chapter section (*Kashiwagi I*; Fig. 1-6: *The Oak Tree I*, sheet two), the slivers of scattered *noge* 野毛 ('wild hairs') are roughly the same thickness as the lightest weighted script, which makes discernment of the lighter characters of the last seven lines of text more difficult, particularly in the upper hemistiches. Compare, for example, the calligraphy brushed over the *noge* in the first five lines of the sheet and notice that although that part of the sheet also has an area of *noge*, since the line weight of the calligraphy is thicker, the characters are more legible.[40] In the final several lines (beginning with the column that starts: '*heki nari ohomu me*') there appears to be a shift in line weight that interacts with the paper design in such a way that the calligraphic strokes in these columns blend in with the decorative elements more than those of previous columns. This is due to the lighter line weight and the coincidence of lightly brushed lines with a thin, loose array of comparably thin hairs. This blending also happens to occur at a point where the columns begin a downward slide towards the leftmost edge of the paper. One way to understand this slight decline is as a brief transitional shift onto the next sheet. The slant on this sheet (Fig. 1-6: *The Oak Tree I*, sheet two) foreshadows the steeper, more dramatic slope on sheet three (Fig. 1-7:

The Oak Tree I, sheet three): there, the columns' descent begins immediately – with the first line – and continues until the third-to-last line of the sheet.

This descent coincides with an increase in brush speed and a more sporadic weighting of characters. The first sheet's columns were all aligned parallel to the uppermost horizontal edge of the paper and the spacing between them – a periodic interstice of about a centimetre – was also consistent. After the fourth column of sheet two, however, the inter-columnar spacing scheme observed on the first sheet of *Kashiwagi I* falters, as does the regularity of line weight.[41] The heads of the columns are generally heavier in tone than the tails, which means that the tendency of the bursts' is to occur at the start of a line and then gradually taper in force as the brush plummets.[42]

In addition to the attenuation of line weight that occurs within some columns, we should also note the striking jump in the numbers of columns from sheet one to sheet two: there is an increase from thirteen columns to twenty (Figs 1-8a, 1-8b: *The Oak Tree I*, sheets one and two.).

In order for these extra seven columns to fit onto a sheet the same length as sheet one, the space between them must contract. We see, for instance, that this contraction in column width does not have to be uniform across all columns, and, in fact, sheet two does not depict a trend of even attenuation. In the first five columns of sheet two (Fig. 1-8b: *The Oak Tree I*, sheet two) the characters are wider and spaced farther apart than those of the subsequent lines. Moreover, from the fifth line on, a shift begins towards columnar superimposition, which, incidentally, also coincides with the intermittent pulses of ink-tone.

Part of this fitful rendering of the text has to do with the calligraphic convention in the *Genji Scrolls* of effecting a differentiation in tightly packed or superimposed columns by arraying them in groups (of three or four, usually) and augmenting the first line of each grouping (Fig. 1-9: *The Oak Tree I*, sheet two, columns four–eight).[43] In addition to making the cramped columns more distinct in their mutual contrast to one another, this technique also gives a sense of depth to the calligraphy, positioning the bolder lead lines with the foreground as the lighter columns seem to recede both below and behind them. The calligraphy is indeed rhythmic, and the dominant tempo appears to pulse with a triplet feel. The sheet begins with every other column made bolder, but near the middle of the sheet – with column seven – there are two consecutive units of three, followed by a swollen unit of four, and then another triple unit as the sheet closes. A simple chart of the oscillating column accents would look like this:[44]

20 19 18 **17** 16 15 **14 13** 12 11 **10** 9 8 **7** 6 5 **4** 3 2 **1**

This suggests that the sheet's implicit calligraphic rhythm involves a triple metre, with an occasional columnar beat added for good measure. The bold oscillation of the lines' tonal force and their movement both suggest a certain musicality. This echoes the textual references made earlier in the chapter to the religious rites taking place at Kashiwagi's bedside: 'The Great Rite and the chanting of the scriptures went forward amid a tremendous din' (T. 676), and 'The tall, fierce ascetic chanted the *darani* with wild and fearful power' (T. 676). Another possibility related to this one is that the muddle comes from Kashiwagi's consternation. For instance, Kashiwagi is shaken by all the noise around him: 'The patient just suffered from vague fears and at times only sobbed' (T. 676). Perhaps the most plausible reason for this disruption, however, is the mounting disruption attending Kashiwagi's illness.

Peeping a little farther ahead, we see that the beat kept on the previous sheet has been tempered slightly, but that the columns then collapse into the calligraphic landslide we witness on the third and final sheet of the *Kashiwagi I* set (Fig. 1-10: *The Oak Tree I*, sheet three).[45] The final sheet of the set sticks to the triplet pattern with a bit more regularity than the preceding sheet:

17 **16** 15 ~ ~ 14 13 12 **11** 10 9 8 7 6 5 4 3 2 **1**

Here, the heavier characters seem more dramatic than their counterparts on the previous sheet because they are moving in more than one dimension: their positions simultaneously change not only with respect to the x-axis, but to the y-axis as well. This accentuates the staggered decline of the columnar landslide.

Since the height of the first fourteen columns falls as we look leftward, the darker lines of characters seem to regulate the speed of the dive, marking its path like points along a parabola. In this case, the intervallic consistency of the emboldened columns' weight mitigates the pitch of the dive because it helps syncopate the columns' steady descent.[46]

One last point I would like to make here with regard to the columnar collapse and the increasing rapidity with which the *midare-gaki* surges ahead is the use of ditto strokes. Comparing sheets one, two and three of *Kashiwagi I*, we find that whereas the first two sheets had a combined total of five ditto marks, sheet three alone has *nine* of the marks. The presence of these stokes is important because it coincides with the increasing speed of the brushwork: the characters written in the *midare-gaki* mode displayed on sheet three are brisk. Consequently, their skimming script abbreviates repeated *kana* with a brief *ten* mark – indicated here with horizontal lines along the right side of the excerpted column – especially near the end of the sheet.[47] Certainly, this kind of abbreviation would be impossible without the allowance provided by certain words. Specifically, in column thirteen, we have: 'かかるこころすすむるや' ('kakaru kokoro susumuru ya') (Fig. 1-10: *The Oak Tree I*, sheet three, detail of column thirteen). We might romanize the ditto-marked phrase as: 'ka^ru ko^ro su^muru ya,' which gives more of a sense of this section's snippety appearance. Rather than the precise delineation of linguistic units, the rush of this ending *midare-gaki* passage signals the use of a brusque brushwork concerned more with displaying the writing's pained rapidity than a clear individuation of characters.

In terms of the paper design, the first sheet of the set is calmer in tone than the sheet that follows it. Although the overall pale greyish colour predominates and gives a dreary air to the sheet, the clusters of gold leaf brighten it a bit. There are three areas of gold leaf sprinkled on this first sheet, which appear to be arranged linearly (Fig. 1-11: *The Oak Tree I*, sheet one). If we were to crop the sheet after the ninth column (there are thirteen on the sheet altogether) and trace a line from the lower right-hand corner to the upper left-hand one, we would find that the clusters fall along that rough 45-degree line at comparable intervals. Each cluster corresponds to a point along that line: the first cluster of gold is the most compact and contains the largest pieces of leaf; the next, medial cluster has the smallest flakes and looks like a fairly dense atomized globe of gold; the line's terminal point is comprised of flakes roughly the same size as those of the first point, but their arrangement is more diffuse than the original clumping.

There are several (I count six) large square-shaped pieces of silver leaf drifting along the top of the sheet.[48] Besides the topmost cluster of gold flakes, these dark silver squares are the design element that is most conspicuous in the upper half of the first sheet; the bottom half is smoked in swaths of silver *mijin* 微塵 ('pulverized dust'), and therefore considerably darker in tone. The sheet is pretty plain, actually – despite the sparkles of gold. The main reasons for this are the overriding pale grey tone of the sheet, the neat regularity of the calligraphy, and the capacious gap that yawns between the areas of oxidized silver spread at the sheet's base and ceiling. That this sheet adjoins one of the most threateningly busy sheets in the entire *Genji Scroll* set flatters it even less, and this juxtaposition highlights the palpable shift in design (and thus mood as well) that takes place along the boundary of the sheet.[49]

A general observation to start with is that sheet two is just more striking than sheet one: the constellations of gold and silver are composed of larger foil flakes, there is much greater variation in the calligraphy's line weight and column height, and there is even a painting of two craggy, sagging, willow branches just to the lower left of centre-sheet (Fig. 1-12: *The Oak Tree I*, sheet two).

Another point of comparison, which was touched upon in the previous paragraph, has to do with the use of open space. There is a vacuum on sheet one that spans the entire length of the sheet and ranges from about ten to sixteen centimetres in height (Fig. 1-11: *The Oak Tree I*, sheet one). I think of this emptiness as the calm before the storm that breaks on the next sheet. There, the vacuum is suddenly filled with significantly darker clouds of silver oxide, massive chunks of gold and silver leaf, hairs, and even painted branches and boulders. There emerges an anticipatory clarity in the design of the first sheet, one that is shattered and sullied once the paper's leftmost border is crossed.

Also note the more crowded vertical orientation of these pieces of leaf in contrast to the amply spaced horizontal bearing of the silver squares at the top of sheet one (Fig. 1-11: *The Oak Tree I*, sheet one). While those of the previous sheet snubbed the pull of gravity, here, the squares of foil leaf seem to fall from the sky. Because these chunks' tumble overlaps with the sudden calligraphic stir that occurs around line five, I read it as an analogous representation of disorder and physical decline.

The area covered by the topple of *kirihaku* squares is also the area in which the calligraphy's columns fall out of line: from 'noshi tamahu' (line four) to 'miki tehu sukoshi' (line nine), the columns and the metallic squares succumb. The constrained bundle of columns echoes the awkward cluster of sliced silver and gold upon which it is brushed. Moreover, the superimposition of the infirm calligraphy over those squares heightens their muddled quality. A quick glance at the column just to the right of the jumble suffices to demonstrate this: since the *kirihaku* clog the gaps between these columns (five through nine), a visual friction is produced that retards a fuller line and inhibits legibility.

Looking at the lower hemistiches of columns six, seven and eight, we see that this sense of visual impediment has an actual material corollary. Specifically, the 'te' of 'mairite' (column six), the 'bito' and 'tsu' of 'hito-bito tsukurohi' (column seven) and the 'shi~ta' joint of kana from 'oroshi-tatematsuru' (column eight), are barely visible because the foil over which they've been brushed has refused their ink. (Fig. 1-12: *The Oak Tree I*, sheet two, detail columns five to nine).[50]

Unlike the surface of unadorned paper, whose plant fibres will absorb ink readily, the surface of metallic materials like the gold and silver *kirihaku* found here are not porous enough to allow ink to permeate easily: they subtly resist inscription. As a result, ink applied to such a surface is not as secure as that which has seeped into the paper, and in this case, it appears that the ink of the particular characters mentioned has been ghosted over the foil leaf squares to leave only the faintest surface trace (if any at all). The coordinated effect of these elements makes for a disturbing spectacle that, as we'll soon discover, is linked to 'Kashiwagi's' emphasis on illness.

The calligraphy's stammering character might also be attributed to the influence of the impinging billows of pulverized silver particles advancing from the sheet's right border. Columns one, three, five and seven of sheet two (Fig. 1-6) are all in contact with the dark grey masses of *mijin*; if the characters brushed over these clouds are to be seen, they must be written with more force than those written over a lighter pigmented background. Moreover, the increase in brush pressure must also be gauged in relation to the perceived impediment of the thicker paper surface. Decorative elements such as *noge*, *unmo* 雲母 (mica powder) and, in this case, *mijin* striations of varying densities, all alter the texture of the paper surface. In turn, they influence both the way ink reacts with the paper as well as the way the calligrapher reacts to the design the elements comprise upon that paper.

Whatever the reason for their emphasis, the characters near the heads of these lines resist the clouds' eclipse by virtue of their audacity. The boldest 'ya' of the entire three-sheet set, for example, is singularly poised directly in the centre of the cloud – the fourth character of the first column (Fig. 1-12: Fig. 1-13: *The Oak Tree I*, sheet two: 'ya-mi'). It is dark and wide, with a broad crossbeam, tight diagonal upswing from its cincture, and a terminal vertical stroke that stands perfectly erect.[51] Since the return stroke of the first 'ya' is a continuous diagonal sweep rather than a halted inward curl, it is more angular than the others, and therefore more commanding. Interestingly, this bold initial 'ya', besides being the strongest character of its kind on any of the sheets of *Kashiwagi I*, also happens to be a component of the first mention of illness to occur on sheet two.

The term sickness ('wazurai' 患ひ) was mentioned by Genji on the previous sheet, and now, here on sheet two, 'illness' ('yami' 病み) is reiterated (Fig. 1-13: *The Oak Tree I*, sheet two).[52] The two relevant phrases referring to illness here are:

わつらひたまふさま
(患い給う様)
'*ailing* appearance' (last line)

and

ことにおもきながやみ
(ことに重き長病み)
'particularly burdensome, prolonged *illness*'[53] (Fig. 1-8a, last line, sheet one, first line, sheet two, Fig. 1-8b)

Illness is a salient theme in the 'Kashiwagi' chapter, and we see here that it has infected the calligraphic array of the *Kashiwagi* scroll sets. These mentions of illness herald the progressive breakdown of the calligraphic order observed on other, more sound, sheets. The ink slackens sharply after the appearance of these phrases: the writing mirrors the protagonist's suffering.[54]

The word 'yowari' is important to note in analysing the calligraphy's visual character here. Its meanings can include 'to exhaust', 'enfeeble', 'break down' and 'weaken'. Looking at the last four characters of sheet two's first line ('yohari [tama]', (Fig. 1-6: *The Oak Tree I*, sheet two),[55] we see that the characters have faded in strength in a very short time; it was just ten characters prior that we glimpsed the vaunted *uber*-Ya. As if taking its cue from the meaning of the word 'yohari', the brushwork has itself weakened considerably. There is, for instance, an obvious discrepancy in line weight between the upper hemistiches of columns one and two, a discrepancy that has been incited with 'sickness' ('**ya**mi') and maintained with 'weakness' ('yowari').

Interestingly, the techniques used to accentuate '**ya**mi' call attention to the destructive force of illness on two types of characters: the *kana* and the protagonists themselves (in other words, 'ji' 字 and 'jin' 人). On this point, we should note that 'mi' homophonically marks the character '身,' which means 'body'. Via semantic overlap, this loosened 'body' is itself a 'character corpus' (*jitai* 字体) that has been altered and riven in response to the gangling body of the 'character' (*jinbutsu* '人物') described in the text. Seen from a polysemic perspective, that the 'み/身' has been broken here is not as strange as it might otherwise seem, because this is precisely the moment at which Onna San no Miya's body shifts to a more sickly state in the narrative depiction of her.[56]

Both the calligraphic techniques used to produce these characters and the style in which they have been written harmonize to highlight the corporeal damage wrought by illness. Instances such as this represent graphic moments at which the semantic and calligraphic registers of words coincide to produce a dramatic visual effect. In 'yami' and 'yowari's' case, we observe this phenomenon clearly.

SOUNDING OUT THE SCRIPT

Art historian Egami Yasushi notes about the paper of *Kashiwagi II* that sheets three to five (Figs 1-14a, 1-14b, 1-15, 1-17: *The Oak Tree II*, sheets three and four, sheet five) have been treated with the same scented dye (*kazome*) and that all three sheets also exhibit roughly the same sizes of sprinkled gold and silver leaf.[57] He goes on to account for the presence of the silver hairs (*gin noge*) by suggesting that they represent a boisterousness amidst an otherwise quiet scene; this is symbolic of the commotion caused by Kashiwagi's constant visitors, in Egami's opinion.[58]

Although I find his interpretation of the *noge* here quite interesting, I have difficulty accepting it, mainly because his characterization is inconsistent. Specifically, whereas in his discussion of the first two sheets of *Kashiwagi I* (Figs 1-8a, 1-8b: *The Oak Tree I*, sheets one and two), the silver hairs are part of a decorative ensemble that 'adds a flamboyance [to the sheet]', when the same material is used on sheet three, its connotation switches to one of disturbance.[59] I do not mean to suggest that Egami's interpretation is implausible; it is merely that by including *noge* among all of the design elements on sheets one and two, and then designating *all* of those different elements as fitting under a single heading, its specific change of use ends up being unaccounted for and its particular relationship to the themes of the chapter is erased.

However, having said that, I do think Egami's characterization of this particular decorative motif in *sonic terms* is both helpful and appropriate. Even the most casual glance at the *kotobagaki* for *Kashiwagi II* reveals a gradual change in mood. To characterize this shift in terms of sound does not seem at all inappropriate to me, but does it not make more sense to attribute this change not to the clumps of *noge*, but instead, to the more brazen bits of gold and silver? After all, these design elements are considerably stronger than the comparably light, measly slivers of silver. They are, for instance, much larger and more reflective than the hairs, so their capacity to alter a sheet's luminescence far outweighs that of *noge*: their visual effect is simply more intense and immediately perceivable. I do believe there is a gradually building discord presented in the *kotobagaki* sheets, but it seems to be more the result of the change in *luminosity* – specifically as a result of the deployment of gold and silver leaf, and cloud-patterned silver powder – than the use of *noge*.[60]

By the third sheet (Fig. 1-16: *The Oak Tree II*, sheet three), as Egami points out, there is a sort of disturbance, and the presence of *noge* in the sheet may in fact be connected to this disturbance; but perhaps not in the way Egami suggests. I think a better way to read the relationship between the wild hairs and the disturbance Egami posits they symbolize involves an examination of the text of the second sheet (Fig. 1-18a: *The Oak Tree II*, sheet two).[61] The pertinent passage is found beginning in column nine of the third sheet with the fourth character, 'hi' (Fig. 1-16; *The Oak Tree II*, sheet three). It runs as follows:

ひころかさなるま〰にはかみひけもみたれものむつかしうけはひかはるわさなるをいよ〰やせさらほひたま〰へるしもしろくものきよけになるさまして[ま]くらをそはたて〰ふしたま〰へり

Hi koro kasanaru mama ni ha,
kami hige mo midare, mono muzukashiu,
kehai kawaru wazanaru wo, iyoiyo
yasesarahohi tamaheru shimo, shiro-
ku mono kiyokenaru sama shite,
makura wo *sobadatete* hushi-tamaheri[62]

As the days wore on one after another, *his hair and beard grew dishevelled*. This would normally be an *unsightly change in appearance*, yet although Kashiwagi had *gradually languished to a frightful thinness*, he was attractively pale, and as he *inclined his pillow a bit* [to listen to Yūgiri] ...[63]

To begin, I think that if one were going to read the presence of 'wild hairs' on the sheet surface as being indicative of some sort of disturbance, it would make sense to link the silver *noge* 'hair' with the hair of the ailing Kashiwagi's beard. Invoking the figure of *midare*, the text notes that Kashiwagi's 'hair and beard grew dishevelled' ('kami hige mo midare'), which seems to be a condition particularly well-suited for representation with 'wild hairs' (Fig. 1-16: *The Oak Tree II*, sheet three).

Another possible *noge* allusion might be to the *noyama* (fields and mountains) mentioned at the beginning of the 'Kashiwagi' chapter in *Genji*. In the passage above, Yūgiri comments on the dishevelled appearance of Kashiwagi's hair and beard; at the start of the chapter, Kashiwagi muses on his disillusionment and his stifled desire to roam the wilderness ('*noyama ni akugaremu michi*').[64] In both instances, there is perturbation of some sort, whether physical or emotional. By tying Kashiwagi's mental discord at the beginning of the chapter and his ill-kempt physical appearance with the rough resonance of the character 'no' ('野' field/wild), we get a clearer idea of the associative overlap of the materiality of a particular substance and its role in assisting the artistic depiction of a textual quotation. This interpretation is thus attractive because it involves both associations of angst and a linguistic link (e.g. 野毛 and 野山) between a particular artistic technique, a concrete textual reference and the mood of the chapter's protagonist. In so doing, I think we get a fuller sense of how textual mood and allusion interact with specific modes of visual artistic representation.

Moving back to *Kashiwagi I*, we glean further meaning from an examination of the paper designs. The last thing I would point out along these lines are the *shita-e* 下絵 ('under-drawings') on the second sheet of *Kashiwagi I* (Fig. 1-6). At the upper right, adjacent to the two clouds of silver, are paintings of mountains;

at the lower left area of sheet two is a painting of craggy tree branches. Both of these pictures fall in accord nicely with the notion of wildness or wilderness discussed just above. The rocky masses near the top of the sheet and the battered branches of the willow tree (柳) pictorially recapitulate the chapter's opening reference to 'fields and mountains' ('noyama' 野山). In the context of the first several lines of the 'Kashiwagi' chapter, it is important to note that these components refer to a landscape that holds unpleasant connotations for Kashiwagi. Early in the chapter, Kashiwagi ponders his past, reflecting:

> ... All of life turned to disappointment. I longed more and more to prepare for the life to come, except that *my parents' distress would then seriously hinder me from wandering moor and mountain*, and I managed one way or another to put the idea aside. Whom but myself have I to blame, if knowing I can never show my face in the world again has brought me in the end to the last pitch of despair?[65]

I quote this passage to show that Kashiwagi's desolation is linked to the 'moor and mountain,' that is, landscape elements that are also depicted on sheet two. In addition, the sagging willow found on the sheet is a melancholic symbol, and as a tree, it also resonates with our ailing protagonist, Kashiwagi, whose name means 'Oak'.

Another applicable arboreal reference in the text involves a pine tree. Kashiwagi muses, 'No one in this world is a thousand-year pine, no one lingers forever' (T. 675). Here, Kashiwagi accepts his fate, and characterizes his impermanence in contrast to the enduring pine, a classic symbol of unwavering fidelity and longevity. In pairing the scroll sheet with the textual references from *Genji*, we have garnered a set of pictorial and textual *engo* 縁語 ('associative words') that serve as an 'adhesive mechanism' linking word and image.[66]

The phrase 'unsightly appearance' ('mono muzukashiu kehai', from the tenth and eleventh columns), used to describe Kashiwagi, could refer just as well to the willow tree painted as part of the bleak, withered landscape backgrounding the sheet of calligraphy, and the phrase would also be applicable to the declining columns of calligraphy that fall within the branches' span (Figs. 1-6, 1-8b: *The Oak Tree I*, sheet two).[67] From 'kotachi no sou' (column ten) to the last column of the sheet, the calligraphy mimics the tree's limp posture: the tops of its columns droop down towards the sheet's edge, halting right where the willow's tip also ends.

We should also stay mindful of the possibility for the 'unsightly' indication to characterize the splotches of silver *mijin* smeared in the upper right quadrant of the sheet.[68] These blots are certainly no more fetching than the gimpy hemistiches of calligraphy they support. Moreover, though, the first horizontal swath of *mijin* coincides exactly with the vertical column containing the 'ya' of 'yami' ('sickness').

This intersection deserves special reiteration because it signifies one particularly resonant locus of the proliferation of valences occurring throughout the graphic terrain of the sheet. Specifically, the 'nakaYAmi' (prolonged illness) reverberates adjacent to the 'noYAma' (fields and mountains), the calligraphic

'や' even referencing calligrammatically the '山' whose shape shadows it; these terms in turn resound against and, indeed, *re*-sound the 'YAnaki' (willow) image in the bottom-left quadrant of the sheet, their sounds echoing amidst the visual landscape configured by illness. Heard and viewed in concert, the sonic image of the focal term *nayami* (illness) dives diagonally along a twisting multivalent arc: from the symbolic, hefty peak of rugged mountain to the gravely peaked image of the willow tree.

What has happened immediately after the writing of this particularly potent 'YA' character is remarkable: with the mention of 'sickness', *the calligraphy begins to look sickly* (Figs. 1-13, 1-6: *The Oak Tree I*, 'yami', first column of sheet two). Looking at the first two lines of sheet two, we observe that right after the brazen 'ya', the characters pale, thinning considerably to a weight roughly half that of the '**kinakaya**' that begins the column and sheet (Fig. 1-6: *The Oak Tree I*, sheet two). *This* shift is so striking because it happens in an instant. This attenuation, after all, occurs not over the course of a few characters, but *immediately* – splitting the word 'yami' in half with the sudden lapse in brush pressure.

Two characters; two very different impressions. The 'ya' is both much broader and darker than the 'mi' below it. We should also notice that whereas the 'ya' is brushed with the *jibo* 字母 ('maternal glyph'/ 'source *kanji*') '也' (which engenders a *hiragana* form), the 'mi' is based on the *kanji* '三' (the basis for a *katakana* form).[69] Although we can only guess at the calligrapher's reason for not using the *hiragana* character 'み' to follow the *hiragana* 'ya,' we can however examine the visual effects caused by the juxtaposition.

For example, there is a clear break between the two characters; the 'mi's' initial stroke is attached to 'ya' with less than a hair's breadth of ink. The 'mi', in turn, stands apart from the 'ni' below it, furthermore, but with less power than the 'ya' above it. Also: that 'ya's' terminal vertical stroke spikes downwards in aim towards the middle of the 'mi'. Along these lines, I would submit that the 'yami' signifying illness (病み) should be read at this juncture as effecting a calligraphic 'interruption' (*yami* 止み) as well. Importantly, these two meanings literally overlap here in the 'darkness' (*yami* 闇) of the silver cloud that begins the sheet. I think this is a crucial intersection of meanings because it signifies the dramatic manner in which the multivalent term '*yami*' performs a pivotal role in interweaving the figurations of 'interruptive darkness' and 'illness' that contour the calligraphic performance of *midare-gaki*.

To give a bit more visual context for this 'dark break', a comparable approximation of the line might look like this:

… きなかやミもはへらす …

The separation effected between the two characters is salient here as well as in the original example. As if having taken a cue from the semantic content of the phrase 'prolonged illness' (なかやみ・長病み), the calligraphy has responded by shifting immediately to another form and thickness. The rest of the line then remains in that weaker register for the duration of the column and the next, switching in its unstable weight from line to line from then on.

In examining the calligraphy with the paper upon which it has been brushed, we observe a double movement: as Kashiwagi's physical body becomes thinner, the silver-powdered clouds fatten up (Figs 1-18a, 18b, 18c: *The Oak Tree II*, sheets two, three and four).

As the viewer moves leftwards, progressing forward in time along the horizontal axis of the scroll, the dark clouds of the paper design gradually swell and proliferate to display a constricted temporality before the tangled-script eclipses normative parameters of time and space on the last sheet. The increase here in the number and size of these markers of darkness signifies the mounting toll of the *yami* steadily consuming Kashiwagi: their tumescence grows in proportion to his degeneration.

Dark grey is the colour of mourning and mourning's shade pervades the sheet's design scheme, evoking the ephemeral hue of Kashiwagi's future at the same time that it symbolizes the stain of his sexual transgression. The sooty masses of smoke mentioned in each of the section's early poems render in concentrated bursts of minced foil the wracking disquiet saturating the section; they make their way into the *kotobagaki* as the material trace of the 'funeral pyre' shading the sheets of *Kashiwagi II*. Within the *Kashiwagi* sections' design scheme, these dark clouds help intimate visually the unsettling subtext and soundtrack that permeates the calligraphy, while at the same time indexing the tensioned temporal deceleration foreshadowing the rapid declines that end the sections. Echoing the split *YA-mi* mentioned earlier, then, these clouds can be thought of as the 'breaking' *ha* (破) that follows the introductory *jo* (序) and ushers in the cadenza-like *kyū* (急) of the section. While I do not want to sidetrack the current discussion of 'Kashiwagi', I think it is important to mention at this juncture that in the section 'Minori', too, the pre-cadenza break arrives swathed in shadow.

Here, on the third of five sheets (Fig. 1-25: *The Law*, sheet three), the ascending step-like horizontal clouds literally foreshadow the spectacular downward *midare-gaki* spirals of the final frame. Extended as the hinge between the glittering bombast of the section's start and the dismal melancholy of its end, this shadow both signifies the nocturnal setting of the deathbed scene and also suggests a protracted temporal interval against which the final calligraphic performance of the characters' desperate poetic exchange can be juxtaposed to most striking effect.

There is, moreover, another overlapping proportionality: the thicker the clouds become, the wider the range of line-weight variation. The calligraphy of the second and third sheets of *Kashiwagi II*, for example, which both exhibit traces of the silver powder cloud arrangements (albeit in fainter form than those of the subsequent sheets), is overall much more uniform in weight than the calligraphy of the fourth sheet. From the fourth sheet on, there is a noticeable change in both the density and size of the characters: the fourth sheet's characters are, on the whole, lighter than those of the previous sheet, and they are slightly smaller as well.[70]

This minute wane in character size results in a slight increase in the number of characters fitted within the columns of the fourth sheet. Specifically, whereas only three columns exceed fourteen characters on the third sheet, there are twice as many 'fourteen-plus' columns on the following sheet. Also, this sheet contains thirteen columns whereas the previous sheet had only twelve. We can understand this jump in character quantity as a calligraphic downshift – the writing is speeding up. Moving onto the next two sheets (the fifth and sixth), this acceleratory trend continues, and the brushwork's speed has risen yet again; what is more, this is evident in thrice the number of columns: eighteen columns now contain greater than fourteen characters.

I mentioned earlier that there was an inversely proportional relationship between the thickening clouds and the thinning calligraphy; I would like to turn to discuss that thinning calligraphy now. Compare, for example, the robust characters of sheet three with the sickly scribbles on the last sheet of the set.[71] As we move from right to left time passes and, over the course of those five sheets, Kashiwagi's condition has worsened considerably. There is a plainly discernible transformation that occurs, one that is manifested in part within the calligraphy of sheets four to eight. The cause of this shift – illness – is clear, and by looking closely we can even pinpoint its onset. This is where it starts:

… いよいよやせさらほひたまへるしもしろ
… iyoiyo yasesarahohi tamaheru shimo, shiro-[72]

Recall the excerpt quoted earlier, in which Kashiwagi was described as languishing with an unkempt beard and leaning up from his pillow to talk with Yūgiri.[73] The phrase just reiterated is key to our understanding of the way in which the Oak Intendant's illness affects the calligraphy in the *Kashiwagi* scroll sets.

This phrase appears in the last two columns of the third sheet of *Kashiwagi II* (Fig. 1-16: *The Oak Tree II*, sheet three). The italicized portion of the phrase represents the hiragana occupying the complete last line of the sheet (the plain 'iyo-iyo' begins from the second to last column). The term I am most concerned with here is *yase-sarahohi* (indicated here with a pair of vertical lines above the relevant columns). The verb stem 'yase-' means 'to become thin' and to this base is added 'sarahohi', which means 'to slim severely'.[74] Together, the two pieces combine to form a forceful compound verb that underscores Kashiwagi's progressive frailty: Kashiwagi is not just thin, he is *emaciated*, and this bodily deterioration advances 'bit by bit' ('iyo-iyo').[75] Remarkably, this bodily attenuation coincides with the gradual attenuation of the script's thickness.

If there were to be any doubts about the central significance of this descriptor of physical deterioration, the artists themselves quell them by *encircling it with silver clouds*. Note in the above image that the key phrase is surrounded by horizontal slivers of darkness, thus focusing the viewer's gaze upon the calligraphically simulated body of the emaciated Kashiwagi. Within the presentational lexicon of the calligraphic preface the dusky ovular design, abetted by a moderately increased brush pressure for the characters, says in fairly unsubtle terms: *Linger over these words*. In short, this juncture, in which the ailing body of Kashiwagi is transfigured into graphic, calligraphic form, represents one site at which shadows and ink collude engrossingly to enact corporeal deterioration.

The last detail I would mention here is that sheet four (Fig. 1-20: *The Oak Tree II*, sheet four) contains one more column than sheet three. As discussed earlier, this increase in the number of columns corresponds to the writing's acceleration. But there is another aspect of this shift: since each sheet is equal in length, the addition of an extra column means that the spacing between columns has been compressed – which happens when the calligraphy's width contracts. This slight horizontal contraction dovetails the 'bit-by-bit' increase in column number, as well as the corresponding thinning of Kashiwagi's body as his illness mounts. This kind of correlation between bodily deterioration and the attenuation of calligraphy is central to an understanding of the inscriptive injuries that occur in the *Genji Scrolls*. We can now begin to get a better grasp of what the terms 'healthy' and 'sick' might denote in calligraphic terms.

Two major criteria for diagnosing inscriptive infirmity are line weight and column width. Just as many diseases cause their sufferers' bodies to wither, we see here that writing too can shrivel in response to its author's ailment. The relationship manifested in the *Genji Scrolls* between body and script becomes more palpable when viewed via the thematic rubric of illness: nowhere else in the *Scrolls* is that link more salient than in *Kashiwagi*.[76] Note that there are only twelve columns on sheet three, as opposed to a staggering twenty-one columns on sheet eight (Fig. 1-19: *The Oak Tree II*, sheet eight). I pointed out above that the increase of one column could affect the width of the calligraphy – just imagine how much more compressed it must become in order to accommodate an extra nine lines. Such a leap in column number would necessitate a collective lateral trimming of characters across the entire sheet, one that coincides with the characters' gradual attenuation of line weight, and their sympathetic thinning in parallel with the ailment's advance.

In more concrete terms: 'yase' is weighted heavier than 'tamahite' in a manner that demonstrates the oppositional interplay between the semantic and symbolic registers of the calligraphy. It is as though the calligrapher is compensating for the word's 'skinny' valence by applying more pressure to his brush, thus making the characters that form 'thin' look **thick**. It is at junctures like this one that we perceive a trace of the calligrapher's kinetic presence through the ink, wherein a particular coordination of presentational and representational registers of the *Genji Scrolls*' calligraphy glints to the foreground not to 'mimic' the thinness of the body, here, but rather to draw the viewer's attention to this calligraphically *enacted* exposure of that body's sinew.

We might also consider the alternation of ink-weight in combination with specific textual references.[77] For example, Kashiwagi strains to hear Yūgiri at his bedside (the scene depicted in the painting), which may coincide with the tonal wane of ink. The end of sheet three, continuing through sheet four (Fig. 1-14: *The Oak Tree II*, sheets three and four) contains the description of Yūgiri's bedside visit with Kashiwagi (Fig. 1-3: *The Oak Tree*, painting):

One saw how very weak [Kashiwagi] was when he raised his pillow and spoke, and one noted the pitiful faintness of his breath. 'You have deteriorated very little, considering how long you have been unwell. Actually, you look even better now than before.' The Commander wiped his eyes nonetheless. 'We promised ourselves that neither of us would go before the other. This is a terrible thing! I cannot even make out why you are so ill. We are so close, and yet I still do not know!'[78]

This passage carries a melodramatic touch. We see in the third column that after the mention of illness ('watsurahi', in this case), the characters grow gaunt for the rest of the hemistiche and the following column as well (Fig. 1-20: *The Oak Tree II*, sheet four). But perhaps the most mawkish example of calligraphic display occurs centre-stage (in the middle of the sheet): this line is part of the sentence wherein Yūgiri starts sobbing about Kashiwagi's impending demise. The ink faded as Kashiwagi struggled to lift his pillow, and now, at the moment when Yūgiri's tears start to fall ('namita otoshite'), there runs a melodramatic swell of ink right in the middle of the sheet emphasizing the moist poignancy of the scene – like the calligraphic equivalent of a calligraphic close-up.[79] Although it is usually the most identifiably 'pictorial' sections of the *Genji Scrolls* that we tend to think of as being in some way 'staged', we observe clearly in passages such as this one, that the calligraphy too bears an actively *affective*, performative quality.

Turning to the *shita-e*, we are presented with a further embellishment of this charged portrayal of Kashiwagi's increasingly dire condition. Considered in reference to the 'bird tracks' ('tori no ato') discussed previously, we find that the birds painted onto the sheet (Fig. 1-21: *The Oak Tree II*, sheet six) are indeed tracks of a sort, in the sense that they are inscriptive traces of a literary image lifted from the pages of *Genji* and then translated to the background of sheet six's own picture-scape:[80] Their sharp wings prick the upper third of the sheet with an insistence of ill portent: they are components of the sinister design that orchestrates Kashiwagi's physical decline and heralds his demise.

On this point, in his book *Medieval History of Physical Appearance and Gesture*, Kuroda Hideo notes the significance of dogs and birds, in particular as 'boundary-like animals' (境界的動物), that both mark spatially the borders between human and inhuman in their movement and, by the same token, often symbolize states of physical or spiritual transition.[81] The birds swoop down from the upper right, tracing two parallel paths. Although the column heights on this sixth sheet are all level, we see that the lines implied by the birds' movement coincide with the plunging columns two sheets later (Fig. 1-19: *The Oak Tree II*, sheet eight). In this sense, the bird design motif serves as a kind of pictorial foreshadowing in that its diagonal movement of decline anticipates that of the calligraphy.

Two sheets later, the 'chicken-scratch' ('tori no ato') mentioned in the text of the chapter – which then resonates further with the placement of the birds on sheet six – manifests itself calligraphically in the snarls of *midare-gaki* plotted across the final sheet. At this point we should return to the 'tori no ato' reference to consider its significance in the context of our discussion of *Kashiwagi*'s calligraphy.⁸² A glance at the polyvalent possibilities of '*ato*' yields several resonant options: bird *tracks*, the sheet's *stains* of silver, the spirit that has *remained* in Kashiwagi's body, and the corporeal *pain* (suggested by the homophonic variant '*ato*' 痕, meaning 'scar') Kashiwagi no doubt feels – as well as the inscriptive injury represented in the ragged calligraphic columns shown here.⁸³

Cleaved from the lofty horizontal standard upheld on every other sheet of its set, sheet eight's calligraphy sprawls down at jagged intervals. The columns' crumble begins from the very start of the sheet: there is a clear, gradual, slump that takes place over the span from '*nomi kikoyuru koto*' (column one) to '*mama ni ito kokoro*' (column eleven). Then there is an upward surge: the twelfth column ('*nari masareha*') starts roughly four centimetres higher than the line before it – in an ink toned several shades darker. This drive barely lasts the length of the line, though, and the next three columns plummet at a steeper angle than the previous ten did. The following two groups of calligraphy, arranged in three-column units, are cramped and scraggly – mashed (just barely) against the leftmost edge of the sheet. If we move to examine 'Minori', another chapter in which illness (this time, Murasaki's) is at work, we get a fuller understanding of the ways in which it commands text, calligraphy and painting in the *Genji Scrolls* (Fig. 1-22: *The Law*, painting).

Like 'Kashiwagi', 'Minori's' very first sentence also concerns the deleterious effects of illness. The chapter opens in the following manner:

> Lady Murasaki's health remained very poor after her serious illness, and she had suffered ever since from a vague, lingering malaise. It was not especially threatening, but all those months and years did not bode well, and by now she was so frail that Genji felt very anxious indeed.⁸⁴

We learn here that Murasaki's body has become weaker as a result of her battle with disease. Looking at the *kotobagaki* that corresponds to this episode in *The Tale of Genji*, we get a sense of the possible effect of such an illness on the calligraphy used to assist in its depiction (Fig. 1-23: *The Law*, sheet one).

The '*no*'s of the second sheet have begun to buckle, losing the robust circularity exhibited by their counterparts on the first sheet. (Fig. 1-24: *The Law*, sheet two). There is less of an effort to complete the circular finishing section of the character here. Compare, for example, the '*no*' (の) of the set's title, *Minori* (Fig. 1-23: *The Law*, sheet one) and the same character found in the fifth column, fifth row, with the '*no*' in the last column of sheet two (the second character). The '*no*'s of the first sheet are rounded perfectly and poised singularly within their immediate contexts; the other '*no*', meanwhile, sags inward with its sides compacted slightly.

Part of this difference in appearance can be attributed to the linkages between '*no*' and the characters that follow it. For example, in columns five and six, of sheet two, the '*no*'s are followed (in order) by the characters '*shi*', '*yo*' and '*ni*', all of which are conventionally lined up in the middle of the column. (Fig. 1-24: *The Law*, sheet two). This means that their vertical component, if linked from above with the tail of the '*no*' loop, will snag that tail stroke before it can pass the column's centre. As a result, a 'no' in this context will tend to have less circularity and will tilt more to the left than one that is autonomous or connected to a character that originates on the left-hand side of the column.

The 'no' of the excerpt's title, *Minori* (御法・みのり), for example, is not tethered to the 'ri' below it; it stands alone as an autonomous linguistic unit. The calligrapher could have used a *renmentai* 連綿体 ('connected character') approach for the three *kana*, yet chose not to. This detail is interesting because it suggests something about the semantic intent of the calligraphy and its choreography in the context of the progressions (temporal and physical) of the scroll.

Clarity seems to be the governing principle behind this kind of writing. This is a commonsensical point to make, certainly, but it has implications for other modes of writing that may not be clear initially. For instance, we need only compare this column (the very first of the *Minori* set) with the last column of the set, to see that the last line, scraggly, cramped, and tilted as it is, was perceived as being radically different in character than this 'mi-no-ri'.[85]

A transformation has gradually taken place over the course of *Minori*'s five sheets, one that I would argue involves a growing prioritization of visual impact over semantic transmission. This is not to say that one kind of calligraphy is more communicative than another. Rather, I mean to emphasize that the visual character of the *midare-gaki* calligraphy of *Minori*'s final sheet (Fig. 1-26: *The Law*, sheet five), by virtue of its rapidity and stricture, is so snarled that the writing's representational capacity pales compared to its presentational dynamism. In other words, I think that *midare-gaki* primarily *performs* for the viewer certain physical conditions depicted in *Genji*, rather than merely *denoting* them. In this regard, *midare-gaki* is more about show than tell, more about the kinetic calligraphic enactment of certain affective and physical conditions than simply their fixed representation.

Using this understanding of *midare-gaki*'s resistance to representational writing, we might then move further to say that in disrupting calligraphy, illness has in turn done injury to the normal signifying order (or at least refigured its contours to impel an altered relation with the reader). Murasaki's sickness affects not only the calligraphy, then, but it also commits towards us, the so-called 'readers' of the *kotobagaki*, a certain violence as well: it impairs our ability to cull semantic content smoothly from the script, relegating us to the position of mere 'viewers'. Our powers of discernment are impaired by this injury, and we are – to some extent – blinded by the writing's intensified figural cant.

Scarry explains this phenomenon in the context of elements of physical pain. She points out:

> A sixth element of physical pain, one that overlaps but is not quite coterminous with the previous element, is its obliteration of the contents of consciousness. Pain annihilates not only the objects of complex thought and emotion but also the objects of the most elemental acts of perception. It may begin by destroying some intricate and demanding allegiance, but it may end (as is implied in the expression 'blinding pain') by destroying one's ability simply to see.[86]

Here, 'destroying one's ability simply to see' should not be taken literally, but read more along the lines of the 'annihilation of objects of complex thought'. In the *Genji Scrolls*, the *midare-gaki* passages are not invisible, but I would like to suggest that their tangles resist a facile legibility. The difficulty a reader might experience when confronting the scrolls stems from the fact that the 'objects of complex thought', that is, the syntactically arranged kana logographs have been enfolded by the illness that has spurred their use in the first place.

Though this semantic impediment may to some extent alter a reader's relation to the calligraphic text, this is not necessarily to suggest a consequential repugnance on the part of the reader.[87] To be sure, the very sight of his own *midare-gaki* calligraphy disgusts Kashiwagi, causing him to '[feel] even worse after this confused effort at writing', but, ironically, what is depicted as grotesque writing in the narrative comes to be stylized as enthralling in the context of the *Scrolls*. In fact, I would argue that this breakdown of the *midare-gaki* 'characters' bodies' (字体) encourages an aesthetic appraisal of the text, one that is based upon (and may in fact depend), on the mirrored deterioration of Murasaki and Kashiwagi's own physical bodies. In this sense, textual, calligraphic and pictorial depictions all permeate one another. Moreover, the 'disruption' or 'mutation' (valences for '*midare*' I here find most pertinent) that occurs to both types of bodies possesses a distinct aesthetic appeal.[88]

Descriptions of *midare-gaki* in *Genji*, for instance, often pose the calligraphic mode as beautiful or striking (in a positive – yet still somewhat destabilized – sense), with examples ranging from an 'uncertain hand' ('ote mo uchi wana nakaruru ni midarekaki') being 'extremely beautiful' ('ito utsukushige nari'), to a 'disordered hand' that is 'quite exquisite' ('ito okashige nari').[89] With these calligraphic characterizations in mind, then, consider the following portrayal of the ailing Murasaki from the 'Minori' chapter:

> She was extremely thin, but her infinitely noble grace gained from precisely that a wonderful new quality, because where once the overflowing richness and brilliance of her looks had evoked the magnificence of worldly blossoms, her beauty now really was sublime, and her pensive air – for she knew that her time was nearly over – was more sorrowful and more profoundly moving than anything in the world.[90]

I would argue that, in a way not unlike that of the calligraphic passages brushed in *midare* mode, this textual excerpt, too, derives its power from a presentational impetus: namely, a desire to display, in this case, the languishing body of Murasaki for the onlooker's scopic pleasure. Certainly, this pleasure depends on our comprehension of the words deployed to convey it, but, even so, there is a sense that this 'telling' is predicated upon a particular mode of 'showing' that is intertwined with and, indeed, predicated upon the force of the illness motif. We should now move to consider the significance of the pictorial portrayal of Murasaki's illness that corresponds to these textual depictions of sickness.

The *onna-e* 女絵 ('woman picture') or *tsukuri-e* 作り絵 ('built picture')[91] style consists of thick pigment use and the overlay of opaque colours to build up a solid, more tactile surface. Colours are stacked and designs are superimposed upon one another.[92] Because of this, in terms of visual mobility, this is a style whose heavy pigments weight the viewer's movement, in turn, clogging progress along a linear axis. Additionally, via the predominantly interior settings and the walls, screens and pillars that comprise them, an incapacitating gauntlet of architectural impedimenta similarly inhibits quick progress through the pictorial realm of the scroll. The *Genji Scrolls* are a prime example of the so-called '*onna-e*' style.[93]

In contrast, the *otoko-e* 男絵 style, of which the *Shigisan-engi* 信貴山縁起 (ca. 1176: *Legends of Mt Shigi*, scroll one) represents a prototypical example, is less weighted: lighter in pigmentation, more fluid ink lines, fewer obstructive architectural elements, and the presence of characters who are scantily clad (if they are even clothed at all); all of these facets contribute to the *otoko-e* handscrolls' emphasis on linear leftward movement and a faster viewing pace.

Akiyama Terukazu writes that in *emakimono* such as the *Genji Scrolls*, 'there is hardly any inclusion of temporal progression within the pictures'.[94] The *Genji Scrolls*' pictures are essentially static. The *Genji Scrolls* are *onna-e* handscrolls structured by a particular textual narrative antecedent and, as such, they were designed to hone in on particular scenes and to stay viewers at each of those scenes, rather than propel them continually forward in time. The painterly techniques used to represent these scenes account for this structured visual hindrance.

For the most part, Akiyama's claim appears to be true, but we do get the sense in the *Minori* picture that there is a hint of mobile temporality even within this stifling, fraught, frame.[95] The painting (Fig. 1-22: *The Law*) depicts Murasaki, Genji and the Akashi Lady grieving within Murasaki's chamber. Murasaki is marked with a curtain tinted purple, to match the plant she is named after, and supports her frail frame upon an armrest, a key symbolic accoutrement in both Murasaki's sickly portrayal and Kashiwagi's. Murasaki is aligned with a downward canted rafter that mimics her feeble tilt, while at the same time suggesting her declining health and the bodily deterioration that ensues. Interestingly, the vector traced by this beam, when juxtaposed with the *midare-gaki* passage that begins the final sheet of the *kotobagaki*, matches the angle of the falling columns' descent.[96] In this case, the *architectural* echoes the *textual* to reinforce archi-textually the tenor of collapse.

Genji too leans forward in anguish, but while both he and his lover loathe their inevitable parting, his grief does not involve the physical affliction that Murasaki's does. Perhaps the most disconcerting aspect of the frame is the upward jutting curtain edge paralleling the pointed shape of the Akashi Lady's head near the middle of the room. This article of furniture interrupts the slant of Murasaki's beam and slices into the otherwise unperturbed visual space she shares with Genji; it displays in pictorial terms the emotional discord among all three characters, as well as the cognitive dissonance evinced in the calligraphy's pitch. Such a juxtaposition between the uneasy silence of the painting and the garrulous *kotobagaki* seems ironic, since the *midare-gaki* calligraphy, in contrast to this muted space, is anything but laconic: something must be said – now, before Murasaki fades away.

There is not the same type of sweeping lateral motion in this painting that we would find in a scroll such as *Shigisan-engi*, but time does indeed pass within this sheet – it just does so at a snail's pace.[97] The key to understanding the temporal shift that occurs in *Minori* lies in the composition's division. The picture is effectively split along a vertical axis by the pillar against which Genji leans.

To be sure, this structure serves as a hindrance to horizontal visual motion along the sheet, and it breaks the sheet into two separate halves. This split denotes a binary of interior versus exterior and, by extension, a temporal binary of before and after: while the interior space depicts the tense, final visit between Genji and Murasaki, the exterior space of the garden depicts the wind-flayed bush clovers (*hagi*) which symbolize Murasaki's demise.[98] This scenic bifurcation, then, splits both the spatial and temporal aspects of the frame into halves of present (left) and future (right) and delineates a border between life and death, as well.

Furthermore, this division effects a visual caesura that echoes the poetic cleft found in the scene's coinciding textual passage. The *kami no ku* ('upper stanza') of Murasaki's final poem reads:

おくと見る　　　ほどぞはかなき　　　ともすれば
'oku to miru　　　hodo zo *hakanaki*　　　to mo sureba'

The word 'hakanaki' ('evanescent/fragile/short-lived') is the main term of the upper stanza, and it denotes the fragility of Murasaki's health and her impending demise; that is, it modifies her *present* condition. The *shimo no ku* ('lower stanza') reads:

風に乱るる　　　萩のうは露
'kaze ni *midaruru*　　　hagi no uha tsuyu'

Here, in the lower stanza, the main term is the verb 'midaruru' ('to disturb/disrupt/tangle/shake') which we might render in the following way:

'kaze ni *midaruru*': '*disturbed* by the wind'
'hagi no uha tsuyu': 'dew atop the bush clover'

What we have, then, is a temporal shift evinced in both *Minori*'s visual and poetic representations. The 'before' depicts a *frail* Murasaki who *is* on the edge of death, weeping to the right of the pillar; the 'after' is the dew that *has been flung* from the bush clover by the wind, on the pillar's left.

Once we have crossed the veranda into the garden (having traversed the vertical pillar boundary), Murasaki has died. Although the interior setting with Murasaki, Genji and the Akashi Empress was undoubtedly hushed, the garden scene seems even more silent. The scene is dour: none of the colour of the interior setting finds its way into this area of the frame. The *hagi* are curved towards the veranda, their wide bend suggesting the wind's forceful influence. Over these long lines of ink is spread a frost of pulverized silver topped with mica powder. This can represent the dew that has dispersed in the wind, or signify that this scene takes place at night.[99] The deployment of this colour also echoes the emotional tenor of the text, in that 'the numbing grief made the world itself seem *like a twilight dream*'.[100] While Seidensticker's translated phrasing here catches the drift of the sad scene, his 'twilight' is a bit misleading. The Japanese phrasing, 明け暗れの夢 maintains some of the shading of the term, but underscores the liminal transition exhibited in the *Scrolls* insofar as it casts Murasaki's death, more accurately, as a 'dream on the dim cusp of dawn'. In addition to its conspicuous dearth of pigment, this side of the sheet also looks desolate because it is a nocturnal scene completely devoid of human presence; only the wind-whipped *hagi* exist in this section:

Also relevant to this split between inside and outside is the juxtaposition, by extension, of private and public. Murasaki's bedchamber is an interior space within which she, Genji and the Akashi Empress share their most intimate moments (and poems) together. The garden, on the contrary, is in contact with this space, yet is external to it, open to view, and thus lacks privacy. The verging of these two locales at the veranda is interesting to consider in terms of Elaine Scarry's notion of representations of pain. She writes:

> This dissolution of the boundary between inside and outside gives rise to a fourth aspect of the felt experience of physical pain, an almost obscene conflation of private and public. It brings with it all the solitude of absolute privacy with none of its safety, all the self-exposure of the utterly public with none of its possibility for camaraderie or shared experience. Artistic objectifications of pain often concentrate on this combination of isolation and exposure.[101]

Here, Scarry describes the private and public spheres' conflation within the context of literary representations of pain. Interestingly, in this case, we see that the distinction's collapse occurs in the visual artistic context of the *Genji Scrolls* as well. One way to understand this blend of spaces is as the result of illness' penetration of Murasaki's body. What makes the two places merge, or, perhaps more accurately, interpenetrate one another, is illness' capability to radically exceed physical boundaries: the logic of contagion according to which it travels undercuts any effort to cordon it off. In this case, disease's violence, while exerting a transformative influence on language, is kinder to spatial perimeters, merely perforating and permeating them in lieu of destroying them completely.

Expanding upon Scarry's notion of pain's power to de-border or collapse interior and exterior zones, we see that an ether of infirmity pervades both this external, natural space, as well as the sheet of calligraphy that precedes it.[102] Both the *hagi* and the handwriting have been disturbed, and a second look at Murasaki's final poem helps us solidify their interlaced connection:

> 'oku to miru   hodo zo *hakanaki*   to mo sureba
> kaze ni *midaruru*   hagi no uha tsuyu'[103]

'Alas, not for long will you see what you do now: any breath of wind may spill from a *hagi* frond the last trembling drop of dew.'[104]

First of all, it is important to note that Murasaki is symbolized by the dewdrops poised upon the bush clover.[105] The poem begins with the word 'oku' which is homophonous with the two contradictory verbs for 'wake up' or 'rise' (起く) and 'put down' or 'settle' (置く). This *kakekotoba* (pivot word) coincides resonantly with Murasaki's precarious, liminal existence: on the brink of death, she hovers tenuously between this world and the next, neither rising into the afterlife nor settling fully within this realm. The term also marks a disjointed temporality in which the moribund body – made prominent by tangled-script – effects a brief hitch in the otherwise smooth transition from past to future in which the immediacy of the present interval of dying is amplified calligraphically.

The ephemerality of Murasaki's life is emphasized further with 'hakanaki', which has valences including 'fragile', 'fleeting' and 'impermanent'. The *kakari-joshi* ('emphatic linking particle') 'zo', which has altered the ending syllable of the adjectival 'hakana**shi**' to become 'hakana**ki**', adds a hard consonant stress to the end of the word, anticipating in the moment of composition the cut to come. What is fascinating about these highlighted phrases is that while they refer ostensibly only to Murasaki's sickly condition, they can also be used to characterize the ailing calligraphy arrayed upon the sheet preceding her.

Like Murasaki, the calligraphy we see on the final sheet of the *Minori kotobagaki* is feeble (Fig. 1-26: *The Law*, sheet five). Its columns rise and fall in an oscillation of height implied by the opposing valences of 'oku'. The mention of 'hakanaki' underscores this debility, and its 'infirm' valence, in particular, resonates with both the subtext of sickness and the script's overtly enacted *instability*; it connotes insubstantiality, transience, weariness, fragility, frailty and sickliness as well. Finally, the verb 'midaruru' (乱るる), the connective stem of which forms half of the term 'midare-gaki' (乱れ書き), is perhaps the most significant word in the poem inasmuch as it codes for Murasaki's death (symbolized by the dew tossed from the bush clover), and because it suggests simultaneously disruptions of bodily and of calligraphic substantiality. 'Tangled-script' is an apt translation of '*midare-gaki*', but instead of 'tangled', other acceptable renderings of 'midare-' would be: 'unkempt', 'disturbed', 'corrupt', 'chaotic', 'confused', 'distorted', 'distressed' and even 'afflicted'. Viewed in combination with Kashiwagi's related condition and read within a calligraphic context, it becomes clear that Murasaki's poetry can disclose as much about her failing health as it can about the analogously ailing script employed to reproduce and strategically foreground that atrophy.

It is precisely in *midare-gaki* passages such as this one that Scarry's notions of pain's destructive influence on language become most pertinent. Illness engenders and sustains a physical and psychological anguish that pervades 'Minori' and 'Kashiwagi', marking the text of *Genji* with scars that consequently manifest themselves in the wounded calligraphy witnessed in the *Genji Scrolls*. This calligraphic damage, though evocative of the psycho-somatic injury endured by its fictional authors, simultaneously represents an aestheticized depiction of the characters' ailing situations as it proffers before our eyes the symbolic scripted bodies of the ill.

This performative artistic display reveals at its marrow an aesthetics of hurt premised on a coaxed voyeurism, one that invites our sympathetic viewing of the sick bodies – both somatic and calligraphic – even as those signifying forms *infirmly resist* facile semantic appraisal. Not only in the calligraphy, but behind it (in the *shita-e*), and beside it (in the painting), as well, are these bodies portrayed in all their engrossing and meticulously staged decay. All of these registers of meaning – although articulated through differing textual, pictorial and calligraphic techniques – are mutually contingent and, as a result, they contribute symbiotically to a choreography of text and image that tangles towards a spectacle of artistry compelled by the force of illness' inscriptive injury.

NOTES

1. I mention the influence of spirit possession (*mono no ke* 物の怪) here because it is cited in the text as being the cause of both Kashiwagi and Murasaki's afflictions.
2. *The Tale of Genji*, translated by Royall Tyler, 677 [hereafter T]. The relevant Japanese passage is: 'itodo naki-masari-tamahite, ohon kaeri, fushi nagara uchi yasumi tsutsu kaitamahu. Kotonoha no tsuzuki mo nau. Ayashiki tori no ato no yau nite' (*Nihon koten bungaku zenshū*, vol. 15, 286). Henceforth, all references to this series will use the acronym NKBZ before volume and page numbers (e.g. 'NKBZ 15: 286'). English excerpts will be taken primarily from Royall Tyler's translation; thus a number that follows an excerpt from *Genji* in English denotes its location in Tyler's translation (T. page). Any English renderings that follow an NKBZ reference without the 'T' designation are my own translations.
3. T. 676. The Japanese phrase is: 'imijiu wananakeba, omohu koto mo mina kaki sashite,' NKBZ 15: 261.
4. Here, I refer to the *midare-gaki* 乱れ書き ('tangled writing') found on the eighth sheet of the *Kashiwagi II* section of the *Genji monogatari emaki* 源氏物語絵巻 (*The Tale of Genji Picture Scroll*), henceforth referred to as the *Genji Scrolls*. See *Genji monogatari emaki: Tokugawa Bijutsukan zōhinshō*, Vol. 2, p. 45.
5. T. 676; emphasis mine.
6. See sheet six of the *Kashiwagi II* section of the *Genji Scrolls* in the *Genji monogatari emaki: Tokugawa Bijutsukan zōhinshō*, 源氏物語絵巻: 徳川美術館蔵品抄, #2 [hereafter GMETBZ], 43. All references to the *Genji Scrolls* will be based primarily on the images in this book, with occasional recourse to the Gotō Museum's *Kokuhō genji monogatari emaki* 国宝源氏物語絵巻 (English title: 'The 40th Anniversary Exhibition: The Illustrated Handscroll of the Tale of Genji'), henceforth referred to as 'Gotō.' The 'swarthy clouds' are dense areas of *gin mijin* 銀微塵 ('silver dust/dust-like sprinkles') arranged in cloud-patterns. They travel to the left, which is where Kashiwagi rests in the painting seen three sheets later; GMETBZ, 46.
7. For images, I will be referring to GMETBZ. All references to the *Genji Scrolls* will be based primarily on the images in this book, with occasional recourse to the 'Gotō'.
8. A few notes about transcription: throughout this chapter I will give the transcribed calligraphic text of pertinent sections of *kotobagaki* 詞書き in both un-spaced hiragana format and romanized Japanese; the first is in an attempt to represent (although only to a decidedly limited extent) the actual Scroll text; the second version is given for ease of reading. In the hiragana portion, I will not include diacritical *nigori* marks, which signal that the syllable is voiced, but I will render the voiced syllables in the romanized version of the text. Each calligraphic column will get its own row in these pages whenever a passage is excerpted, and the romanized version will follow suit. The karat mark (^) will represent the repetition of a single character that was dittoed in the original calligraphic

text; a tilde (~) will represent the repetition of a two-syllable unit. Brackets around a character mean that the character was omitted on the original sheet of calligraphy and has been subsequently added here.
9. Specifically, I will be dealing with the 'Kashiwagi' chapter from *Genji*, and the *Kashiwagi I* and *Kashiwagi II* sets from the *Genji Scrolls*. The context should provide guidance when I write only 'Kashiwagi'.
10. T. 676.
11. T. 675–6, emphasis mine.
12. NKBZ15: 286.
13. T. 677, emphasis mine.
14. Kashiwagi's writing is characterized this way in 'Hashihime' as well, where his calligraphy is not only akin to strange bird tracks, but also 'lumpy' ('tsubu-tsubu').
15. This was a cosmological/medical guide that related various illnesses to certain constellations and their (often inauspicious) shifting celestial positions; its author was Kai'e (b. 1172). See Rosenfield, John M., *The Courtly Tradition in Japanese Art and Literature: Selections from the Hofer and Hyde Collections* (Cambridge, Mass.: Fogg Art Museum, Harvard University, 1973). The two images to which I refer here can be found on pp. 29 and 102, respectively.
16. Ibid., pp. 102–103. This reference is also interesting for what it suggests about the violent penetrative capacity of illness *vis-à-vis* the human body.
17. Here I have italicized the words with which 'ato' shares a valence. Another pun on the word '後' (after/future/descendant/successor) resonates with Kashiwagi's lack of a legitimate male heir, due to his illicit liaison with Onna San no Miya (which produced Kaoru, who is assumed to be Genji's son).
18. We should also keep in mind the aesthetic implications of this splintering; namely: this kind of writing is not considered attractive. This is, for all intents and purposes, 'bad calligraphy'. For more on the *Genji* textual references dealing with 'good,' 'bad,' 'calm,' 'careless' and various other types of calligraphy, see Komai Gasei 1988: 254–76.
19 Elaine Scarry, *The Body in Pain: The Making and Unmaking of the World* (New York: Oxford University Press, 1985), p. 54. Scarry goes on to assert that another element of pain is 'its obliteration of the contents of consciousness', which ties in nicely with the wracked appearance of the *midare-gaki* passages portraying ill characters such as Kashiwagi and Onna San no Miya in *The Oak Tree* ('Kashiwagi') and Murasaki in *The Law* ('Minori').
20. I feel this is a tenable claim not so much because there is a sense of Kashiwagi being in acute pain in the context of his depictions (although he is certainly weak and anguished), but because of the palpable corollary between pain and illness' effects on language.
21. This shift may seem a bit abrupt, but I will return to engage Scarry's observations more fully later in the paper.
22. Akiyama Terukazu 2000: Vol. 1, p. 90.
23. Nagoya 1999: 35.
24. See Sano Midori 2000: 4.
25. See Kohitsugaku Kenkyūjo, ed. 1994: 29–44 for a detailed account of the calligraphic groupings and stylistic traits of the script in relation to other Heian calligraphy.
26. For information on women's involvement in Heian painting and their possible role in the production of the *Genji Scrolls*, see Akiyama Terukazu, 'Women Painters at the Heian Court', translated by Marybeth Graybill, in Marsha Weidner, ed., *Flowering in the Shadows: Women in the History of Chinese and Japanese Painting* (Honolulu: University of Hawaii Press, 1990), pp. 172–6.
27. Many of the *Genji Scroll kotobagaki* have been lost. Twenty-nine *kotobagaki* sections remain; ten of those are fragments, most of which were at some point culled from larger sections of the text and used as private calligraphy samples.
28. It is believed that nobles competed for the opportunity to choose which paper was

most appropriate for a certain scene. See Akiyama Terukazu: 2000, Vol. 1, pp. 90–3, and Sano Midori 2004: 87–100 for background on the production and composition of the scrolls. For more on the materials used to produce the *Genji Scrolls*, plus a filmed re-enactment of particular aspects of their composition, see Videochamp's *The Tale of Genji* (videocassette).

29. For an extended in-depth study of these two important works in relation to a broader art historical trend of decorating paper see Egami Yasushi's essays on each of the works in *Nihon no Bijutsu*, No. 397 (1999): 38–50 and 70–76. For excellent full length studies of the *Heike Nōgyō*, in particular, see Julia Meech-Pekarik, *Taira Kiyomori and the Heike Nōgyō* (Cambridge, Mass.: Harvard University, 1976, an unpublished Ph.D. thesis), and Komatsu Shigemi 2005.

30. The telling irony of this is that only the most skilled calligrapher was allowed to simulate such a maladroit hand as Kashiwagi's.

31. Gotō, pp. 62–3.

32. An Edo period attribution posited the calligrapher as being Fujiwari no Korefusa 藤原伊房 (1030–96), but scholars now believe this attribution to be too early. See Shimizu Yoshiaki, 'The rite of writing: Thoughts on the Oldest Genji Text'. *RES* 16, (Autumn, 1980), p. 62.

33. These two sections have been classed – according to both painting style and calligraphic style – as '1A'. *Minori* and *Suzumushi* also fit within this category. The similarity in styles has also led scholars to believe that these sections were once part of the same scroll and that each calligrapher probably split the scrolls up, doing two apiece. For more on this taxonomy, see Akiyama Terukazu: 1964, p. 266.

34. For more on the establishment of the Kōzei style and the development of the Sessonji lineage, see Shimizu Yoshiaki and John M. Rosenfield, *Masters of Japanese Calligraphy* (New York: Asia Society Galleries, 1984), pp. 48–50. For information regarding this school's development in competition with the Hosshōji school, founded by Fujiwara no Tadamichi 藤原忠通 (1097–1164) and characterized by more forceful execution and a tilted brush, see Gary DeCoker, 'Secret Teachings in Medieval Calligraphy: Jubokusho and Saiyosho', *Monumenta Nipponica*, Vol. 43, Issue 2 (Summer, 1988) pp. 197–228. A characterization of Kōzei's calligraphy may also be found in the *Yakakuteikinshō* 夜鶴庭訓抄; see Komatsu Shigemi: 1970, 40. It should also be noted that calligraphy done according to Kōzei's model is often designated as 'Kōya-gire A style', in reference to a three-class system of calligraphic identification associated with writing samples kept at Mt Kōya.

35. Sano Midori refers to the calligraphic style used for the *Minori* and *Kashiwagi* sections in the following terms: '[a style] that has inherited the gracefully delicate classic Japanese style perfected by Fujiwara Yukinari' (藤原行成が大成した優美繊細な上代和様を受け継ぐもの), Sano 2000: 42.

36. See Nagoya 1999: 26–35 for dates and sample images of these works. See also, Haruna Yoshishige 1993: 93–5 and 255–64, for physical descriptions of the papers used for the works and a survey of their calligraphers' stylistic attributes, respectively.

37. See *Sumi supesharu: Ōchō kana shodōshi* 墨スペシャル, No. 27 (Spring 1996), pp. 60–1, for more on the Kōya-gire 2 style and other tilted brush-point styles that derive from it. Minamoto Kaneyuki 源兼行 (1023?–74?) has been posited as the calligrapher.

38. This phrase comes from Mushanokōji 1990: 58–9.

39. This phrase is used by *emakimono* scholar Okudaira Hideo as part of his description of *The Tale of Genji* as 'romanticist literature that takes Hikaru Genji as its central [interest]' (光源氏を中心とするロマン主義の文学) in Okudaira 1987: 128–9. While perhaps less prevalent an idea among more recent scholars of *Genji*, the idea espoused by Okudaira in his popular writings on *emakimono* play into and promote prevailing, culturally essentialist, assumptions about *Genji*'s relation to traditional Japanese sensibilities, e.g. emotional attunement to the vicissitudes of the seasons, aesthetic investment in representing the 'sadness of things' (*mono no aware*) etc. Needless to say, I

should like to resist these types of interpretations as much as possible here. See, Richard Okada, 'Domesticating the Tale of Genji', *Journal of the American Oriental Society*, Vol. 110, No. 1 (Jan. – Mar., 1990), pp. 60–70, for an account of the stakes and consequences attending certain (exclusionary) interpretive stances with regard to works of Heian literature.

40. The images I refer to can be found in GMETBZ, 32–3. Legibility might seem an odd, or even superfluous quality to discuss, but I bring it up partially as a means of understanding better the interaction between brush, ink and paper, and the coordination of elements of the paper's design with the writing brushed over it. For various reasons, I do not believe legibility of the calligraphy was of prime importance to the people who experienced the completed scrolls. Two factors that would account for this are their close familiarity with the subject matter of *Genji* (which would obviate the need for reading with a goal of comprehension), and the common salon practice of having one person read the text aloud while the others looked at the pictures, a reading practice itself portrayed in the *Azumaya I* section of the *Genji Scrolls* themselves. I think that for the most part, the aristocrats who enjoyed the *Genji Scrolls* did so more as well-versed readers for whom the content of the narratives was already known to the extent that the calligraphy was probably appreciated less for its communicative properties than for its performative ones.

41. There is no doubt about the collapsing columns and the more varied line weight here on sheet two, however, I should note that part of the reason this variation is so clear is tied to the physical condition of the scroll. The second sheet has been preserved better than the first, and does not show nearly the degree of wear that sheet one does. Sheet one is lined throughout with conspicuous fissures in the paper surface (mainly along the horizontal dimension). The most severe cracks are visible along the middle of the sheet, starting from the rightmost edge, where a sizeable patch of mica powder shows through.

42. The convention of re-inking the brush may partially account for this but even so, the instances of characters positioned lower in columns that are comparable in tone to higher characters implies that brush pressure – not just ink quantity – plays a crucial part.

43. The preferred method of augmentation is an increase in line weight, even though the calligraphers could conceivably also alter speed or position as a primary means of columnar differentiation.

44. I have arranged the column numbers this way in accordance with the *emakimono* right-to-left reading/viewing pattern.

45. See GMETBZ, 34. Spirit possession is at work here too.

46. I use 'pitch' here for both its musical and aeronautical valences. The tildes in the diagrammatic line represent a gap in text that occurs after the fourteenth column. I consider them akin to two silent beats in that they represent the amount of space used elsewhere on the sheet for two columns of calligraphy, but there are no columns on the sheet. Yet, the spatial rhythm still implies a unit of three, counting the fourteenth column and the two (absent) lines after it. I did not attach this footnote to the diagrammatic line for the sake of visual clarity.

47. See in particular the thirteenth column of sheet three: GMETBZ, 34.

48. More specifically, they all float within the uppermost quarter of the sheet.

49. I should point out that in terms of material composition and colour scheme, these two adjacent sheets are nearly identical: with the exception of the second sheet's presence of an under-painting, both employ exactly the same materials. The second sheet is dyed to a tone roughly the same as that of sheet one, but with a bit more warmth. Egami calls the colour a dye of 'light brown added in several places' (Egami 1999: 8).

50. Looking closely, it actually looks as if the bold 'te' sitting between lines six and seven might have been rewritten after the first pass of brushwork did not show clearly enough. I say this because there is a 'te' in line six that is right next to this 'te', but is

almost invisible, due to the foil leaves' resilience to ink; the 'te' also makes no sense in the context of column seven. Therefore, my guess is that the calligrapher inserted this bolder 'te' in order to compensate for the excessively light one to its right.

51. The three other characters that stand out against the silver *mijin* clouds here are the 'i' of the third column (fourth position), the 'ki' of the fifth column (sixth position), and the 'ko' of the third column (sixth position). This 'ko' is interesting because the two parallel strokes that comprise the character are utterly shunned in lieu of a vertical line. This suggests that a calligraphic tendency implemented when writing over dark horizontal design elements is to stress a character's verticality: this can be observed clearly with the first 'ya', the 'ko' and the 'ki'.

52. I should point out here that 'watsurahi' can also mean 'anxiety' or 'worry'. In that case, the appropriate *kanji* would be '煩'. Since the calligraphy uses *kana* to write the word and not *kanji*, I have ventured, on the basis of context, to determine that the 'watsurahi' should be read as 'sickness', a valence that, curiously, the vast majority of scholars seem to ignore. I suspect that this meaning, though equally as feasible a rendering as 'anxiety', has been repeatedly overlooked, in part, due to a hermeneutic residue sedimented over decades of scholarship. Since the earliest glosses of 'watsurahi' substituted the *kana* with the *kanji* for 'worry', subsequent readers also participated in this reading; I do not, for my purposes here. The pun does, however, resonate well in this context and is apt as an appended valence.

53. Emphases mine.

54. For Onna San no Miya in this case, and Kashiwagi, too. However, here the physical weakness embodied by this calligraphy strengthens my argument.

55. I realize that there are actually five syllables represented here, but the bracketed 'tama' signifies the use of *kanji* for the two sounds: therefore [tama]hu = [給]ふ.

56. This happens despite that which the wheedling Genji would have Suzaku-in believe about his daughter's condition.

57. Egami 1999: 9.

58. Ibid.

59. Ibid. The full sentence in Japanese is: 'Gin no mijin, chūkirihaku, sakihaku, noge, kin no shō-, chū-, ōkirihaku, sakihaku ga hanayakasa wo soeru.' ('The silver dust-like sprinkles and medium-sized flakes of leaf, leaf shards, wild hairs, small, medium, and large leaf gold flakes and foil shards add flamboyance.')

60. I will discuss this progression a bit later in the chapter.

61. I mean 'better' here only in terms of tenability with regard to correspondence with the *Genji* text. I should point out that Egami uses the textual reference 'hito sawagishū sawagi-michi tari' (Egami 1999: 8) to account for his interpretation of the '*noge* agitation'.

62. Adapted from GMETBZ, 40–1.

63. Emphases in the three versions are mine. I have not indented them because such formatting would inhibit my attempt to display the approximated composition of calligraphy more in line with the way it has been done in the *Scrolls*.

64. *Genji monogatari*, *Shōgakukan nihon koten bungaku zenshū* (NKBZ) Vol. 4: 279.

65. T. 675, emphasis mine.

66. Here I use Richard Okada's phrase. For more on *engo* and their role in *Genji* narration, see Richard Okada, *Figures of Resistance: Language, Poetry and Narrating in The Tale of Genji and Other Mid-Heian Texts* (Durham, North Carolina and London: Duke University Press, 1991), pp. 108–11.

67. We should also keep in mind that 'kehai' 気配 can also mean 'sign' or, even more apt in the context of this paper, 'symptom'.

68. Here I am talking about sheet two of *Kashiwagi I*. See GMETBZ, 33.

69. I realize that the *hiragana* / *katakana* distinction may not have been as rigid during the time of the *Scroll*'s production; I distinguish here in order to characterize other differences in appearance between the characters.

70. Only the column in the very centre of the fourth sheet (column seven of thirteen), the line that begins: '[na]mita otoshite', is weighted consistently as heavily as those of the third sheet; four lines earlier than that, the third column's upper hemistiche is also weighted similarly.
71. I will explain what I mean by 'robust' and 'sickly' in subsequent paragraphs.
72. The emphasis here is mine. Refer to the passage quoted earlier for a longer translation.
73. Although I am now shifting gears slightly to discuss the notion of calligraphic health, and not 'wildness', I think the dishevelled appearance of Kashiwagi's hair and beard, the 'wild hairs' that represent it, and the ragged writing to be treated in the following paragraphs, are all related.
74. The word 'sarahohi' is the connective form (ren'yōkei 連用形) of the verb 'sarabohu,' which means 'to slim severely' ('hidoku yaseru'). The linking of the two verbs makes for a particularly emphatic rendering of 'to become thin'.
75. 'Iyo-iyo' is often rendered as 'gradually', but I think 'bit by bit' is an accurate variant that retains the adverb's onomatopoeic quality.
76. For more on the relationship between pain (to which illness is connected) and textual creation, see Elaine Scarry's *The Body in Pain*, 'Pain and Imagining' (New York: Oxford University Press, 1987), pp.161–80.
77. For this observation, I will be referring briefly to sheets three and four of *Kashiwagi II*, GMETBZ, 40–1.
78. T. 683.
79. Refer to GMETBZ, 41, column seven.
80. These geese also effect a pictorial pun in that they evoke the character of Kumoi no kari ('geese entering the clouds'); these are wild geese going into the clouds of silver oxide. See GMETBZ, 43.
81. See Kuroda 1986: 162–8.
82. At this point, please refer to the earlier examples of the 'tori no ato' passages quoted earlier in this paper.
83. Here I have italicized the words with which 'ato' shares a valence. Another pun on the word ('後' after/future/descendant/successor) resonates with Kashiwagi's lack of a legitimate male heir, due to his illicit liaison with Onna San no Miya (which produced Kaoru, who is assumed to be Genji's son).
84. T. 755. (His fear is warranted: spirit possession is to blame.)
85. See GMETBZ, 86.
86. Scarry (1985), op. cit., p.54.
87. In some cases, *midare-gaki* has strongly positive aesthetic value, as in the cases of Genji and Lady Rokujō's calligraphy. On this point, see Komai's classifications in Komai 1988: 269.
88. For more on this type of appeal, see Shimizu, 'The rite of writing', op. cit., p. 60, which glosses several *Genji* descriptions of *midare-gaki* in the context of their attractiveness. See also, Komai 1988: 270–1.
89. These are examples that occur in the *Yūgao* and *Suma* chapters, respectively.
90. T. 759. The phrase used to describe Murasaki's body, 'yase-hosori tama[hu]', is a more delicate rendering than the 'yase-sarahohi' used in Kashiwagi's portrayal. That said, the confluence of terms delineates a link between the two ill characters.
91. I use the term 'built' here to connote some of the layering of pigment that occurs in producing this type of painting. The term 'onna-e' is used in opposition to 'otoko-e'. I am assuming the gendered distinction between the two genres is based upon ideas of masculine art being lively and full of dynamic movement, whereas feminine pictures are characterized by their subdued quality and relative lack of movement. There are apparently also spatial differences: *onna-e* tend to be situated with their characters gathered indoors while *otoko-e* paintings are often set outdoors, allowing their characters greater freedom of movement.

92. The paintings were designed by a master painter, who composed the scene and drew the outlines. Then his apprentices would fill in those outlines with opaque mineral pigments. Finally, the master would go over the paint with ink again in order to add details and contour lines.

93. Other related examples from the same period that employ these techniques include *Nezame monogatari emaki* 寝覚物語絵巻, and the *Heike Nōgyō* 平家納経 (1164). In terms of paper design, the *Heike Nōgyō* is similar to the *Genji Scrolls* as is the contemporaneous *Sanjūrokunin kashū* 三十六人歌集 (*The Thirty-six Poets' Anthology*, 1112). For more on the relationship between the *Genji Scrolls* and the *Thirty-six Poets' Anthology*, see Akiyama Terukazu's essay 'Emakimono no hassei to tenkai', the section entitled: 'Dō jidai no ihin; 'Sanjyūrokunin shū' nado' ('Relics of the Same Period: The Thirty-Six Poets' Anthology, et al.'), Akiyama Terukazu: 2000, vol. 1, pp. 26–8. For more on the techniques involved in constructing *tsukuri-e*, see, in the same volume, 'Tsukuri-e no gihō' 作り絵の技法 ('The Techniques of *Tsukuri-e*'), pp. 24–5.

94. 'E no naka ni, jikanteki na keika wo hotondo fukamanai' is the phrase, in Akiyama, 'Emaki no hassei to tenkai,' ibid., p. 5.

95. Please refer to pp. 88 and 89 in the GMETBZ for images. See also Sano Midori's argument on this picture in chapter 2 of this volume.

96. I have superimposed a line onto several of the few columns of the *midare-gaki* sheet here to emphasize this angular coincidence.

97. Or, considered differently: instantaneously.

98. Bush clover (*hagi*) and dew (*tsuyu*) are the main poetic images of the chapter. The most emotionally charged poem in the chapter is produced by Murasaki a little while before she expires, and contains both of these words, as does Genji's response.

99. Silver is often used in the depiction of nocturnal scenes, particularly as a pigment for the moon or moonlight.

100. *Genji*, S.718. Emphasis mine.

101. Scarry, op. cit., p. 53.

102. I use the word 'delirium' here because it denotes both bodily trembling and incoherent speech, two traits related to *midare-gaki*.

103. NKBZ 4: 491, emphasis mine.

104. T. 759.

105. Shimizu notes that 'The metaphor of tangled leaves and evanescent dew is the crucial theme in the second half of the text and calligraphy.' Shimizu, 'The rite of writing, op. cit., p. 57.

2

THE NARRATION OF TALES, THE NARRATION OF PAINTINGS

SANO MIDORI

TRANSLATED BY SINEAD KEHOE

❧

UNDERSTANDING NARRATIVE, UNDERSTANDING PAINTINGS

This chapter considers the narrative 'method' of the *Tale of Genji* as it is presented in the narrative scroll paintings owned by the Tokugawa and Goto Museums. In attempting to 'read' the *Tale of Genji* in this format, one must first address the somewhat fluid and inconsistent boundaries of the word 'narrative'. The parameters of 'narrative' could be described as follows:

i. narratives have plots
ii. narratives give form to time
iii. narratives are operated by the act of narrating
iv. narratives require a reader.

The plot is the organization of the events.[1] These events (which took place, or were anticipated) are described by different narrative voices (via various deliveries, or perspectives), and the 'narration' or 'reading' of the incidents coincides with the 'experiencing' of time. That is to say, however, it is not simply the causal relation and continuity of the incidents that conceptualizes time. Instead, one could say that the locus of narration is also the locus where time is manifest.

Enomoto Masazumi, for example, has written that *The Tale of Genji*'s basic temporal structure is:

> … the sense of time that a reader takes away from *The Tale of Genji* … [is] … one of presence and 'presentness' at the locus of narration, giving the impression that the action is occurring 'now' right before one's eyes.[2]

Enomoto's focus upon narration as giving 'form to time' augments a similar discussion by Shimizu Yoshiko's who notes that in any scene:

The author [of *The Tale of Genji*] exhaustively pursues the precise and the vague ticking away of time. Therefore, although the pace may appear to slow down suddenly, or even condense on a single point, one scene clearly ticks out the detailed time of its content and the overall action proceeds. Although the scene central to the chapter is conceived by the author as a single static painting, the event is conveyed in the world of language, in which the quality of continuous narration is not lost.[3]

Nakayama Masahiko, citing the peculiar nature of the 'voice convention'[4] of Japanese adjectives (of emotion or desire) and verbs (of feeling and thought) writes:

... of course the finitive form of these terms expresses the present tense, and that present is taken as far as possible to correspond to pure, localized present time.[5]

He observes that the text of *The Tale of Genji* possesses the peculiar features of that localized present time, and of a manifested subject of textual action. This is to say, Nakayama explains that the narration of *The Tale of Genji* is such that the reader identifies himself/herself with the basis of textual action as 'here and now' and the subject of that action as 'I'.

In Shimizu's thought-provoking critique, narrative time is continuously unfolding even within a static framed scene.[6] Enomoto, in the piece mentioned above, follows Shimizu's argument and focuses on narrative and time. Although in another essay Enomoto deviates from the idea of the 'presence and "presentness" of the locus of narration' in the text, he points to a quality of 'now-ness' found in the painted scenes of the *Genji Scrolls*, noting that the auxiliary verbal suffix 'けり' (which defines a past event) is excluded from the excerpt for this purpose, and discusses the 'here and now' manifested in the *Genji Scrolls* narrative format.[7] Nakayama presents an argument interpreting the narrative composition of *The Tale of Genji* by comparing it to its French translation.

These arguments are persuasive and special attention should be given to the fact that this type of analysis performed on this particular work (*The Tale of Genji*) has initiated a wider debate redolent with possibilities. Specifically, however, they are particularly noteworthy for taking up the realm of 'time' as a narrative problem.

This issue of the 'presentness' of narrative does not end with the peculiar qualities of the text of *The Tale of Genji*; nor does it end with the debate on the peculiarities of the Japanese language. Rather we are led to an examination of the basic theoretical arguments of narrative itself. To begin with, let us ask the following question: is not narrating – be it textual or oral – the sort of action which generates a space in which the reader and the listener can hold in common the present?[8] Narrating not only manifests the localized time of 'now' and 'here' (in other words, time without breadth). Narrating is also a manipulation (productive action) which combines localized moments of 'now' and 'here,' and gives them form – something we must not lose sight of.

Furthermore the narrated 'now' (the 'now' held in common by the reader/listener) is positioned in relation to the expansion of memory and anticipation as shown below in my description of the 'reading' of the *Genji Scrolls*. That is to say, the manifestation of time (in its infinitesimal existence, or point of 'now') is something that continuously produces the vectors of anticipation which direct the future, and the vectors of memory which direct the past. The divisions of time, and the sections of a narrative, are 'imaged' (in the case of the writer) or 're-imaged' (in the case of the reader), as continuous: a continuation from the past to the future; or the connection of twisted or reversed time in the story. Time is the negotiation between the narrative's sequence and the reader's reading. Narrating manifests the 'here and now', and shares it with the reader, while simultaneously recovering it and allocating it in the narrative sequence. As this continuous tug of war recurs, the intersection of the two worlds (the world of the text and the reader) pulls the narrative along and achieves the expansion of time.

I now turn to the *aporia* of time to see how people have approached it: time as an entity without existence; and time as existence only to be verified through experience. How is it that *logos* can capture *chronos*? Certainly, it was through telling stories that people humanized time.[9] Narrative is the 'imaging', as well as the 're-imaging' of time, by means of some code of language (in the broad sense of the word).

Narratives can be divided into two main categories: 'content' and 'form'. Content indicates that which is narrated (linguistic content), while form indicates the narrating itself (linguistic action).[10] The recent preoccupation with 'form' may account for the trail blazed to new horizons of narrative theory, but let us not forget the importance of 'content' too. 'Individual pieces' are not something left only to the narrative 'method' (the type of narrating). As the 'intercepts' of a story emerge, the narrating which manages these 'intercepts' carves out the contours of the 'individual pieces' of the narrative. The content of the narrative (that which is narrated), collides with the various aspects (forms) of the narrating, thereby constructing the 'individual pieces' of the narrative's sequence.

This chapter attempts to develop the argument that it is necessary to identify the basic features of these written narratives (the imaging of time and the re-imaging of time), that is the structural elements that support the narrative. I shall, therefore, pay particular attention to the three elements: plot, narrating and reading. To reiterate, these three fundamental elements are: the narrative 'must have a plot',[11] and then it must also have the two constitutive elements of narrative activity – 'narrating' and 'reader'.[12]

The next question might be how to establish the parameters of 'painting'? In comparing painting with literature, the first thing to note is its material character. Painting cannot be realized without the tangible structure – painted surface (paper, wood and cloth) and painting materials (ink and pigments), and the visual structure of the painting plane which is visually constructed from line and colour. What is depicted therein guides the viewer to some kind of image and delivers meaning – regardless of the viewer's capacity to interpret it. The characteristics of painting may be enumerated as follows:

i. materiality
ii. representational qualities
iii. technical properties
iv. two-dimensionality.[13]

Painting, in its tangible form, pre-exists as a frame which establishes the visual domain through its materials (canvas and paints) and by the scale and shape of its surface. The reader's (viewer's) gaze scans that total visual domain, reading (or viewing) the 'text' that is the painting. The main difference between both texts – the 'language-text' and the 'painting-text' – is that the former has a story-line, while the latter reveals the story. The characteristic of a painting is that typically what is depicted is visually experienced comprehensively or simultaneously in what I term here the 'all at once experience'.[14] The level of expression or the entire picture plane is, of course, not homogenous. The strength of its 'visual verifiability' (or 'visual impact') lies, naturally, in the consistency of the depiction; system of symbolic placement of forms; colour and line; and the effect of its forms – all of which ingeniously guide the reader's gaze. Thus guided, the image (both its parts and as the sum of its parts) and the sequence of the meaning is read on the picture plane 'all at once'. Painting has a particular form as text, in the sense that it is expressed within the frame of the visual domain, and that within the frame (putting visual verifiability aside) the gaze moves over the whole and its parts simultaneously.

This being the case, a painting which is the object of a comprehensive gaze allows, fundamentally, for the manifestation of 'here and now', that is to say, for the manifestation of the represented objects and events in the present. We would do well to recall Lessing who categorized painting as a spatial art.[15] Painting, in many cases, and in the case of narrative painting in particular, causes the reader/viewer to pick up a sense of time which has breadth.[16]

Let us consider the following. The 'presentness' of the depicted objects and events generally lacks a connection to the temporal construction of the reader's actual world, and their positions cannot be determined with respect to it. In other words, the 'presentness' freely arises from the reader's absolute chronological temporal structure. The reader pulls this omnipresent time towards himself as he reads, and the depicted scene (the painting-text) thus anchors itself in the sequential time existing beyond (the text). That is, in essence, the starting point of 'grand narrative'.[17]

Secondly, there is what is called 'intratextual' time. The actualization of sequential time by reading – of course not in 'real time' – is not a self-willed construction of the reader. That is to say that it is not something the reader embraces absolutely. The producer's subjective time, or the sequential time (the text's autonomous time) which the depicted scene (the painting) allows to bleed outside of the text, is reflected in the sequential time of reading. In other words, the painting-text is already, in essence, located within that which sets the narrative in motion. In the case of narrative painting (including here, for example, the genre of 'history painting') the 'here and now' of the picture plane follows the sequence of the original text of the narrative. At the same time, however, the collision of variously parsed aspects within the picture plane results in an oscillation between the severing and fusing of the 'here and now' on various levels. The relative importance of the meanings are played out through the motifs, the opacity of the pigments and the continuity of one form to another. Together these serve to reveal the 'now and here' structure of time within the picture plane.

In other words, the 'painted frame' (that which sets the narrative in motion in the painting) constitutes that which 'narrates' the painting. I wish now to consider the narrative 'method' (the perspective and method of expression in narrative painting) and will take as an example, the *Genji Scrolls* owned by the Tokugawa and Gotō Museums.

NARRATING IN *THE TALE OF GENJI SCROLLS*

The Tale of Genji Scrolls is the oldest extant painted version of *The Tale of Genji*. The ingenious composition and superior descriptive power of this work speak to the maturation of Japanese narrative painting in the first half of the twelfth century. The extant sections come from only twenty chapters of *The Tale of Genji* and it is presumed that the original might have comprised leaves from all fifty-four chapters, assembled as a long illustrated narrative scroll, perhaps in a set of about twelve scrolls.[18]

It is a work of relatively small format measuring approximately 22 centimetres from top to bottom. The text is copied across several sheets of paper, and each 'scene' is punctuated by a single-sheet painting, thus giving it a 'paragraph format' (*danraku shiki* 段落式). This format stands in strong contrast to that of the illustrated handscrolls of '*setsuwa* 説話' (Buddhist narratives such as, for example, *The Miraculous Origins of Mt Shigi* 信貴山縁起絵巻) or the format of handscroll narratives like *The Story of the Chancellor Ban Dainagon* 伴大納言絵巻. These are also twelfth century scrolls, but consist of long paintings running across a number of sheets of paper. That is to say, these narrative paintings employ '*renzoku shiki* 連続式', a continuous format, and the style of their paintings has a light, playful quality similar to animation. The linearity of such works is characterized as the punctuated format (*senbyō shugi* 線描主義) and it contrasts with the *Genji Scrolls* (T/G), which presents a romantic, suspended moment (*seitaiteki* 静態的), finely articulated in beautiful polychromy using such techniques known as a 'line-for-an-eye and a hook-for-a-nose' and 'blown-away-roof'.

We find four varieties of painting styles, and five calligraphic styles in the extant *Genji Scrolls* (T/G).[19] Accordingly, it may be considered to be a collaborative work involving several groups. The paintings command intense descriptive power and the calligraphy is written over beautiful sheets of paper sprinkled with gold and silver foil; the surface lavished with high quality pigments which express the sensibility of the narrative. Both paintings and calligraphy are the shining achievements of each group vying with one another.

We may speculate that the production of the original *Genji Scrolls* was the result of a competition like a '*mono awase* 物合' (a competitive matching of things) conducted by the courtiers of the imperial court.[20]

We can surmise, from the extant segments that survive in the T/G version, that each leaf includes a selection of one to three scenes extracted from the original text.[21] From these scenes a text has been created (suitably edited and adapted) and a painting appended. The composition may be considered to be a slightly adapted or edited version (*shōshutsubon* 抄出本) of *The Tale of Genji*, the premise being that the reader is already familiar with the complete text. These scrolls are not targeted, therefore, at readers unacquainted with the original text; in fact, only readers very well acquainted with the original can fully appreciate and enjoy the way in which the world of the narrative has been visualized through this form of illustration; and the scrolls anticipate such enjoyment.

It must be said that, in this sense, that the T/G version is fundamentally different in concept from the illustrated versions of the woodblock printed editions. The woodblock prints were published with the dual purpose of being guides to understanding and to popularizing the text of *The Tale of Genji*; for example, Yamamoto Shunshō's 山本春正 *The Illustrated Tale of Genji* (*E-iri Genji monogatari* 絵入源氏物語).[22] Unlike these 'popular' versions, the scrolls had a 'summarizing sequence': a concept not found in the production of the *Genji* sets of poetry slips and fans. Painted with scenes from *Genji*, such poem-slips and fans were popular from the end of the middle ages into the pre-modern era; the artists painstakingly indexing the *Genji* narrative as they carved out, scene by scene, these vehicles of *Genji* images.[23]

Many have already examined the subject of narrative expression in the *Genji Scrolls* (T/G). One such scholar, Enomoto, discusses these *Genji Scrolls* by examining and comparing the original text with the handscroll texts, as well as Seidensticker's English translation. Although I, too, have contributed to these discussions elsewhere, Enomoto's provocative arguments conclude that there is still, however, an abundance of topics crying out for further analysis. If I were to summarize, somewhat approximately, these scholarly debates on narrative expression, I would note that most attention has been paid to two issues: 'scene' and 'viewpoint'.[24] Against the background of this ongoing research, I wish to consider the issues of 'plurality of perspective' and the description provided by the narrator from the 'perspective of narrating'. Seeing the reader as 'a subject of the action of the narrative' is essential to my argument about 'perspective' and 'narrator'.

Plurality of perspective
I would like to refer to the painting from the chapter titled *The Law* (*Minori*) discussed in chapter 1 of this volume by Reginald Jackson (Fig. 1–22). The excerpt narrates Murasaki's death including exchange poetry between Murasaki, the Empress and Genji.[25] Its composition, based on lines slanting from right to left, positions the interior of the room to the right and the garden on the left. In contrast to the carefully reproduced interior, the garden is

portrayed, essentially symbolically, simply by grasses waving in the wind against a silvery background.

The interior and exterior is clearly contrasted by colour and descriptive direction, with little sense of spatial consistency. Moreover, there is a disjunctive angle of vision; a division created by the confrontational breaking away of the view of autumnal grass from the rest of the composition, the bird's-eye view. The tie-beams are abruptly truncated at an angle, and the bold, sharp diagonal lines running parallel to each other add to the sense of anxiety expressed in Murasaki's position as she leans against the armrest. The silvery air sweeps against the backs of Genji and the Empress and the sorrow of all three finds its metaphor in the wind-swept grasses of autumn.

It has often been pointed out that this illustration brings together three different viewpoints. First, there is the bird's-eye view provided by the 'blown-away roof' composition. This is the view of a world below glimpsed through the eyes of a god, or the view seen by a girl who has removed the roof of her doll's house and is peering inside. Next, there is the 'high angle view' where the viewer seems to be very close to the figures within the painting (as, for example, in the case of Genji and Murasaki, who are too large relative to the scale of the room). Finally, there is 'the interior perspective': the view of the figures within the painting. The grasses of the garden, for example, a counterbalance in the composition, establish the view reflected in the eyes of the figures in the painting.

The reader's glance sweeps across the whole painting, encompassing all these views as one. First we look 'down' from the upper right, dominant end of the slanted room; then into the situation 'within' the room (where the three figures of Murasaki, Genji and the Empress are arranged); and finally the reader's glance takes in the entire painting and sees the garden and the swaying grasses. The gaze, framing the narrative world, then moves on to the details of the painting. It is not unusual in this type of feminine painting (*onna-e*) to see a female form, like the figure of the Empress here, shown from the back and depicted so small that all scale and balance is lost. It lacks strength or any sense of visual recognizability.[26] By contrast, the depiction of the two oversized figures (in relation to the architecture) directs the reader's scrutiny first to Genji and Murasaki and then to what they touch, hold and look at: Murasaki leans against an armrest and Genji holds a fan. Thus our gaze moves from behind Genji to face Murasaki, and on to the autumn grasses at which Murasaki may have been looking. It moves from the so-called 'zero focalization' to the 'focalization' of the figures in the painting.[27] The gaze of the reader (from Genji to Murasaki) is integrated with Genji's angle of vision; similarly the gaze towards the autumn grasses seems to correspond to that of Murasaki's view.

The painter clearly positions these images in a way that directs the reader's gaze. In this scene, we read the connection between Genji and Murasaki. The artist depicts them sitting close to one another, counterbalanced by the juxtaposition of the garden, as seen by through Murasaki's eyes. This view supports the reader's expectations, based on prior knowledge of the scroll text, and these limit the reader's freedom of interpretive choices. Furthermore, the original written text is a world of myriad voices; one in which the subject of the narrating voice is incessantly changing from the 'omniscient narrator' to the 'voiced narrator' and to the voice of the characters in the narrative. In other words, the scene of the narration is nested like so many Russian dolls.[28]

However, the reader's gaze does not stop: it oscillates between observing the whole, its parts and back again; moving from a bird's eye view of the entire scene ('zero focalization'), down to the scrutiny of its separate parts ('the focalization' of its figures), and back to acknowledge the whole painting. The reader knows that the gaze towards the autumn grasses is Murasaki's angle of vision, and that at the same time it is also the angle of the Empress and Genji.[29] In the memory of the reader, primed by the text, the focus does not stop at Murasaki, although in the painting she is brought into focus by the gaze and 'narrated' by the poems of Genji and the Empress. Moving from one figure to another, approaching and retreating, the gaze oscillates between the objectivized world of the narrative and the subjective assimilation of the viewpoints of the figures.

Neither the 'omniscient narrator', nor the narrators living in the world of the narrative are given form. However, the viewpoint which moves across the entire world of the narrative exists and thus the very action of the reader's reading, or viewing from one particular viewpoint, establishes an omniscient viewpoint outside the work; bringing to mind the eye of the camera. There is something operating within the reader's 'reading', that functions to control the cause and effect of action and to work out its sequence, allowing the entire scene into the field of vision.

At the root of the syntax of a painting is the text's 'voice', rendered as third person narrative. The 'bird's-eye view' technique used in narrative painting clearly establishes the 'omniscient reader', the narrative's transcendental omniscient viewpoint (an omniscient viewpoint that is manifest at the level of the reader's logic).[30]

It goes without saying, therefore, that the author of the *Genji Scrolls* is none other than the reader.[31] Let us take the example of a 'competent reader' of *The Tale of Genji*. Figures 2-1 and 2-2, also illustrate 'The Law' ('Minori') chapter, this time taken from Yamato Waki's appealing *manga* comic adaptation of *The Tale of Genji, Asaki yume mishi* (*Passing Dreams*).[32] The two-page section reproduced here follows the dialogue between the Empress Akashi and Murasaki which is expanded into four pages and is followed by Murasaki's death.

Incidentally, *Passing Dreams* narrates the story primarily through the techniques of direct speech and interior monologue. Events are narrated exclusively by the characters involved; the events emerge from the dialogue between the characters written in balloons and from their thoughts and feelings written as narration. Of course, this does not mean that the 'narrator' has completely vanished. There are a number of exceptions – the so-called author interventions.[33] There is no case, however, where a figure appears suddenly at the locus of the narration (giving life to the world of the narrative from within), or in

Figs. 2-1 (A and B)[35]

Fig. 2-1(B)

(B1): From top left, right edge
Murasaki 'No! ... that is not it ... really, I was happy'

(B2): Left
Murasaki 'To have been able to love someone, and to love this world ... to have been loved ...'

(B3):
Genji: 'Oh! – strange that it happened ...'

(B4): Below right
Genji appears:
Princess: 'Daddy ...
Genji: 'So how long has it been since you looked out over the flowers ...?'

(B5): Left of that, top
Genji 'Oh, so the Empress's coming has changed you.'

(B6): Below that
Murasaki: 'Ah, poor you ...
'I cannot possibly leave you, when you are so weak ...'

Fig. 2-1(A)

(A1): From top right:
Murasaki 'No, it is not alright to be like me ...'

(A2): Below it:
Empress 'Mummy! ...'

(A3): Below that, right:
Murasaki 'To live like me just to be at the beck and call of the love of a Lord is by no means the best way to live!'
'You are someone who can have a way of life that is not like mine!'

Below:
Murasaki 'I want you to live as someone who would like to live with dignity as a woman, who is not at the mercy of a great lord.'

(A4–6): To left of that:
Empress 'Mummy! ... Then you have not been happy?'
Murasaki 'I was not happy ...'

Fig. 2-2 (C)

From top right
Murasaki   'Transient alas, those dew drops settled on the clover leaves
Soon to be scattered by the autumn wind' [Waka #1: IM. 80]
Murasaki [modern Japanese version]
Though I can sit up now, my life is transient, like those dew drops on the clover leaves scattering by the autumn wind.
Genji   '... My lady...'
Genji   'In this frail world
Where every dewdrop struggles to be the first to go
Let neither of us leave the other one behind' [Waka #2: IM. 80]
Genji [modern Japanese version]
In any case, life is as fragile as the dew that competes to be the first to fly away, I cannot bear to be the last to leave.

(3):   Below that
Empress: 'Daddy, Mummy, you say nothing but tragic words...'

(4):   Below that
Murasaki   '..... ......'

which – phantasmagorically – the narrator appears (through being assimilated into the characters in the work).[34]

Let us track these frames which, for convenience, I have numbered sequentially. The opening scene (A1) is Murasaki's full face. As the dialogue clearly shows, the reader looks at Murasaki from the same perspective or viewpoint as that of the Empress as she converses with Murasaki (A2). Next is Murasaki's interior monologue (A3). The viewpoint maintains a considerable distance from Murasaki and the reader 'images' Murasaki's thoughts in the frame. Then in frame (B3) Genji makes his debut as a 'voice' and in (B4) Murasaki and the

Empress are in the background, while Genji is in the foreground; all figures in the scene are present. In (B5), Genji's thoughts are directed to Murasaki as words and, in this frame, Murasaki, who was depicted in the background in (B4) is drawn considerably closer in, while in (B6) the viewpoint seems to move to Murasaki. The composition of this frame is further complicated by its many layers of construction: the reader is looking at Murasaki; stares at Genji's entire figure; and reads Murasaki's thoughts. In staring at Genji, the reader assumes Murasaki's viewpoint, but at the same time, the reader is looking at Murasaki, the protagonist of the frame (B6).

Next, the sequences (C) – (2) and (3)) focus on Murasaki, Genji and the Empress, consecutively and the former two express poems of their internal thoughts. In C-(4), the reader's perspective takes in all three people objectively. That is, the narrating which, from the visit of the Empress to the composing of poems by the two people, changes from one viewpoint to the next in each frame is now in C4 governed by the 'narration frame' of the 'author' or 'omniscient narrator' established as external to the work. This 'author' or 'omniscient narrator' is inscribed in the auxiliary verb (けり) of the original written text, at the end of the passage: 'It was indescribably sad' (かけとめん方なきぞ悲しけれ). The perspective of such narrating is something beyond the picture plane.

The twelfth-century single sheet painting of *The Law*, and the modern, continuous frame composition of Fig. 2-1, and Fig. 2-2 both render the climax of *The Tale of Genji*'s chapter 'The Law' as painting. The modern version, dividing the story into these slices or 'frames', painstakingly traces the changes in perspective in the original text and reproduces the linearity of the text. The twelfth-century version slices out a particular scene from the story, and folds within it, as layers, a number of different perspectives. However, in contrast to the layering seen in the cartoon, the twelfth-century version has the Russian doll effect of moving from outside the narrative world to inside the narrative world, from a panoramic view to a close-up. Yet, common to both is the framework: one in which the 'omniscient viewpoint' is placed outside the picture plane, and exterior to the narrative world.

We see in the T/G composition of *The Law* a plurality of perspectives: views that 'come and go' 'inside and outside' of the painted world. At the same time the painting recreates the 'narrating' of the original text – the 'narrating' it creates is not necessarily the same as that of the text. One might almost say that the 'narrating' of the painting under discussion requires a 'reading' that incessantly consults the text, and that the point of the narration may in fact lie in the dynamics of such interaction.

Depiction of Ladies-in-Waiting[36]
In the previous section, we saw the narrating frame bound by the omniscient viewpoint which does not clearly reveal its form in the world of narrative. We also saw the viewpoint which attaches itself to the figures in the narrative world, and is assimilated to their viewpoints: these figures we might call 'transparent

narrators'. At the same time as they frame the scene, these narrators (who possess an unbalanced, phantasmagoric viewpoint within the scene) share the same technique of narrating as the reader. However, just as the 'voiced narrator' appears from time to time in the original text of *The Tale of Genji*, a type of narrating distinct from 'transparent narrating' can appear within the scene, that is to say, a narrator possessed of form.

Take, for example, the painting of the scene from the chapter, 'Evening Mist' (Fig. 2-2). A *shōji* 障子 screen partitions off the two ladies-in-waiting on one side of the painting, while the leftward line of the tie-beam descends into the main room which is where we find the principle couple, Yūgiri and Kumoinokari. The ladies-in-waiting are shown to be peripheral both in their placement within the picture plane, and by the way they are depicted. The painting is clearly about the central figures (Yūgiri and Kumoinokari) as she steals up behind her husband intending to snatch away a letter from the Ichijō mansion. In the neighbouring room, two ladies-in-waiting are positioned to overhear the couple's imminent quarrel.

Neither the scroll text (which corresponds to this scene) nor the original text makes any mention of the existence of these ladies-in-waiting; although any reader would be right to assume the presence of such ladies-in-waiting in the context of an aristocratic Heian household of this period. In our role as visual readers of this scene, we rescue those ladies-in-waiting from their transparent existence. They are no longer just figures who shore up a scene; they have become animated. We have turned them into characters who begin to move in the narrative. While never directly participating, they observe and can be said to substitute for us, the readers.

We should, perhaps, first verify how we scan the picture plane, the motion of our viewpoint as readers, when we see, or read, this scene. As in most East Asian painting, and in the illustrated narrative scroll format in particular (although this one no longer has its original form), the reader's gaze first sweeps across the entire scene, flowing from the right. Directing the eye is the diagonal line of the tie-beam which slants down from the right, discriminating between Yūgiri and Kumoinokari (on the left) and the ladies-in-waiting (on the right). Our viewpoint, pushed back to the black chest (running parallel to the tie-beam to the back left of the painting), focuses on the action taking place between the main protagonists and then, only then, encompasses the intriguing image of two ladies spying from the next room. These eavesdropping ladies-in-waiting frame the reader's viewpoint: that is to say they guide our scrutiny of events.

The first scene of *The Ivy* (Fig. 2-3) is somewhat similar. Kaoru and the Emperor are playing a game of *go* 碁 while two ladies-in-waiting spy on them from the next room. These ladies-in-waiting 'witness' the marvellous Kaoru as a suitable son-in-law for the Emperor while the Emperor loses his game (losses which determine Kaoru's engagement). When the Emperor allows Kaoru to take the chrysanthemum from the garden, it also symbolizes the understanding between them that the second princess is to be married to Kaoru.[37]

The court ladies portrayed in this painting never participate in the central events. Placed at the periphery of the narrative, they simply exist as eyes trained on those events; 'witnesses' who take on the role of narrating what they have seen and heard. Cannot these witnesses be said, therefore, to be the 'narrators of the narrative'? They bring to mind the 'false frame' of *The Tale of Genji*; reminiscent of those ladies of old; women who spied and eavesdropped on all the events and who were probably the very same ladies-in-waiting who later told 'tales'. In the original text, there were 'floating narrators': their voices heard as they came in and out of the text, but their forms never seen. In the *Genji Scrolls*, these floating narrators are given a physical presence.

As witnesses, they observe but only imperfectly: their ears pricked up but listening from neighbouring rooms; their eyes peeled but only to spy through blinds. They are neither participants in the events, nor complete observers and certainly not true (or expert) witnesses. These events are therefore narrated by those whom I call 'inadequate observers': ladies who happen to be present at the event, but who never participate directly in, nor completely see or hear, such events.

Incidentally, Murasaki Shikibu, who bore a heavy responsibility as the *Auspicious Event Reporter* of the Midō Kampaku's residence, often makes the remark in her diary (*The Diary of Murasaki Shikibu*), 'I did not see all the details' (くはしく見はべらず).[38] This kind of excuse can often be found in the diaries of poetry contests which Murasaki Shikibu probably referred to when she recorded the auspicious birth of the imperial prince. The records as narrated by ladies-in-waiting, who are not in total possession of all the facts, may contain obscurations of these facts, slight fabrications and praise – all of which is allowed for in the romantic structure.[39] The very fact that the narrator's voice is 'heard' transforms perhaps a 'chronicle' into a 'narrative'.[40]

In any case, narrative text, once it takes as its starting point the narration of events, is immediately limited by the perceptions of the narrator; in effect, the omniscient viewpoint of the narrative. So if, as argued above, an omniscient viewpoint does in fact exist, then the question arises as to where is it situated and who possesses it.[41]

The narrator within the narrative is fundamentally an 'inadequate observer', a witness who is not allowed within a certain distance of the occurrences; an interpreter who has lost her sense of balance. The reader is the counterpart of the 'inadequate observer' (the observer, witness, interpreter) and so, in this way, the omniscient viewpoint is given to the reader.

The painting of the second scene of *The Oak Tree* (Fig. 1–3) provides a perfect illustration of narrative symbolism. The ladies-in-waiting milling around at the lower left-hand corner of the painting, are not positioned to view the other side of the screen. They do not turn to look towards Yūgiri and Kashiwagi and, in denial, they thus refuse to see and acknowledge the tragic death scene.

CONCLUSIONS AND AMENDMENTS – THE READER BEYOND THE PLOT

I have stated above that the T/G version of the *Genji Scrolls* presupposes a reader already familiar with the *Tale of Genji*, and I have drawn attention to the fact that enjoyment of this T/G version relies on the enthusiastic reader of the original text. I wish here to scrutinize such texts once more, as compositions open only to a select group of readers, and examine what kind of 'narrating' such 'texts' succeed in creating.

Take, for example, *The Bell Cricket II* (Fig. 2-4). On the evening of the full moon, Genji and the young courtiers visit the Retired Emperor Reizei (from here on called the Reizei-in).[42] Of all twenty scenes that exist today, this scene has the most especially controlled and intimate composition. The palette is extremely limited; the composition clear-cut and powerful; and in the ordered depiction of the room, the figures are handled masterfully. The pale green of the *tatami* and the (orange) brown of the floorboards provide rhythmically repeating sashes of colour, guiding the reader's gaze from right to left; from the lower right-hand side of the painting to the upper left. The painting's compositional lines (parallel lines of architectural colour running diagonally from upper right to lower left) run counter to, and right across, the diagonal lines of the picture plane (the seated figures). We see the flute-playing nobleman in the front, Genji in the centre, and Reizei-in at the top left in this composition. Genji and Reizei-in are like mirrored reflections of one another, manifesting both the import and meaning of their confrontation in the narrative. We can, perhaps, add to this pair another two. The flute-playing lord can be paired off with his fellow nobleman in the lower part of the verandah (likely playing a *shō* 笙 [panpipes]). The counterpart of Hotaru, His Highness of War[43] (the figure in the lower left edge of the painting, at the base of the pillar) is the aristocrat, placed centrally on the verandah who is probably keeping time. Other figures which can be seen as 'matching' pairs are those squeezed in between each pair. These 'in-between pairs', however, completely lack the solidity of Genji and Reizei-in; and the solid mirror image of Genji and Reizei-in, enclosed by the two considerably looser mirrored pairs, is a deliberate attempt to emphasize the nucleus of the scene: Genji and Reizei-in.

The line-up of these figures (first Reizei-in, then Genji and then the flautist) along the diagonal axis of the picture plane is suggestive of the plot development revolving around the flute. In the chapter, 'Evening Mist', Kashiwagi's widow, the Princess Ochiba, gives her husband's beloved flute to Yūgiri and, in 'The Flute' chapter, as he plays it that night, Kashiwagi appears to him in a dream. Genji then takes possession of the flute from Yūgiri, intending to give it to its rightful owner (see 'The Bell Cricket' chapter). Furthermore, at the moon-viewing fête at the Rokujō palace (an event narrated in the original written text, but one which takes place just before the scene illustrated here in the T/G version *Bell Cricket*) Genji is seen to lament the death of Kashiwagi, famed for his talented flute playing.[44] The role of 'The Bell Cricket' chapter must be that, based on a poem by Bai Juyi (772–846) 'On the fifteenth night, I'll see the colour of the new moon, and think of my deceased friend two thousand *li* away',⁴⁵ thoughts of a distant friend, deceased Kashiwagi, are summoned by the moon into the context of the narrative, and Genji's pardon of him, and thus the reader's lamentation, is confirmed.⁴⁶ This being the case, it is appropriate if the figure seen to be playing the flute is Yūgiri.

In other words, the composition is such that Reizei-in and Yūgiri are lined up with Genji placed in the middle. Genji occupies almost the centre of the picture plane. The reader experiences the thrill of suspense when he views this expressive figural arrangement and recognizes in it the parent-child relationship. In the narratives Genji and Reizei-in are known to be exactly like one another, and in the picture plane they are painted as complementary mirror images. Yet, it is no secret that they are in fact father and child. Also Yūgiri, positioned with his back to Genji's is portrayed in the narrative as Genji's son (who inherits Genji's attributes) but here he is shown instead as a figure who lives by a different design.

There is another point well worth noting in this painting as its diagonal axis narrates the positioning of the one child hidden from the world (Genji's child: Reizei-in) and the other recognized by the world (his child: Yūgiri). Readers already familiar with the original text will undoubtedly recall the existence of another of Genji's sons, Kaoru showing that things depicted (Reizei-in and Yūgiri) can also announce motifs not present (the absence of Kaoru). Yūgiri plays the flute while his gaze fixes at a point beyond the picture plane. It is somewhere, right at the painting's edge, where nothing is depicted save a large swathe of silver, so that the reader might imagine Kaoru who though recognized by the world, is the son who is not really a son.⁴⁷

Since, in the original text of *The Tale of Genji*, there is no scene where in the Reizei-in's palace the noblemen play music, this picture is thought to be a unifying image and seen to be an intervention of the painter.⁴⁸ In the original text of *The Tale of Genji*, the scene which precedes the text of the *Genji Scrolls* shows Yūgiri and other courtiers playing music in ox-drawn palanquins approaching Reizei-in. The reader should note that such scenes, although outside the narrative fragments excerpted for the actual *Genji Scrolls* texts, nevertheless get brought into the picture plane. The reader of the *Genji Scrolls* delights in recalling the original text, not just experiencing the text and the paintings before him. Excerpted scenes are not concentrated at a single time (rendered as painted scenes) but acknowledge that they are a fusion of various scene-fragments – a synthesized scene. In a 'reading' illuminated by the memory of the original text, these static paintings achieve the breadth of the narrative's time. It is worth noting that the work of 'clipping out', the texts of *Genji Scrolls*, which are like excerpted versions of narratives, has the function of drawing the reader's attention to what comes before and after the excerpted sections. Sections coming both before and after these 'clipped out' excerpts from the texts are included within the scenes of the *Genji Scrolls* paintings.

Incidentally, in *Poetics*, Aristotle explains the importance of plot (the organization of the incidents) as an aspect of the construction of tragedy. He discusses it as something rational and having inevitable consequences. In other words, the plots of well constructed tragedies should exclude intrusions of anything non-inevitable. However, it appears that there is a recognition that the plot also includes that which is external to the plot. I do not here have the latitude to trace the arguments of Aristotle's *Poetics*, but Aristotle's statement on things 'external to the plot' is appealing and provocative.[49]

The text of the *Genji Scrolls* (T/G) excises a segment from the text of the original narrative, and presents a scene before the reader. The picture plane is principally a painted representation of the scene in the excerpted text, but at times motifs from scenes prior to or following the text are included. So the reader interprets and reads the narrative world expanding before his eyes as he reads the scroll's text, contemplates the painting, and has recurring memories of the original text. Even if the *Genji Scrolls* highlights the production of a world, at the same time it is bound to the features of the narrative of the original text which remains external to it. In other words, the reader interprets the *Genji Scrolls* before his eyes within the greater context of the narrative (the reader has captured).

The plot, as it is represented unravelling before one's eyes, is in constant consultation with that which is external to it given the fixed relationship between the *Genji Scrolls* and the original text. I would like to revisit this anew, in the context of the mutual actions of the narrative and the reader.

In reading the *Genji Scrolls*, that which is external to the consulted plot is not necessarily limited to that written in the original text. Take, for instance, the previously considered second scene of *The Bell Cricket* (Fig. 2-4). To the reader reading along in the original text, up until the point when chapter references Bai Juyi's poem, the elements external to the plot of the original text of *The Tale of Genji* are none other than the 'entire image of the scene'[50] of the narrative, which stands as the background of the world of the production of the original text. Of course, it is expected that this will be subtly different from reader to reader. This point is not limited to illustrated handscrolls – the secondary productions. The issue I problematize here is that each time the book is opened, the text is created anew.[51] Each time the reader reconstructs the 'narrating of the text'; it is a live narration. *The Bell Cricket II* (Fig. 2-4) presents itself as a good model for this argument. If there is a structure in which the reading of the visual text and the reading of the written text interact, it is because the 'reading' of the images requires constant consultation with the written text, as we verified in the first section on the plurality of viewpoints.

Let us take one more painting as an example. In Fig. 2-5, we see the third scene of *The Illustrated Tale of Wakeful Sleep* (*Nezame monogatari emaki*), considered to have been produced around the middle of the twelfth century. Generally speaking, the explanatory aspect of *The Illustrated Tale of Wakeful Sleep* is secondary to the moving and atmospheric aspect of its picture plane. In this third scene, one is deliberately made to view the form of Masakonokimi, the protagonist, by peeping into the interior through an open shutter left.

The corridor running from the upper right to lower left, divides the picture plane into two: on the left is a woman inside a room; and to the right, there is a garden with trees. One might associate this painting with the *Bamboo River I* of the *Genji Scrolls* (T/G) (Fig. 2-6). In the third scene of *The Illustrated Tale of Wakeful Sleep* (Fig. 2-5), the view of the garden is executed in a stylized pattern and, as previously stated, the protagonist Masakonokimi's form is also only but suggested in what is an extremely vague painting. Though these points are different, the similarity between the images from *The Tale of Wakeful Sleep* and the 'Bamboo River' chapter of *The Tale of Genji* is clear. I would like to cite my earlier remarks on *The Illustrated Tale of Wakeful Sleep*:

> When one views *The Illustrated Tale of Wakeful Sleep* qua illustration of a narrative, one finds that it diverges from the original text (the written text). That is, the text positively refuses to be pictorialized (in a literal sense). In composition, the handscroll takes the stance of putting forth the frame of an 'image' quoted from a scene in the narrative, and that 'image' is then laid as an imitation of that scene. It is reasonable to say that this is the location of a 'reading' which, taking the original text as an entrance, makes a comparatively large narrative emerge. Furthermore, three of the four extant paintings of *The Illustrated Tale of Wakeful Sleep* adopt an extremely distinct story expression, as even the figure of the protagonist who carries the plot does not occupy a clear position within the picture plane. With symbolic scenes that dismiss the main characters, the paintings show how the process of signification brings about estrangement from the story.[52]

The third scene of *The Illustrated Tale of Wakeful Sleep* renders visible for the reader the fact that the original text of *The Tale of Wakeful Sleep* references *The Tale of Genji*. We now peek, one scene after another, through the chain of associations, into the recesses of the entwined narratives.[53] Plot normally coexists with that external to the plot, narrative is manufactured with each 'reading', and the reader finds many paths through the forest of images. Does not painting's 'narration' elucidate for us the root of the debate on narrative's 'narration'? That is to say, works which express forms by the reader's reading present a twisting together of the various plots within the work and the reader's memory and expectations, elements which are external to the plot.

I have been extending an intricate discussion on narrative and painting above. I now hope to make this convoluted discussion more accessible by elucidating its very beginnings. Through the analysis of a single work (the painting-text) of the *Genji Scrolls* (T/G), I have discussed the manufacture of narration by the omniscient viewpoint of the reader. This idea occurred to me when I remarked upon the concept of that which is 'external to the plot' in Aristotle's *Poetics*.[54] Aristotle, as is well known, argued that plot (the organization of events) must be both logical and natural, and that the non-essential elements of the gods and fates should be eliminated. Yet at the same time, Aristotle said that the play could include those aspects which had to be excluded. In other words, he is saying that the drama that unravels on-stage causes the audience to recall things off-stage (not in the play). In other words, Aristotle suggests a dramaturgic method in which the irrational elements are excluded with great care from the surface of the text by the playwright, but nonetheless are called forth in the actions the audience sees, and are intertwined with the incidents on stage.

I do not here intend to enter into a debate on Aristotle, nor do I have the qualifications to do so and I am unclear whether the impressions recorded above are, in fact, valid interpretations of Aristotle. Yet, to me, the phrase 'external to the plot' was just like a light illuminating a path when one is lost.

With regard to the narrating of painting, I wish to take up once more the issue of the omniscient viewpoint, which I discussed elsewhere in 1992.[55] That time, I pigeonholed the question of who holds the omniscient viewpoint: the author or the reader? Therefore, in prioritizing the narrative painting which visually expresses text, the issue of 'reading' as the production (or creation) of narrative remained untouched as a large topic for future debate. Later in my discussion on narrative viewpoint, the discussion gradually turned to 'the reader whom the narrative transcendently possesses'. This reader exists external to the work, and also presents that which is external to the plot. My discussion is now concerned with the fact that 'that which is external to the plot', in other words, 'the entire view of the scene' is entrusted to the reader.

At the same time, I must make clear that I have drawn inspiration, for my discussion relating to the narrative activity which occurs at the intersection between the 'author's text' and the 'reader's text', from Umberto Eco's discourse on text, Paul Ricoeur's discourse on time, which I took up in the introduction,[56] and Aristotle's concept of that which is 'external to the plot': these severally are the wellsprings of my ideas.

Elsewhere I have discussed how the narrative's internal context in *The Illustrated Tale of Wakeful Sleep* is established by means of quoting antecedent images[57] and here I would like to take this opportunity of reviewing this. From the perspective of the work manifested in the reader's 'reading', it is not sufficient to speak of the general outline of the production's internal context. This presupposes what might be called a fixed (or definite) text view. The important thing, instead, is the context of the individual worlds that the individual reader establishes. So, in that sense, I wish to add another term to the one previously published, namely, the 'view of the entire scene',[58] and add to that notion, the importance of another: 'the form of memory arising from the reader's experience and expectations'.

NOTES

1. When using the term 'plot' here, I have in mind the plot *(mythos)* of Aristotle's *Poetics*. Aristotle said that plot is the structure of the action. In *Poetics*, plot building consists of the technique of structuring, and thus the internal connection of the plot is a logical, not a chronological, one. Furthermore, Aristotle considered the purpose of tragedy to be action, not a character, and seeing the *mythos* of tragedy to be locating the various paths by which an exalted individual action is cast into misfortune. That is to say, the structure of the plot is something that should work to lead the disharmony of the misfortune of the exalted individual action and the feelings of the audience (fear and pity) to being something probable and comprehensible (harmonious). Thus, as the six factors of the construction of tragedy, Aristotle posits (i) things which are the vehicles of imitation: 'diction' and 'song'; (ii) things which are the methods of imitation: 'the ornament of spectacle'; and (iii) things which are the object of imitation: 'plot', 'characters'

and 'reasoning'. He states that 'the most important of these is the structure of the incidents'. See Aristotle, *Poetics I with The Tractatus Coislinianus, A Hypothetical Reconstruction of Poetics II, The Fragments of the 'On Poets'*, translated by Richard Janko (Indianapolis: Hackett Publishing Company, 1987), p. 8. Furthermore, Aristotle says that: 'The plot ... is the first principle ... of a tragedy.' Matsumoto Nisuke and Oka Michio's commentary interprets this point as: 'For each part of a tragedy (aspect of construction), the purpose is to actualize the (expression of) form that exhibits the function ... the plot is this form, and is to be viewed as the principle which actualizes this form'; see Matsumoto and Oka (eds.), *Shigaku (Aristotle's Poetics), Iwanami bunko* (Tokyo: Iwanami Shoten, 1997), vol. 1, Ch. 6, note 17, p. 143.

2. Enomoto 1990. This issue – the presentness of the site of the narration – is one which is not confined to the analysis of *The Tale of Genji* in particular.

3. Shimizu Yoshiko 1980. First published in Shimizu Yoshiko 1966.

4. This means that, in case of Japanese adjectives which indicate one's emotion or desire and verbs which show one's feeling and thought, the subject of the textual action is the same as the subject of the textual expression.

5. Nakayama 1995: Ch. 2, p. 39.

6. The continuously unfolding time mentioned here moves forward in the sense of the act of narrating constructing time. However, the forward motion does not stipulate that narrated time is progressing on the time axis.

7. Enomoto 1992. Concerning けり, see Murakami Fuminobu's discussion in chapter 4 of this volume. Also see Jeremy Tambling's chapter 5.

8. As seen in the frame comprising, for example, the first words of *The Tale of the Bamboo Cutter* (*Taketori monogatari* 竹取物語), 'Now [it is] long ago' (今は昔), and its conclusion, 'And so it is told' (とぞいひ傳へたる), the various forms of narrating used in classical Japanese literature are, as pointed out by Takahashi Tōru, 'devices of psychological perspective camouflaging the continuity between the fictitious "long ago" and the readers' "now".' We must now take up anew Takahashi's argument on this point in the process of investigating the immediacy of narrating; see Takahashi Tōru 1991a.

9. 'Le temps devient temps humain dans la mesure où il est articulé sur un mode narratif' (Time becomes human time in so far as it is articulated in a narrative mode), Paul Ricoeur, *Temps et Récit*, vol. 1 (Paris: Seuil, 1983), p. 105.

10. The propositions which must be problematized here are Gérard Genette's '*histoire*' (narrative content), '*récit*' (narrative discourse) and '*narration*' (narrating). In Genette's idea, the third concept of '*narration*' turns to the discussion of narrating as an act of the author. This is a framework that divides narrating into mode and action (and Genette performed a concrete and structural analysis of the modes of narrating in the section on '*récit*'). I have not adopted these three divisions in this study. See his *Narrative Discourse: An Essay in Method* (Ithaca: Cornell University Press, 1980).

11. One might say, in other words, that to have a plot means to involve the possibility of summarizing, or the rules governing the causal relation and the time axis.

12. The reader shapes the text from outside the text. In the three aspects of communication of 'sender-information-recipient,' communication is not established unless there is movement from the sender to the recipient. And reading comprehension (to follow Ricoeur, op. cit.) is the end of the imaging of the text.

13. Arikawa Haruo divides paintings into the following four levels in order to discuss their compositions: material phenomena (material existence, materials); forms (visual existence, line, colour, form, design); illusions (object, image); and representations (symbolic existence). Arikawa Haruo, *Seiyō kaiga zenkai* (Interpreting Western Painting), unpublished manuscript. Besides expressing my appreciation for access to the manuscript, with its valuable investigative discussion, I am eagerly awaiting its publication.

14. Yet, of course, there are methods of appreciating paintings of the non-tableau variety (like illustrated handscrolls), which do not stipulate viewing all the features of a painting at the same time.

15. Gotthold E. Lessing, *Laocoon: An Essay Upon the Limits of Painting and Poetry, With Remarks Illustrative of Various Points in the History of Ancient Art*, translated by Ellen Frothingham (Boston: Roberts Brothers, 1893).
16. Even in the case of abstract painting, which is considered greatly distanced from narrative, for example in the paintings of the abstract expressionist Jackson Pollock, in all likelihood the material conditions of the weight of the paints and the dripping materials and so forth rouse the reader to a sense of time. Perhaps that may be understood as the reader setting the narrative in motion by giving physicality to time through viewing the material conditions.
17. See Jean François Lyotard, *The Postmodern Condition* (Manchester: Manchester University Press, 1984).
18. The paintings and text excerpts for nineteen scenes survive: *A Waste of Weeds*; *At the Pass*; *The Oak Tree I, II, III*; *The Flute*; *The Bell Cricket I, II*; *Evening Mist*; *The Law*; *Bamboo River I, II*; *The Maiden of the Bridge*; *Bracken Shoots*; *The Ivy I, II, III*; and *The Eastern Cottage I, II*. In addition, there remains the text excerpt of *A Picture Contest*, as well as the eight leaves of text (excerpt) fragments which have been passed down in albums and so forth: *Young Murasaki*; *The Safflower*; *Wind in the Pines*; *Wisps of Cloud*; *The Maidens*; *The Fireflies*; *The Pink*; and *The Oak Tree*. If we include lost chapters among them, the extant parts run from the fifth chapter, 'Young Murasaki' to the fiftieth 'The Eastern Cottage', then we may surmise that originally the work was meant to represent all the chapters from 'The Paulownia Pavilion' to 'The Bridge of Floating Dreams'. Aside from these there is also the painting from *Young Murasaki* housed at the Tokyo National Museum, which has been verified as having been a part of the T/G version; see Akiyama Terukazu 1978.
19. In the T/G paintings, four 'hands' can be identified by the size of the figures and the patterns on the clothing and so forth. The painting styles range from the considerable technical experience evident in the *Bamboo River* and *The Maiden of the Bridge* group; to the expository depiction of the *Young Murasaki* and *Bracken Roots* to the *Eastern Cottage* group; the special character of the drawn out symbolic expression with fine depictions seen in the group covering from *The Oak Tree* to *The Law*; and the group comprising *A Waste of Weeds* and *At the Pass* with its simple compositions. Those features reflect the stylistic preferences of the various painters in charge of the painting production. Leaving aside, for the moment, issues of these stylistic preferences of the various painters, I shall instead analyse the narrative of the painting of the T/G version as a whole, as an example of narrative painting expression in the first half of the twelfth century.
20. I have situated *The Genji Scrolls* (T/G) as part of the *ōchō no fūryū* (elegance in the Heian period) of the first part of the twelfth century. On this point, see the following essays: Sano Midori, 'Ōchō no fūryū' (Elegance in the Heian Period) and '*Genji monogatari emaki* no sekai' (The world of the *The Tale of Genji Scrolls*) in Sano 1997.
21. For instance, the group from *The Oak Tree* to *The Law* (which is considered to have survived as an undivided scroll) provides three scenes from the 'Oak Tree' chapter and two scenes from 'The Bell Cricket' chapter. The others take only one scene from the chapter. How it was determined which scenes would be selected from each chapter, as well as what kind of dynamics were at the base of those selections, is an important issue for this kind of excerpted version.
22. For example, the afterword of *The Illustrated Tale of Genji* (*E-iri Genji monogatari*) states: 'From long ago, there have been people with an interest in putting illustrations in books, so now, too, at places where the poems and phrases are particularly worthy of attention, I have augmented the text by humbly appending illustrations.' And in *The Overall Meanings and Fine Details of Genji* (*Genji no kōmoku* 源氏綱目), published by Yao Kambei 八尾勘兵衛 in Manji 3 (1660), it is said, 'Since long ago, there have been many mistakes in the illustrations with regard to depicting rank in appropriate clothing. For that reason, I have put in illustrations next to the text that should be illustrated.' According to Yoshida Kōichi's detailed research, *The Illustrated Tale of Genji* (*E-iri Genji monogatari*) was first published privately in Keian 3 (1650), after which it was published

in Jōō 3 (1654) by the bookseller Ikadō Setsurin 一華堂切臨, when additional woodcuts were added. See Yoshida 1984 and 1985. Concerning the construction of the designs of these enormously popular seventeenth century woodblock printed editions, I have pointed out the intersection of conventional principles (traditionalism) and the principles of the text (realism), and will discuss this issue concretely in the future (Sano 1994a).

23. In the case of these painted fans and poem-slips depicting *The Tale of Genji*, even when text is appended, in most cases it is only poems from the original text, and cases in which the poems and depicted scenes do not match one another are not rare. On the compositions of these medieval and premodern, small format paintings of *The Tale of Genji*, which pile upon one another patternistic style and indexed motifs, see the various versions compiled in Akiyama Ken and Taguchi Eiichi (eds) 1988.

24. In painting analysis, the term 'viewpoint' typically refers to the angle from which the scene is described. For that reason, it differs subtly from 'viewpoint' as it is taken in literary criticism, as either the narrator's or the author's viewpoint. Yet, in the narrative painting under discussion here, the issue of viewpoint is actually none other than a debate about narration. Incidentally, as a rule, it is rare that a single so-called fixed viewpoint unifies an entire painting. Especially in premodern Japanese painting, which was not guided by the one-point perspective method found in European Renaissance painting, there was no consciousness of a logical, rational viewpoint, and it was extremely common to have a multiplicity of viewpoints composing the picture plane. For instance, it is quite obvious in Sesshū's 雪舟 early sixteenth century *Bridge of Heaven* (*Ama no hashidate* 天橋立) that the expanse of mountains lined up along the bottom of the picture plane and the presentation of the curving expanse of scenery in the middle to the top of the picture plane which leads from Jikō-ji/Kokubun-ji to the promontory of Hashidate are captured from different perspectives. The painter, in composing the painting, unifies views from various angles and heights. Even this *Ama no hashidate*, notable amongst medieval Japanese paintings as a landscape painting based on an actual view, is not at all the sort of painting produced like a camera-shot with a fixed point of view. Turning to the fabrication that is painting, the painter transforms her own visual experience into a montage. Furthermore, one can find a clear discussion of the manifestation of different shapes of time achieved through compounding such different viewpoints in Chino 1988.

25. The scroll's text corresponds to the text of the original appearing in Iwanami ed., *Genji monogatari* (*The Tale of Genji*), SNKBT, vol. 4, p. 169, line 13 – p. 171, line 5. If one looks closely at the *Genji Scrolls*' text, it is clear that it is not an abridged version of the original. Furthermore, in relation to Enomoto's essay (1992), I wish to call attention to the dropping of the auxiliary verb of past tense, 'けり' in the scroll's text, which has the Empress visit Murasaki as, '[She] goes to the palace [みやぞまいりたまふ]' in place of, '[She] went to the palace [宮ぞ渡り給ける]'.

26. There needs to be a separate discussion of this type of female figure, drawn very small and from the back. To give a rough account of the points of debate, the problems might be, for example, a form shown from the back may imply that it is denied subjectivity or empathy, and small may mean that the figure is portrayed from a distance. In addition, there are the issues of why it is that small-sized figures viewed from the rear appear only as women, and the extent to which we find the application of this syntax throughout history and across genres.

27. Genette, op. cit., IV, 'Focus', pp. 222–7.

28. Enomoto (1992) has already meticulously argued this point, but I would like to identify once more the movement of the narrating viewpoint in the original text. At the risk of being lengthy, let us take a look at the text as we do so. See 'The Rites' (SNKBT IV: 169–71), *The Tale of Genji*, translated by Royall Tyler [T. 759–60], and Ivan Morris, *The Tale of Genji Scroll* (Tokyo and Palo Alto: Kodansha International, 1971) [Hereafter 'IM']. First of all, at the beginning of the text, the Empress Akashi visits Murasaki (1) '中宮はまいり給なむとあるを … こなたに御しつらひことにせさせ給' (Her Majesty would soon return to the palace, … and she had her rooms done up specially for the

occasion) [T. 759]. Here, the narrator directs her viewpoint close to the Empress's and Murasaki's inner thoughts as she narrates the circumstances. And reflecting upon Murasaki in the past, the formerly abundantly charming beauty, the narrator describes the present Murasaki who is now racked with illness, 'あてになまめかしきことの限りなさも' (she was more beautiful than ever; Seidensticker, 1981, p. 717, hereafter cited as 'S') and how '限りもなくらうたげにおかしげなる御さまにて' (her beauty now really was sublime) [T. 759]. Then, (2) 'いとかりそめに … 心ぐるしく、すゞろにものがなし' (For the empress the slight figure before her, the very serenity bespeaking evanescence, was utter sadness) [S. 717] gives rise to the narrator's viewpoint seen in 'この世の花のかほりにもよそへられ給しを' (because where once the overflowing richness and brilliance of her looks had evoked the magnificence of worldly blossoms) [T. 759]. At the same time, the locus of the narrative frame seems to gaze on Murasaki from the Empress's viewpoint. Next, (3) '風すごく … はればれしげなめりかしと聞こえ給' (a violent wind had started, and Murasaki was sitting up, leaning against her armrest, so that she might gaze at the trees and plants in the garden as they swayed in the gusts) [IM. 80]. This marks Genji's arrival, and narrows the focus down to Genji's viewpoint. And then (4), the text presents Murasaki's words, 'かばかりの隙あるをも … 萩の上露' (With a pang she saw how happy her little reprieve had made him, and she grieved to imagine him soon in despair. '*Alas, not for long will you see what you do now: any breath of wind may spill from a* hagi *frond the last trembling drop of dew*') which includes her poem [T. 759]. This marks the return to an internal focus, namely Murasaki's, as Genette would have it. Then, regarding the passage which includes poetry exchange between Genji and the Empress's (5) 'げにぞおれかへりとまるべうもあらぬ、… かけとめん方なきぞかなしかりける' (but the moment could not last …. though he wished it endure for a thousand years. He mourned that nothing could detain someone destined to go) [T. 759]. This (5), moves from Genji (3) as the character with the viewpoint, back to the narrator. And then, lastly (6), which includes the conversation between the Empress and Murasaki, 'いまは渡らせ給ひね。… 明けはつるほどに消えはて給ひぬ' (Please leave me … She died with the coming of day) [T. 759] provides a sentence in which the narrator informs readers of the circumstances, though the viewpoint closes on Genji's inner thoughts. While the categorization may not be flawless, (4) corresponds to Genette's internal focalization. Segment (2) displays a wavering of viewpoint, that is while taking the form of (the Empress's) internal focalization, the narrator 'supplements' the reflection upon Murasaki's features which the Empress would not be expected to know (while Enomoto describes as 'supplementing,' Takahashi Tōru calls this the ghostlike narrator). The other viewpoints are drawn close to those of Genji and the Empress, at the same time their thoughts are handled within the frame of the narrator's narrating, and by so doing they are objectified.

29. The 'model' reader, by way of knowing the scroll's text and the original text of *The Tale of Genji*, is expected to know that Murasaki, the Empress and Genji are exchanging poems about their mental image of the autumn grasses.
30. Sano 1996 and 1997.
31. I have in mind here the author of the *Genji Scrolls* who is not simply the painter, but is the producer of the illustrated scroll in a broader sense. For instance, in the production of *Genji Scrolls*, the person who worked out the basis upon which scenes were chosen and again how to abstract the scroll's text from the original (the person in charge of production), was probably also giving orders to painters concerning the completion of the painting.
32. Here I use Kōdansha Comics Mimi-Books (Nov. 1980 – July 1993). Note that (A) and (B) are not facing pages in the original. (A) is on the left-hand page, while (B) is on the reversed right-hand side.
33. See, for example, *Genji monogatari*, SNKBT (Iwanami ed.), vol. 1, p. 106.
34. In *Asaki yume mishi* (*Passing Dreams*), we should note that Genji's wet-nurse Taifu no Myōbu is vividly constructed. In that way, the fabrication of 'old woman's tales of

times long past' (古女房の昔話) of the original text of *The Tale of Genji* is instead placed concretely in the form of a narrator within the world of the narrative.

35. Figures 2-1 (A and B) and 2-2 (C) are from Yamato Waki's 'The Law' ('Minori') cartoons in *Asaki yume mishi*. Dialogue translated by Richard Stanley-Baker and *waka* by Ivan Morris, *The Tale of Genji Scroll*, with an introduction by Yoshinobu Tokugawa (Tokyo: Kodansha International, 1971), p. 80.

36. I have discussed this issue elsewhere, but will enlarge on it here again. See Sano 1994b and 1997.

37. In the original text's 'Oak Tree' chapter the marriage of the second princess is only narrated through the metaphor of the wager of the *go* game, that is, it is narrated in the thoroughly personal understanding of personal space. This conception may be considered to be echoed in the conception of the T/G version, which even depicts retired Emperor Reizei's form.

38. Sano 1994c. See also Murakami Fuminobu's discussion on 'き' which is used when the narrator discloses herself in *sōshiji* (commentary) as a commentator in chapter 4 of this volume.

39. When one considers that writing in the phonetic syllabary of *kana* permits such incompleteness, such personal character, the issue naturally carries us to the feminine axis of narrative in discourse on gender.

40. That which I wish to bring to mind here is the pre-history of narrative seen by the viewpoint of women's history. Orikuchi Shinobu (1965, vol. 1) says that to begin with, narratives were words handed down from the gods. If that is the case, then are not records based on the obscured personal viewpoints of ladies-in-waiting the reverse of formal records in Chinese characters by men, and do they not draw us closer to the 'narratives of the gods' by overcoming the boundary between personal and formal (private/public)? They are one's distant memory of the primeval narratives of the heavenly maidens (*miko*), or the revival of the memory of lost ancient times. For that reason, the inadequate observations of ladies-in-waiting secure the legitimacy of the narrative. In *The Tale of Genji*, the author has Genji say, 'これら（物語）にこそ道々しく詳しきことはあらめ' (It is tales that contain the truly rewarding particulars!). In this context the importance of which is the understanding that narrative overcomes the two opposing stances of private and public, and establishes an absolute axis.

41. On the one hand, the fabricated narrative structure of historical narratives (*kagami mono*) such as the *Ōkagami* (*The Great Mirror* 大鏡) takes the form of vesting the narrator within the work with an omniscient viewpoint. At the very least, in these narratives of succession (*yotsugi monogatari* 世継物語), we see that men appear to appropriate female narrators' exclusive rights to narrative *a priori* of the heavenly maidens.

42. Emperors, ruling from a very young age, usually 'retired', taking holy orders, after a short reign.

43. This lord is easily judged to be Hotaru based on his placement within the room. That is to say, these three figures, Genji, Reizei-in and this figure are within the eaves of the mansion, while the lords playing music are in the corridor. Genji responds to the sudden summons of Reizei-in, taking along the lords to gather at the Rokujō palace (Hotaru, Yūgiri and the young lords). That is to say, in this scene, a figure who is depicted on the same spatial level as Genji and Reizei-in would naturally be one of their kin, and could be none other than Hotaru, who is of the imperial line.

44. *Genji monogatari*, NKBZ (Shōgakukan ed.), vol. 4: 371.

45. Bai Juyi 白居易, *Bai Juyi ji* 白居易集 (Peking: Zhunghua shuju, 1979), vol. I, pp. 274–5; see also Katayama 2001, pp. 18–19.

46. Genji remembers the deceased upon looking at the full moon and says, 'Every moonlit night has its own mood, but the moon's brilliance tonight sends one's thoughts soaring far beyond this world…' [T. 713]. This is referenced in the poem of Fujiwara Masatada 藤原雅正 in the *Gosenshū* 後撰集 (*Later Collection of Japanese Poetry*), 'いつとても月見ぬ秋はなきものを、わきて今宵のめずらしきかな' (There has been no autumn when I have not seen the moon, so this night is especially strange), and also

takes one line from its source poem in *Hakushi monjū* 白氏文集 (*The Bai Juyi Collection*). Furthermore, regarding the moonlight which calls to mind the deceased in 'The Bell Cricket' chapter, see Takahashi Bunji 1985 and Sano 1991.

47. Furthermore, this scene has been pointed out as being 'homo-social'. See Inamoto 1999. Certainly, of the nineteen extant scenes, this is the only one in which women do not appear. The meaning is that even female narrators are excluded from the narrative of lineage of Genji and his sons presented in this scene, and male society is shown in a straightforward fashion. At the same time, the reader must also witness the opposite of such a homo-social composition. This is because both the narrator and the reader know the actual parentage of Reizei-in and Kaoru, as opposed to the parentage as the world understands it. (Regarding the painting from 'Young Murasaki', it is unclear whether the extant painting is complete, so it is excluded for the time being. But judging from the designs of later *Tale of Genji* paintings, this scene may, just as Inamoto says, also be called homo-social.)

48. Chino 1988.

49. Aristotle writes in his *Poetics*, 'Part of every tragedy is the complication, and [part] is the solution. The [incidents] outside [the tragedy] and often some of those inside it are the complication, and the rest is the solution' (*Poetics*, op cit., p. 22). In the notes of the Matsumoto and Oka translation, this passage is interpreted as follows: 'Matters which are "external to the play" point to matters which occur before the beginning of the play,' and they are, 'taken as one part of the plot'. Furthermore, with regard to 'the fact that the oracle for some reason ordered him to go there, is outside the general plan of the play', seen in the example of *Iphigenia of Tauris* taken up in *Poetics*, op cit., Chapter 17, as the universal form of the argument of drama, the notes similarly say 'that which is external to the plot' (exō tū mythu) and 'that which is external to the play', are conceptually the same.

50. Sano 1989.

51. In this discussion I have consulted Umberto Eco, Lector in *Fabula* (Milano, 1979).

52. Sano, 'Emaki no hyōgen' (The Expression of Illustrated Handscrolls) in Sano 1997: 515, note 6.

53. Sano 1997: 506.

54. The author's understanding of Aristotle's *Poetics* derives exclusively from Japanese translations, and is therefore somewhat lacking as adequate interpretation.

55. As presented in my oral presentation, 'Sculptural Expressions in Narrative Painting', given at *The Human Form, The Human Body*, The International Symposium of the Tokyo Cultural Properties Research Institute, Tokyo, 1992. See Sano 1994d.

56. Paul Ricoeur, *Time and Narrative*, translated by Kathleen McLaughlin and David Pellauer (Chicago: Chicago University Press, 1984), p. 49.

57. Sano, 'Emaki no hyōgen' in Sano 1997: 506.

58. See my discussion in 'The Grammar of Buddhist Narrative Painting' in Sano 1997: 420.

Part 2

Reading the *Genji* Texts

3

DISPLACEMENTS OF CONQUEST, OR EXILE, *THE TALE OF GENJI*, AND POST-COLD WAR LEARNING

RICHARD H. OKADA

☙

In its narrow sense a political banishment, exile in its broad sense designates every kind of estrangement or displacement, from the physical and geographical to the spiritual.
Susan Rubin Suleiman, Exile and Creativity

The last point I want to make is that this book is an exile's book.
Edward Said, Culture and Imperialism

Who reads *The Tale of Genji*? Talk to people in Japan and they will tell you that the only time they read the narrative was in their *kokugo* (national language) class in high school, and perhaps a few lines in preparation for their college entrance exams. Ask them what the greatest work of Japanese literature is and they will probably say *The Tale of Genji*. Americans, on the other hand, who were assigned the *Genji* tale in college literature or history courses, no doubt heard it touted by their professors as the greatest Japanese literary work. The place where the *Genji* text(s) remains a central focus of attention – besides those 'cultural centres' where affluent housewives (*shufu*) congregate to 'read' classical texts with a noted authority – is that part of the scholarly world known since Meiji times as *kokubungaku* 'national literature'. This is an arena that encompasses colleges and universities, university professors, commercial publishing houses that produce major *kokubungaku* journals (like Gakutōsha and Shibundō), university presses and, occasionally, those public intellectuals known as *hyōronka*. Specialists expend enormous amounts of energy each year writing hundreds, if not thousands, of pages on the text and contributing to the periodic 'special issue' of a journal devoted to *Genji* often in the context of a trendy, if not theoretical, topic. Similar to the attitude of Japanologists in the West, *kokubungaku* scholars have, by and large, resisted the implementation of theoretical perspectives, a trend that still exists in both areas today.

What we have with the *Genji* text is, in other words, a largely unread tale that occupies the apex of Japanese literature. Another 'classic' tale thus emerges, that of a text embedded in a nation's cultural unconscious, a text functioning primarily as a symbol that allows for the construction of a privileged 'past', a symbol that can be ceaselessly mobilized to validate a modern national identity. The Heian period (794–1192) from which this particular text derives has, not coincidentally, been regarded by Western scholars as one dominated by 'the rule of taste'.[1]

I begin with the above because it is incumbent upon those of us who teach in the new millennium academy – in the context of the global transformations that have occurred in the wake of the Cold War – to refocus our attention continually on the inter-relations of 'literature,' scholarship and national identity, as well as on the position of the scholar herself/himself. As a result of theoretical developments in many different fields of study, such perspectives are fast becoming integral and necessary to the analysis of any 'literary' text, be it from contemporary America or tenth and eleventh century Heian Japan.

This chapter attempts to be mindful of the connections between scholarship, gender and the nation-state in particular,[2] as they concern the category of the 'aesthetic', which the *Genji* tale and the Heian period as a whole, have been thought by modern scholarship to exemplify and, especially, the relationship of that category to the exilic condition. The aesthetic, or culture in general, often formed a locus of masculinist displacement of the violence of territorial conquests that marked the processes of modernization during the nation-state era. The aesthetic has constituted a crucial aspect of modern 'literature' as nations utilized the emblems created by artists and writers to help consolidate their 'imagined communities', and scholars and critics complicit, albeit often unwittingly, with the nationalist programme emphasized the aesthetic qualities of literary works thought to 'reflect' nature and the good life. This essay explores the exclusionary effects of aesthetic displacements with a particular focus on questions of exile, transgression and the consequences for the marriage practices of women of mid-Heian.

Among the instances of the constructing of a nation as aesthetically oriented, the case of Japan during the early stages of the post-Second World War period stands as one of the most obvious, yet it was such an easily accepted naturalizing process at the time that no contemporary observer could realize its full import. The impulse towards the postwar aestheticizing move lies in the need to counter the negative wartime image and was constructed by scholars working together with the US military to study Japan's national character.[3] It was Sir George Sansom's *A Short History of Japan*, published in 1962, however, that contained the characterization of Japan that remains canonical today. An eminent historian of Japan, Sansom called the culture of Heian Japan 'unique' precisely because it was 'almost entirely aesthetic'[4] and governed by a 'rule of taste'.[5] Sansom's statement forms part of a larger postwar effort to construct a peaceful, cultured nation that, together with the economic trope of hard work implied in the rally cry in Japan of 'high level growth' (*kōdo seichō*), served to counteract both the image of imperialist aggressor in the Second World War and the hold that Marxism had among the intelligentsia. It also obfuscated the turn in US policy towards the support of men who had been purged directly after the war and of conservative politics in the wake of fighting on the Korean peninsula. The formulation might have been original, but Sansom's aestheticizing gesture itself was not; as we see from this statement, written in 1955, by another founding member of postwar Japanology, Donald Keene. In comparing *Genji* with *A la Recherche du Temps Perdu*, Keene observed, 'In both the barons are noted less for their hunting and fishing than for their surpassing musical abilities, their flawless taste and their brilliant conversation.'[6] American scholars, therefore, have actively participated in creating the cultural image of a beauty-loving nation to buttress the peace-loving image forced upon it by constitutional revision.[7]

The valorization of the aesthetic in Sansom's desire to make Heian Japan and, by implication, native *kana* works of the period 'almost entirely aesthetic' might be startling in any age, but it would have been just as surprising, given the ideological climate, for anyone in the early postwar period to gainsay an eminent scholar like Sir George Sansom. It was easy for others subsequently to jump on the 'aestheticizing' bandwagon and promote texts like *The Tale of Genji*, and the female diaries, thereby helping to construct a Heian period (the name is written with characters meaning 'peace and tranquillity') dominated by aesthetic 'taste'.

One such scholar was Ivan Morris. In his *The World of the Shining Prince*, published in 1964, Morris makes the 'rule of taste' play a major regulatory role in amorous relations of the time.[8] In the longest chapter in his book, 'The Women of Heian and their Relations with Men', he relates the aesthetic to sexual mores, particularly those of women.[9] Take, for example, the following: 'for the vast majority of young, upper-class women the most engaging interest was their relations with men ... women ... were above all absorbed in their relations with their husband or lover, or lovers; and it was the attitude of these men that mainly governed their existence'.[10] But, notes Morris, not only were women 'all absorbed' with men, some of them, especially 'unattached women, like Sei Shōnagon, tended to be extremely promiscuous'[11] and, he continues, 'even a relatively strait laced observer like Murasaki is more likely to censure a colleague for her taste in matching the colours of her robes than for having numerous lovers'. Clearly Morris is nonplussed to discover that even straight-laced women condoned promiscuous behaviour and his censorious attitude is evident in his characterization of 'the **lax sexual mores** that prevailed in the Heian period'.[12]

What saves such women for Morris is the primacy of the aesthetic, and especially a masculine embodiment of it. Heian aristocracy, which for Morris is 'marked by a curious mixture of depravity and decorum', is prevented from 'degenerating into something crass and sordid' by 'the dominant part played by the rule of taste'.[13] The aesthetic allows Morris a way to reconcile what for him, and for many of his readers, are morally repugnant sexual customs. He then proceeds to cite long passages from different texts (one from *The Diary of Izumi Shikibu* and three from *The Pillow Book*), before delivering the following:

It is small wonder, then, that the hope of every Heian woman was to secure the affections of a man who, however many concubines and mistresses he might have, would be sure to protect her from the vicissitudes to which she was subject in a polygamous society. Such a man is Prince Genji. It is not just because of his looks, his sensitivity and his artistic talents that he emerges in Murasaki's novel as the ideal male, but because, once he has given his support to a woman, he never withdraws it, even though he may have lost all interest in her as a mistress.[14]

Genji emerges in Morris's portrayal as the handsome, sensitive, loyal and ever-so-solicitous figure who can save women from their loose ways, while the women appear as over-sexed, passive creatures who must resign themselves to periods of sorrowful waiting for their man's next visit. A character like the male Genji functions here as handmaiden (manservant?) to a masculinist aestheticism that enables him to reconcile what he calls a 'mixture of depravity and decorum'.

What I would like to suggest here is that Hikaru Genji occupies in Morris's discourse a position much like the United States does in the following statement by Gayatri Spivak:

At the end of the Second World War, the self-representation of the United States ... was that of a saviour, both militarily and, as architect of the Marshall Plan, in the economic and therefore sociocultural sphere.[15]

In Morris' reading, Genji, like America, firmly possesses a 'rule of taste' that allows him to be a 'saviour', an unquestioned civilizing, as well as subjugating, force.[16]

Aesthetic displacements – effected by scholars like Sansom and Keene – and patriarchal gender displacements – effected by scholars like Morris – appear now as attempts by Western scholars to circumscribe the potentially unruly elements of a native text by installing behind it a timeless, iconic, image of a peaceful, beauty-loving nation; an image that Kawabata Yasunari evoked in 1968 in his Nobel Prize acceptance speech which he titled 'Japan the Beautiful and Myself'. We must also remember that the *Genji* narrative is usually read as a 'romance', centring around Genji and Murasaki, a predictable adjunct to the aesthetic and masculinist displacements I have just discussed.[17]

Given the aestheticizing sedimentation, we could of course elect to stop teaching and writing about premodern literature, or any literature at all for that matter, since to do so would be to remain complicit with nation-state agendas that ceaselessly co-opt alternative readings. Or, we could, as the following attempts to do, continue to teach and analyse literary texts but transform them as we do so into useful sites for the interrogation of the requisites of modern reception and, especially, the primacy accorded the aesthetic.

When we begin to reread the *Tale of Genji*, for example, we might begin by remembering that the Heian period was marked by moments of violence and exclusionary practices during the century or so leading up to Murasaki Shikibu's time (late tenth and early eleventh centuries), hardly a period of 'peace and tranquility'. The ruling family was a branch of the Fujiwara clan that ousted political rivals by sending them into exile and then inserting themselves into the imperial lineage through a complex combination of intermarriage and political overseeing. Since *monogatari* were not the bounded objects that modern criticism often purports literary texts to be, it is perhaps not surprising that events like exile and the effects of the Fujiwara ruling practice on women form major intertexts of the narrative. I shall argue that, far from being preoccupied with matters of aesthetic taste – 'love' – or 'romance', as the dominant *Genji* readings would have it, the narrative situates many of its most important scenes at intersections involving displacements produced by exile (or other forms of exclusion and transgression) and patriarchally determined marital situations, particularly the practice of sending daughters to court, a kind of feminized exile. It goes without saying that the *Genji* narrator does not present the 'aesthetic' as comprising isolated entities/events, or leisurely pursuits but continually suggests its intimate relation to political and other matters. We must also remember in this regard that certain Heian 'arts', especially poetry and prose, were often the preserve of writers, both male and female, whose ancestors had been expelled or marginalized by the Fujiwara rulers. Rather than simply oppose the exilic to the aesthetic, what we need to do is to interrogate how one is continually implicated in the other.

First of all, as I have stated, in order to solidify their power, Fujiwara leaders ruthlessly ousted rivals, whether potential or otherwise, and whether they belonged to another clan or to their own, exiling them to different regions of Japan. One infamous locus of exile was Tsukushi (modern-day Kyushu), where the victim was sent after being 'appointed' Provisional Governor-General of Dazaifu (*Dazai gon no sotsu*), an administrative headquarters and military outpost on the island. More often than not persons expelled from the capital seem to have been victims of trumped up charges. The most famous such exile in Japanese history is Sugawara no Michizane (845–903) who, while Minister of the Right, was appointed Provisional Governor-General of Dazaifu and exiled to Tsukushi in 901 by then Minister of the Left and Fujiwara hegemon, Fujiwara no Tokihira. Another relevant figure appointed to the position was Ariwara no Yukihira (818–893) in 873. Persons exiled to Tsukushi closer to Murasaki Shikibu's time, again as Provisional Governors General of Dazaifu, include Minamoto no Takaakira (914–982), during the Anna Incident in 969 and, a couple of decades later, the two Fujiwaras, Korechika (974–1010) and his brother Takaie (979–1044), in 996. The former was sent to Dazaifu as Provisional Governor-General. A celebrated case of self-imposed exile is that of Minamoto no Tōru (822–895) who built a mansion at a site that partly corresponds to Genji's fictional Rokujō mansion and who also held land southeast of the capital in Uji, the locus of the final ten chapters of the *Genji* narrative. It is not surprising that later commentaries cite such men as models for the fictional Genji.[18]

What emerges here is the suggestion that the post of provincial governor, often held by men of great learning like Murasaki Shikibu's father and comprising a class of bureaucrats called *zuryō*, was in many ways tantamount to the bureaucratically sanctioned exile of talented officials. The appointee was required to embark on a tour of duty that kept him away from the capital for three or four years, even longer in those cases where he was appointed successively to different regions. He sometimes left his family behind, as in the case of the author of *Kagerō nikki*, although it is important to remember that others such as Murasaki Shikibu, Sei Shōnagon and the author of *Sarashina nikki* accompanied their fathers to their regions of appointment. In any case, what I want to argue here is that the 'appointment' of an official as Provisional Governor-General of Dazaifu can be viewed as an exilic intertext that is inscribed within all such official designations. Historical exiles, if they didn't die in their far-off province as Michizane did, were usually pardoned and returned to the capital after a few years, although they were never able to regain their former political status. Genji's case is highly unusual if measured by historical examples since his political fortunes rise after his return.[19] I am, by the way, not suggesting that men appointed to regional posts thought they were being exiled; on the contrary, many seem to have eagerly sought such posts for economic as well as political reasons and were bitterly disappointed when they either did not gain the appointment as provincial governor at all or did not receive the desired province.[20] What I do mean to suggest is that provincial governors in the *Genji* text are legible metonyms for exile and that the narrative continually stages its most important events at the nodes of the displacements resulting from exile and fatherly ambition.

Second, we might do well to be attentive to a crucial aspect of Fujiwara strategy that involved marrying off their daughters to the emperor or crown prince and then attaining the position of either Regent (*sesshō*) to a child emperor or Prime Minister (*kampaku*) to an adult one. It was a ruling method that depended on an uncertain factor, namely, that the daughter would give birth to a male heir.[21] If the union were successful, the Fujiwara could then manipulate the son into the position of crown prince, have him appointed the next emperor, and continue to influence his every decision – the Kokiden faction in the *Genji* tale is an excellent example of this. The Fujiwara could do this partly because of the power accorded the mother's family by Heian society. The presence or absence of strong maternal backing (which Genji lacks) meant success or failure for a woman in the polygamously oriented, highly competitive, structure of marriage. If, in other words, nature took its hoped-for course, the Fujiwara hegemon would achieve a position of supreme power as maternal grandparent (*gaisofu*) to an emperor.

We can note here that the Fujiwara also had to deal with the practice of reducing royal sons to 'commoner' status with a granted surname, usually 'Gen' or Minamoto, although several other surnames, like 'Hei' (Taira) and 'Zai' (Ariwara), were also used. The move, made out of economic or political expediency, excluded (exiled?) the child from imperial succession but created an individual who, as he took his place among the other officials in political life, often presented an unwelcome challenge to the Fujiwara leaders. The *Genji* tale explores the far-reaching consequences of one such 'demotion', which can also be viewed as another displacement similar to that of exile. In this regard, it is noteworthy that the Minamotos mentioned above in connection with different forms of exile, Takaakira and Tōru, were first-generation 'genji'.

At any rate, Fujiwara power depended partly on their sending their daughters to court and having them be appropriately fertile. The general practice, called 'serving at the palace' (*miyazukae*), consisted of mid- to high-ranking courtiers placing their daughters into imperial service where the latter faced confinement as a kind of hostage to the court in exchange for benefits granted her and the family. The women were given court rank and rooms at the palace and returned to their families only on special occasions, such as childbirth, other celebrations, illness or if the palace burned down. The status of the women, depending on the ranks of their fathers, ranged from several ranks of common attendants to junior or senior consort (*kōi* or *nyōgo*). The daughters of Fujiwara hegemons usually achieved the elevated rank of senior consort and had the best opportunity eventually to rise one rank higher and be named empress, the ultimate sign of success for a Heian aristocratic family. Many empresses actually exerted great influence on both their husbands and their grandfathers. Murasaki Shikibu and other celebrated Heian women writers were lower-ranking court attendants who served empresses (who presided over palace 'salons') and who had risen from among the ruling northern branch of the Fujiwara family. In the *Genji* text, the marriage of daughters of high-ranking families often takes centre stage in the form of fatherly desire and the determination to find appropriate husbands and situations, whether as imperial consorts or as wives of prominent courtiers.

The woman introduced in the opening lines of the text, Genji's mother, is a junior consort (*kōi*) of the reigning Kiritsubo Emperor and a victim of just such fatherly ambition and desire. We learn from Genji's grandmother after her daughter's untimely death that her husband, now dead, had wanted his wife to do everything in her power to assure their daughter was accepted at court. Genji's mother, soon after giving birth to him and without the all-important backing of a politically powerful father, is virtually hounded to death by her court rivals.[22] Ignoring precedent, the Emperor spends all of his time with her rather than apportion his visitations among all of his women, especially his highest-ranking senior consort and Genji's nemesis, Kokiden, daughter of the Minister of the Right.

The narrative thus opens in an ominous, not to say tragic, manner, but many readers misinterpret the Emperor's relationship with Genji's mother and the subsequent birth of her jewel-like son. Rather than originating in 'love' or amorous passion as some would have it, the narrator seems to be showing us the tragic underside of a male desire that depends for the prosperity of a family lineage on a feminine presence at the same time that it ignores the consequences of the practice for the women themselves, leaving them, in many cases, self-conscious and homeless. The Emperor's 'love', then, is not a positive virtue but must be viewed in the fatal context of a woman's double victimization, by a fiercely ambitious father and an irresponsibly obsessive Emperor.

Among other notable fathers with similar ambitions for their daughters are Genji's rival, Tō no Chūjō, first son of the Minister of the Left and a Fujiwara, whose oldest daughter loses out in a competition for an emperor's affections with the woman Genji supports (the Rokujō lady's daughter, Akikonomu); the Akashi lay priest, who manages to counter Fujiwara practice by marrying off his daughter, not to an emperor, but an emperor *manqué* – i.e. Genji – and the father of the Lady of the Locust Shell (Utsusemi). Other instances include the Retired Suzaku Emperor who represents sovereigns who had difficulty finding suitable husbands among the ranks of commoners, and the Eighth Prince, an important figure in the last ten 'Uji' chapters. But whether marrying up or down, the narrative clearly suggests that the outcome cannot but be an unhappy one for the women, who end up displaced within the machinations of male ambition.

The figure of Genji himself, a product, then, of his grandfather's ambitions, combines the tragedy of his mother with the element of exile when he voluntarily leaves the capital before the Kokiden faction can take official action against him. Genji's 'exile', related in part to his lack of strong maternal backing, is the most famous and obvious one in the narrative and the chapters devoted to this, namely 'Suma' and 'Akashi', are among the most celebrated.[23] Those chapters evoke earlier historical exiles and others who were sent to, or were associated in some way with, the area that Genji selects. The most notable of these were Fujiwara no Korechika, noted above, and Ariwara no Yukihira. Is it a coincidence that the latter, a royal son lowered like Genji to commoner status, was Senior Assistant Governor-General of Dazaifu, that unmistakable locus of exile? Furthermore, Yukihira is also said to have lived at Suma, perhaps like Genji in self-imposed exile. When Korechika was exiled to Dazaifu, he tried to hide out in his sister Sadako's chambers, then was granted permission to remain in Harima Province for about five months. Harima, of course, is where Akashi is located. The man Genji meets in Akashi, a former provincial governor known as the Akashi lay priest, is himself living in a state of self-imposed exile after his family had experienced unnamed setbacks in the capital. The family must once have been quite illustrious since we learn that the priest's father had been a minister. It is possible to surmise, therefore, that the father might also have been a victim of exile (the strong suggestion here of Korechika and his father Michitaka cannot be dismissed). The political is then intertwined with the genealogical when we discover that he and Genji's mother are first cousins. A final tie to exile lies buried in the text: Genji's primary wet-nurse. That woman, who is Koremitsu's mother, is the wife of a Senior Assistant Governor-General of Dazaifu.

Genji's 'exile,' then, whether self-imposed or not brings him together first with a blood relative who has chosen to leave the capital in a similar gesture of voluntary, though in his case permanent, exile, and then with the man's daughter, the Akashi lady, Genji's second cousin. She is the woman who will bear him the girl who ultimately allows him to seize supreme power as the maternal grandfather to an emperor, the mark of political success at least as it was defined by Fujiwara practice but here a brilliant displacement of that practice. The kinship tie is echoed by the ambitions, similar to those of Genji's grandfather, that the Akashi priest harbours for his daughter: he refuses to give her to just anyone and has been grooming her for just the right man he was certain, due to his ceaseless prayers to the Sumiyoshi deity, would come along, a man just like the shining Genji. It is important to note here that the 'aesthetic', in the form of the lady's skill on the *koto*, serves as a powerful lure to attract Genji and realize the priest's hopes. Perhaps due to political setback, the Akashi priest, in contrast to Genji's grandfather, does not have court alliances in mind for his daughter. Patriarchal desire, however, produces similar results insofar as the Akashi lady, although not subject to the fatal humiliation that Genji's mother had to endure, is forced to give her daughter over to Murasaki's care and is constantly self-conscious of her lowly status. The 'success' of the Akashi family, which includes Genji's mother's lineage, demonstrates the powerful will that members of the provincial governor class, marginalized by the ruling house, possessed. At the same time, the narrative forcefully re-marks the great sacrifices that such women had to make.

Among the other instances of fatherly ambition, the case of Tō no Chūjō and his first daughter would seem a repetition of the historical case of Fujiwara daughters since he belongs to that clan. The situation to which I refer involves Tō no Chūjō's desire to send his daughter to court thus bringing her into direct competition with Genji's own foster daughter (the Rokujō lady's child) for the attentions of the Emperor. Desire and exclusion are again at issue as the latter girl's father was a man who had been appointed crown prince only to fail ignominiously and be deposed; he is dead at the beginning of the narrative. Again, the details are not given but both women are helpless in the face of parental ambition: the Rokujō lady, one of Genji's early lovers, desperately wants Genji to support her daughter and make her a royal consort, while Tō no Chūjō desperately wants his daughter to become primary consort and then Empress so that he can strengthen his own position.

Noteworthy here is that the woman from the displaced Rokujō family, Akikonomu, ultimately gets the upper hand in a manner that, once again, interconnects aesthetics and politics. Tō no Chūjō's daughter holds the initial advantage since she is sent to court first. What enables Akikonomu to win the crown prince's favour, however, is her skill at drawing, which the crown prince also loves and is good at – as in the Akashi lady's case, the aesthetic here serves the political. The manoeuvre allows Genji and his crucial political ally and enduring obsession, Fujitsubo, to manipulate imperial succession at an early stage, thereby preparing the way for the next stage when his own daughter by the Akashi lady can become primary consort and, finally, empress. The amorous and the political also become intertwined as the narrating leaves us with this suspicion: did the Rokujō lady utilize Genji's attentions, which she was successful in winning due in part to her skill in calligraphy and poetry, in order to secure a political future for her daughter?[24] Finally, the aesthetic again plays a role in further consolidating Akikonomu's position in the 'Picture

Contest' chapter when Genji's sketches drawn during his exile at Suma carry the day to ensure victory for his faction.

Besides signifying the political suppression of Tō no Chūjō's line, the situation relates to my concerns insofar as it brings together, in spectacular fashion, two characters marked by exclusion and/or transgression. The Emperor in question happens to be the 'illicit' child (later known as the Reizei Emperor) born to Genji and his father's consort, Fujitsubo. The exact nature of the transgression involving Genji and Fujitsubo is a complex issue that has been long debated by scholars. Lest readers be worried that imperial succession is tainted forever, the narrator makes sure that the Akikonomu-Reizei pair do not produce an heir.

Tō no Chūjō and his progeny may be defeated politically but, surprisingly, it is his lineage and not Genji's that provides the focus of a large part of the narrative. The cases of Tamakazura (Tō no Chūjō's daughter) and Kaoru (his grandson but presumed to be Genji's son) are the most startling examples and, more important for my purposes, their tales are both associated clearly with exile and transgression. Genji's progeny on the other hand – the nondescript Reizei Emperor, the sober Yūgiri, the flippant Niou and the largely absent Akashi Empress – pale in comparison.

I have written about Tamakazura's fictional figuration elsewhere but let me make explicit here her link to exile.[25] After the death of her mother, Yūgao, she is taken to Tsukushi by her mother's wet-nurse, whose husband is being relocated there as Junior Assistant Governor-General (*shōni*) of Dazaifu. There she grows into adulthood at which time her foster father, the nurse's husband, dies and the family ends up staying in the far-off region. When we meet her, she is pursued by a wealthy man of military might from a neighbouring region who wants her for his bride. Tamakazura's foster family tries to dissuade him by appeals to a fictitious 'handicap' she suffers from, but when he remains undaunted her stepbrother whisks her away to the capital. Tamakazura's tale contains another echo of exile besides Tsukushi: the inscription in her figure of an earlier tale, *The Tale of the Bamboo Cutter*. In that text as we have it today, we find that the central female character, Kaguya-hime, has been sent to earth because of misdeeds committed in her former world, represented by the moon. When her time on earth is up, she must abandon her present existence and return home. What is important for my analysis is that her figure co-mingles courtship and marriage with the hint of exile.[26] She is the focus of male desire in the form of six suitors. As with the ambitious fathers noted above, the old bamboo cutter, a foster father, urges her to choose one of them. The wooing of her by six men (including the Emperor) who fail, variously and sometimes ignominiously, at winning her forms the major segments of the tale.

Tamakazura, while confined by Genji to a room in his Rokujō mansion, is forced to become the target of a similar case of male desire. As with Kaguya-hime, all of the obvious candidates for her hand fail, including the Emperor. Of course, Tamakazura doesn't return to the moon or wander back to a far-off land like Tsukushi but she suddenly becomes the wife of a man who was barely hinted at in the narrative.²⁷ What is intriguing is that Murasaki Shikibu, through the *Genji* narrator, explicitly singled out *The Tale of the Bamboo Cutter* as the 'ancestor of all tales'.²⁸ That she did so suggests the importance of interrogating the larger implications of exile and marriage practices. In Tamakazura's case, we find another version of a father sending his daughter to court, but in a mode of reversals that constitute her character and that begin to undermine whatever power and prestige Genji had obtained up until then. Rather than a 'real' father trying to give her away in a socially sanctioned manner, we have Genji, like the old bamboo cutter, performing a surrogate role as a doting father (the narrator calls him a 'mother' as well) with ulterior motives. Like the Akashi priest, he will not hand her over to just anyone but, unlike the former, he seriously considers sending her to court, to his half-'brother' (actually son) the Reizei Emperor. Also unlike the Akashi situation, Genji's 'foster' role allows him to make sexual overtures to her himself and to discover, often to his dismay, that Tamakazura has a strong will of her own. That General Higekuro is able ultimately to steal into her quarters, a clear transgression of Genji's space, and claim her as his prize might have been due as much to her manipulative talents as to the General's unmistakable ardour. Tamakazura does enter court service for a time but is not trapped by it.

Tamakazura's tale is told within the context of Genji's Rokujō Mansion. The mansion is often seen primarily as a locus of aesthetic activities – music, poetry, painting, seasonal motifs, etc. – but here, too, what seems an aesthetic or 'romantic' context of wooing Tamakazura is also another site of feminine confinement that begins the undoing of the figure who will serve to transform the narrative from Genji's lineage to that of Tō no Chūjō: Kashiwagi, Tō no Chūjō's oldest son. As a result of Genji's ruse that involves keeping Tamakazura from her father and pretending that she is his own daughter, Kashiwagi feels betrayed when he discovers that Tamakazura, whom he had been encouraged to pursue, was really his half-sister.²⁹

After the experience with Tamakazura the narrative begins, or rather continues, its inexorable shift of focus to Tō no Chūjō's lineage. The 'Wisteria Leaves' chapter in which Genji achieves his greatest political success – he is accorded the status and emoluments of a Retired Emperor – further undermines his lineage as it simultaneously presents the narration of the marriage of Yūgiri and Tō no Chūjō's second daughter, Kumoinokari. The marriage of the two, regarding which Kashiwagi plays a major intermediary role, effects a re-appropriation of the 'official' part of Genji's lineage back into the lineage of Genji's in-laws (Yūgiri's mother, the Aoi lady, who was Genji's official wife, was Tō no Chūjō's sister).

Soon thereafter Genji yields to imagined pressure from his half-brother, the retired Suzaku Emperor, and agrees to marry the Emperor's third daughter. Known as the Third Princess, the girl is the daughter of a woman who was a 'female Genji', a princess demoted like Genji to commoner status.³⁰ The marriage turns out to be a disaster in every respect. It deeply wounds Murasaki and hastens her death; the girl, her father's pet, is immature and empty-headed and has almost nothing to offer besides her royal status; the man who succeeds in sexually possessing her and making her pregnant ends up dying an early death. The fatherly desire manifested by the Suzaku Emperor can be read, moreover, as a parody of the earlier cases. Since he is retired and studying to become a monk, marriage in his case brings no political advantage; it is more a gesture of futility by a sad, befuddled and motherless emperor. That the narrative, however, makes much of such a gesture by linking it both with a 'female Genji' and a fateful transgression attests to its importance in the text.

The man in question is Kashiwagi, the oldest son of Tō no Chūjō. He completely loses his head over the Third Princess after accidentally spying her through curtains at a 'football' contest. A character consistently marked by missteps, Kashiwagi manages to enter her chambers, no doubt by bribing an attendant, and spend a fateful night with her, after which she becomes pregnant. The child born of the liaison, Kaoru, is thought to be Genji's child and becomes the major male figure of the final ten 'Uji' chapters. Like Genji, a product of male obsession and transgression, albeit at a lower social level, Kaoru's figure embodies the various displacements of Genji's lineage. It is interesting, though not surprising, that the narrator makes him keep company after his father's death first with Genji's own child of a similar transgression, the Reizei Emperor, and then with Genji's younger half-brother, the Eighth Prince of Uji.

Kashiwagi's act further displaces Genji and institutes the child as the main male figure of the narrative at the same time that it marks Kaoru, much as he is marked by his effusive personal scent, as a figure of transgression. While in the presence of the Reizei Emperor, Kaoru overhears a conversation about a man at Uji who has devoted his life to Buddhist texts. Kaoru's interest is piqued and when he visits Uji to meet and study with the prince, he happens also to discover the prince's two daughters living in seclusion. Music again serves to lure a man from the capital, this time to women whose father is living in exile (see below); in this case, however, the results differ vastly from the Genji-Akashi case.

The Eighth Prince is one of Genji's younger half-brothers[31] and the second character in the narrative to experience political defeat in a contest for imperial succession (the Rokujō lady's husband was the first). We learn that he was implicated in a plot hatched by the Kokiden lady to eliminate the then crown prince, Reizei, and replace him with the Eighth Prince. As usual, we are not given the details but are told that he moved to Uji after his house in the capital burned down. If we remember that a similar conflagration befell Minamoto no Takaakira's mansion in the capital when he was expelled to Dazaifu, the case becomes stronger for viewing the prince's move to Uji as another instance of exile. Uji itself presents a non-capital space that, as mentioned before, metonymically evokes Minamoto no Tōru, but also ancient scenarios of struggle for imperial succession, self-imposed exile and suicide.[32]

The Eighth Prince, like his pupil Kaoru, is thoroughly compromised by transgressive acts and exile. His main worldly concerns are his two daughters, both born in Uji, the second birth resulting in his wife's death. His character thus recalls the Akashi priest. However, as if obeying the pattern of reversals and displacements inaugurated by Tamakazura, and further reinforced by the Suzaku Emperor's inability to make a firm decision regarding a suitable husband for his daughter, the Eighth Prince's daughters by his official wife and a third daughter by another woman all face lives of sorrow, tragedy and displacement. Perhaps due to his disillusionment with political life, his advice to the first two daughters regarding Kaoru is ambivalent and he rejects the third altogether. The third daughter's mother ends up married to a boorish but wealthy provincial governor in whose household Ukifune grows up.

Oigimi, the oldest daughter, rebuffs Kaoru's advances, which are equivocal at best, until she dies, a death due to mysterious causes although it is possible to read it as a kind of suicide. The second daughter, Nakanokimi, ends up marrying Niou and moving to the capital where, rather than the celebrated spouse of a prince, she acquires a status that is not much better than that of palace attendant. Oigimi adamantly refuses to yield to Kaoru as if learning from the hardship that earlier women experienced in yielding, or being forced to yield, to men of high station and good breeding: Genji's mother, the Rokujō lady, Yūgao, the Akashi lady, the Second Princess (Kashiwagi's official wife), and the Third Princess. In line with the present analysis, it is interesting that the governess for the two daughters, Ben no kimi, was taken by a man to a place referred to only as 'the farthest reaches of the western sea', which again suggests the Dazaifu area, and spent ten years there before returning (like Tamakazura) to the capital after the man's death.

The third daughter, Ukifune, is the final, extended focus of the narrative and so it is not surprising that her character incorporates all the factors discussed so far. The suggestion of exile obtains both from her father, the Eighth Prince, and metonymically from her current status as stepdaughter of a provincial governor. The narrator pointedly remarks that in fathering her, the Eighth Prince committed an act of transgression against his beloved wife, an act which he regrets so much that he refuses to acknowledge Ukifune's existence. Her mother eventually marries a provincial governor who becomes her stepfather, a man reminiscent of the one who pursued Tamakazura in Tsukushi, both men of wealth but devoid of cultural grace and sophistication. And, as with Tamakazura, her story evokes *The Tale of the Bamboo Cutter*. As with Tamakazura and Kaguya-hime, she becomes the focus of male suitors, although in her case, as with Akikonomu, it is her mother and her stepsister, Nakanokimi, rather than a male, who are most anxious to find her a mate/home. Her character, most importantly, is inscribed by figures that enact displacement: 'fiction', writing, the substitute/ simulacrum. She is 'fictional' in a genealogical sense as the stepdaughter of the Governor of Hitachi; her very introduction into the narrative plays on her substitutive image when she is conjured up by Nakanokimi (in 'The Ivy' chapter); she is further marked by the activity of calligraphic brush-writing, or more precisely, 'writing practice' (*tenarai*), which involves a repetitive process that blurs the lines between 'original' and 'copy'. She tries to take her life but she is saved and a 'cremation' held for her becomes a bodiless displacement. She is taken to Ono but her life from then on is conspicuously marked by 'silence' (although, echoing Yūgao (Chapter 5), 'silence' was a part of her character from the beginning) which performs the ultimate displacement of language, of narrative, of the very narrative that, like Kaoru and Niou, would seek to enclose her. As the narrative moves towards its end, Ukifune only grows more determined to remain silent. In her silent, dream-like state after her 'death', a state in which even memory is erased (she continually pleads amnesia), she eludes her would-be conquerors, and refuses to be co-opted back into life in the capital. All she is left with is her speechless, homeless condition.

We can read Ukifune's thoroughly displaced and homeless situation as the narrator's criticism of the patriarchal practices where male desire for the maintenance of family lineage is continually blind to the question of feminine victimization. Her 'unresolved' narration, then, provides a fitting 'end' to a narrative that, as I've been reading it, relentlessly traces the effects of displacement, especially as it is produced by Fujiwara political and marital practices. Her life, from the start, is very much that of an exile, displaced from society and continually forced to live as a surrogate for others. The difference in her case is that, whereas exiles often did return to the capital, she adamantly refuses to allow herself to be co-opted back into a society that mainly marginalizes and excludes women.

By inextricably associating major characters with exile and transgression, Murasaki Shikibu traces the myriad ramifications of political displacement for the lives of both women and men. In such a scheme, the status of exile becomes a powerful trope for life itself for Heian courtiers caught in a social order dominated by Fujiwara ruling practices. The *Genji* tale does not single out any one of the major sociopolitical factions (the imperial family, the Fujiwara, the Genji, or the provincial governors) for direct criticism. We might have expected Murasaki Shikibu to paint a glowing picture of a Michinaga-like figure since she was in his daughter's employ at court for a number of years. In fact, however, the Fujiwara do not come off very well, although Tō no Chūjō's lineage, which means a branch of the Fujiwara clan, produces the major characters for much of the narrative. As I have suggested, rather than proffer models (political, amorous or marital) of power or success, the *Genji* text continually inscribes forces of exile and displacement especially as they relate to women like the Rokujō lady, Akikonomu, the Akashi lady, Tamakazura, Ukifune and her Uji stepsisters. Even Genji's relationship with Murasaki, thought by many critics to be the most romantic and ideal in the text, participates clearly in the mode of transgression and displacement: Genji 'abducts', enslaves and makes of her his most private possession. We also learn that her mother's father was an Azechi Major Counsellor, another kind of provincial official as well as another trope of exile.

In its ever-changing movement of displacement, the Genji text demonstrates dramatically that nothing is established without exclusionary effects and, simultaneously and more important, that whatever is established will in turn be displaced: whether it be the shining Genji; his father and imperial succession; Genji's lineage; masculinist ambition; or the topos of the capital. Rather than simply a generalized rhythmic oscillation ('the mighty must fall,' for example), Murasaki Shikibu elects to focus sharply on the effects of exile and patriarchal desire on women and those men ousted from official life in the capital. The final example of Ukifune's condition is perhaps the most radical and telling case of exile and displacement.

Alternative readings are inevitable to some degree and therefore in need of constant critique and displacement. If, however, such readings of literature acknowledge their degree of impossibility and, at the same time, attempt to keep destabilized their own positions, alternative readings might be one way of beginning to negotiate a global condition; one where notions like subjectivity and identity based on old and inadequate nation-state parameters can be displaced both to reveal their ongoing complicity with violence and exclusion, and also to look towards a different world(s) of analysis.

NOTES

1. See George B. Sansom, 'The Rule of Taste', *A History of Japan To 1334* (Stanford: Stanford University Press, 1958).
2. Of course, we can simply decide not to read literary texts, especially those of the pre-modern period, at all. One of the premises of this essay is that literary texts often provide the best examples of the hidden ideology at work in their readings; thus to address those examples while at the same time offering reconfigurations provides an excellent means by which to demystify both the 'literary' and the assumed coherence of the nation-state.
3. For a discussion of the wartime images – Japanese as primitive and barbaric, infantile, and susceptible to mental and emotional instability – of the Japanese national character that later scholars had to counter by installing the category of the aesthetic, see John W. Dower, *War Without Mercy: Race and Power in the Pacific War* (New York: Pantheon Books, 1986), Chapter 6.
4. George Sansom, *Japan: A Short Cultural History* (London: The Cresset Press, 1962), p. 238.
5. George Sansom, *A History of Japan to 1334*, op. cit., p. 178. Sansom was perhaps not coincidentally echoing Motoori Norinaga's proto-nationalistic, eighteenth century, valorization of *mono no aware* as the key to *The Tale of Genji*.
6. Donald Keene, *Japanese Literature: An Introduction for Western Readers* (New York: Grove Press, 1955), p. 75.
7. Let us also remember the postwar translations of Japanese literature that often became aestheticizing exercises that de-politicized and sanitized their linguistic objects (I am thinking of translations of Kawabata and Tanizaki, for example).
8. Morris's translations include *The Pillow Book of Sei Shōnagon*, 2 vols. (New York: Columbia University Press, 1967); *As I Crossed a Bridge of Dreams: Recollections of a Woman in Eleventh-Century Japan* (London: Penguin books; New York: The Dial Press, 1971). See also Ivan Morris, *The World of the Shining Prince: Court Life in Ancient Japan* (New York: Alfred A. Knopf, 1964); this study has recently been reprinted thereby attesting to its status as the canonical study of Heian culture.
9. To be questioned first and foremost would be Morris's use of 'fictional' texts to underwrite his 'descriptions' of Heian society, but I shall set that aside, and take a look at a few of his statements.

10. Morris, *The World of the Shining Prince*, op. cit., p. 224.
11. Ibid., p. 226. And also prone to jealousy, as in his characterization of *The Kagerō Diary* as 'one long wail of jealousy.' To be fair, I must note that Morris does suggest, although he does not pursue, a strong feminine subject position for women: 'Many of them (i.e. women like Sei Shōnagon) had their own houses and, being economically independent, were free to have such relations as they wished and also to terminate them. They could refuse their favour to a man; they could keep him waiting; they could send him away at any time, or replace him by another lover,' ibid., p. 226.
12. Here Morris echoes the words, written more than half a century earlier, of Aston, a British forefather of Japanese literary studies: 'Another subject much dwelt on by native critics is the morality of the *Genji*, some denouncing it, *as it deserves*, while others strive to defend what even from the Japanese point of view is indefensible. Truth to say, the laxity of morals which it depicts is deplorable.' W.G. Aston, *A History of Japanese Literature* (New York: D. Appleton and Company, 1899; my emphasis), p. 97. In a review of the first installment of Arthur Waley's translation of *Genji*, Virginia Woolf takes a different view: 'but we would wrong her [Murasaki] deeply if, thus seduced, we prettified and sentimentalized an art which, exquisite as it is, is without a touch of decadence, which, for all its sensibility, is fresh and childlike and without a trace of exaggeration or languor of an outworn civilization'. V. Woolf, '"The Tale of Genji": The First Volume of Mr. Arthur Waley's Translation of a Great Japanese Novel by the Lady Murasaki,' reprinted in *Literature East and West*, vol. 11, no. 4 (Dec. 1967), p. 426.
13. Morris, *The World of the Shining Prince*, op. cit., p. 227.
14. Ibid., p. 242. Let us also remember that at the end of the chapter he refers to an expression of the most 'dramatic' effects of polygamy: 'the emotion of jealousy'. His preoccupation with the emotion leads him, among other things, to an over reading of *Kagerō nikki* (*The Gossamer Years*), which Morris sees as 'one long wail of jealousy by a woman in whom the emotion has attained hysterical proportions, and who gives vent in her writing to all the complaints, all the bitterness, all the tension …'
15. Gayatri Spivak, 'The Making of Americans, the Teaching of English, and the Future of Culture Studies,' *New Literary History*, vol. 21, no. 4 (Autumn 1990), p. 789.
16. Recall also Edward Seidensticker's translation of the *Genji* (New York: Knopf, 1976). Perhaps arising out of a perceived necessity to clean up the often impossibly complex Heian *kana* (or *onna-de*, 'women's hand') syntax as employed by Murasaki Shikibu involving absent pronominals, unstated honorific references, all-too frequent ellipses, and discrepancies resulting from textual variants, Seidensticker chooses to naturalize *Genji* in crisp cadences reminiscent of the style of that paragon of American masculinity, Ernest Hemingway, thereby displacing Arthur Waley's earlier rendition with its flowing rhythms reminiscent of a Victorian Bloomsbury world. The 1970s, of course, was a decade that saw an urgent need for remasculinization and cultural retrenchment after America's defeat in Vietnam, a time that witnessed debates on and the establishment, notably at Harvard (from 1974 to 1978), of a core curriculum, and also the rise of the Right and its PC attacks during the Reagan-Bush years, the effects of which we are still feeling today.
17. For a later example of the maintenance of the aesthetic construction of *Genji*, see Andrew Pekarik ed., *Ukifune: Love in 'The Tale of Genji'* (New York: Columbia University Press, 1982).
18. One of the most often cited commentaries is *Kakaishō*, the fourteenth century text by Yotsutsuji Yoshinari. The commentary cites possible models for Genji but emphasizes the exiled Minamoto no Takaakira as a prime candidate. See Yotsutsuji 1978.
19. Genji's exile is often seen in the context of a mythical and narrative paradigm in which men of noble blood are fated to wander for a time before returning. Exile is often transformed by modern scholarship into the more romanticized state of 'wandering'. For a discussion of the mythic elements in *Genji*, see Haruo Shirane, *The Bridge of Dreams: A Poetics of 'The Tale of Genji'* (Stanford: Stanford University Press, 1987), pp. 77–80.

20. For example, Murasaki Shikibu's father, Tametoki, appealed his case after receiving the province of Awaji. Michinaga intervened and Tametoki was given Echizen, the province to which Shikibu accompanied her father. See, Imai 1976. Some posts, moreover, were honorary ones that allowed the appointee to remain in the capital.
21. For a concise discussion of Fujiwara practices with a focus on Minamoto no Takaakira, see Oyama 1991.
22. Her father is a Major Counsellor, rather than a Minister.
23. Scholars have debated whether Genji was exiled or voluntarily left the capital. It seems best to see his move to Suma and Akashi as an evocation of earlier historical figures, both those exiled and those who voluntarily retreated from public life. See the discussion of several historical cases of exile by Fujikoge 1981.
24. When her daughter is appointed High Priestess of Ise and the Rokujō lady leaves the capital, she can be seen as performing another instance of self-imposed exile.
25. See my *Figures of Resistance: Language, Poetry and Narrating in The Tale of Genji and Other Mid-Heian Texts* (Durham, North Carolina and London: Duke University Press, 1991), Chapter 9.
26. See the discussion of the Kaguya-hime in the context of other tales of 'transgression' and wandering by Takahashi Tōru 1987: Part 2, Chapter 1.
27. She also disappears from the narrative for one chapter, 'Branch of Plum', immediately following her abduction.
28. The remark appears in 'A Picture Contest', *The Tale of Genji*, translated by Edward Seidensticker, 1976 (Penguin Books, 1976), p. 311.
29. Genji's mansion, on part of the land belonging to the Rokujō lady, has been seen as a way to appease her spirit but it can also be seen as more than a casual nod towards that self-imposed exile, See Fujii 1980: Chapter 8, for a discussion of the mansion and the Rokujō lady.
30. The narrative thus begins anew, with two chapters appropriately called 'New Herbs' (Chapters 34, 35) by repeating the political move seen in 'The Paulownia Court' (Chapter 1), only this time with a gender reversal.
31. 'He himself was the tenth son of the family, younger than his brother at Uji,' Seidensticker, 1976, p.781.
32. The Uji figure involved is Uji no Waki Iratsuko, who had been crown prince but, when his father the emperor dies, refuses to accede to the throne; becomes involved in a power struggle with his elder brother; retires to Uji; and ultimately commits suicide. See the discussion by Ishihara Shōhei (1981).

4

PERSON, HONORIFICS AND TENSE IN *THE TALE OF GENJI*

MURAKAMI FUMINOBU

☙

PERSON AND HONORIFICS

The aim of this chapter is to illustrate in the *Genji* text how classical Japanese personal references, honorifics and temporal suffixes mark narratorial standpoints and also to see briefly, as an initial attempt, how a similar effect can be achieved in English translation which does not have honorifics and whose temporal and personal reference systems are different. I have previously published a similar study of classical Japanese modal suffixes and sensation/emotion adjectives which determine the narrative distance in *The Tale of Genji*.[1] This chapter constitutes the latter half of my complete narrative study of the *Genji* text. As in the previous study, the issues examined here have two different aims: first to identify and second to differentiate the narrator and the characters.[2] Thus, my discussion will be focused on the cases in which classical Japanese personal references, honorifics and temporal suffixes function as identifying mediators between the narrator and the characters, the occasions on which they distinguish them, and the effects that they produce in each case. In this first section I will start with the personal references and honorifics.

There are three main types of honorifics in classical Japanese, i.e. the 'respect', 'humble' and 'polite'' forms.[3] Those important for our discussion are the first two: the respect and humble forms. The respect form is made either by adding such suffixes as 'たまふ', 'す', 'さす', 'る', 'らる', etc. to a verb, e.g. 'おもひたまふ' (to think + respect), or adding prefixes such as 'ご', 'み' or 'おほん' to a noun, e.g. 'みこころ' (respect + his or her mind). Another way to make a respect form is to change the verb, e.g. from 'いふ' (to say) to 'のたまふ' (to say + respect). The humble form is made by adding suffixes 'たてまつる', 'きこゆ' or 'まうす' to a verb, e.g. '聞きたてまつる' (to hear + humble), or by changing the verb, e.g. from 'いふ' (to say) to 'さうす' (to say + humble).

In classical Japanese, more than modern Japanese, personal references are scarcely used in literary texts. The agent of an action or the bearer of consciousness is often distinguished by honorifics rather than by personal references. I would like to call this type of sentence 'person-less' sentences. They can be found in the following passage from the 'Wisteria Leaves' chapter where Murasaki and Akashi meet.[4] The former starts talking about the Akashi princess, the daughter of the latter:

「かく大人びたまふけぢめになん、年月のほども知られはべれば、うとうとしき隔ては残るまじくや」と、なつかしう [1] のたまひて [hon.]、物語など [2] したまふ [hon.]。これも [3] うちとけぬるはじめなめり。ものなどうち [4] 言ひたるけはひなど、むべこそはと、めざましう [5] 見たまふ [hon.]。またいと気高う盛りなる [6] 御けしき [hon.] を、かたみにめでたしと [7] 見て、そこらの御中にもすぐれたる御心ざしにて、並びなきさまに [8] 定まりたまひ [hon.] けるも、いと道理と [9] 思ひ知らるるに、かうまで [10] 立ち並びきこゆる [hum.] 契りおろかなりやは、と [11] 思ふものから、[12] 出でたまふ [hon.] 儀式のいとことによそほしく、御輦車など [13] ゆるされたまひて、女御の御ありさまに異ならぬを、[14] 思ひくらぶるに、さすがなる身のほどなり。(NKBZ III: 442–3)

'The sight of (her) becoming a fine young lady makes (us) aware how much time has passed, and (I) hope that (we) shall be friends' – (she) [1]*says* in a friendly manner, and [2]*has* a talk. For this one too, this is the first note of [3]*becoming intimate*.[5] In the way that (she) [4]*has said*, (she) [5]*sees* the reason (why Genji has been so strongly drawn to her). (She), from her point of view, [7]*sees* how elegant and dignified (her) [6]*appearance* is, and [9] *understands* why (she) [8]*remains* in (her) place of eminence; and though (she) [11]*thinks* it is the most remarkable good fortune that (she) [10]*is* in such company, the feeling of inferiority comes back as (she) [14]*compares* (herself with her) who [12]*leaves* court [13]*being allowed* to ride in a royal carriage, as if (she) were one of the royal consorts.

(Here and in the following, unless otherwise stated, bold italics and numbers in brackets are mine. **[hon.]** indicates a verb with honorifics, **[hum.]** humble form.)

No personal reference is supplied in this part. Only 'これ' (this) can be interpreted as suggesting a person, but alone it does not clarify whether it is Murasaki or Akashi. The reader might be confused as to which lady each 'she/her' in my English rendition refers to. Without the guide of personal references, however, the reader of the original version can recognize who the agent of any specific verb is. Murasaki is described with honorifics and Akashi without them.[6]

Specifically, the verbs and nouns which describe Murasaki's actions and appearance are expressed in respect forms : [1] 'のたまひ' (to say); [2] '物語などしたまふ' (to tell a story); [5] '見たまふ' (to see); [6] '御けしき' (her appearance); [8] '定まりたまひ' (to remain in a position)'; [12] '出でたまふ' (to leave); and [13] 'ゆるされたまひ' (to be allowed). In contrast, the verbs which describe Akashi's actions or consciousness are stated without honorifics, or with a humble form addressed to Murasaki: [3] 'うちとけ' (to become intimate); [4] '言ひ' (to say); [7] '見' (to see); [9] '思ひ知らるる' (to understand);

[10] '立ち並びきこゆる' (to be in someone's company); [11] '思ふ' (to think); and [14] '思ひくらぶる' (to compare). Refer to the following rendition:

> 'The sight of her becoming a fine young lady makes us aware how much time has passed, and I hope that we shall be friends' – she **says [hon.]** in a friendly manner, and **has [hon.]** a talk. For this one too, this is the first note of ***becoming intimate***. In the way that she **has said**, she **sees [hon.]** the reason why Genji has been so strongly drawn to her. She, from her point of view, **sees** how elegant and dignified her ***appearance [hon.]*** is, and **understands** why she **remains [hon.]** in her place of eminence; and though she **thinks** it is the most remarkable good fortune that she **is** in such company, the feeling of inferiority comes back as she ***compares*** herself with her who **leaves [hon.]** court ***being allowed [hon.]*** to ride in a royal carriage, as if she were one of the royal consorts.

As has been demonstrated in the above passage, the usage of honorifics is one of the means that assist the reader, as well as the narrator, in identifying a character without her or his personal references. The absence of personal references and the usage of honorifics, typical in classical Japanese fictional language, bring about some specific features. Firstly, the shift of narrative perspective and voice is often made by changing the usage of honorifics rather than by turning the personal reference. Amanda Stinchecum mentioned that the 'use of the honorific verbs *tamau* ... reflects the linguistic situation, in which the speaker's social relation to both the addressee and the topic is expressed' (italics are original).[7] But the narrator uses honorifics in talking about a certain character (such as Murasaki) not only from her own viewpoint, but she also often assumes the perspective of other characters in the story (such as Akashi). That is, the narrator can represent one character's respect for another character, as well as expressing her own respect for characters.[8] By skilfully using honorifics, the narrative perspective and voice drastically and swiftly shift from the narrator to the character or from one character to another.

Observe the following passage from the 'Beneath the Oak' chapter where Kaoru meets Oigimi:

> [1] 思す **[hon.]** らんさま、また [2] のたまひ契り **[hon.]** しことなど、いとこまやかになつかしう [3] 言ひて、うたて男々しきけはひなどは [4] 見えたまは **[hon.]** ぬ人なれば、けうとくすずろはしくなどは [5] あらねど、[6] 知らぬ人にかく声を [7] 聞かせたてまつり **[hum.]** 、すずろに [8] 頼み顔なることなどもありつる日ごろを [9] 思ひつづくるもさすがに [10] 苦しうて、つつましけれど、ほのかに一言など [11] 答へきこえたまふ **[hon. + hum.]** さまの、げによろづ [12] 思ひほれたまへ **[hon.]** るけはひなれば、いとあはれと [13] 聞きたてまつりたまふ **[hon. + hum.]**。(NKBZ V: 189)

> How (he) [1]***feels [hon.]***, and how (he) [2]***made [hon.]*** certain promises – [3]***telling*** in the gentle and friendly way – nothing insistent [4]***can be seen [hon.]***, so (she) [5]***feels*** neither constraint nor apprehension, yet, after all, (she) [7]***has [hum.]*** [6]***an unfamiliar*** person ***hear*** the voice, and, over the weeks, (she) [8]***has come to look*** to (that person) vaguely for support – [9]***keeps thinking*** – though it [10]***is still too painful***, the way (she) [11]***answers [hon. + hum.]*** (him) a little [12]***seems to be so grieved [hon.]*** that (he) [13]***hears [hon. + hum.]*** it as pitiful.

The usage of a 'perception verb' – [4] '見え' (to be seen to her) – suggests that the narrative perspective in the first half of the above passage is Oigimi's.[9] If we compare [13] '聞き' (to hear Oigimi) with [7] '聞かせ' (to have Kaoru hear), we can see there the shift of the narrative perspective from Oigimi to Kaoru. It is important to examine the perception verbs to see the narrative perspective and to hear the voice in the text. In the above passage, when the narrator says that Kaoru induces neither constraint nor apprehension, this is his appearance not so much to the narrator as to Oigimi. Thus, the narrator as well as the reader can share Oigimi's perception and the narrative perspective and voice is hers.

In the above part, however, besides the usage of perception verbs, honorifics play an important role in setting the narrative point of view and voice. In the first half, except [3] '言ひ' (to tell), Kaoru's actions and thought are described in respect forms: [1] '思す' (to think); [2] 'のたまひ契り' (to make certain promises); and [4] '見えたまは' (to be seen). Oigimi's actions and thoughts, on the other hand, are depicted without honorifics or with a humble form to Kaoru: [5] 'あら' (to be in a mental state); [6] '知ら' (to know); [7] '聞かせたてまつり' (to have him hear); [8] '頼み顔なることなどもあり' (to look to him for support); [9] '思ひつづくる' (to keep thinking); and [10] '苦しうて、つつましけれど' (to be painful). All this proves that the narrative perspective is Oigimi's in this part. The narrator's usage of honorifics is identical with that of Oigimi. The scene is presented from Oigimi's point of view, and Kaoru is described from her angle with her respect and humble honorifics for him.

From 'ほのかに一言など答へきこえたまふさまの' (the way she answers) onwards, the usage of honorifics shifts. Firstly, [11] '答へきこえたまふ' (to answer) includes two different honorifics; Oigimi's humble attitude to Kaoru (きこえ) and the narrator's respect to Oigimi (たまふ). Then, Oigimi's mental activity [12] '思ひほれたまへる' (to grieve) is described in respect form (たまへ). Further, in the last part of the quote, Kaoru's perceptive activity [13] '聞きたてまつりたまふ' (to hear Oigimi talking) is, contrary to the case in [11], depicted with his humble attitude to Oigimi (たてまつり) and the narrator's respect to Kaoru (たまふ). This shows that the narrative perspective shifts in this part from Oigimi to Kaoru.

To use honorifics in describing Kaoru from Oigimi's perspective results in an identification of the narrator with Oigimi. By using honorifics which are supposed to be used by Oigimi, the narrator can share her perspective. When the narrator changes the usage of honorifics and expresses Kaoru's respect for Oigimi, she can be assimilated into Kaoru's consciousness. Honorifics here realize the integration between the narrator and the character in question. This sort of shift of narrative perspective and the identification between the narrator and the character can often be accomplished in classical Japanese literary language by manipulating honorifics.[10]

The second characteristic of honorifics is to widen the narrative distance between the narrator and the character. Initially, this may seem to contradict the first feature of honorifics which realizes the integration between the narrator and the character. But they are actually two sides of the same coin. In the case of psychological descriptions the more the narrator's consciousness emerges distinctively and independently from the character's perceptive, from his or her emotional, mental or thought processes, the wider the narrative distance between them. And, conversely, the more the narrator's and the character's mental activities are integrated into one, the narrower the narrative distance.[11] Honorifics in the authorial narrative situation,[12] that is the honorifics which exclusively indicate the narrator's respect for a character, are one of the instances in which the narrator's consciousness appears as separate from the character's mental activity. When no proper character is around in a scene as a vehicle for expressing respect to a person whom the narrator is describing, the usage of honorifics must be attributed to the narrator. Then, the honorific discloses the character of the narrator. It widens the narrative distance and often changes the sentence mode from *showing* to *telling*.[13] Besides expressing respect or humbleness, honorifics play a role as *narrative modal markers*.[14]

In Japanese psychological description, the distinction between the *showing* and *telling* modes is crucial. Observe the following two person-less sentences:

(1) 悲しとおもふ。 (Someone) feels sad.
(2) 悲しとおもひたまふ。 (Someone) feels (+ **honorific**) sad.

As I have pointed out before in my former study,[15] in Japanese, one must narrate others' mental activities in the *telling* mode; one cannot display others' psychology in the *showing* mode. We can say, therefore, that if such verbs as 'おもふ' (to think), 'せむ' (to want to do), 'おぼゆ' (to feel), etc., which indicate one's mental activities, appear in the *showing* mode of person-less sentences, they should be considered either to represent the character's monologue or the narrator's own thinking. If one exposes the psychology of others in *showing* mode, it results in a grammatically unacceptable sentence in conversational situations. This sort of ungrammatical sentence is, however, often used in fictional language (*monogatari*). We can find many sentences in literary works in which it appears from the context that a third-person character *thinks* in *showing* mode in the narrator's narration. These ungrammatical sentences seem to play the role of obscuring the distinction between the narrator and the character, especially in person-less sentences. Thus, in the above single-folded *showing* sentence (1), if it is used in fictional language, the narrator's narration ('he thinks') and the character's monologue ('I think') can be merged. Whereas in the *telling* sentence (2) the character's mental activity '*omou*' (to think) is described with an honorific (*tamau*). While the *showing* sentence (1) has no room for the narrator to distinctively appear, the *telling* sentence (2) does have room in the honorific. The narrative distance between the narrator and the character in sentence (2) is wider than that in (1).

As has been pointed out, we have to take cases into consideration in which the narrator uses honorifics to a character (A) from another character's (B's) perspective. The narrator's respect for one character (A) is then indistinguishable from the other character's (B's) respect for that character (A). In this case, by using honorifics the narrator can identify himself or herself with the character (B) and the narrative distance between them becomes shorter.[16] By contrast, when the honorifics apparently disclose the narrator's own respect, that is, when they are used in the authorial narrative situation, they serve to reveal his or her own cognitive activity and thus widen the narrative distance. On the other hand, the lack of honorifics for a key person who carries the narrative perspective results in the assimilation of the narrator into that character.[17]

Consequently, we can say that although psychological predicates in personless sentences tend to produce a single-folded *showing* mode in which the characters' mental activities are directly revealed without the narrator's independent consciousness, if honorifics are added to the psychological predicates, they tend to indicate the duplicated psychological description of the character by the narrator. It can be seen in the following passage taken from the part in which Genji first meets young Murasaki:

「何ごとぞや。童べと腹立ちたまへるか」とて、尼君の見上げたるに、すこしおぼえたるところあれば、子なめりと ［1］見たまふ **[hon.]**。「雀の子を犬君が逃がしつる。伏籠の中に籠めたりつるものを」とて、いと口惜しと ［2］思へり。(NKBZ I: 280)

'What is it? Fight with children?' saying so, the nun has looked up, (he) [1]***sees [hon.]*** a resemblance, perhaps (they) are mother and daughter. 'Inuki let my baby sparrows loose. (I) had them in a basket.' – (she) [2]***thinks*** it regretful.

Genji's action and perception [1] '見' (to see) is expressed with an honorific 'たまふ' and young Murasaki's inner thought [2] '思へり' (to think) without honorifics. If the last sentence were reformulated with an honorific, such as '思ひたまふ', it would turn into the *telling* mode, told by the narrator (a lady-in-waiting) who respects young Murasaki. If the agent of the mental activity '思ふ', that is the character Murasaki, appears in the sentence as a personal pronoun / noun, the narrator has a place where she can disclose herself as the one who refers to the character in the third person. But there are neither honorifics nor personal references in the above sentence. The result is a close description of Murasaki's mental activity.[18]

It should not be overlooked that the suffix 'り', which indicates the completion of action, is added to [2] 'おもふ' and thus displays the narrator's cognitive activity. But her consciousness as revealed in the aspectual suffix seems less remarkable than that in the honorific. Further, it must also be taken into consideration that Genji's official and family rank is high enough to be respected, but that Murasaki, still an unknown child, does not have to be accorded respect.[19] Yet, from the point of view of narrative mode, it can be said that while Genji's perception in the first sentence is depicted from the outside viewpoint with the honorific in duplicated *telling* mode, Murasaki's inner thought is described more directly without the narrator's distinctive consciousness. The narrative distance between the narrator and Murasaki is much shorter than that between the narrator and Genji. This is realized by the usage of honorifics.

The function of honorifics is not confined to changing the narrative distance between the narrator and the various characters. By virtue of honorifics, the narrator can also alter the narrative distance to one character depending on the situation she or he narrates. This is the case in the following passage from the 'Festival of the Cherry Blossoms' chapter where Genji happens to catch at the sleeve of a lady who is later discovered to be Oborozukiyo:

> わななくわななく、「ここに、人」と [1] <u>のたまへ</u> **[hon.]** ど、「まろは、皆人にゆるされたれば、召し寄せたりとも、なむでふことかあらん。ただ忍びてこそ」とのたまふ声に、この君なりけり、と [2] 聞き定めて、いささか [3] 慰めけり。
> わびしと [4] 思へるものから、情なくこはごはしうは見えじ、と [5] 思へり。
> (NKBZ I: 427)

> Trembling and trembling again, (she) [1]***calls [hon.]*** for help saying 'A strange man is here,' but, 'Since I am always allowed my way, calling someone will do (you) no good. Just be quiet.' [2]***Recognizing*** the voice, [3]***somewhat reassured***.
> Though of course [4]***upset***, (she) [5]***thought*** that (she) should not look to (him) as wanting in good manners.

In the first instance Oborozukiyo's action [1] 'のたまへ' (to call) is described in the honorific form of 'いふ' (to call). Later, her mental activities: [2] '聞き定め' (to recognize); [3] '慰め' (to be reassured); [4] '思へる' (to think); and [5] '思へり' (to think) are expressed without any honorifics. It indicates that the narrator firstly narrates Oborozukiyo's action in the wider narrative distance with an honorific which conveys the narrator's distinctive cognitive activity, and that later she restricts the apparent presence of her own consciousness. In this manner, the narrator here comes closer into Oborozukiyo's mental activities in this crucial climax scene.

The omission of honorifics in the narrator's authorial narrative situation in *Genji* is one of the signs which display which character in which scene the narrator identifies with. In this sense, by examining the omission of honorifics one can see who the character is that the narrator sympathizes with in a particular part of the story. It may be possible to say that in a critical part of the story in which a close description of a character's mental activities is necessary, honorifics are often avoided. By so doing, the narrator can narrate the scene reducing her own independent appearance.[20] Let me quote a rather long passage from the 'Typhoon' chapter in which Yūgiri, Genji's son, glances at Murasaki. His perception, thinking and actions are narrated mostly without honorifics:

> 大臣は、姫君の御方におはしますほどに、中将の君<u>参りたまひ</u> **[hon.]** て、東の渡殿の小障子の上より、妻戸の開きたる隙を何心なく<u>見入れたまへ</u> **[hon.]** るに、女房のあまた見ゆれば、立ちとまりて音もせで見る。御屏風も、風のいたく吹きければ、押したたみ寄せたるに、見通しあらはなる廂の御座にゐたまへる人、ものに紛るべくもあらず、気高くきよらに、さとにほふ心地して、春の曙の霞

の間より、おもしろき樺桜の咲き乱れたるを見る心地す。あぢきなく、見たてまつるわが顔にも移り来るやうに、愛敬はにほひ散りて、またなくめづらしき人の御さまなり。御簾の吹き上げらるるを、人々押へて、いかにしたるにかあらむ、うち笑ひたまへる、いといみじく見ゆ。花どもを心苦しがりて、え見棄てて入りたまはず。御前なる人々も、さまざまにものきよげなる姿どもは見わたさるれど、目移るべくもあらず。大臣のいとけ遠くに遥かにもてなしたまへるは、かく、見る人ただにはえ思ふまじき御ありさまを、至り深き御心にて、もしかかることもやと思すなりけり、と思ふに、けはひ恐ろしうて、立ち去るにぞ、西の御方より、内の御障子ひき開けて渡りたまふ。
「いとうたて、あわたたしき風なめり。御障子おろしてよ。男どもあるらむを。あらはにもこそあれ」と聞こえたまふを、また寄りて見れば、もの聞こえて、大臣もほほ笑みて、見たてまつりたまふ。親ともおぼえず、若くきよげになまめきて、いみじき御容貌のさかりなり。女もねびととのひ、飽かぬことなき御さまどもなるを身にしむばかりおぼゆれど、この渡殿の格子も吹き放ちて、立てる所のあらはになれば、恐ろしうて立ち退きぬ。今参れるやうにうち声づくりて、簀子の方に歩み出でたまへれ **[hon.]** ば、「さればよ。あらはなりつらむ」とて、かの妻戸の開きたりけるよ、と今ぞ見とがめたまふ。(NKBZ III: 256–8)

Genji was with his daughter. ***Approaching [hon.] along the east gallery, Yūgiri saw [hon.] over a low screen that a door was open at a corner of the main hall***. He stopped to look at the women inside. The screen having been folded and put away, the view was unobstructed. The lady at the veranda – it would be Murasaki. Her noble beauty made him think of a fine birch cherry blooming through the hazes of spring. It was a gentle flow which seemed to come to him and sweep over him. She laughed as her women fought with the unruly blinds, though he was too far away to make out what she said to them, and the bloom was more radiant. She stood surveying the scene, seeing what the winds had done to each of the flowers. Her women were all very pretty too, but he did not really look at them. It almost frightened him to think why Genji had so kept him at a distance. Such beauty was irresistible, and just such inadvertencies as this were to be avoided at all costs.

As he started to leave, Genji came through one of the doors to the west, separating Murasaki's rooms from his daughter's.

'An irritable, impatient sort of wind,' he said. 'You must close your shutters. There are men about and you are very visible.'

Yūgiri looked back. Smiling at Murasaki, Genji was so young and handsome that Yūgiri found it hard to believe he was looking at his own father. Murasaki too was at her best. Nowhere could there be a nearer approach to perfection than the two of them, thought Yūgiri, with a stabbing thrill of pleasure. The wind had blown open the shutters along the gallery to make him feel rather exposed. He withdrew. ***Then, going up [hon.] to the veranda, he coughed as if to announce that he had just arrived.***

'See,' said Genji, pointing to the open door. 'You have been quite naked.' (S. 458–9)

Honorifics to Yūgiri are added to the sentences in bold italics (in Seidensticker's translation). Between these two sentences, honorifics are not applied to him.[21] This assures that the narrator describes the scene from the viewpoint close to that of Yūgiri.

So far, we have examined two important features of honorifics. Firstly, when the narrator uses honorifics to a certain character (A) from the perspective of another character (B), that is, when the narrator represents (B)'s respect for (A), the narrator's respect for (A) is indistinguishable from (B)'s respect for (A). The narrator can in this case identify himself or herself with (B), and the narrative distance between them shortens. Secondly, when the narrator uses honorifics exclusively expressing his or her own respect, that is, when the honorifics are used in the authorial narrative situation, they serve to reveal the narrator's cognitive activity and widen the narrative distance. On the other hand, the lack of honorifics to a key person in whom the narrative perspective is set results in the assimilation of the narrator's consciousness into the character's. Since nobody except the emperor normally uses honorifics to apply to himself or herself, these two characteristics can be summarized to say that the closer the usage of the honorific comes to that of a character, the vaguer the distinction between narrator's and the character's consciousness.

With or without honorifics in a particular situation, the narrator of the Japanese classical literary language can be close to or far from the character's mentality. How can a similar effect be achieved in English which does not have honorifics? We will see in the next two examples how Seidensticker and Tyler have translated the original text into English. First, there is the following example of Kashiwagi's thoughts from the 'New Herbs (Part 2)' chapter. Kashiwagi (son of Tō no Chūjō) is attracted to Genji's wife, the Third Princess, and is in agony. Although he is frightened of Genji, he cannot get her out of his mind:

> みづからも、大殿を [1] 見たてまつる **[hum.]** に気恐ろしくまばゆく、「かかる心はあるべきものか。なのめならむにてだに、けしからず人に点つかるべきふるまひはせじ、と [2] 思ふものを、ましておほけなきこと」と [3] 思ひわびては、「かのありし猫をだに得てしがな。思ふこと語らふべくはあらねど、かたはらさびしき慰めにもなつけむ」と [4] 思ふに、もの狂ほしく、いかでかは盗み出でむと、それさへぞ難きことなりける。(NKBZ IV: 147)

> When (he) [1]*looks [hum.]* at Genji, frightened. Do thoughts like this really exist? Should not conduct what is to be blamed by others – (I / he) [2]*think(s)*. Even such a monstrous thing – (he) [3]*thinks in agony*. Could have the cat. May not be able to talk of this unhappiness with it, perhaps, but may be less lonely. Wish to tame it – (I / he) [4]*think(s)*. The thought is like an obsession – how to steal it? – but that is not easy.

Kashiwagi's inner thinking is consistently depicted without honorifics. Though his humble attitude to Genji is mentioned in [1] 'たてまつる', the narrator's respect for him does not appear. The personal reference used in this part is not 'he' but the vaguer 'self' (みづから). No quotation marks are supplied in the original handwritten text. These features result in the ambiguity between the character's monologue and the narrator's narration.[22] Whose voice is [2] '思ふ' (to think) and [4] '思ふ' – Kashiwagi or the narrator?

Another interesting point here is the combination between the volitional suffix and 'と思ふ' (to think that): [2] 'せじ、と思ふ' (I think I do not want to do = I do not want to do), and [4] 'なつけむと思ふ' (I think I want to tame =

I want to tame). This sort of double expression is frequently used still in modern Japanese language, as in '食べようと思う' (I think I will eat ...). As was mentioned earlier, the Japanese psychological predicate can, in the *showing* mode, only express the speaker's mentalities. Thus, in the psychological predicates in person-less sentences of fictional language which indicate the character's mental activities, the narrator's narration and the character's monologue can be easily merged. But the combination of two psychological words produces a different effect. It can be a double fold *telling* mode narration, just like the result of 'psychological predicate + honorific'. In order to narrate one's own mental activity in the *telling* mode, this pattern is often used in Japanese.

In English 'I want to go to Tokyo' or 'I will go to Tokyo' is probably enough to make the sentence acceptable as describing oneself. A corresponding Japanese sentence '東京に行こう' (Let's go to Tokyo) or '東京に行きたい' (I want to go to Tokyo) is not sufficient to 'narrate' oneself. They are not in *telling* but in *showing* mode. The speaker's will is directly exposed without his or her recognizing activity. These two expressions are therefore appropriate only for the speaker's inner monologue (in the latter sentence) or as a means of exposing his or her wish to the listener it produces an invitation ('Let's go to Tokyo' in the former sentence).

In order to change the mode from *showing* to *telling* in modern Japanese, so that the sentence becomes suitable as a narrative description of the speaker's mental state made by the speaker herself or himself, one must add a modal marker to indicate the speaker's cognition, such as 'のだ'. In case of 'たい', this works; the sentence '東京に行きたいんだ'[23] (I tell you that I want to go to Tokyo) is sufficient to narrate the speaker's intention in the *telling* mode. In the case of volitional conjugated forms of verbs this does not work. '東京に行こうのだ' (I tell you that let's go to Tokyo) is unacceptable. Since 'のだ' cannot be added to the volitional conjugated form of a verb, the only way to change the *showing* mode sentence ending with its volitional conjugated form of verb into the *telling* mode is to add 'と思う' (to think); '東京に行こうと思う' (I tell you that I will go to Tokyo). Most probably, 'と思う' in modern Japanese plays a similar role of narrative modal marker as does 'のだ'. By adding 'と思う' or further 'と思うんだ', one can change the narrative mode from *showing* to *telling*. It seems that this rule can be also adapted to apply to classical Japanese.

Perhaps the duplicated consciousness expressed in the above examples is typical in any language. Language is presumably a product of duplicated consciousness. It seems that personal references in English play an important role in this duplication. When a character is referred to as 'he', the speaker is implicit as 'I'; even when a character is referred to as 'I', the one who calls this character 'I' also appears as the bearer of individual cognitive activity. Since Japanese personal references are scarcely mentioned, the speaker's duplicated cognition must surface elsewhere in such narrative modal markers as 'のだ' or 'と思う'.

If this twofold expression 'volitional conjugated form + と思う'

('ようと思う' in modern Japanese or 'むと思ふ' in classical Japanese is used in person-less sentences in fictional language, there are two possible interpretations. (1) 'I (the character) think 'I (the character) want to do …'' and (2) 'he (the character) thinks 'I (the character) want to do …'' Since psychological predicates including the above volitional conjugated forms indicate only the speaker's (the first person's) mental activities, the one who wants to do something is in most cases the character. But, the point is who recognizes this, the character or the narrator? In (1), 'と思う' (I think) is included in the character's monologue, whereas in (2), 'と思う' (he thinks) is the narrator's narration. While in (1) the character's consciousness is revealed, in (2) the narrator's cognitive activity is exposed. In this ambiguity, the reader, if unconsciously, hears the two different voices in one word. This must be another reason why in [2] 'せじ、と思ふ' (to think not to want to do) and [4] 'なつけむと思ふ' (to think to want to tame) the narrator's and the character's voices are integrated.

Seidensticker translated this passage as follows:

> Kashiwagi was afraid to look at Genji. He knew that he was thinking forbidden thoughts. He was always concerned to behave with complete correctness and much worried about appearances. [5]**What then was he to make of so monstrous a thing as this?** He thought of the princess's cat and suddenly longed to have it for himself. [6]**He could not share his unhappiness with it, perhaps, but he might be less lonely**. The thought became an obsession. [7]**Perhaps, he could steal it – but that would not be easy.** (S. 588)

In this English translated version a similar effect of merging two different voices is achieved by different means. Firstly, the sentence [5]'What then was he to make of so monstrous a thing as this?' catches the reader's attention. The sentence is certainly depicted from the outside viewpoint with the third person personal pronoun 'he' and past tense 'was'. The narrator's distinctive cognition appears there. But the contents of the sentence and the consciousness of asking seem to belong to the character Kashiwagi rather than to the narrator. As pointed out by many, this style is called a *narrated monologue* or *free indirect style*.[24]

Furthermore, the sentences [6]'He could not share his unhappiness with it, perhaps, but he might be less lonely' and [7]'perhaps, he could steal it – but that would not be easy' are also the authorial narrative situation with the third person personal pronoun (he/his) and the past tense (could/might/would). But here again it seems possible to infer that the person who recognizes the possibility and expresses it by 'perhaps' and 'could/might/would' is the character Kashiwagi, as well as the narrator.

By contrast, Royall Tyler translated the same passage as follows:

> The Intendant, who looked on His Grace with dazzled awe, shrank from his own thoughts, since he would never have wished to give the least offence and this one was beyond the pale, but he longed in his trouble at least to have the cat – not that I could pour out my heart to it, he thought, but it would be a comfort when I am feeling lonely – and he schemed frantically to steal it for himself. That alone would be tricky enough, though. (T. 628)

Tyler's version distinguishes the narrator's and Kashiwagi's voices clearer than Seidensticker's. For instance, 'The Intendant ... shrank from his own thoughts, since he would never have wished to give the least offence ..., but he longed in his trouble at least to have the cat' is clearly narrated by the narrator's voice. Then, in the part between two dashes '– not that I could pour out my heart to it, he thought, but it would be a comfort when I am feeling lonely –', 'he thought' is narrator's voice, and the other part is narrated by Kashiwagi's voice. Although the narrative distance within Kashiwagi's mentality is widen by using 'could/would', the first person pronoun 'I' avoids the merge between the narrator's and the character's consciousness. Lastly, 'he schemed frantically to steal it for himself' again, by using the third person pronoun 'he/himself', emphasizes the narrator's voice, and therefore the following sentence 'That alone would be tricky enough, though' also shows the narrator's consciousness.

Let me take one more similar example from the 'New Herbs (Part 2)' chapter in which Kashiwagi first meets the Third Princess. Kashiwagi expects a proud lady at first, but when he sees her, he finds her very different:

よその思ひやりはいつくしく、もの馴れて見えたてまつらむも恥づかしく推しはかられ [1] たまふ **[hon.]** に、ただかばかり思ひつめたる片はし聞こえ知らせて、なかなかかけかけしき事はなくてやみなん、と [2] 思ひしかど、いとさばかり気高う恥づかしげにはあらで、なつかしくらうたげに、やはやはとのみ見えたまふ御けはひの、あてにいみじく思ゆることぞ、人に似させたまはざりける。さかしく思ひしづむる心もうせて、いづちもいづちも率て隠したてまつりて、わが身も世に経るさまならず、跡絶えてやみなばや、とまで [3] 思ひ乱れぬ。

　ただいささかまどろむともなき夢に、この手馴らしし猫のいとらうたげにうちなきて来たるを、この宮に奉らむ [3'] とてわが率て来たると [4] 思しきを、何しに奉りつらむ、と [5] 思ふほどに、おどろきて、いかに見えつるならむ、と [6] 思ふ (NKBZ. IV: 216–17)

Thinking of her from a distance, (he) [1]***expects [hon.]*** a proud lady whom it is not easy to talk to, so just to tell (her) a little of this unhappiness, and say nothing that appears to be regrettable later – (I / he) [2]***thought***, but, (she) is not proud and not difficult to talk to, friendly, pretty, and the way looks gentle is graceful and elegant, different from most ladies. Calm mind disappears. Could bring and hide (her) somewhere, and die there (with her), (he) [3]***has thought***.

　In the dream, though not falling asleep, the cat which (he) tamed comes up mewing prettily. I have brought it here, because (I / he) [3]***think(s)*** that I want to give it to her – (I / he) [4]***felt***. But why should give (it to her), – (I / he) [5]***think(s)***. Then wake up; why have had such a dream? – (I / he) [6]***think(s)***.

The narrator starts with the description of Kashiwagi from the outside viewpoint using an honorific [1] '推しはかられたまふ' (to expect), and then comes closer to his mentality by omitting honorifics in [2] '思ひ' (to think); [3] '思ひ乱れぬ' (to think without control); [4] '思し' (to feel); [5] '思ふ' (to think); and [6] '思ふ' (to think).[25] The combination between volitional suffixes and 'と思ふ' (to think) can be also found in the passages: 'やみなん、と [2] 思ひしかど' (I just want to stop – (I / he) [2]think(s)); 'この宮に奉らむ [3'] と [思ひ]て'[26] (I want to give it to her – (I/he) [3]think(s)); '何しに奉りつらむ、[5] 思ふ' (why should give – (I / he) [5]think(s)). The narrator's and Kashiwagi's voices in these expressions are so deeply assimilated into one that it is almost impossible to distinguish between them.

Again, let me quote Seidensticker's translation:

> He had expected a proud lady whom it would not be easy to talk to. He would tell her a little of his unhappiness, he had thought, and say nothing he might later regret. But he found her very different. She was pretty and gentle and unresisting, and far more graceful and elegant, in a winsome way, than most ladies he had known. His passion was suddenly more than he could control. [7] ***Was there no hiding place to which they might run off together?***
>
> He presently dozed off (it cannot be said that he fell asleep) and dreamed of the cat of which he had been so fond. It came up to him mewing prettily. He seemed to be dreaming that he had brought it back to the princess. As he awoke he was asking himself why he should have done that. [8] ***And what might the dream have meant?*** [S. 613–14]

The sentence [7] 'Was there no hiding place to which they might run off together?' is in a sense again a narrated monologue, in which the narrator's voice meshes with Kashiwagi's voice by the use of the third-person personal pronoun ('they') and the past tense ('was'). The sentence [8] 'And what might the dream have meant?' also shows the identification between the voices of the narrator and Kashiwagi.

Tyler translated the same passage as follows:

> Having imagined her haughty from a distance and forbidding in intimacy, he had resolved merely to hint at his torment and to try nothing more daring, but when he discovered less lofty pride than a sweet, nobly yielding and captivating charm, he took her to be unique among women. Every thought of wise self-restraint vanished, and he longed in confusion only to carry her off into hiding somewhere, anywhere, so as to vanish forever from life in the world.
>
> Upon dozing off a moment he dreamed that the cat he had made into such a pet came to him, mewing sweetly, and that he brought it to Her Highness as a gift. He awoke wondering why and perplexed about what his dream meant. (T.651)

In this part, 'Every thought of wise self-restraint vanished, and he longed in confusion only to carry her off into hiding somewhere, anywhere, so as to vanish forever from life in the world' and 'He awoke wondering why and perplexed about what his dream meant' are narrated by the narrator's voice and consciousness. They are narrated in the very stable authorial narrative situation. We can say that in the above two examples an effect similar to that of honorifics and 'volitional suffix + と思ふ' in the original *Genji* is achieved by the narrated monologue in Seidensticker's English translation. By contrast, Tyler's translation is narrated by the narrator's unified voice in the authorial narrative situation.

'き' (*KI*) AND 'けり' (*KERI*)

Like personal references and honorifics, the use of suffixes 'き' and 'けり' is also related to narrative modes. We firstly have to distinguish them.[27] An examination of the text of *Genji*, as has been pointed out by many, reveals that 'けり' is often used in current synchronic descriptions. That is, even if the narrative perspective is closely related to the time when the story took place, namely the story **Now**,[28] frequently 'けり' is used. On the other hand, 'き' apparently shows past actions and occurrences recollected from the present narrating moment.

The difference between 'き' and 'けり' can be precisely seen in the following example from 'The Paulownia Court' chapter in which a messenger comes from the palace to the house of the late Lady Kiritsubo's mother:

内裏より御使あり。三位の位贈りたまふよし、勅使来て、その宣命読むなん、悲しきことなり [1] ける。女御とだに言はせずなりぬるが、あかず口惜しう思さるれば、いま一階の位をだにと、贈らせたまふなり [2] けり。これにつけても、憎みたまふ人々多かり。
　もの思ひ知りたまふは、さま容貌などのめでたかり [3] しこと、心ばせのなだらかにめやすく、憎みがたかり [4] しことなど、今ぞ思し出づる。さまあしき御もてなしゆゑこそ、すげなうそねみたまひ [5] しか、人がらのあはれに、情あり [6] し御心を、上の女房なども恋ひしのびあへり。「なくてぞ」とは、かかるをりにやと見えたり (NKBZ I: 101)[29]

A messenger comes from the palace. That a nunciary arrives and reads the official order that (the Emperor) offers (the lady) the Third Rank [1]*is [keru]* grievous. (The Emperor) unbearably regrets the fact that (he) has not appointed (her) an imperial consort, so (he) thinks even if it is one higher rank and *offers [keri]* it (to her). There are many who resent even this favour.

Others who have a more sensitive nature, remember now what a beautiful lady (she) [3]*was [shi]*, how simple and gentle, and how difficult to find fault in (her heart) [4]*was [shi]*. Because of excessive favour (of the emperor) (they) [5]*had [shika]* malice towards (her), but the grand ladies are now reminded of how sympathetic and unassuming (she) [6]*was [shi]*. The phrase 'how well one knows' must be invented for just such an occasion.

The narrator's usage of the present tense verbs, 'あり' (to be), '来て' (to come), and '読む' (to read) at the beginning indicates that she is within the story time in this part. At the end of the second sentence, [1] 'ける' is used. But this does not change the tense. As Richard Okada pointed out, けり here should be considered as a sort of narrative modal marker.[30] But the point is, as Shirane argued, that 'exactly what kind of mood it defines'.[31] Amanda Stinchecum says on this point that けり 'implies the presence of a speaking subject, i.e. a narrator; it implies further that the narrator is making a statement of judgement, something like, "I'm telling you that it is so that …"'[32] The function of 'けり' as defined by Stinchecum could be interpreted as the narrator's *cognitive narrative modality*. It indicates the narrator's cognitive activity and thus the narrative distance between the narrator and the events in the story. In the following sentence (the Emperor regrets, so he promotes her, and many resent this favour), [2] 'けり' is also considered as being synchronic narrative and showing the narrator's cognition of the events in the story (story **Now**).

In the next three sentences, the late Lady Kiritsubo is lamented by others and by the narrator. She is depicted from the story's present point of view. In this part 'き' ([3] 'し', [4] 'し', [5] 'しか' and [6] 'し') instead of 'けり' is used. 'き' appears only in the description of what she was like and what the grand ladies did when she was alive (story **Past**). It depicts events that occurred in the past viewed from the present moment of the story.

There is also the following similar example from the 'Evening Faces' chapter in which we can compare 'き' and 'けり' again. After the death of Yūgao, Genji has a dream about her:

は夢をだに見ばやと思しわたるに、この法事したまひてまたの夜、ほのかに、かのあり [1] し院ながら、添ひたり [2] し女のさまも同じやうにて見え [3] ければ、...... (NKBZ I: 267–8)

Genji thinks '(I) want to see a glimpse of (the dead girl), if only in a dream', then, on the day after the services (he) [3]***has [kere]*** a fleeting dream of the woman who [2]***lay [shi]*** beside (him) in that house exactly as it [1]***was [shi]***.

Here again, 'き' is added to events that occurred in the past (story **Past**) as seen from the story's present moment.

The English tense system, to risk oversimplification, consists of the discourse **Now**, the story **Now** and the story **Past**. It is based upon just one standard – present narrating discourse time. Seymour Chatman considers that generally the discourse **Now** is expressed in the present or present progressive, the story **Now** in the past or past progressive, thus the story **Past** can be expressed in the past perfect.[33] However, this argument is not applicable to the Japanese story. It is pointed out that in Japanese the discourse **Now** shifts easily to story **Now**.[34] Therefore, if the concept of tense requires the standard, zero-point, the here-and-now,[35] it would be better to assume that 'き' in Japanese is not a past tense marker, and just indicates the temporal distance between the narrating time and the narrated time. By disclosing the temporal distance, 'き' plays two significant roles; firstly by means of narrating the story **Past** with 'き', to set the narrative perspective in the story **Now**; and secondly, by way of narrating the story **Now** with 'き', to visualize the narrator at the discourse **Now**.[36] In contrast, 'けり' is used to show the story **Now** described from the contemporary synchronic time in the story **Now**. It does not mark any temporal distance, but rather shows a cognitive distance. It may be possible to say that the sentence typical of the opening part of fiction, '昔男ありけり' (Once upon a time there was a man) indicates not only that the narrator is narrating about a man in the past, but also that the narrative perspective is already set in the story **Now**. '昔男ありき' (Once upon a time there was a man), on the other hand, shows that the narrative perspective is in the present narrating moment (discourse **Now**) and the narrator is recollecting the past event (story **Now**) from the present view point.

Even if 'き' is used at the beginning of chapter, it often indicates the past event looked at not from the discourse **Now**, but from the story **Now**. Compare the following two passages, one from the well-known opening passage of *Genji* in which 'けり' is used, and one from the beginning of 'The Wormwood Patch' chapter where 'き' is used:

いづれの御時にか、女御更衣あまたさぶらひたまひける中に、いとやむごとなき際にはあらぬが、すぐれて時めきたまふありけり。(NKBZ I: 93)

In a certain reign, among many ladies who were / are in the court, there was / is a lady not of the first rank but deeply loved by the Emperor.

藻塩たれつつわびたまひ [1] しころほひ、都にも、さまざま思し嘆く人多かり [2] しを、さてもわが御身の拠りどころあるは、一方の思ひこそ苦しげなり [3] しか、......(NKBZ II: 315)

In those days of sea grass [1]*steeped [shi]* in brine, in the city there [2]*were [shi]* many ladies lamenting Genji's absence, but for ladies in secure places, the problem [3]*was [shika]* just loneliness in his absence.

The content of the first passage above certainly occurred in the past. It is, however, more likely that the consciousness of the past is displayed not by 'けり', but rather by 'いづれの御時にか' (In a certain reign). 'けり' does not here serve to indicate the temporal distance between the narrating time and the narrated time and make the present moment, the moment at which the narrator is narrating, appear clearly. It only shows the narrator's cognitive activity.

In the second passage (the opening lines of 'The Wormwood Patch'), after Genji's return to Kyoto from his exile in Suma and Akashi, the narrator narrates the miserable states of the ladies who were not openly recognized as Genji's wives. The usage of 'き' in this part indicates that the narrator recollects the story **Past** (when Genji was in exile) from the viewpoint of the story **Now** (after his return to Kyoto). Compared with 'けり' in the first passage, 'き' in the second citation should be regarded as simply indicating past events or occurrences (story **Past**) recollected by the narrator from the story **Now**.

In the following opening lines from 'The Gatehouse' chapter, 'き' should also be interpreted as not indicating the past tense seen from the discourse **Now**, but the past tense recollected from the story **Now**:

伊予介といひ [1] しは、故院崩れさせたまひてまたの年、常陸になりて下り [2] しかば、かの箒木もいざなはれに [3] けり。(NKBZ II: 349)

A man who [1]*was [shi]* called Vice-Governor of Iyo the year after the death of Genji's father [2]*became [shika]* **Vice-Governor of Hitachi and [2]went [shika]**[37] there, hence, his wife, the lady Hahakigi [3]*goes [keri]* with him to his post.

In this passage, the Vice-Governor of Iyo becoming Vice-Governor of Hitachi and going there are described as the story **Past** viewed from the story **Now** (after Genji's return to Kyoto) by the use of 'き'. And that his wife, the Lady of the Locust Shell, went with him is described as the story **Now** by using 'けり'. It shows that the narrator's temporal perspective shifts from the story **Now** (after Genji's return from his exile) to the story **Past** (when the Vice-Governor of Iyo became Vice-Governor of Hitachi and went there) with the use of 'けり' at the end of the sentence. By employing 'き' in the above two passages, the narrator suggests that her discourse **Now** is subsequent to Genji's return to Kyoto (the story **Now**) and that she recollects the events in the story **Past** (when Genji was in Suma and Akashi).

Given that 'き' shows temporal distance between the narrating and narrated times, when 'き' is added to an action that occurred in the present moment of the story (story **Now**), instead of in the past of the story (story **Past**), the narrator can appear in the present moment of narrating time (discourse **Now**). This kind of usage of 'き' is not often found in *Genji*, but certainly exists, as in the following passage from the 'New Herbs (Part 1)' chapter where Murasaki replies in a letter to the Emperor Suzaku:

御返りはいかがなど、聞こえにくく思したれど、ことごとしくおもしろかるべきをりの事ならねば、ただ心を述べて、
　背く世のうしろめたくはさりがたきほだしをしひてかけな離れそなどやうにぞ**あめりし**。(NKBZ IV: 69)

How to reply – (Murasaki) thinks it difficult, and this is neither ceremonious nor cheerful occasion, so (she) just expresses her mind and,

　　'If your thoughts are upon the world you leave behind,
　　You should not make a point of cutting your ties.'
　　The poem ***was probably [an meri shi]*** like the above.

The temporal suffix in the last line is 'き'. This 'き', together with 'めり' which shows the narrator's conjecture, suddenly and clearly visualizes the narrator who is recollecting the past event (story **Now**) with assumptions formed in the discourse **Now**. Perhaps it is because the poem is sent to the Emperor, and it is unlikely that the narrator has seen it. She must explain the situation to the reader. And by so doing, she makes herself appear before us by using 'き'.

A similar example can be found in the 'Bamboo River' chapter where people around Tamakazura regret the decision to marry her older daughter to the Emperor Reizei. Tamakazura is criticized by them:

少将なり [1] しも、三位中将とかいひておぼえあり。「容貌さへあらまほしかり [2] きや」など、なま心わろき仕うまつり人は、うち忍びつつ、「うるさげなる御ありさまよりは」など言ふもありて、いとほしうぞ見え [3] し。(NKBZ V: 99–100)

The one who [1]***was [shi]*** lieutenant is called captain now and much admired. '(He) [2]***was [ki]*** so good-looking,' whispers one of the cattier women, 'and much better than the one surrounded by nasty women'; (Tamakazura) [3]***looked [shi]*** pitiful.

'き' appears three times. The first two indicate the past states (story **Past**) seen from the present moment of the story (story **Now**) and show the temporal distance between the two. The last one is different. It depicts the story present (story **Now**). If in the last sentence 'けり' were used instead of 'き', i.e. 'いとほしうぞ見えける', it would become a normal description in classical Japanese fictional language; the narrator would be narrating the past event (story **Now**) from the contemporary synchronic viewpoint (story **Now**). But 'き' in the above passage produces a temporal distance between the discourse **Now** (narrating **Now**) and the story **Now**. It makes the narrator appear in the narrating time. The effect is to give a description of the scene as if the narrator had been there and recollected the event later.

This kind of 'き' therefore can be used when the narrator discloses herself in *sōshiji* 草子地 (commentary) as a commentator.[38] This is so in the following passage from the 'Sacred Tree' chapter, in which the narrator apologizes for not writing down all the poems composed in the scene, due to their lack of merit:

多かめりし言どもも、かうやうなるをりのまほならぬこと数々に書きつくる、心地なきわざとか、貫之が諫め、たうるる方にて、むつかしければとどめつ。(NKBZ II: 134–5)

There probably **were [shi]** numerous other poems; but it is in bad taste to write down unserious ones from such occasion, Tsurayuki has warned, so I have not troubled myself to write them down.

The narrator in this part is observing events from the discourse **Now**. One more similar example can be found in the 'Ivy' chapter in which poems are again quoted. Before Kaoru moves his wife, the Second Princess, from the palace to his Sanjō mansion, the Emperor holds a wisteria viewing party in her mother's apartment. Their guests place their poems upon the lectern at this occasion:

例の、いかにあやしげに古めきたりけんと思ひやれば、あながちにみなも尋ね書かず。上の町も、上臈とて、御口つきどもは、ことなること見えざめれど、しるしばかりとて、一つ二つぞ問ひ聞きたり [1] し。… かたへはひが言にもやありけん。かやうに、ことなるをかしきふしもなくのみぞあなり [2] し。(NKBZ V: 471–2)

As usual, I think that the poems are of the fusty sort, so I do not write all of them down. Though they are in high positions, high rank bears little relation to performance as a poet, but by way of remembering the occasion (I) [1]**asked [shi]** (them) to make note of a few … Some of them may be mistakenly transcribed. But seen in the above none [2]**was [shi]** conspicuous for its originality.

Here again by using 'き', the narrator in the discourse **Now** appears as an informed witness to the past occasion, that is in the story **Now**.

CONCLUSION

In conclusion, I will briefly summarize this chapter. In the first section I have illustrated how classical Japanese personal references and honorifics increase the sense of indirect free discourse where the character and the narrator's thoughts blend, and how they increase a sense of personal subjectivity on the narrator's part. By examining each individual part of the *Genji* text, I have summarized the characteristics of the usage of honorifics by simply saying that the closer the usage of the honorific comes to that of a character, the vaguer the distinction between the narrator's and the character's consciousness.

In the second section I have examined the usage of temporal suffixes, 'けり' and 'き', from the perspective of narratorial standpoint. It can be concluded that when 'き' is added to the story **Past** in the narration, it indicates the narrator's recollection from the story **Now**. It shows that the narrator is in the story **Now**. In contrast, when 'き' is added to the story **Now** in the narration, it reveals the narrator in the discourse **Now**. That is, in classical Japanese the narrator can reveal her figure by using 'き' for the story **Now** in the narration. Consequently we have seen how the narrator of *Genji*, by skilfully using honorifics and temporal suffixes, drastically and swiftly shifts the narrative perspective and voice from the narrator to the character or from one character to another, and takes a different narrative distance in each occasion.

NOTES

1. Murakami Fuminobu, 'Using Epistemic Modal Suffixes and Sensation/ Emotion Adjectives to Determine Narrative Distance in *The Tale of Genji*,' *Journal of the Association of Teachers of Japanese*, 32: 2 (1998). Concerning the narrative study of *The Tale of Genji*, see also Nakayama Masahiko 1995.
2. Since *The Tale of Genji* is shaped as a narration by ladies-in-waiting, the narrator in this paper will be referred to by the feminine pronouns 'she/ her/ herself'. Concerning the relations between honorifics, epistemic modality and the narrative distance and perspective, see Itoi Michihiro's studies in Itoi 1981, 1986, 1992, 1993 and 1995.
3. Concerning the previous literature and classification of honorifics, see Kitahara (ed.) 1978. For the usage of honorifics in classical literary works and/or *Genji*, see Tamagami 1964–1969: *Bekkan* 1, pp. 26–41, 156–82; Morino 1966, 1972 and 1975; Akita 1976; Negoro 1983 and 1991; Akiyama Ken 1984: 198–224; and Mori 1985, 1986.
4. In most cases, I have supplied two versions of the *Genji* text in citations: (1) a version of the original in Japanese script Shōgakukan ed., *Genji monogatari*, NKBZ and (2) my literal rendition made by referring to Seidensticker's English translation ('S') and by amending it so as to be as faithful as possible to the original syntax.
5. Though Seidensticker translated this sentence into: 'It was the first note of intimacy between them,' the original text: 'これもうちとけぬるはじめなめり' allows another interpretation as: 'For this one too this is the first note of intimacy' (NKBZ III: 442, headnote 17). If we take the latter reading, the one for whom this is the first note of intimacy must be not Murasaki but only Akashi, for honorifics are not added to the verb 'うちとけ' (to become intimate).
6. See Akiyama Ken 1984: 212–17.
7. See Amanda Stinchecum, 'Narrative Voice in the *Genji monogatari*,' Ph.D. thesis (Columbia University, 1980, Ann Arbor, Michigan: University Microfilms International), p. 23.
8. See Mori 1985: 73–4 and 1986: 55.
9. I would like to use a term 'perception verb' for the verb which indicates perception, like to see, to look, to hear, to sound, to sniff, to smell, to taste, to feel, etc.
10. See Kaneoka 1962: 41.
11. See Gerald Prince, *A Dictionary of Narratology* (Lincoln: University of Nebraska Press, 1987), p. 22; and Murakami Fuminobu, *Ideology and Narrative in Modern Japanese Literature* (Assen: Van Gorcum, 1996), p. 13.
12. See Franz Stanzel, *A Theory of Narrative*, translated by Charlotte Goedsche (Cambridge: Cambridge University Press, 1984), p. 5.
13. In this paper, as in my previous studies, *showing* can be defined, from the linguistic point of view, as a mode in which the sentence is produced with minimum intrusion of the narrator's external consciousness or cognition, whereas in *telling* the narrator's psychological attitude towards the proposition is distinctively expressed through modality in its broad sense. While in the *showing* mode the narrator appears only circumstantially, in the *telling* mode she or he is clearly present. The more constituents a sentence has in which the narrator's independent consciousness appears, the more it is considered to be in *telling* mode. In this sense, the *showing* and *telling* modes are closely related to the narrative distance between the narrator and the character. The wider the narrative distance, the closer the text is to the *telling* mode. The narrower the narrative

distance, the closer the text is to the *showing* mode. While the *telling* expresses a duplicated consciousness, the *showing* is a single-folded mode. Thus *showing/ telling* can be defined in terms of the relative degree of constructing / withholding the presence of a narrator. The constituents of sentences which convey the narrator's distinctive cognition will be in this chapter termed the *narrative modal markers*.

14. See Akita 1969: 3; Mitani 1978: 43, 1969–1982: vol. IV, pp. 182–97, and 1989: 162–86; and Itoi 1995, pp. 181–3.
15. See Murakami 1994, 1996, op. cit., pp. 70–5, and 1998, op. cit., pp. 12–14. Also see Itoi 1995, p. 175.
16. In this sense, as Derrida mentioned, we can say that the difference between the subject and the object of literary language is barely maintained. Derrida writes: 'The "subject" of writing does not exist if we mean by that some sovereign solitude of the author. The subject of writing is a system of relations between strata ...' See Jacques Derrida, *Writing and Difference* (London: Routledge & Kegan Paul, 1978a), pp. 226–7.
17. See Shimazu 1947, pp. 186–8; and Mori 1985, p. 77.
18. See Sugiyama 1973, p. 56.
19. See Mori 1986, p. 43.
20. See Shimazu 1947, pp. 186–8; Tamagami 1964–1969: *Bekkan* 1, pp. 175–6; Ishida 1971, pp. 26–7; and Shimizu Yoshiko 1980, pp. 96–7. Concerning the omission of honorifics, Yoshizawa Yoshinori presented a different interpretation: he noted that when the narrator criticizes or blames a character, he or she often does not use honorifics for the character; hence, this sort of omission of honorifics reveals the narrator's accusation of the character. See Yoshizawa 1940, pp. 86–90. Yokoyama (1941: 48–80) supported Yoshizawa's interpretation.
21. *Kawachi-bon* supplies one honorific to Yūgiri at '音もせで見たまふ' (He stopped to look at the women inside + respect). Concerning the honorifics in this part, see Higashihara 2004, p. 72.
22. See Amanda Stinchecum, 'Who Tells the Tale? '*Ukifune*': A Study in Narrative Voice', *Monumenta Nipponica*, XXXV: 4, 1980, p. 377.
23. '*n da*' is another form of '*no da*' used in conversational situations.
24. See Seymour Chatman, *Story and Discourse* (Ithaca, N.Y.: Cornell University Press, 1978), p. 203; Dorrit Cohn, *Transparent Minds* (Princeton, N.J.: Princeton University Press, 1978), p. 105; and Wallace Martin, *Recent Theories of Narrative* (Ithaca, N.Y.: Cornell University Press, 1986), pp. 136–42. See also Bakhtin's concept of 'polyphony' in Mikhail Bakhtin, *Problems of Dostoevsky's Poetics*, edited and translated by Caryl Emerson; Introduction by Wayne C. Booth, (Minneapolis, Minnesota: University of Minnesota Press, 1984).
25. See Takehara 1977, p. 62.
26. 'とて' here should be interpreted as a short form of 'と（思ひ）て.'
27. Among numerous studies on 'けり' and 'き', especially concerning 'けり' and 'き' in fictional language, see Takeoka 1963; Enomoto 1976, pp. 15–19; Yoshioka 1976, pp. 149–93, 1977a, pp. 1–22, and 1977b, pp. 127–91; Negoro 1977, pp. 17–22; Takahashi Tōru 1982, pp. 218–19; Itoi 1981, pp. 107–39, and 1995, pp. 184–8, 195–7; Kumakura 1990, pp. 38–47; Higashihara 2004, pp. 16–17; Richard Okada, *Figures of Resistance: Language, Poetry and Narrating in The Tale of Genji and Other Mid-Heian Texts*, 1991, pp. 35–42; and Haruo Shirane, 'Review of *Figures of Resistance* by Richard Okada,' *The Journal of Japanese Studies*, 20:1 (1994), pp. 221–8.
28. See Seymour Chatman, 1978, op. cit., p. 80.
29. 'し' and 'しか' are other forms of 'き.'
30. Richard Okada, *Figures of Resistance: Language, Poetry and Narrating in* The Tale of Genji *and Other Mid-Heian Texts* (Durham and London: Duke University Press, 1991), pp. 41–2.
31. See Haruo Shirane, 1994, op. cit., p. 224.
32. See Stinchecum, 1980, op. cit., p. 27.

33. See Seymour Chatman, 1978, op. cit., p. 80.
34. See Mitani 1978: 50.
35. See William Frawley, *Linguistic Semantics* (Hillsdale, N.Y.: Lawrence Erbaum Associates, 1992), pp. 337–8.
36. Itoi Michihiro pointed out the two different usages of 'き'; to indicate a state different from the narrating present and to show a state different from the present time in the story. See Itoi 1981: 123, 134.
37. 'なりて' in the original text is not past tense. But the phrase should be interpreted as being connected to the following verb '下り'. The tense marker 'しか' covers both.
38. See Yoshioka 1977b: 127–91.

Part 3
Reading the *Genji* Romance

5

'KIRITSUBO': *GENJI*, SPACING AND NAMING

JEREMY TAMBLING

☙

INTRODUCTION

For Bakhtin, the 'novel' form – always given a subsidiary place in relation to poetry and drama, because always seen as potentially subversive and parodic – is marked by heterogeneity, since it carries in it the discourse of the other; it is many voiced, 'polyphonic', the term associated for Bakhtin with Dostoyevsky. Poetry and the epic and drama are in Bakhtin by contrast more homogeneous, tending towards exclusion of the other, moving towards a total statement, through the finality of metaphor which can make diverse, different seeming things be perceived as one, homogeneous. *The Tale of Genji* includes in it these two forms of writing, and in addition, its narrative includes 795 court poems (*waka*), many of which are used in exchanges between characters, plus numerous other poems which are alluded to, and much historical commentary on it focused on its poetic qualities; so that it contains contradictory tendencies towards diversity and towards homogeneity at once.[1] This chapter explores the implications of these two movements.

The homogeneity, however, is not all in the text's poetic, literary language. It is there in the novel form too. The nineteenth and twentieth century European and American novel is more homogeneous than Bakhtin's example of Dostoyevsky allows, and Roland Barthes, discussing it in its 'classic realist' phase shows how a tendency towards the plural and the different is countered by a tendency to centre the text, to control the reader's response. In *S/Z*, Barthes's analysis of Balzac's short story *Sarrasine*, Barthes shows how the realist text is structured by codes which enable reading to seem spontaneous, the action of a free agent who arrives at the same conclusions that the author's text already possesses, as if spontaneously. To be brief, there are five codes, the first two being the '*action code*', which impels the reader forward, and the '*hermeneutic code*', which keeps in the mind the suggestion that there is a mystery to be elucidated which reading to the end will solve. Three other codes keep the reader in place at any point within the text. The '*semic*' enables connotations about the characters to rise in the mind: a few selected adjectives applied to each character connote various aspects of his personality. The '*symbolic*' sets up a series of antitheses around which the action moves and implies the range of ideas around which the text is mobilized, which always follow binary oppositions (e.g. masculine / feminine). The '*cultural*' appears when reference is made to events or things the reader knows of already, and their appearance gives to the text its appearance of familiarity with what there is to be known.

These codes are put together to account for nineteenth-century popular fiction produced in 'mass' conditions by a writer who was conscious of the market; they are far from the world of the shining prince and from a woman writing a single manuscript to be copied by her readers and not intended for a market, so not needing to flag the work with constant references to keep that readership together. But Barthes did not simply read *Sarrasine* for the codes. He divided it up (see *S/Z*, Section vii) into *lexias*, 'brief continuous fragments, ... units of reading', variable in length, 561 in all. These unpack several codes and bring out the plural nature of the text. The codes are not all there is, they do not stand out by themselves, they need something else to display them. They imply a textual unconscious, so that to read it is not to engage only with consciously deployed meanings; they suggest that behind the narrative are other prior narratives at work enabling this type of narrative both to be written and to be read. The applicability of this insight, derived from texts where a bourgeois ideology undergirds a narrative (like *Sarrasine*), is problematic when it is taken over to such a text as *The Tale of Genji*. What can it demonstrate of a textual unconscious? Will not a reading that uses this critical theory be likely only to prove points already known about the place of men and women in Heian society?

Nonetheless, there are elements in *Genji* that prompt discussion which can be aware of Barthes's terms. In the discussion of *monogatari* in Chapter 25, 'Fireflies' ('Hotaru'), Genji comments on the alliance of women with literature:

> They know perfectly well that in all these old stories there is scarcely a shred of truth, and yet they are captured and made sport of the whole range of trivialities and go on scribbling them down.

So that old stories are mocked by the patriarchal Genji who concedes however:

> But amid all the fabrication I must admit that I do find real emotions and plausible chains of events. We can be quite aware of the frivolity and the idleness and still be moved ... Sometimes a series of absurd and grotesque incidents which we know to be quite improbable holds our interest, and afterwards we must blush that it was so.[2]

Genji's charge is that fiction is lying; he prefers real emotions, and a chain of events – which implies causality, a textual movement that is not simply digressive. He continues:

But story-telling ... does not consist of simply relating all the events of a person's life in the order in which they occurred. [Nonetheless, *Genji* is very focused on one man's life from birth to death.] On the contrary, stories come into being in the first place because the author cannot keep enclosed within his heart what he has seen and heard of the endlessly fascinating and various ways of men in this world, both the good and evil of them, a store of observations which he desires to pass on to later generations. If he decides to bring out the good in people he will search the world over for examples of the good; or if, on the other hand, he wishes to follow the popular fancy, he may make a collection of the evil and unusual. In either case the writer's materials are all drawn from life in this world.[3]

The last sentence makes literature mimetic, following on from life, raising questions of its 'real' quality. How people see reality and judge something to be real is, however, consensual, the effect of ideology, and Barthes shows how narrative codes seduce the reader into agreement with authorial positions which seem passive, reflecting how life is, effacing their own construction of what is signified in the text as real. In this chapter of *Genji*, the desire for the real mixes with a claim with which mimeticism must be in contrast, that the text is moral, didactic, moving within the orbit of Buddhism. *Genji* exists within these contradictory claims for fiction, and using Barthes, who unveils the devices by which the reader thinks she is getting a reflection of life as it is, I want to give here a reading of the first chapter of *The Tale of Genji*. Since it opens everything up, no reader need feel debarred from looking at it on the basis of lack of familiarity with the narrative. I am working with translation, using not Waley, but Seidensticker and Helen McCullough, who have both translated this chapter, as well as Royall Tyler.[4] This is my ignorance of Japanese; yet the non-specialist contemporary Japanese reader also tends to read *Genji* in modern Japanese translation. And any reading of *Genji* is an act of cultural translation; there can be no pretence that this Heian world can be entered upon in any other way than by transposing its states, admitting that any reading of a text of such alterity is inevitably a rewriting into terms the critic knows, whether that is acknowledged as rewriting or not.

READING THE MEDIEVAL TEXT

'Kiritsubo' is translated by Seidensticker as 'The Paulownia Court', 'a name taken from a tree planted in the garden of Kiritsubo lady's Rear Palace apartments'. In the same way, the name of Fujitsubo, who appears later, means 'wisteria court'. The Kiritsubo lady is defined by the building of that name in the imperial court which in turn derives by metonymic association from the tree. The title identifies the person through topography, giving precedence to the latter. In analysing this chapter, which is intended to be a Barthes-like 're-reading', to bring out the 'return of the different',[5] little depends on a question which has caused controversy: when it was written in relation to other chapters. It has been held both that it was written first and that it came later.[6] If it was written out of sequence, its thematic importance becomes more focused, though the chapter may serve formally as a beginning, there is no sense that conflicts find their origin in it: they are already there.

In setting up this reading, I use a second comparison, not from the Western realist or modernist texts (though Proust has been the subject of one comparison with *The Tale of Genji*),[7] but from the European medieval – assuming that any generalizations may be made about this literature. In thinking of the French *roman* of the twelfth century, questions need not be asked about the novel/romance distinction – one only available in English – since the term *roman* includes all narratives and would translate the term *monogatari* ('a telling of things'). In *The Bridge of Dreams: A Poetics of The Tale of Genji*, Haruo Shirane sees 'horizontal amplification as the basic movement of the thirteenth century Arthurian romances'. It is a narrative pattern not of 'monocentric unity (vertical extension) but constant digression'.[8] He sees it also operative in *The Tale of Genji*. Shirane is, implicitly, discussing the twelfth century Chrétien de Troyes, who as shown in the opening of *The Knight of the Cart*, wrote for Marie de Champagne, president of a literary court in France, using the Arthurian legends of Geoffrey of Monmouth (1136–37), written 120 years after the death of Murasaki Shikibu (c. 975–1025).[9] Chrétien contrasts with Murasaki Shikibu in the Heian period, writing more privately, and possibly in a serial manner in the court of the Empress Shōshi. In patriarchal terms, a man writing for women gives literature as an institution more credibility than a woman writing for women, with the added ambiguous alliance of literature with love, so that there is something tendentially erotic about Chrétien's narrative.

A familiar argument links European medieval narratives to Gothic space, whether in cathedrals (part of 'the twelfth century renaissance') or in manuscripts, where the page allows for separate forms of representation, differentiated from each other. For Arnold Hauser: 'Gothic art leads the onlooker from one detail to another and causes him, as has been well said, to "unravel" the successive parts of the work one after the other.'[10] But the separate spaces of Gothic have equivalents in the art form of the Heian, the picture-scroll. Ivan Morris quotes Dietrich Seckel on the 'parallel perspectives' set up within the scroll through the varied slant of the lines of depth, represented by beams, screens and curtains. 'It creates a clearly defined pictorial area in which all objects and events find their natural place. At the same time it remains open on all sides, and fits smoothly and without breaks into the picture's continuous motion.'[11] Though the word 'natural' is problematic, needing the critique Barthes performs on realist representation in fiction, yet the point is relevant: the sense of continuous movement links separate spaces. What follows will discuss space as it is represented in *The Tale of Genji*. Here, following Shirane, and noting how buildings in Heian Japan were usually single-story, horizontality is at work; as opposed to cathedrals which despite their interior separations of space, tend towards verticality, and integration of the various separate parts, so that each part is analogous to another. The impression in *The Tale of Genji* is of separated spaces, of a spreading out, of separate pockets.[12]

Chrétien implies in his writing a sense of the importance of the French nation, an aspect of his interest in integration. *Cligés* opens referring to what the author has written before, and the announcement that he has a new tale, drawn from old books. 'Our books have taught us that chivalry and learning first flourished in Greece; then to Rome came chivalry and the sum of knowledge which now has come to France.'[13]

There is an alliance between literature, the nation and a didacticism which centres the text. Didacticism emerges in the Prologue to *Erec and Enide*:

> The peasant in his proverb says that one might find oneself holding in contempt something that is worth much more than one believes; therefore a man does well to make good use of his learning according to whatever understanding he has, for he who neglects his learning may easily keep silent something that would later give much pleasure. And so Chrétien de Troyes says that it is reasonable for everyone to think and strive in every way to speak and to teach well, and from a tale of adventure he draws a beautifully ordered composition that clearly proves that a man does not act intelligently if he does not give free rein to his knowledge for as long as God gives him the grace to do so.[14]

Chrétien signs himself in the opening so giving the text a coherence around himself. Murasaki Shikibu never does this throughout *The Tale of Genji*. Chrétien says what he is doing: from a tale of adventure he draws a '*molt bel conjointure*'. The '*conjointure*' (composition, putting together) gives coherence, harmonizes, like marriage as a *conjointure*, and the phrase draws attention to the beautiful form wherein the moral is conveyed. To the inscription of authority and of intention is added attention to the beauty of the form. This term is called 'interlacing', so used by Ferdinand Lot, in 1918; he is said to have 'traced a large number of themes and episodes [in *Lancelot*] which the poet would introduce, drop and resume many pages later, sometimes many times'.[15] Design is emphasized, while the typical plot of a romance by Chrétien centres on the narrative of a quest, which is presented in different forms so that each part has an analogy to each other, and a pattern is discernible. 'First, the hero achieves a high degree of personal happiness and worldly success in an initial and usually self-contained sequence. Then he is made aware of an error or flaw which invalidates that happiness and success. Finally, in the major portion of the poem, he undertakes a series of adventures in order to correct the error and thereby recover his happiness.'[16] This pattern, for Per Nykrog, means that Chrétien's heroes show an '*interior* conflict that opposes them to *themselves* or to their implicit images of themselves'. He is thinking of such things as Yvain's madness, which precedes his movement towards reintegration, and with this sense of psychic conflict it is unsurprising that Nykrog refers to a tradition of 'Occidental individualism' of which he takes the romance to be an early example.[17] Accordingly, near the opening of *Yvain*, the knight Calogrenant gives a narrative with an appeal made seven times over that his words may reach the 'hearts' of his audience. The ear hears, but the heart must 'take and enclose and retain the word when it hears it'.[18] The narrative is allegorical; its hidden or spiritual meaning relates to inner individuality.[19]

OPENINGS AND PRIOR NARRATIVES

No Prologue opens *The Tale of Genji*, to give a transition from present to past. Murasaki begins, as Shirane translates, 'Which imperial reign was it?' as does Bowring, who also shows how the narrator's time disappears, and the past becomes present, and that 'the Emperor, his ladies and his favourite are placed in this [first] sentence in such a way that those ladies come between the Emperor and his favourite, causing friction syntactically as well as socially'.[20] The opening is a question, addressing and implicating the reader, asking the reader to guess, or to work at creating the time of the events, setting up a dialogism, refusing omniscience (a rhetorical ploy):

> In which reign was it, among the many lesser consorts and ladies of the wardrobe serving the Emperor is one who, though not of the highest rank, is favoured above the rest. The other ladies, each of whom have from the outset thought proudly, 'I am the one,' are scornful and jealous of this presumptuous upstart.[21] [B.58]

Seidensticker reads:

> In a certain reign there was a lady not of the first rank whom the Emperor loved more than any of the others. The grand ladies with high ambitions thought her a presumptuous upstart, and lesser ladies were still more resentful. Everything she did offended someone. Probably aware of what was happening, she fell seriously ill and came to spend more time at home than at court. The Emperor's pity and affection quite passed bounds. No longer caring what his ladies and courtiers might say, he behaved as if intent upon stirring gossip. [S. 3]

As with Chrétien, the narrative picks up from events far back in time (the point was also noted in 'The Fireflies' ('Hotaru'), quoted earlier). In Bowring's reading, the conflicts are similar to those that Genji in Chapter 21, 'The Maiden' ('Otome'), tries to prevent by setting up the 'four parks' in Rokujō, where he can have everyone near him, including 'the people [women] who were still off in the country' [S. 382]. The Rokujō mansion, with Akikonomu's autumn garden in the southwest, and the northeast given to the lady of the orange blossoms, the northwest to the Akashi lady (the winter garden) and the southeast to Murasaki's spring garden, is the attempt to produce space suggesting diversity of place and of time. In this chapter, space, implied in the title, the space of the court, will be contested.

In McCullough, there is no reference to love; instead, the lady enjoyed imperial favour. She grows 'seriously ill' in Seidensticker, but 'grew frail and melancholy' in McCullough. 'Melancholy' as a clue-word, suggests the state of recognition of pathos as a law of life.[22] McCullough translates that the Emperor's way of treating her 'seemed destined to go down in history as an exemplar of favouritism' – which prompts consideration of this as an historical text, so distanced from its writer, who is writing an historical record, while the translation implicitly blames the Emperor for his partiality.

> His court looked with very great misgiving upon what seemed a reckless infatuation. In China just such an unreasoning passion had been the undoing of an

emperor and had spread turmoil through the land. As the resentment grew, the example of Yang Guifei the one most frequently cited against the lady. [S. 3]

The example of Yang Guifei, the favourite concubine of Emperor Tang Xuanzong (ruled 712–56), executed in 756, blames the woman for the fall of the state. The reference to history in McCullough is continued in this paragraph, which looks back to a Chinese example (history being read for its display of examples). Yang Guifei and the Emperor become figural[23] for this 'modern' example which works through a consideration of the Emperor and his management of the land. The woman disrupts the land; excessive passion or affection (McCullough) is failure of rule. In the first paragraph, the women were resentful; in the second, the criticism comes from the court. Yang Guifei becomes an important reference within the text, part of the symbolic code, and through the action code, prompting thought about the death of the lady. The violence it prompts speculation about is not fulfilled, for this text remains throughout very nonviolent. The lady will not be killed, as Yang Guifei was; she will simply be allowed to return home. She will not do anything to incur resentment, she simply has a son: this text's sober realism.

The Japanese text makes no comparisons with the Tang: an implicit contrast to the strategy of the opening of *Cligés*. It stresses continuity between the two civilizations. Shirane says that 'the opening chapter represents a variation on the Tang poet Bai Juyi, and his *Changheng ge* (The Song of Everlasting Sorrow), which describes Tang Xuanzong's scandalous infatuation with Yang Guifei, which disrupted his reign and resulted in the consort's death at the hands of his own subjects'.[24] The Emperor's love for the Kiritsubo *kōi* – (Intimate),[25] like Xuanzong's passion for the lowborn but incomparably beautiful Yang Guifei, threatens public order and ultimately contributes to the woman's death.

Bai Juyi's 'Song of Everlasting Sorrow' Waley calls 'a narrative poem of 120 lines in seven-syllable verse'.[26] It describes the relationship between the Emperor Xuanzong and the lady, and her death in 756 when An Lushan marched against the Emperor, and the Emperor's soldiers demanded she should be trampled to death. It tells how he is haunted by her memory, until a Taoist priest finds her, as Waley puts it: 'in one of the Taoist paradises'. She gives him 'certain keepsakes, tokens of their deep love, a blue-enamelled box and a golden hairpin to take back with him into the world of men'.[27] It is a recreation, fifty years after the event of Yang Guifei's death, in 806 or 807, by a poet who never knew the events first-hand. The account is already mythicized and is non-epic in taking the part of the sufferer, the victim. It illustrates an antagonism between various antitheses that in Barthes's terms would belong to the symbolic code that is marshalled here: love and power; the private and the public; men's worlds and the world of women; love and war; reality and ideality; age and youth; the powerless emperor and the woman who has gained dignity; and who has the final word:

> 'Our souls belong together,' she said, 'like this gold and this shell –
> Somewhere, sometimes, on earth or in heaven, we shall surely meet.'

> And she sent him, by his messenger, a sentence reminding him
> Of vows which had been known only to their two hearts.
> 'On the seventh day of the Seventh-month, in the Palace of Long Life,
> We told each other secretly in the quiet midnight world
> That we wished to fly in heaven, two birds with the wings of one,
> And to grow together on the earth, two branches of one tree.'
> Earth endures, heaven endures, sometime both shall end,
> While this unending sorrow goes on and on for ever.[28]

The last two lines step out of the narrative mode to comment, which both makes the sorrow eternal – the sense of あはれ, or pathos, in *Genji* is comparable to this, as are references to melancholy going through the first chapter – and which also proclaims the eternality of the text. The last line names the poem: 'unending sorrow'. The ending announces that there is no ending. The close of the poem announces the triumph of art over everything else. The authority of the last line of Bai Juyi's text carries the poem over into *Genji*, so that this text is written under the shadow of a precedent, though the precedent is not an original.

The third paragraph of the first chapter fills in details about the lady the Emperor loves. Her father, a major councillor, is dead, so she has no male to speak for her; her mother is declared an old-fashioned lady of good lineage, attentive to the smallest details of etiquette. She is without 'strong backing' at court. These details point to the absence of the patriarchal. A disorder here is corrected in the next paragraph, which begins with the logic of 'it may have been because of a bond in a former life that she bore the Emperor a beautiful son, a jewel beyond compare' (replacing the lost father with a new male). The logic which refers to a previous life casts the present events under the shadow of repetition. There is no original event and the linear narrative (established on the line of generations) is not simply that, for events follow absent causes, pointing to alternative narratives which can hardly be mapped – this being a difference from the realist nineteenth century narrative. The birth of the new child leads to the outbreak of factionalism again, since the child is as beautiful as the mother, and it leads to the narrative of the jealous older woman (Kokiden, daughter of the Minister of the Right), whose son is put in the shade by this new prince. The narrative sets up antitheses (the symbolic code): private/ public; favour/affection; primogeniture and the law of narrative (which follows sequentiality, as in the model of father handing on to the son) versus a love which threatens to break down narrative altogether:

> On public occasions, the Emperor continued to favour his eldest son. The new child was a private treasure ... on which to lavish uninhibited affection. [S. 4]

Uninhibited affection goes with 'unreasonable demands' which the Emperor places on the mother, and with 'immoderate habits'. The absence of restraint finishes a narrative line of action, by setting up the boy as the 'Emperor's favourite'.

The following paragraph sets up a narrative which continues the topic of resentment, which takes on the character of the semic code – as does the 'seme'

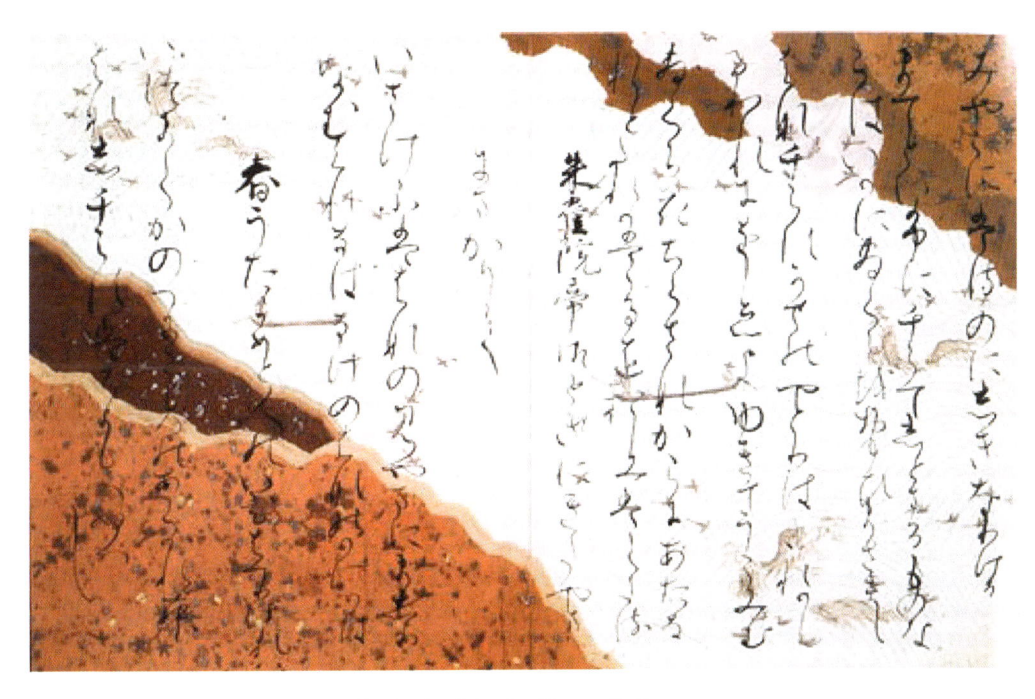

Sanjūrokunin kashū, Honganji, Kyoto.

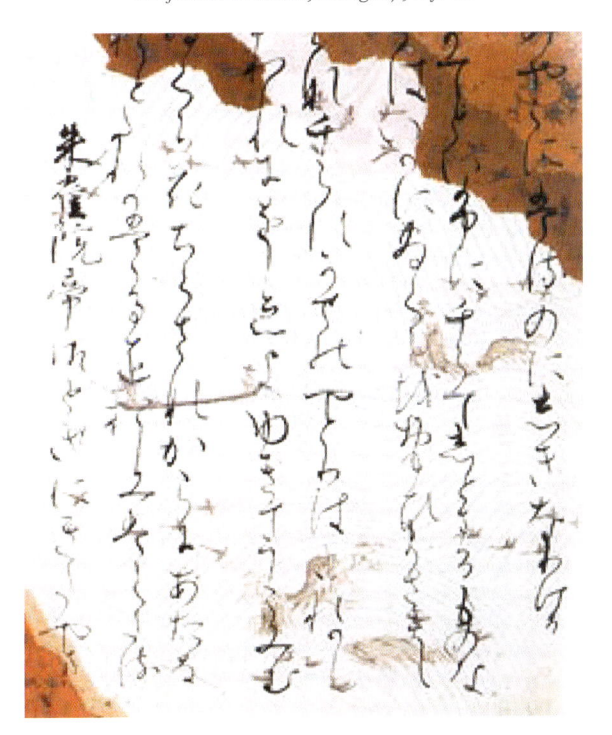

1.2

Heike Nōkyō: Preface, frontispiece (Illustrated Lotus Sutra scrolls, offered by Heike clan; Jō-bon:*mikaeshi*). Itsukushima Shrine.

The Oak Tree II. Painting. Tokugawa Museum, Nagoya.

1.4

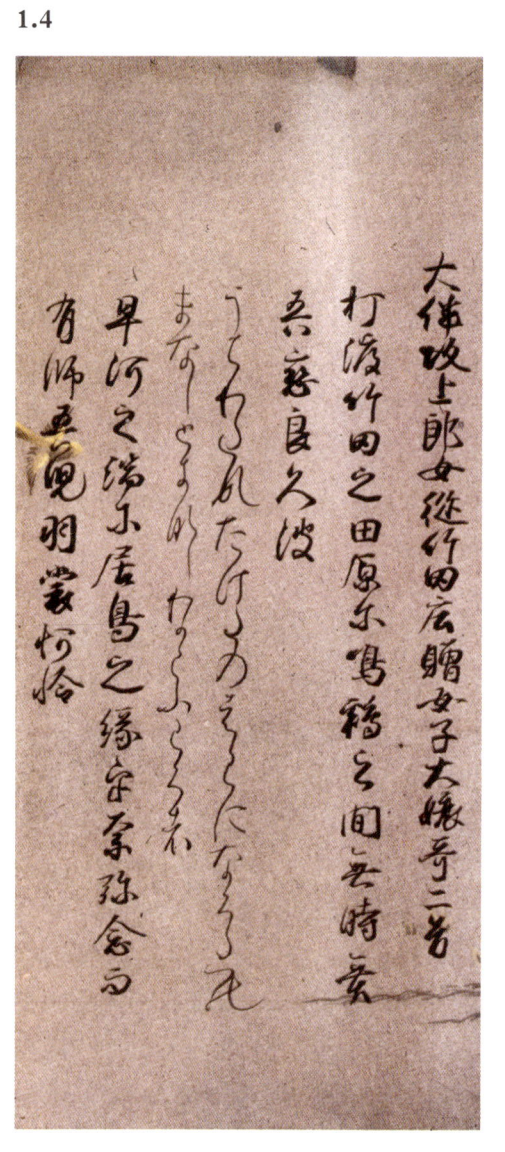

大伴坂上郎女從竹田庄贈女子大嬢歌二首

打渡竹田之田原乎鳴鶴之間無時裳
吾戀良久波

うつたへにた河志ろもあらねと
なとかなみたのうつらふるかも

早河之瀬尓居鳥之縁乎奈久弥會布
有師画売羽裳何怜

Katsura-bon Man'yōshū. Yamato Bunkakan Museum, Nara.

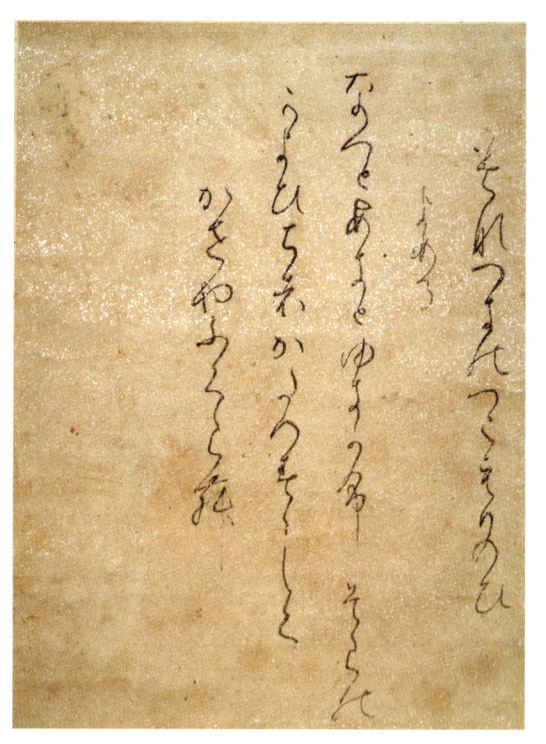

1.5

[waka in kana]

Kōya-gire 2 Kokin wakashū. Mitsui Bunkō, Tokyo.

The Oak Tree I, sheet 2. Tokugawa Museum, Nagoya.

1.7

The Oak Tree I, sheet 3. Tokugawa Museum, Nagoya.

The Oak Tree I, sheet 1. Tokugawa Museum, Nagoya.

1.8b

The Oak Tree I, sheet 2. Tokugawa Museum, Nagoya.

The Oak Tree I, sheet 2, detail, columns 4–8.

The Oak Tree I, sheet 3, detail of column 13: '*kakaru kokoro susumuru ya*'.

The Oak Tree 1, sheet 1. Tokugawa Museum, Nagoya.

1.12

The Oak Tree I, sheet 2, detail columns 5–9, with willow tree.

1.13

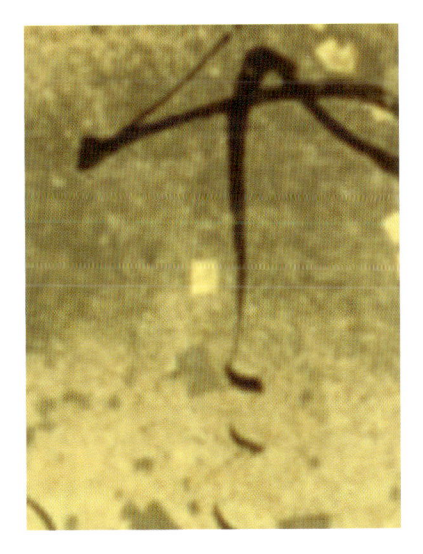

The Oak Tree I, 'yami', first column of sheet 2.

1.14a

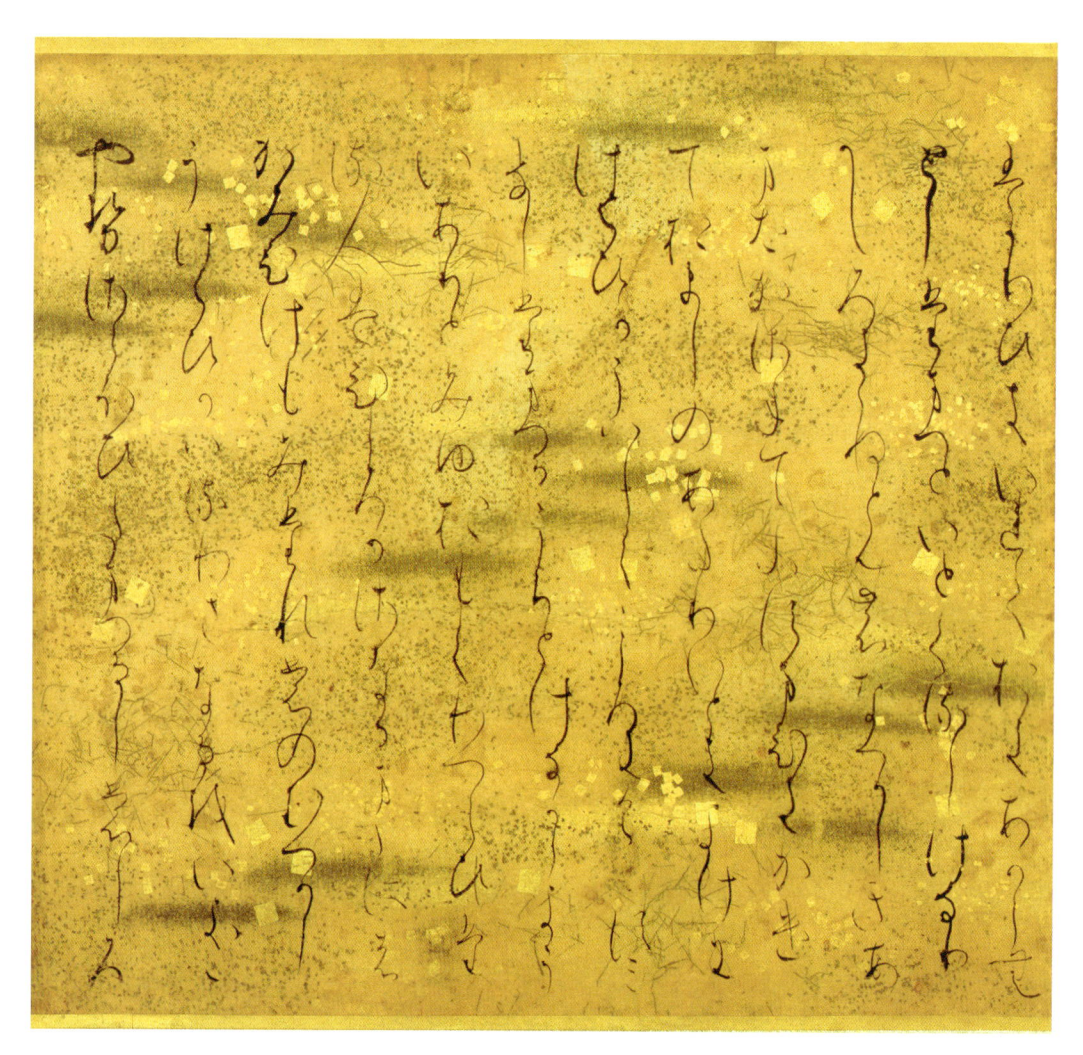

The Oak Tree II, sheet 3. Tokugawa Museum, Nagoya.

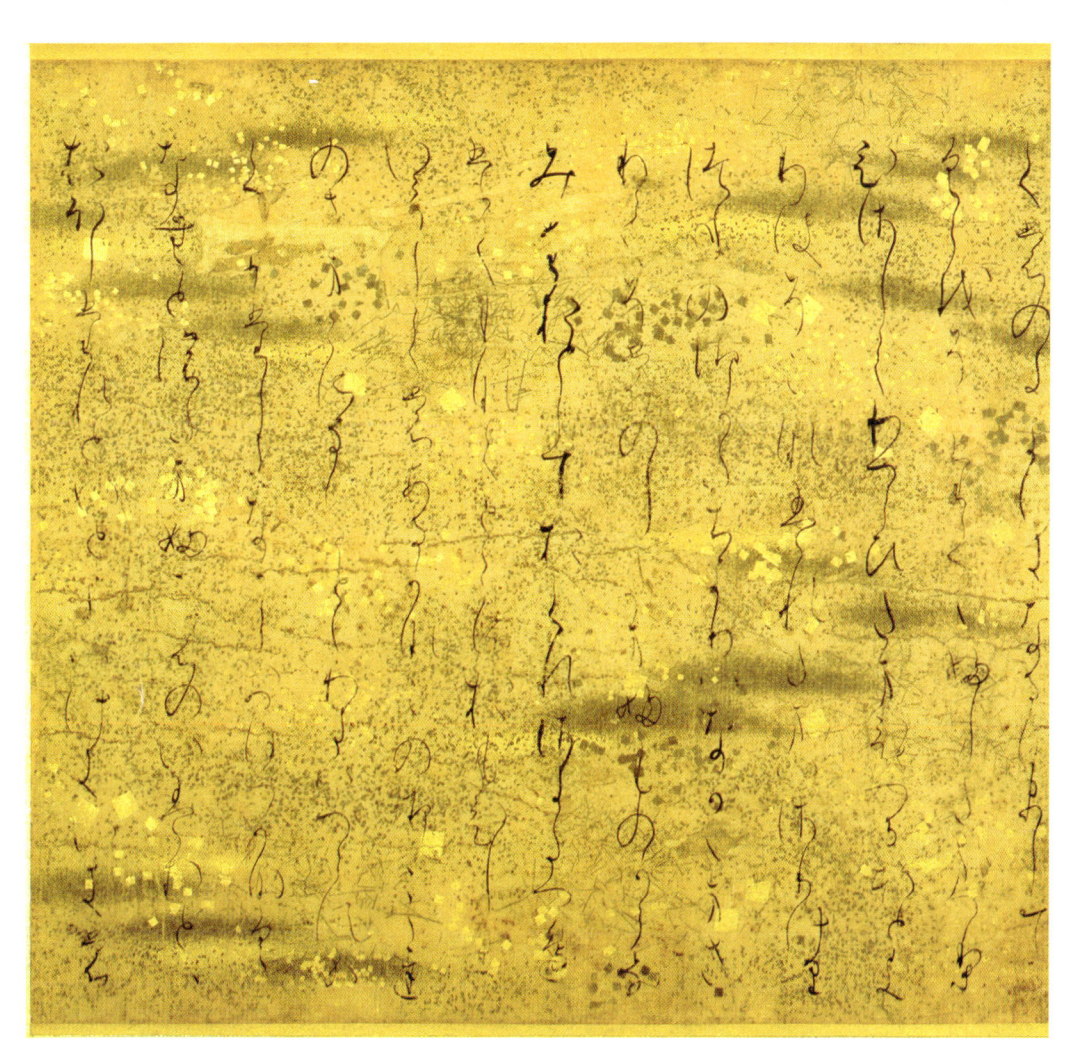

The Oak Tree II, sheet 4. Tokugawa Museum, Nagoya.

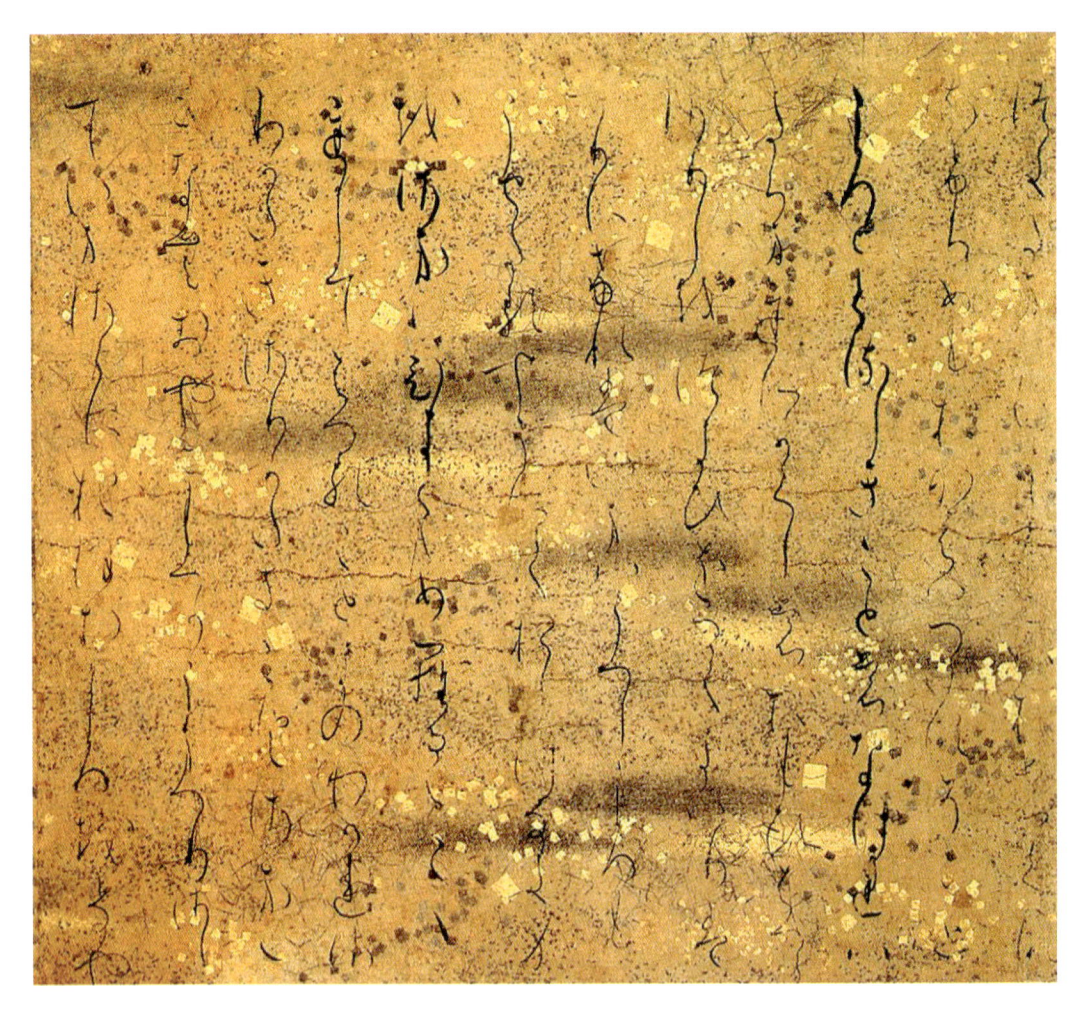

The Oak Tree II, sheet 5. Tokugawa Museum, Nagoya.

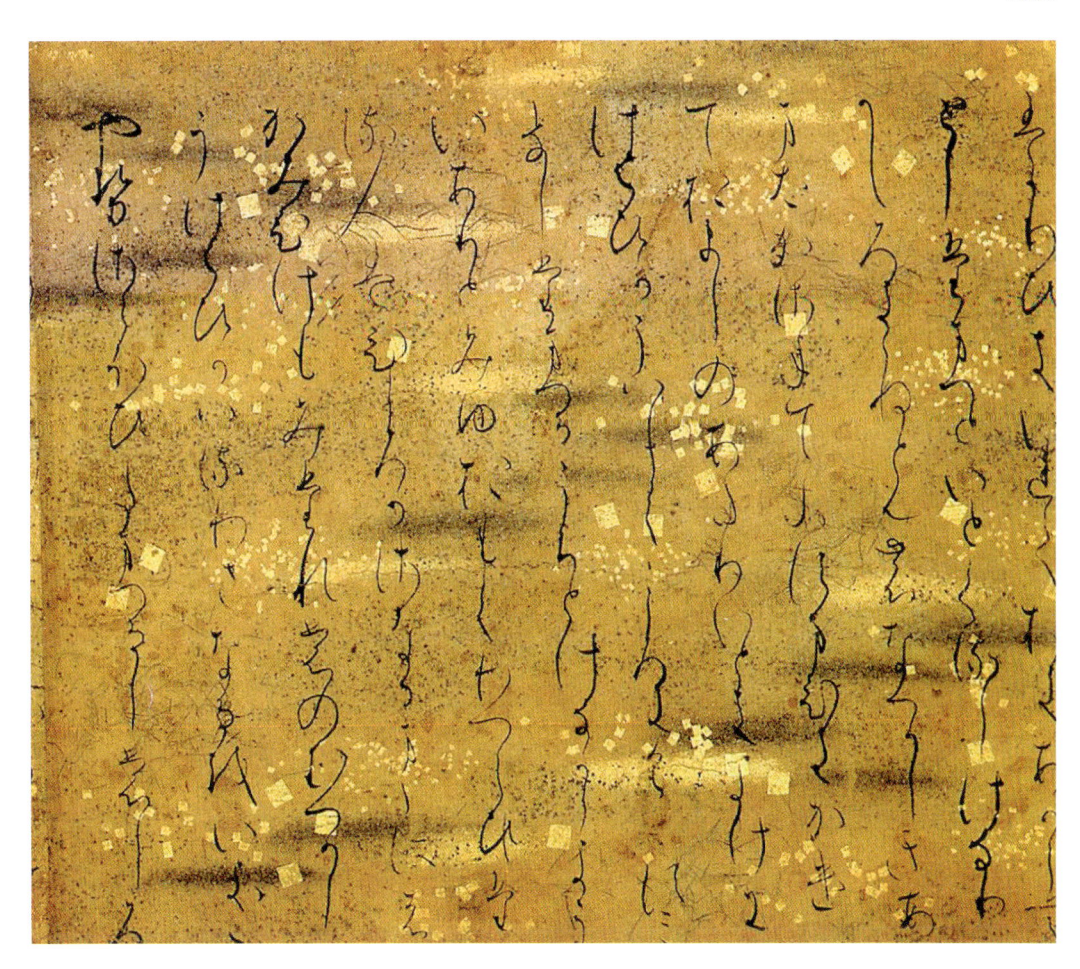

The Oak Tree II, sheet 3. Tokugawa Museum, Nagoya.

The Oak Tree II, sheets 3 and 4. Tokugawa Museum, Nagoya.

The Oak Tree II, sheet 2. Tokugawa Museum, Nagoya.

1.18b

The Oak Tree II, sheet 3. Tokugawa Museum, Nagoya.

The Oak Tree II, sheet 4. Tokugawa Museum, Nagoya.

1.19

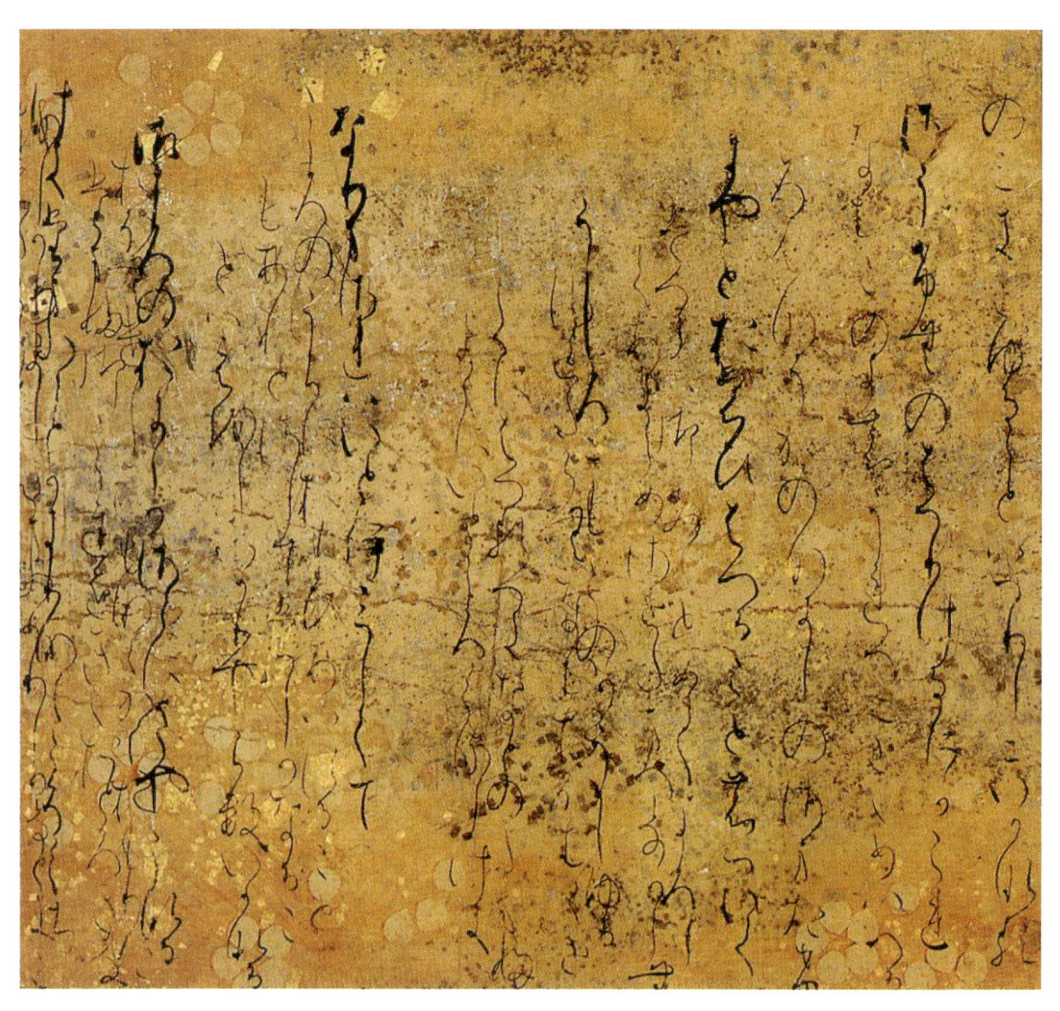

The Oak Tree II, sheet 8. Tokugawa Museum, Nagoya.

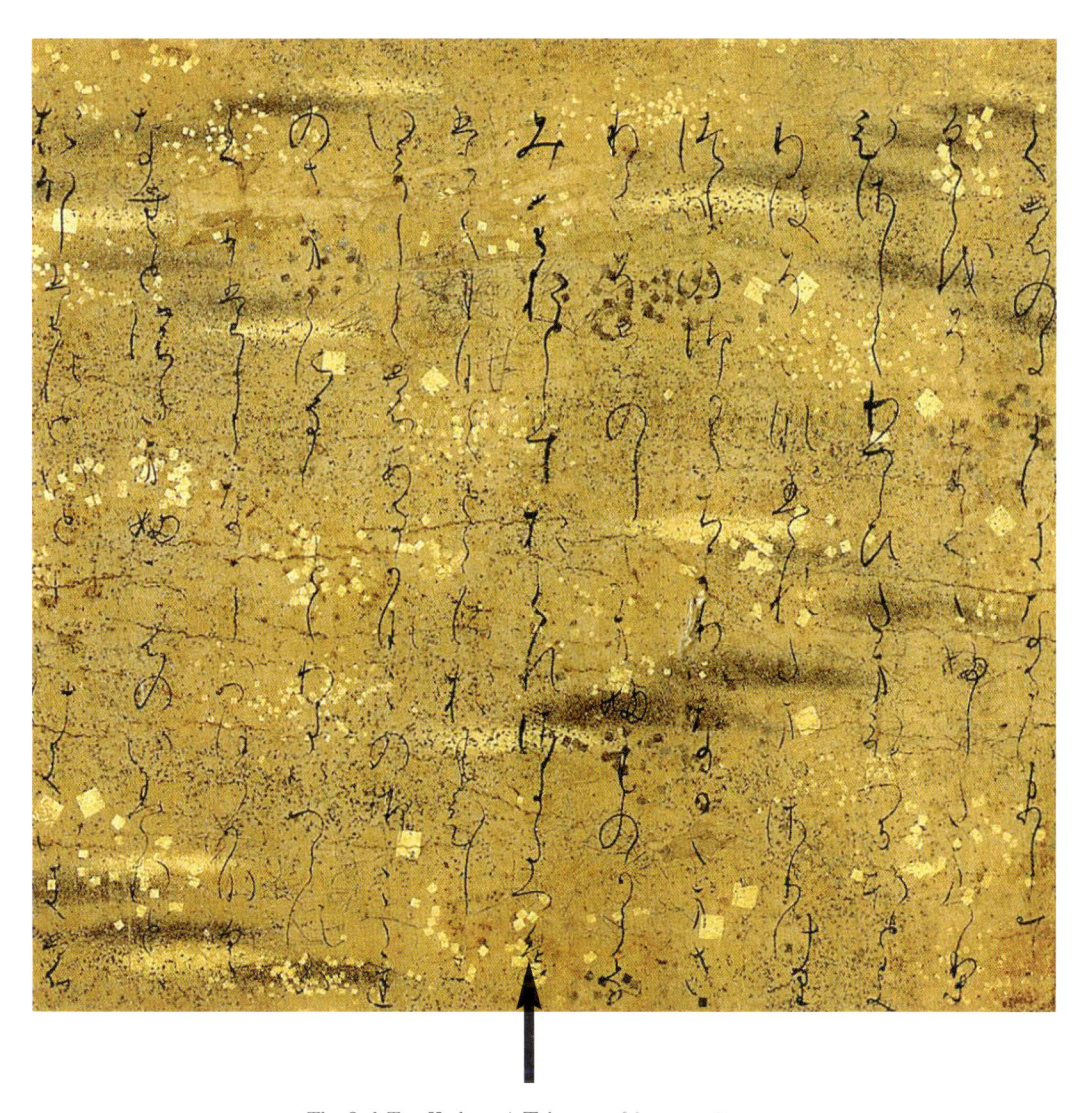

The Oak Tree II, sheet 4. Tokugawa Museum, Nagoya.

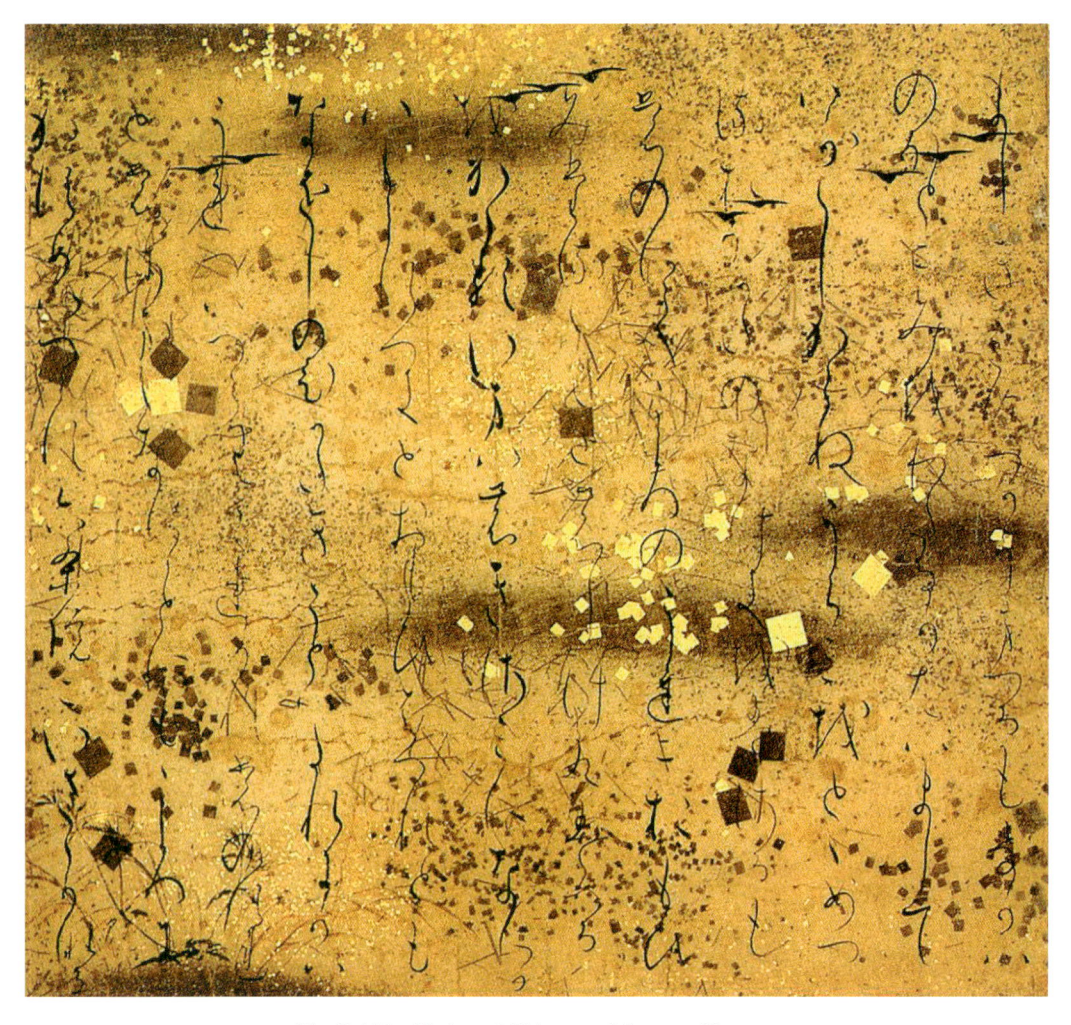

The Oak Tree II, sheet 6. Tokugawa Museum, Nagoya.

1.22

The Law: painting. The Gotō Museum, Tokyo.

The Law, sheet 1. The Gotō Museum, Tokyo.

The Law, sheet 2. The Gotō Museum, Tokyo.

1.25

The Law, sheet 3. The Gotō Museum, Tokyo.

The Law, sheet 5: *midare-gaki*. The Gotō Museum, Tokyo.

2.2

Evening Mist. Gotoh Museum, Tokyo.

The Ivy I. Tokugawa Museum, Nagoya.

2.4

The Bell Cricket II. Gotoh Museum, Tokyo.

From *The Illustrated Tale of Wakeful Sleep* (*Nezame monogatari emaki*).
Yamato Bunkakan Museum, Nara.

2.6

Bamboo River I. Tokugawa Museum, Nagoya.

6.1

From *The Roman de la Rose*. Harley 4425, British Library.

6.2

The Kajūji villa, Kyoto.

6.3

Hōjūji reconstructed; Kanagawa Prefectural Museum, Yokohama.

6.4

The Lady at the Bridge. Tokugawa Museum, Nagoya.

6.5

From the *Haft Paykar*, by Nizami. British Library

Bamboo River II. Tokugawa Museum, Nagoya.

The Bell Cricket I. Gotoh Museum, Tokyo.

6.8

From the *Annual Ceremonies* scrolls, Tanaka collection.

Mōtsuji temple, Hiraizumi.

of excessive emotion, and another code, of detraction: the theme of slander, which, as in Western texts, such as Shakespeare, is linked especially to the court, making a court/pastoral antithesis. These are recognizable emotions. The symbolic code works through the antithesis of order and violation of order. The passage uses the cultural code, prominent in this early chapter which sets up so much, through defining how court space works, and what rituals have to be observed. Two spaces are mentioned: the Paulownia Court and the Kōrōden, and two women are made to swap places; the change of place implying the change of identity:

> Though the mother of the new son had the emperor's love, her detractors were numerous and alert to the slightest inadvertency. She was in continuous torment, feeling that she had nowhere to turn. She lived in the Paulownia Court ['the building called Kiritsubo'; M. 26]. The Emperor had to pass through the apartments of other ladies to reach hers, and it must be admitted that their resentment at his constant comings and goings was not unreasonable. Her visits to the royal chambers were equally frequent. The robes of her women were in a scandalous state from trash strewn along bridges and galleries. Once some women conspired to have both doors of a gallery she must pass bolted shut, and so she found herself unable to advance or retreat. Her anguish over the mounting list of insults was presently more than the Emperor could bear. He moved a lady out of rooms adjacent to his own [away from the Kōrōden, where she had always lived; M. 26] and assigned them to the lady of the Paulownia Court, and so, of course, aroused new resentment. [S. 4]

The text becomes particular, and chronological. The prince reaches the age of three [S. 4], followed by 'the summer' [S. 5], followed by the lady's death, and that autumn [S. 7] and then the spring [S. 13], and the boy becoming six and then seven [S. 13]. Months and years [S. 15] bring Genji to twelve [S. 16] and he is given to the daughter of the Minister of the Left, in symmetry with his father. These are textual moments giving 'the effect of the real' as Barthes says of the realist text; gestures setting up the narration as a particular kind, detailed, non-rhetorical. The chronology contrasts with the other, speaking of an earlier life, and indeed the events – the death of the lady, Genji coming to court – are mythic; they must happen to fulfil the pattern of resentment and of exposure to the stepmother. Further, the other chronology, that makes Genji miraculous, something from another life, reappears, 'among the more discriminating ... were some who marvelled that such a paragon had been born into this world' [S. 5]; 'a tremor of apprehension passed over the Emperor – might it be that such a prodigy was not to be long for this world?' [S. 13]. These suggest Barthes' hermeneutic code; making something about Genji undecidable, they set up narrative expectations.

MOURNING AND MELANCHOLIA

The lady's sickness and her journey home is overcoded by another, the 'road we all must go' [S. 6] – 'the road to death' [M. 27]. The lady dies that same night, and the boy is taken to the house of mourning, following 'precedent' (the cultural code). The text follows this up with a note of what in a medieval Western text would be called *sententiae*: 'The death of a parent is sad under any circumstances, and this one was indescribably sad' [S. 6]. The reader is kept in place via the cultural code – a reference to what we all know – which is itself also part of the semic code: 'indescribably moving' [M. 28] says nothing, does not enter the feelings of the boy. Thus the feelings of the mother, of the Emperor and of the partially repentant court ladies are only conventional. The Emperor lapses into a mourning which becomes melancholia: there is no eroticism, as the other ladies are not summoned to his bed. 'His serving women were plunged into dew-drenched autumn' [S. 7]. The Kokiden lady, 'mother of his eldest son' who refuses to share the mood of sadness, implies by that gesture that she is outside this world: she is distanced from the erotic. In contrast, 'the Emperor's thoughts were with this youngest son even when he was with his eldest'. This repeats the public / private distinction noticed before [S. 4], how the Emperor behaves with regard to both sons; but it intensifies it so much that the Emperor now can be seen almost as a subject divided between conscious and unconscious thoughts. It is this which appears in the next paragraph, in a section where the signifiers: dew, autumn, tears and melancholy persist throughout the section which describes the autumn tempest [S. 7] and the chilly evenings (symbolic code: decline, disorder, death).

> The autumn tempests blew and suddenly the evenings were chilly. Lost in his grief, the Emperor sent off a note to the grandmother. His messenger was a woman of middle rank called Myōbu, whose father was a guards officer. It was on a beautiful moonlit night that he dispatched her, a night that brought memories. On such nights he and the dead lady had played the *koto* for each other. Her *koto* had somehow had overtones lacking in the other instruments, and when she would interrupt the music to speak, the words too carried echoes of their own. Her face, her manner – they seemed to cling to him, but with 'no more substance than the lucent dream'.

Autumn is the most overdetermined motif in the text: its associations of beauty, violence and melancholy persist throughout, as in Chapter 47 'Trefoil Knots' ('Agemaki') – 'Autumn nights are sad in the most ordinary of places' [S. 828]. In Barthes' terms, it fits the semic code. The typhoon motif reappears in Chapter 28, 'The Typhoon' ('Nowaki'), where it blows into Akikonomu's garden and destroys her flowers, and Yūgiri, Genji's son, is enabled to see Murasaki with Genji, as the shutters have not been properly fastened and the winds have blown the shutters along the gallery [S. 457–9]. The storm is metaphorical, and produces more than form of instability: it seems to be a form of madness, as it is for Yūgiri. The typhoon in Chapter 1 makes a separation between what has gone before and what happens now, for it rouses the Emperor into action; indeed it might almost be said to mark the beginning, since as a result of it Genji is brought to court. (The second typhoon marks a displacing of Genji, as his control over women is about to be replaced by that of his son.) The typhoon rather than closing an episode of love produces a mad action; it also induces memories. The same paragraph puts the tempest alongside 'beautiful moonlit nights' as though these two could co-exist in time. The point seems to be the doubleness in the Emperor; the typhoon exists alongside the memories which 'echo' as the voice is described to do, and as the poetry echoes from the *Kokinshū* imperial anthology of 905, 'reality ... has no more substance than the lucent dream'. [S. 7][29] The writing echoes throughout, with repetitions of tears, dew and autumn; indeed the writing here tends towards homogeneity – as happens with metaphor, which claims that one thing is describable in terms of another. In that sense, the attitude of the Kokiden woman to the Emperor becomes a marker of difference, the sign that not everything can be brought within the same metaphorical force, just as, later on, the marker of the Rokujō lady, who appears as a rejected figure between Chapters 4 and 14, is her difference, her non-assimilation into the order given to women in the *Genji*.

Myōbu's journey to the grandmother's house conveys spatial difference. Her carriage is drawn through the gate, and she discovers it to be desolate: dark, surrounded by weeds and with the autumn winds tearing at the garden. 'Only the rays of the moon managed to make their way through the tangles.' There is a stress on difficulty of access to this space, like the trash thrown down in the court passageways to keep the Kiritsubo lady from the Emperor. As in the previous paragraph, the moon is the signifier of love and femininity, and its arrival in the garden coincides with Myōbu's. Everything echoes; the writing all tends to one end, with only slight marks of difference, as with the Kokiden lady. Even the reference to the moonlight quotes from a poem which Shirane translates as:

> Though no visitors
> Call upon this dwelling
> Spring arrives
> Unhindered by the tangled weeds.[30]

The incident of visiting the lonely woman is repeated more than once in *Genji*, perhaps most beautifully in Chapter 15, also spatially named, 'The Wormwood Patch' [in Waley, 'The Palace in the Tangled Woods'], which refers back to an earlier incident in Chapter 6. There, Genji had visited the daughter of the late Prince Hitachi in her ruined house and rejected her after catching sight of her red nose. Chapter 15 returns to her isolation and describes her gardens as overgrown and infested with foxes and owls and tree-spirits. The princess refuses to leave in the belief that Genji will one day come to her. In the Fourth Month, Genji slips out for what might be a sexual expedition, and comes across the house which he eventually realizes he has been at before. As he sends Koremitsu, his foster-nurse's son and his own servant, into the house to see what is happening, she wakes up from a dream of her father and sets servants to clean the house, and to do something about the rainwater. Koremitsu speaks to a servant and returns to Genji, who reflects that he ought to go in:

'It is very wet, sir. Suppose you wait until I have shaken a little of it away.'

> 'Myself will I break a path through towering weeds
> And ask: does a constant spirit dwell within?'

Genji spoke as if to himself, and despite Koremitsu's warnings got from his carriage.

Koremitsu beat at the grass with a horsewhip. The drops from the trees were like a chilly autumn shower.

'I have an umbrella,' said Koremitsu. 'These groves shed the most fearful torrents.'

Genji's feet and ankles were soaking. Even in the old days the passage through the south gallery had been more obstacle than passage. Now the gallery had caved in, and Genji's entrance was a most ungraceful one. He was glad there were no witnesses. [S. 299–300]

Coming in, he speaks 'gracefully' to the lady:

> 'Although we have seen so little of one another,' said Genji, 'I have not ceased to think of you all this time. I have waited impatiently for some sign that you too still care. Although I did not detect any welcoming cedars this evening, I did somehow feel these groves pulling at me. And so you have won the game.' [S. 300]

It is not autumn, but autumn is referred to. Rain indicates the desolation and gives the effect of the real, though it also refers back to a text: Seidensticker references Koremitsu's speech 'I have an umbrella' from the *Kokinshū* (no. 1091):

> Your master, good sirs, must not be without an umbrella
> These groves at Miyagino shed the most fearful torrents.

The most famous umbrella in Western literary theory is in Derrida's *Spurs*, playing with 'I have forgotten my umbrella,'[31] an unsigned statement in quotation marks found among Nietzsche's papers. Derrida plays with 'all the possibilities of significance' (the phallic; the importance of the veil; or of the fold; or of the importance of living close to the lightning; or the question of what is entailed in forgetting) to suggest, however, that the umbrella need not signify. The umbrella Genji's servant gives him need not be fully accounted for by a reference, nor be explained in terms of a desire to keep the reader in the sense of the 'real'. It covers his shoulders, but his feet are soaking. The way to the lady is as difficult as is the way for the Kiritsubo lady to the Emperor in the first chapter, since the passage through the south gallery has collapsed, the rain is falling, and movement is impeded by the necessity of walking in time to an umbrella. The text idealizes and de-idealizes at once.

The reference to 'welcoming cedars' [S. 300] reverts to an earlier visit, an autumn one, to a neglected woman in Chapter 10, 'The Sacred Tree' ('Sakaki'). The Rokujō lady, at the Shinto shrine, refuses to admit him, and he thrusts in a branch of the Shinto sacred tree, the *sakaki*, an evergreen used in purification rituals, but here tendered as an apology. She replies:

> 'You err with your sacred tree and sacred gate
> No beckoning cedars stand before my house'

which Seidensticker annotates from the *Kokinshū* (no. 982):

> 'Should you seek my house at the foot of Mount Miwa
> You need only look for the cedars by the gate.' [S. 187]

The text is so interwoven that the reference in Chapter 16 evokes this earlier one, as though Genji has learned from the Rokujō lady, and speaks her language, dialogically, as he now speaks to the Safflower princess.

Visiting an abandoned or desolate scene that requires a difficult crossing of space, that is marked by an *aporia*, which suggests both a problem of access and the pre-existence of the ruin, and the sense that in each different space there is an abandoned woman who is either in retreat or who has been forced out into such an area, becomes very suggestive. Each woman, each space, evokes a memory, and implies a subjectivity built up on lost chances, lost chances to integrate. A passage in Freud may help:

> When it happens that a person has to give up a sexual object, there quite often ensues an alteration of his ego which can only be described as a setting up of the object inside the ego, as it occurs in melancholia ... [Freud speculates on how this might occur] ... At any rate, the process, especially in the early phases of development, is a very frequent one, and it makes it possible to suppose that the character of the ego is a precipitate of abandoned object-cathexes and that it contains the history of those object-choices ... there are varying degrees of capacity for resistance, which decide the extent to which a person's character fends off or accepts the influences of the history of his erotic object-choices. In women who have had many experiences in love there seems to be no difficulty in finding vestiges of their object-cathexes in the traits of their character.[32]

It looks as if the Safflower lady embodies features of her dead father: she has been dreaming of him at the moment that Genji, who had been, momentarily, her lover, arrives at her desolate house. But I am not trying to read psychoanalytically, which would be likely to result in homogeneity in relation to a text with the alterity of *Genji*: I am more interested in trying to work out the implications of these spatial differences. Genji tries to bring four women together in the Rokujō mansion; the discovery that seems to be made so often in *Genji monogatari* is of spaces occupied by abandoned figures – the last ten chapters of the book will come to mind – and they help evoke a landscape which is not continuous, because each space is marked by a difficult access, and which is above all, marked by melancholia (which itself may eroticize them). Freud allows the thought that subjectivity may comprise different loved objects, all internalized and that memory is of those, but they are differently installed within the subject, not related each to each, so that consciousness would be like a mosaic of different fragments of object-choices. Perhaps something like this is produced in the landscapes and the spaces of *Genji*. To take Ivan Morris's title 'The World of the Shining Prince', it may be suggested that the landscape and the places are the expression of Genji, the dissemination of his subjectivity – or his attempt to impose himself, to inhabit a space.

The pathos in *Genji*, more than nostalgia and courtly sensibility, is awareness of the always-fragmented nature of things. The desolate house of the mother of the Kiritsubo lady – desolate within a few months of the daughter's death – implies the always-already abandoned nature of subjectivity, filled with spaces which record loss. Myōbu arrives, and is received, according to McCullough, 'at the south entrance to the main hall' [M. 29]. The mother feels the embarrassment of her having had to 'grope her way through the dews of these mugwort-choked grounds' [M. 29]. Myōbu opens up by alluding to a previous visitor who had come there: 'Naishi-no-suke told His Majesty she felt much worse – really devastated [the woman become like the place] after she came here and saw things for herself' [M. 29]. Thus the first detailed visit becomes a repetition of another, an earlier. Events which have happened seem anticipated in dreams, as the message from the Emperor is that he has been either dreaming or is as in a dream:

> He has said that for a time it seemed as if he were wandering in a nightmare [dream, M. 29] and that then when his agitation subsided, he came to see that the nightmare would not end. If only he had a companion in his grief, he thought – and it occurred to him that you, my lady, might be persuaded to come unobtrusively to court. He cannot bear to think of the child languishing in this house of tears [house of mourning, M. 30] and hopes that you will come quickly and bring him with you. He was more than once interrupted by sobs as he spoke, and it was apparent to all of us that he feared having us think him inexcusably weak. I came away without hearing him to the end. [S. 8]

The narration details what the Emperor said, giving a later order to the narrative events, which have related barely what he did in dispatching Myōbu. Similarly, only now will the contents of the note be revealed. The breaking of chronology confirms that events have no priority one to another. The tears of the Emperor grow in intensity, as it were, after the description of the house of mourning in which the mother lives. Genji will go from one house of tears to another, as though mourning were primal.

The lady takes the letter ('I cannot see for tears ... let these sublime words give me light') but cannot read the letter through to the attached poem because she can no longer see through her tears. The symmetry and the incremental nature of tears go together. Her reply in McCullough implies one of the reference-points of the text:

> Knowing as I do that longevity is a curse, I feel ashamed even to imagine the thoughts of the Takasago pines, and I surely could not presume to come and go at the imperial palace. [M. 30]

Longevity as a trial, and the Takasago pines as symbols of longevity, the reference being to a poem, recall the text's cultural code. The text slips in the assumption easily. Genji must not stay with the mother who feels she 'bears a curse from a previous existence' [S. 9] – a reason why, in this text, there can be no origins, nor any beginning of mourning or of melancholy. She continues giving a narrative of the perils of ambition, which runs on gender lines (the father wanting something for the daughter while the mother does not); this resonate throughout *Genji*:

All of our hopes were on the girl, I say again, from the day she was born, and until he died her father did not let me forget that she must go to court, that his own death, if it came early, should not deter me. I knew that another sort of life would be happier for a girl without strong backing, but I could not forget his wishes and sent her to court as I had promised. [S. 9]

The reluctance of the mother to let the boy go to the court is the theme of Chrétien's *The Story of the Grail*; in both texts there is the cultural code of the court as dangerous. But Perceval and his mother live initially in the forest, which, like the forest of Brocéliande in *Yvain* is another space, irreconcilable with court values, and perhaps not in a spatial continuum with it. It is the 'Other world',[33] evocative of a psychic state as when Yvain, mad, runs to the woods and becomes a wild man. There is less emphasis on an 'other world' in *Genji*.[34] Otherness is conveyed through mansions that become desolate. There is no opposition between the forest and the court, which makes defective the court/pastoral comparison mentioned before. There is only one space to be occupied.

The mother's words look back on the daughter's plight, and anticipate Genji's destiny, as though belonging to the action code, and asking what will that destiny be in the future (the hermeneutic code). She ends her speech by putting it down as 'the mad wanderings of a heart that is darkness' and the Emperor is similarly reported by Myōbu as feeling that 'he must seem dreadfully eccentric' – with the sense of guilt from a previous existence [S. 10, M. 30]. Myōbu leaves the mother in a text full of the signifiers of autumn, tears and landscape sounds (the insects) which would by themselves have bought tears. A homogeneity exists between Myōbu and the grandmother (the poems they exchange; Myōbu's hesitation in leaving) and this totalizing glimpse is one of the idealizing drives within the text, as is the emphasis on the divided heart of the grandmother (not wanting to go to court, in contrast to the young women, not wanting to lose Genji) and the divided state of Myōbu and the Emperor.

HOMOGENEITY AND HETEROGENEITY

Myōbu returns to the court and:

... was much moved to find the Emperor waiting up for her. Making it seem that his attention was on the small and beautifully planted garden before him, now in full bloom, he was talking quietly with four or five women, among the most sensitive of his attendants. He had become addicted to illustrations by the Emperor Uda for 'The Song of Everlasting Sorrow' and to poems by Ise and Tsurayuki on that subject, and to Chinese poems as well. [S. 10–11]

The autumn garden, as in the scenes of the Rokujō mansion, is the most select. Autumn appears in Akikonomu, whose name means 'Preferring Autumn'. The daughter of the Rokujō lady, Genji stands in relation to her as though she were his daughter-in-law, since she is married to the Reizei Emperor, Genji's son. Talking to her at autumn time, with a soft rain falling, he thinks back, and debates the relative merits of spring and autumn:

> I have been told that in China nothing is held to surpass the brocades of spring, but in the poetry of our own country [the alliance of poetry with nationalism goes with the binary oppositions set up here] the preference would seem to be for the wistful notes of autumn.

She replies:

> ... for me the autumn wind which poets have found so strange and compelling – in the dews I sense a fleeting link with my mother.

He replies in verse:

> Then we too feel alike. You know my secret
> For me it is the autumn winds that pierce. [S. 345–6]

The Rokujō lady had died at the end of the year [S. 287]. But the autumn winds here have a sexual force: Genji is trying to attract Akikonomu, as in the *Kokinshū* poem no. 546, based on lines of Bai Juyi:

> There is no time when
> I do not suffer the pangs
> of love for you but
> miraculously yearning
> grows on autumn evenings.[35]

Autumn, part of a cultural code, continues to gather resonances, and as though everything were implicit in that first chapter. The Emperor in his garden fashions his subjectivity on gardens, illustrations and poetry: the narrative recalls Bai Juyi's poem (as though the journey to see the mother were equivalent to the journey made to see Yang Guifei after her death); and then illustrations by the Emperor Uda (reigned 887–897) one of whose concubines was Lady Ise. The other name mentioned, Tsurayuki (884?–946?), compiled the *Kokinshū*. Lady Ise and Tsurayuki are combined again later in the anniversary rites for the Uji princesses' father, where Kaoru participates and quotes the poems. 'Old poems, they could see, had much to say about the unchanging human heart' [S. 822]. The maxim (*sententia*) in its wisdom about the uses of literature suggests the cultural code and the opposition of old/unchanging the symbolic code. Poetry is here the opposite of the novelistic form, in that it brings emotions, thoughts and images together, into a form of homogeneity; perpetuating a feeling which remains the same, as with the Emperor.

As before, only at this stage are the contents of the letter and its poem, which echoes the Emperor's, revealed, where their maximal intensity can be felt since they are being read by the people for whom they are intended. Letter writing, in addition to the existence of a messenger, doubles the space of representation (as opposed to an epistolary novel of the eighteenth century, the writers of both letters are also kept visible before the reader, and they are not known only by their letters). The mother's poem alludes to the father who had wished the Kiritsubo lady to come to court, as 'the tree that gave them shelter' [S. 11]. The Emperor is silently defined in terms of his lack of patriarchy, especially when the grandmother's 'devotion' [S. 12] to her dead husband's wishes is recalled (i.e. in sending the daughter to the court).

The narrative contrasts this grief with Kokiden's pleasure [S. 12] but before that the Emperor dwells on the 'keepsakes' Myōbu has brought back from the mother, with, again, an implication of the difficulty of having traversed space, so that the presents seem to have come from the dead, as the Tang poem makes so much of separate spaces: and brings up presents from the dead:

> ... he thought of what a comfort it would be if some wizard were to bring him, like that Chinese Emperor, a comb from the world where his lost love was dwelling. He whispered:
>
> > 'And will no wizard search her out for me,
> > That even he may tell me where she is?'
>
> There are limits to the powers of the most gifted artist. The Chinese lady in the paintings did not have the lustre of life. Yang Kuei-fei was said to have resembled the lotus of the Sublime Pond, the willows of the Timeless Hall. No doubt she was very beautiful in her Chinese finery. When he tried to remember the quiet charm of his lost lady, he found that there was no colour of flower, no song of bird, to summon her up. Morning and night, over and over again, they had repeated to each other the lines from 'The Song of Everlasting Sorrow':
>
> > 'In the sky, as birds that share a wing.
> > On earth, as trees that share a branch.'
>
> It had been their vow, and the shortness of her life had made it an empty dream. [S. 12]

In the Kokiden lady's parallel apartments, music creates a heterogeneity which is seen as 'bad taste', 'unnecessary injury' and part of the lady's 'arrogant and intractable nature' so that the text moves in two directions at once, criticizing both the homogeneity set up round the Emperor (through the Kokiden lady's actions) and the heterogeneity. Though the text proceeds with the Emperor's reflection far into the night, his poem and his sleeplessness, and with a citation from Ise, speaking as the Emperor in a reflection on 'The Song of Everlasting Sorrow', it appears as excessive, presented as such openly, if indirectly, through the courtiers whose voices remain unattributed:

> Not all voices were sympathetic. Perhaps, some said, it had all been foreordained, but he had dismissed the talk and ignored the resentment [a refrain word in Seidensticker] and let the affair quite pass the bounds of reason; and now to neglect his duties so – it was altogether too much. Some even cited the example of the Chinese Emperor who had brought ruin upon himself and his country. [S. 13]

Before, it was the Kiritsubo lady who had been criticized, now it is the Emperor, in a moment where history is seen to furnish examples. The Emperor's identification with the Chinese Emperor, Xuanzong, had been private and comforting, but here it is read differently. The Emperor has become feminized, and his subjects can see it. As in the Lacan analysis of the Poe short story 'The Purloined Letter', taking up a subject position is feminizing and weakening, and comes about from the structural position the person is brought into within the symbolic order.[36] In the light of this feminizing, Genji appears at the court. The incident of the autumn night – seven pages in Seidensticker –

is followed by 'the months passed' and a different sense of pace, 'the following spring'. This relates to the new spirit of action Genji evokes – note the speed with which he reads the Chinese classics. In contrast, the Emperor, frustrated in his desire to have him named as crown prince (markers of his femininity, his fear of the relations of the Kokiden lady) has that failure labelled as discretion by his people. The grandmother dies, having prayed 'to be with her daughter' [S. 13] or 'that she might be allowed to go in search of her daughter' [M. 34]. The reference is again to space; where the living and the dead do not inhabit radically heterogeneous spaces, but exist at long distances from each other.

MASCULINITY AND FEMININITY

The boy's behaviour in the Kokiden pavilion, in its 'inner chambers', behind the blinds, in front of ladies not ashamed to show their faces, is a narrative attempt to bring together the disparate attitudes that had been allowed to exist with regards to the Emperor and the Kokiden lady. The Kokiden lady smiles at him, but so would a stern warrior have done so. Genji's masculinity and femininity are interchangeable (do the women respond to a precocious boy or to a girl, that they are so even with him?) and these dual aspects recall the theory of the erotic interest with which Shakespeare's boy actors were invested.[37] Genji evokes masculinity, which relates to the heterogeneity evoked by the Kokiden lady, when the Emperor's grief aligned him to the feminine. The feminine then becomes the homogeneous while to do justice to the heterogeneous elements, a masculinity that is also a femininity is needed (there is no 'mere' masculinity here). This enables a re-coding of those elements that went along with the homogeneous: autumn, evening, dew, tears, melancholy, death, as feminine, while the 'Shining Prince' fits with the day, with action and with a masculinity that is not simply that. The narrative, then, in gender terms, might be broadly said to show the ascendancy of the feminine throughout, even though the heterogeneous, as here, wins out at times. The heterogeneous includes the homoerotic; in Chapter 2, Genji's companions 'almost wished that he were a woman' [S. 24].[38] They cannot imagine a woman who would satisfy him. 'To see him was to sense the difficulty of choosing a woman who could be completely worthy of him, even if she were the highest of the high' [M. 44]. A homoeroticism the female author notes, is coded in terms implying a rationalization is at work, for the sexual appeal is noted in the narration but not in the explanation. If the explanation is taken literally, the text refuses to think in terms of symmetry between the sexes and their desires. That desire cannot be met, that the subject is created through desire, makes narrative possible and makes it endlessly metonymic in character. Freud, in discussing male sexuality, says:

> It is my belief that, however strange it may sound, we must reckon with the possibility that something in the nature of the sexual instinct itself is unfavourable to the realization of complete satisfaction ... The final object of the sexual instinct is never any longer the original object, but only a surrogate for it ... when the original

object of a wishful impulse has been lost as a result of repression, it is frequently represented by a series of substitute objects.[39]

The series of substitute objects is what is meant by metonymy (a change of name), and it implies that narrative is a continuous provision or desire for supplementary substitutions which will compensate for a lost original event and which will prevent any cessation of narrative since there can be no transcendental signifier, and so no point of closure.

LANGUAGE AND DESIRE

The narrator bows to heterogeneity when, after alluding to both his accomplishments in Chinese and in music, she says 'to recount all his virtues would, I fear, give rise to a suspicion that I distort the truth' [S. 14]. Heterogeneity continues with the ambassadors from Korea; homogeneity with the Emperor's recall of the edict of Uda, whose feminine significance will seem apparent from the earlier reference to him [S. 11] and the injunction not to receive foreigners (the cultural code). The ambassadors are lodged at the Kōroden mansion (the cultural code, in defining the proper place) and the boy is smuggled in to see the physiognomist, in another suggestion of the difficulty of traversing space. The physiognomist's words about the future (the action code) lay bare the tendency of the narrative, while they also propose a mystery (the hermeneutic code): what can this boy be if he is to be neither emperor nor emperor's surrogate? Strictly, he will have *no* place; the tale is of someone who is unnamed, if naming implies a firm subject position. The name 'Genji' applies to someone for whom ambiguity *is* their state; it could be argued that this aligns Genji to women, who within patriarchy have no assigned position. It makes him truly heterogeneous, and double: the Korean contributes a Chinese poem in which he expresses both joy and sorrow at seeing Genji. The heterogeneity is further noted when an Indian astrologer confirms the Japanese and Korean intuitions, but as it is confirmation of a position, it is also marking the text's drive towards sameness, even if it means that in narrative terms, Genji is styled a commoner.

The text then turns to a reflection upon that homogeneity. The Emperor cannot find someone who resembles the dead Kiritsubo, and then he does find the woman: the Fourth Princess, daughter of a former emperor. The growth of this one from girlhood to womanhood parallels Genji's growth, as do the circumstances where the mother is unwilling to send her to court (as Genji's grandmother was reluctant with both Kiritsubo and Genji), and details are given which confirm that there is no beginning of the narratives of resentment at the court [S. 15]. Eventually, on the advice of her elder brother, Prince Hyōbu, Fujitsubo arrives. 'The resemblance to the dead lady was indeed astonishing' [S. 16]. McCullough does not translate the words as 'the dead lady', reading simply 'the Kiritsubo lady' [M. 36] but in Seidensticker the woman is already, if lightly, marked by death (as indeed she will die, in Chapter 19).[40]

As in Western medieval texts and in contrast to realist novels, the lady's beauty is not described; it remains general, ideal. The effect generalizes beauty, and diminishes individuality, but means that there is no questioning the proposition whether the lady looks like the dead mother or not. The matter would be impossible to decide; the dead woman is not available for comparison; any comparison would be memory-based, or desire-based. Is the narrative statement that she looked like the dead lady what 'they say' or authoritative, or indirect discourse, unattributable? The point is left open, but means that the similarity need never be tested. The resemblance of one woman to another is textual, not empirically real, and desire is mobilized textually. When Genji loves Fujitsubo because of her relationship to the mother, that is absence (she becomes less and less visible) which is premised on absence – for not only is the mother dead, so that he has no idea what she looked like, but it is untested whether Fujitsubo ever could be like the mother. As with deconstruction, for whom the lack of origins is the point, and where experience is never pre-textual, desire is shown to be created textually rather than through the power of experience.

A double of the Kiritsubo lady, she supplements her loss by providing 'boundless comfort' – indeed the text recalls at this point that the Kiritsubo lady had been the victim of 'a love too intense' so that though the Emperor may not consciously think much on her, the text stresses how the lost object of desire gives character to this new love. Desire of a particular person becomes a rationalization, and the commentary registers this with its own rationalizing: 'So it is with the affairs of this world.'[41] The point about the lost object is more developed with Genji. He wants to be with the lady because he has never seen his mother and has been told that this lady resembles her. Desire which is desire for an unattainable fantasized object, the dead mother, increases since he can only catch occasional glimpses of her face. His desire is matched by the desire engendered by the narrative (there is a possible application of the action-code): the question is whether he will see her clearly, and ultimately whether they will become lovers. She seems to become even more virginal (with 'child-like shyness') after she has been associated with the Emperor than she was before: an increase of femininity, a decrease in the power of homogeneity. The effect sets her up as an object of desire that crosses the generations (the Emperor's generation and Genji's), that makes her not quite codifiable (she is a wife, and yet also a child): as a wife she seems to conclude one narrative, to do with the Emperor's desire, as a girl, she opens up another narrative, which is her relationship with Genji, which is signalled to the reader in the physicality of her description, and above all in the sense that though married, she is still to be won. He brings her presents of 'cherry blossoms or autumn leaves' [M. 37][42] – spring and autumn joined, with the meanings that these two seasons will later develop already implicit.

Fujitsubo's destiny is to be named as something she is not: as the Kiritsubo lady, as Genji's mother, as, ultimately, after Genji has been given his new name, 'the shining one', 'the lady of the radiant sun'. The woman's difference is not affirmed, and it is interesting that while this is not consciously marked in the text as a point of criticism, again the Kokiden lady becomes emblematic of what is unsatisfactory about this for the woman. Again she feels 'resentment' and though that is rationalized by the text (her son, who will become the Suzaku Emperor, is not as attractive as Genji), it is also a possible form of resistance to the woman's destiny.

The following paragraph in Seidensticker ('It seemed a pity') propels Genji forward in the comparison of generations: if Fujitsubo seems childlike, Genji leaves his 'boyish attire' behind, receiving the cap of an adult. To the themes of attraction to Fujitsubo, and resentment felt by the Kokiden lady is added a third: male, fraternal, rivalry with the Crown Prince, whose capping has taken place already in the Grand Hall. Its sequence leads to a fourth theme, when the Minister of the Left gives his daughter to become Genji's 'bedmate' [M. 38], with the assumption that she will become the principal wife later. The narrative logic sets up a contrast with the Minister of the Right, whose ascendancy seems assured. The narrative theme, Genji's destiny, is set out in relation to four relationships, four rivalries: with the father and mother; with the stepmother; with the brother; and with the Minister of the Left – which sets up a political theme. In all this, the situations impose a logic of their own – two wives; two sons; two Ministers; which provides further balancings: attraction to one woman, but bedding another.

The change has gender implications: before the hair is cut the boy resembles his mother, (feminine); afterwards, wearing adult trousers, he is the 'son' that the Emperor delights in, who has the potential to make the Emperor, the father, feel old. This masculinity is increased by reference to marriage. Signifying the importance of the contractual relationship, which will further debar him from Kiritsubo, and continue the process of definition of the subject, the contractual arrangements are presented in much more detail than the capping ceremony. There is an emphasis on spatial arrangements, which begins with the throne facing east (the sun) on the porch and Genji coming in from the east, like the shining prince. Genji goes from the capping ceremony to the courtier's waiting room where he takes a seat below the last of the imperial princes when it becomes time for the company to drink. The Minister must cross to the royal apartments. Here a present is offered (coming from the greater to the lower, in ceremonial terms at least) and poems are exchanged which as a formal act repeats both the meaning of the speech-act of the poems and their actual sense. The minister descends from the royal apartments to the courtyard by way of a long garden bridge, an act which isolates him and brings him out, and at the foot of the stairs there are waiting senior nobles and imperial princes. The food 'overflowed the premises' – the only thing that steps out of a spatial order, but it fits within the cultural coding that the generosity should overflow the measure. At the end of the sequence, Genji is sent to the other house – home of the Minister of the Left. The attention to the correctness of spatial arrangements, which fits with the later discussion of the gardens, means that the text keeps the reader within the sense of borders and boundaries, within the proper. The point should be remembered in considering the quasi-transgressive nature of Genji's quasi-incestuous future relationship with

Fujitsubo, and in considering too how the text is not on the side of excess, or the heterogeneous. The details of Japanese architecture and gardens belong to an ideology assigning to each subject their own space and hence a way for visualizing their position.

However much of order there is, the text still responds to the non-relationship of subjects to the ideological positioning they have been assigned. McCullough makes more of the femininity in Genji and of his erotic appeal to the man (like the appeal to the father) than Seidensticker does:

> Genji was still very childish in appearance, and to the host he looked almost frighteningly sweet and appealing. But to the daughter, who was a little the elder of the two, the match seemed unsuitable and embarrassing. [M. 39]

This lady, Aoi,[43] does not quite fit into the sexual stereotypings; just like the Kokiden lady, and the hint of disharmony will lead Genji to feel that they are not suited, so that this, as everything else, becomes symptomatic behaviour.

Alliance to the Minister of the Left brings out the fourth rivalry: his son by his principal wife, older than Genji and an officer, and later called Tō no Chūjō,[44] is married to the fourth daughter of the Minister of the Right. Tō no Chūjō is brother-in-law to Genji, since he is Aoi's brother, which repeats the earlier rivalry with the other brother; he is also allied to the Minister of the Right, which aligns him also with the Kokiden lady, and makes him by marriage Genji's stepuncle. Finally, as another male, he is a rival in love, which touches the issue of relationships with Fujitsubo. This first chapter interlaces and repeats many potential sources for conflict, the result being to tease the reader to know which of them – all of them? – will be taken up. We move from the Emperor, whose obsessions started the chapter, to the two Ministers and their families. The chapter redefines the interest, not as relating to the Emperor, who is comparatively marginal politically, that being expressed in his love and his melancholia, with which it is inseparable. The marker of being displaced is that private grief becomes centre-stage. The point holds for such a different text as *Hamlet*, and indicates how narrative is set up structurally; narrative situations are generated by the structure of texts, and so subjectivity is constructed textually.

The last three paragraphs in Seidensticker return to Genji in relation to his father, the Emperor, and thus imply that Genji's destiny may be that of comparative marginality, which makes him comparable at least lightly, to women's marginality. Having begun with private love in relation to the public realm, the chapter circles back there. Genji does not go much to the Sanjō mansion of his bride. 'Fujitsubo was for him a vision of sublime beauty' [S. 18] – and she is doubly interdicted, first because of his attachment to his bride, about whom he feels that 'he was not at all sure that they were meant for each other' and secondly by his father, because, being of age 'he no longer had his father's permission to go behind her curtains'. He is enabled (he is of age) and disabled at the same time, reduced to a child by the father: the contradiction seems structural. He plays the phallic flute; Kiritsubo the *koto*, which allows her to sing also, so that eroticism is carried by the voice through the curtains. Feminist criticism stresses the power of seeing as patriarchal, the power of the voice as maternal; ironically the position of being the man (which should make him patriarchal) means that he is pushed into a new reliance on the maternal, upon the woman identified with the lost mother, which implies emotional dependency. Subject-positions seem structural, not personal (the point that is stressed in Lacan's analysis of 'The Purloined Letter'): subjectivity comes about from the subject's positioning within the symbolic order. The Lacanian point may be seen more easily through the Japanese text when personal names which seem to guarantee identity do not exist (there is no equivalent to Chrétien de Troyes signing himself) but where the name floats metonymically as the effect of a place, or a position, or an office.

The paragraph beginning 'The minister selected' implies the non-relationship between what the subject possesses, and the space of desire. Genji has two homes stocked with women; in addition, he is assigned the Paulownia Court, which emphasizes his kinship with his mother at every level: keeps him feminine, marginal, reminds him of his contradictory position in being both favoured and denied at the same time, and associates him with women rather than with patriarchal power. Not only does he live where his mother used to, but also his mother's family home is remodelled. It had been desolate, presumably, with the death of the grandmother: now it is begun again, in a way that also suggests new narrative beginnings, premised on the removal of the old melancholy:

> The plantings and the artificial hills had always been remarkably tasteful, and the grounds now swarmed with workmen widening the lake. If only, thought Genji, he could have with him the lady he yearned for. [S. 19]

The renovations and the busy activity imply the desire to have a new narrative, and accordingly they fit with the ending of a first chapter. But changing the ground – widening the lake, with all that this implies in terms of providing new material for hills – cannot cope with the buried past, cannot wipe out melancholia, because the house is associated with the dead mother – even though Genji has no personal awareness of her. The ending shows space to be saturated with the past – but it is not that the past can be thought of in simple chronological terms as the past. The past is created as surely as the workmen excavate the lake, which in itself has associations with absence, and with the abyssal. In making the lake over anew, the effect is to open up an area which can be invested with desire, and that labelled as the past, which is created retroactively.

The return to the house, first seen in the chapter in its autumnal desolation, marks the beginning of building to parallel the point that this is a chapter of beginnings. Genji returns to this estate after his exile, in Chapter 14, 'Channel Buoys' ('Miotsukushi'), and then:

> ... he had most splendidly remodelled the lodge to the east of his mansion. He had inherited it from his father and his plan was that it be home for the lady of the orange blossoms and other neglected favourites. [S. 273]

One way of describing *The Tale of Genji* is in terms of the attempt to define and enlarge a space for the subject since the subject is defined by space – which is also history. In Chapter 18, he finishes the eastern lodge and defines thereby a particular space:

> The eastern lodge at Nijō was finished and the lady of the orange blossoms moved in. Genji turned the west wing and adjacent galleries into offices and reserved the east wing for the Akashi lady. The north wing was both spacious and ingeniously partitioned, so that he might assign its various rooms to lesser ladies who were dependent on him, and so make them happy too. He reserved the main hall for his own occasional use. [S. 318]

Again, different spaces are related to women. This gathering, and desire to integrate the scattered women of his life is, in Freud's terms, a melancholic attempt to deal with a prior fragmentation, and it commences with the building that takes place in Chapter 1. In Chapter 31 he buys the four parks in Rokujō, near the eastern limits of the city, including the lands of the Rokujō lady [S. 382–3]. The impulse to integrate is inseparable from the imperialistic drive to possess, to become powerful, and also from the desire to change a history of loss, expressed in the Rokujō lady's vengeful spirit possession (yet to reappear, in relation to Murasaki, in Chapter 35).

Making the space 'perfect' as McCullough translates, is the attempt to order things, but in ordering, an unconscious is opened up; and significantly, since it is desire that is important here, not an actual woman, the lady Genji yearns for is not named. 'It is of course, Fujitsubo that he would like to see installed,' writes Norma Field,[45] but apart from the openness of the desire, which connects his unspecified desire to the reader's drive to continue with the narrative, it must be said that there is no closure here on a specific woman, nor is there until after the meeting with Murasaki in Chapter 5, where the sight of a girl prompts thoughts of a grown woman. 'How deeply affecting are the ways of the heart' indeed.[46] The desire for integration in linear terms can never be fulfilled as long as one woman is a metonymy for another; in vertical terms it cannot be fulfilled because each place contains its buried memory. This loss of integration, borne out fully in the Ukifune chapters, contrasts with Chrétien de Troyes, with whom, perhaps, there can be narrative closure around one woman.

There is no name for the woman who could live in this space, because the woman has no name; is she – for instance, Fujitsubo – moved into this other space she would be different, as though newly identified. Lack of naming conveys the impossibility of desire ever being satisfied, and recalls the lack of a known name for the author of *Genji*: Murasaki (purple, or lavender) comes from the character in the *Tale* who dies in Chapter 40. By the end of the following chapter, Genji will have died. The death of this figure, both heterogeneous (outside Genji's sphere) and homogeneous (brought into it, part of the text) whose existence enables the author to exist, as though in a form of *prosopopoeia*[47] and the death of Genji come together. As she has brought the author into existence, so has Genji, similarly unnamed by being dis-owned, and dis-placed: he has given a second life to the author, has made her the author indeed. In a sense, Murasaki engenders Genji. First seen in Chapter 5, 'Wakamurasaki', the chapter where Genji sleeps with Fujitsubo, she seems to speak in the place of that which enables narrative – Genji realizes who he desires, Fujitsubo. But what enables narrative is itself narrative; for the story that the bishop tells Genji about Murasaki's mother [S. 90] is identical to the narrative of what happened to Genji's mother; it repeats the events of 'Kiritsubo'.[48] There is no point of origin; this narrative's 'primal scene' is folded into other narratives which baffle notions of narrative time, and make the present tense the only possible one in which narrative can take place. Unsurprisingly, for the metonymies of desire which generate narrative, when Genji first sees Murasaki she reminds him of Fujitsubo [S. 88] who reminds him of Kiritsubo, so Murasaki becomes a figure for what originates the text.

When Genji sleeps with Fujitsubo, the resultant child, assumed to be the son of the old Emperor, and so Genji's half-brother, becomes Emperor in his turn in Chapter 14, as the Reizei Emperor. Genji in this way becomes unacknowledged father of the Emperor, though the line is illegitimate (the point prevented Tanizaki from translating these sections in 1939). As Murasaki engenders the text, so it continues in a way which is subversive of the official narrative: it could be taken as another of Okada's instances of the text figuring resistance. Narrative in the Western model is patriarchal in that it follows the model of inheritance: father to son. It misses out the mother entirely in this; the mother is the metaphor which enables a transition from one generation to another (from one narrative step to another). If narrative is so patrilinear in mode, it becomes the more interesting that *Genji* makes clear its actual 'improper' character – the proper / improper distinction being one that deconstruction attacks. The central issue of the illegitimacy of the Emperor, guarantor of patriarchal authority and of the 'name of the father' becomes an instance of the text's opposition to narrative. That is to go further than Genji concedes when he refers to the Chinese-written history of Japan, the *Nihon shoki* (720) and says that 'the *Chronicles of Japan* and the rest are a mere fragment of the whole truth. It is your romances [*monogatari*] which fill in the details.' [S. 437] The text is more subversive as anti-narrative, where it has, as part of its richness which refuses to settle on a single centre, shown up narrative to be a repressive structure, always keeping out of view the metaphor which enables movement from one narrative point to another. The *monogatari* form contains within it a critique of its own narrative, as much as Genji sees the *monogatari* narrative as a critique of the national histories in *kanbun* (Chinese text).

The chapter has concluded with Genji aged twelve. Though this chapter shows the passing of time and indicates growth, its mood does not imply that time is other than fragmentation, continuation of melancholy, and this relates to the impression of slowness and detail in the narrative. There is a movement back and forth between the stability of different places, and the attempt to establish a space, and the feeling of desolation and of places falling into decay;

and the narrative tempo is deliberate, constructing time-schemes (mythic and chronological) that do not give the subject the power of initiation. There is a contrast with Chrétien de Troyes, whose texts are organized round a repeated, and centring and patriarchal theme, the quest. In *Yvain*, the first sixty lines set up a narrative of the knights preparing to hear a tale given by Calogrenant, who is about to speak of something that is to his disgrace. A sense of disorder in the court, premised on the absence of the King, accords with this (this is Chrétien's art of analogy), but Calogrenant begins his narrative at line 149 by telling us what had happened to him more than seven years ago when he was questing for adventures.[49] He concludes and Yvain tells him his determination to avenge his shame. The King, who has emerged from his chamber, says that he will go with a party to the site of the adventure, but Yvain determines to go first, achieves his quest, wins a wife, and is ready to greet King Arthur's party when it arrives, but feels he must go back temporarily to the life of that court, and leaves his wife for a year. He forgets his promise to return, is condemned by her messenger and told that he has lost her love. He rushes from the court, going mad in the wilderness. The narrative returns to the quest theme, whereby Yvain comes back to his senses, made fit to win his wife's love again. Interlaced with the story of Yvain is Gawain, whose adventures parallel his. The ending secures a resolution, but with no sense that the passage of years makes a difference, or that any deep-rooted change to modes of perception has taken place in the narrative, despite the successive adventures, each analogous to the other. It is potentially more triumphalist in form, more masculine and it does not allow for fragmentation. Interlacing keeps everything in place, suspends time. The Japanese text thinks differently. If it discovers in the writing that which it tracks down as the image of what allows it to write, it inscribes that with temporality. Murasaki and Genji both die. The last thirteen chapters of *Genji* exist posthumously in relation to those people the text has brought into being who now have no name, no space.

The man desires completeness, in relation both to his estate and the woman who evokes for him another woman and so on endlessly, but the text's melancholy comes from the perception that she is marked by lack, also shared by Genji, in the conditions in which he loves Fujitsubo and relating also to his lack of a name. 'The sobriquet, "the shining Genji", one hears, was bestowed upon him by the Korean.' [S. 19] 'The name Minamoto or Genji' was conferred upon him when he was made a commoner by his father as has been said earlier [S. 15]. Does the name mark heterogeneity or homogeneity? If Genji is made central, he is marked with desire, and a heteroclite voice has named him as the heterogeneous within Heian society. It is the heterogeneous that the text returns to: those points which show that what supports a system – of patriarchy, of history, of narrative – is that which is outside and which is simultaneously on the inside, working to undo any single structure, and to show its secret, and feminine, life.

NOTES

1. Bakhtin's classic statements on the novel appear in *The Dialogic Imagination: Four Essays* by M. M. Bakhtin, edited by Michael Holquist; translated by Caryl Emerson and Michael Holquist (Austin: University of Texas Press, 1981). The use of the terms 'heterogeneous' and 'homogeneous' here derive from Georges Bataille, 'The Psychological Structure of Fascism', Allan Stoekl ed., *Georges Bataille: Visions of Excess: Selected Writings 1927–1939* (Minneapolis: University of Minnesota Press, 1985).
2. Edward G. Seidensticker, trans., *The Tale of Genji*. Eighth Edition (1985), p. 437 [hereafter 'S']. I will also cite the Helen Craig McCullough trans., *Selections from Genji and Heike* (1994), [hereafter 'M'].
3. Translation by Edwin A. Cranston, in 'Murasaki's "Art of Fiction",' *Japan Quarterly* 18 (1971), pp. 207–13, especially p. 209. Compare S. 437.
4. Tyler's translation appeared after this chapter was written, and though I have consulted it I have not made it central to this chapter, which is not, after all, concerned with the merits of translation.
5. Roland Barthes, *S/Z*, translated by Richard Howard (New York: Hill and Wang, 1970), p. 16.
6. For the arguments, including a view that Chapter 1 was written after Chapter 12, see Aileen Patricia Gatten, *The Secluded Forest: Textual Problems in the Genji Monogatari* (Ann Arbor: Michigan, University Microfilms International, 1981), pp. 257–77.
7. Shirley M. Loui, *Murasaki's Genji and Proust's Recherche: A Comparative Study* (Lewiston: East Mellen Press, 1991).
8. Haruo Shirane, *The Bridge of Dreams: A Poetics of 'The Tale of Genji'* (Stanford, California: Stanford University Press, 1987), p. 57.
9. 'The Knight of the Cart' ('Lancelot'), *Arthurian Romances* translated by Carleton W. Carroll (Harmondsworth: Penguin, 1991), p. 207.
10. I quote the comment in my *Dante and Difference: Writing in the Commedia* (Cambridge, Mass.: Cambridge University Press, 1988), p. 122. The classic statement aligning Gothic and Chaucer was that of Robert M. Jordan, *Chaucer and the Shape of Creation: The Aesthetic Possibilities of Inorganic Structure* (Cambridge: Harvard University Press, 1967).
11. Ivan Morris, *The Tale of Genji Scroll*, with an Introduction by Tokugawa Yoshinobu (Tokyo: Kodansha International, 1971), p. 142.
12. On the layout of Japanese mansions, see Appendix 1 in *The Diary of Lady Murasaki*, translated by Richard Bowring (Harmondsworth: Penguin, 1966) (hereafter cited as 'B'), pp. 68–74. Also, Ivan Morris, *The World of the Shining Prince: Court Life in Ancient Japan* (New York: Kodansha International, 1994, c1964), pp. 37–54.
13. Chrétien de Troyes, '*Cligés*', in *Arthurian Romances* (London: Dent, 1967), p. 123.
14. Chrétien de Troyes, 'Eric and Enide', ibid., p. 37.
15. Norris J. Lacy, *The Craft of Chrétien de Troyes: An Essay on Narrative Art* (Leiden: E. J. Brill, 1980), p. 67.
16. William S. Woods, 'The Plot Structure in Four Romances of Chrétien de Troyes', *Studies in Philology*, Vol. L (January 1953), Number 1, summarized by Lacy.
17. Per Nykrog, 'Two Creators of Narrative Form in Twelfth Century France: Gautier d'Arras – Chrétien de Troyes', *Speculum* 48 (1973a), pp. 266–7.
18. 'The Knight with the Lion' ('Yvain'), *Arthurian Romances*, op. cit., p. 227.
19. Here the difference with *The Tale of Genji* seems to be one of degree, for Genji tells Tamakazura that 'even in the writ which the Buddha drew from his noble heart are parables, devices for pointing obliquely at the truth. To the ignorant they may seem to operate at cross-purposes. The Great Vehicle is full of them, but the general burden is always the same' [S. 438].
20. Kumakura Chiyuki, *The Narrative Time of 'Genji monogatari'* (Ann Arbor: University Microfilms International, 1980), p. 76. See the analysis of the first chapter, pp. 76–96.
21. See also H. Richard Okada, *Figures of Resistance: Language, Poetry and Narrating in*

The Tale of Genji *and Other Mid-Heian Texts* (Durham and London: Duke University Press, 1991), p. 183. Okada discusses the 'Kiritsubo' (pp. 183–196) and his translations are critical of Seidensticker's, particularly on the question of narrative time. He argues that the present tense of the narrative is 'tenseless narrative' where 'the narrating valorizes each of its moments or instances, rather like a picture scroll or slide show, viewed frame by frame, matched with a running commentary, each moment susceptible to extensions and amplifications and also appropriate elisions' (p. 178), quoting the first paragraph of 'Kiritsubo' for this. He contrasts this with Gerard Genette's analysis of 'simultaneous narrating' – 'narrative in the present contemporaneous with the action' where Genette sees either a tendency towards the effacement of the narrator or to the narrative becoming interior monologue. Seeing this view as limited by its 'Eurocentric' tendency – which favours the subject/object dichotomy – to its usefulness in discussing a *monogatari* text, he takes the latter as a mode 'that privileges the narrating [i.e. the performative event] without becoming subjective' (p. 179). The view he is drawing on is that of Tamagami Takuya, who in 1950 proposed a view of *monogatari* coming into play through reading aloud. Tyler's comments on tense should be added: he translates into the past tense, like Seidensticker, and says: 'English lacks such a verbal mode of narrative immediacy, and translating into the present would not help, since the present is still a tense, not a mode [he takes the verbal inflection – __ as indicative of a verbal mode rather than a tense], and is in any case difficult to sustain successfully through a long narration' (Introduction, p. xxviii). See also Sano Midori's and Murakami Fuminobu's chapters of this book.
22. The theme of the criticism of the Japanese Tokugawa period, specifically Motoori Norinaga (1730–1801).
23. In 'figura', the term from Erich Auerbach, the later character / event derives greater reality from being overladen by the former. See Auerbach, *'Figura', Scenes from the Drama of European Literature*, translated by R. Mannheim (Chicago: University of Chicago Press, 1959).
24. Shirane, op. cit., p. 123.
25. The *kōi*, or Intimates, were a rank lower than that of Imperial Consort.
26. Arthur Waley, *The Life and Times of Po Chu-I* (London: Allen and Unwin, 1949), p. 44.
27. The poem is translated by Witter Brynner in Cyril Birch, compiled and edited, Donald Keene, associate ed., *Anthology of Chinese Literature* (New York: Grove Press, 1965), pp. 266–9, and by Dore J. Levy, *Chinese Narrative Poetry: The Late Han Through Tang Dynasties* (Durham: Duke University Press, 1988), pp. 129–33; and see pp. 70–5 for analysis.
28. Birch, op. cit., p. 269.
29. See also *Kokinshū: A Collection of Poems Ancient and Modern* translated and annotated by Laurel Rasplica Rodd with Mary Catherine Henkenius (Tokyo: University of Tokyo Press, 1984), no. 647, p. 235.
30. Shirane, op. cit., p. 121.
31. Jacques Derrida, *Spurs: Nietzsche's Styles*, translated by Barbara Harlow (Chicago: University of Chicago Press, 1978), pp. 123–43.
32. Freud, 'The Ego and the Id', *Penguin Freud* vol. 11 (Harmondsworth: Penguin, 1977), pp. 368–9.
33. See Brigitte Cazelles, *The Unholy Grail: A Social Reading of Chrétien de Troyes's Conte du Graal* (Stanford: Stanford University Press, 1995), p. 42.
34. This must be qualified by the magical journey Genji makes by boat to Akashi (Chapter 13), and the last ten chapters at Uji resonate with suggestions of an Other world. But these are substantial places. The other world in *Genji* is that of spirit possession: see Doris Bargen, *A Woman's Weapon: Spirit Possession in 'The Tale of Genji'* (Honolulu: University of Hawaii Press, 1997).
35. *Kokinshū*, op. cit., p. 205.

36. Lacan's essay is translated by Jeffrey Mehlman in *Yale French Studies* 48 (1972), pp. 38–72. The critique of it by Derrida, 'The purveyor of truth', *The Postcard: From Socrates to Freud and Beyond*, translated by Alan Bass (Chicago: University of Chicago Press, 1987) is the supplement to it: see John P. Muller and William J. Richardson, eds, *The Purloined Poe: Lacan, Derrida and Psychoanalytic Reading* (Baltimore: Johns Hopkins University Press, 1988). The letter (which is language) imposes a subject-position on whoever comes into contact with it, and compelling each person held by it (they think they hold the letter) to repeat the actions performed by the earlier holder. The possessor, therefore, is weakened, paralysed as to capacity for action, feminized. The implications for narrative theory which Lacan's essay serves, are that the symbolic order is constitutive for the subject: fiction demonstrates the laws of the symbolic order, which are the conditions for the possibilities of fiction, as they are conditions for the possibility of subjectivity.

37. The classic statement remains Lisa Jardine, *Still Harping on Daughters* (Brighton: Harvester Press, 1983).

38. Okada, op. cit., p. 204, reads this differently from Seidensticker: 'He is wearing layers of soft white singlets under only a loosely slung, informal court robe, and has left his collar ties dangling; lying on his side in the lamplight – most beautiful, one would want to see him as a woman.' Okada criticizes Seidensticker for missing the transformative aspect of the desire – the wish to turn Genji into a woman, which he relates to the woman authoring the text and writing for women, desiring Genji, ambivalently positioned in terms of his court-position, to be like them.

39. Freud, 'On the Universal Tendency to Debasement in the Sphere of Love', *On Sexuality: The Penguin Freud 7* (Harmondsworth: Penguin, 1977), p. 258.

40. In the original sentence no personal reference is supplied. The resemblance to the lady who died is mentioned elsewhere.

41. A good example of where Okada (op. cit., p. 193) faults Seidensticker, when he translates this as 'How deeply affecting are the ways of the heart,' showing, in his commentary, that 'something as accidental as resemblance can and often does arouse strong emotions,' so 'foregrounding the accidental at the heart of the originary'.

42. Seidensticker has 'flower or tinted leaf' [S. 16]. In this context, 'flowers' usually meant cherry blossoms.

43. No name is given here: the name appears in Chapter 9 (see Seidensticker's Note, p. 164) as a chapter title ('Heartvine'), and as the name of the lady who dies in the chapter.

44. The name derives from the office: he serves 'in the dual capacity of head chamberlain (頭) and middle captain (中将)' [M. 4].

45. Norma Field, *The Splendor of Longing in the Tale of Genji* (Princeton: Princeton University Press, 1987), p. 103.

46. The episode recalls Roland Barthes's *Camera Lucida* (New York: Hill and Wang, 1980) pp. 67–73 where Barthes finds the only adequate photograph to represent his dead mother is the Winter Gardens picture, where she is seen as a young girl with her young brother, posing as wife and husband – in a way Barthes could never have seen her in life.

47. The term Paul de Man uses in 'Autobiography as De-Facement', *The Rhetoric of Romanticism* (New York: Columbia University Press, 1984), p. 76: 'Prospopoeia is the trope of autobiography by which one's name ... is made as intelligible and memorable as a face.'

48. Okada's analysis of this chapter (op. cit., pp. 250–65) should be consulted for this.

49. Auerbach's discussion of *Yvain*, its idealism of tone, and omission of everything outside the spheres of love and arms, should be consulted; see Erich Auerbach, 'The Knight Sets Forth', *Mimesis: The Representation of Reality in Western Literature*, translated by Willard Trask (Princeton: Princeton University Press, 1953), pp. 123–42. The contrast with *Genji*'s 'representation of reality' is striking.

6

GENJI AND THE GARDENS OF MEDIEVAL ROMANCE

RICHARD STANLEY-BAKER

☙

INTRODUCTION

In *The Tale of Genji*, gardens are frequently loci for the advancement of romance, and function in some respects as gardens of love. This chapter compares the literary gardens of love in *The Tale of Genji* with traditions of medieval romance in Europe and Persia. Literature in several major cultures throughout the world reveals a common concern with love, courtship and sexual encounters during the medieval. These directions were often set in an ironic, or contrapuntal relationship with the central religious doctrines of their time; in addition, they quite frequently evoke, or ironize, gnostic ontologies of spiritual union.[1] Establishing a locus of irony with regard to the ideal form of love is found to be a common trope in these medieval works, and invites further interrogation of the subversive potential of romantic love and its literature.[2] C. S. Lewis was the first to explore this theme in 1936, and it has been much expanded by Ernst Curtius, Peter Dronke, John Fleming, A. C. Spearing, David Hult, Maria Rose Menocal, Julie Scott Meisami and others.[3] The expression of such tropes required some degree of accommodation with the dominant religions of each culture. In Europe medieval scholars were rediscovering via Arab translations and commentaries the major elements of the distant, pagan canons of Greece and Rome. Arab culture was also responding to those same classical traditions as preserved and re-interpreted by Arab scholars. And out of this blend, particularly in Muslim southern Spain, al-Andalus, the foundations of the new love literature emerged.[4]

The love literatures of the medieval showed an increasing preference for the vernacular language, as opposed to hitherto hallowed canonical languages, such as Latin, or Chinese. Japan developed a love literature couched in the vernacular language, found in the lyric verse of *waka* poems. The validation of the vernacular in the new love literatures is highlighted by Dante in *Vita nuova*, where he observes that his audience were 'ladies, for whom it was difficult to understand Latin verses'; this may be read, globally, to mean the classics or *auctoritates* of ancient tradition.[5] Read in generic terms, the object of romantic love and literary homage was a real person (not sainted, or a figure of the imagination), who was unlikely to be wooed successfully with literary homage in a canonical or classical language such as Chinese. Japan was among the first of medieval cultures to validate to a substantial degree love lyrics in the vernacular, as seen in Imperial *waka* anthologies like *Kokinshū* (905), or *Ise monogatari*.[6]

MEDIEVAL ROMANCE: GLOBAL MARKERS

In these several and distinct medieval cultures, romantic love, the central topic for romance literature, presented a potentially subversive subject, one often condemned by the religious orders of these cultures. Associated with these challenges, and possibly a form of response, is the reification and deification of the feminine, especially as seen in the increasing tendency to worship Mary as an icon of purity, or as Queen of Heaven, as seen in the works of St Bernard of Clairvaux. From Bernard to Dante, we encounter an increasingly classicized image of the feminine, one of holiness, purity and beauty. By the eleventh and twelfth centuries, feminine or feminized images also emerge from Buddhism in China and Japan, as seen in the merciful icon of the white-robed Guanyin.[7] By Dante's time the purest symbol of this nature was the white rose, symbolizing the Host and much more, as seen in *Paradiso* 1.

The poetry of romantic love is found in these cultures to be couched quite frequently in various forms of allegory, ranging from the veiled truths or '*integumenta*' of William of Conches, to the figures discussed by Dante in *Convivio*,[8] offering a religious justification for writings on romantic passion. Further, such allegory – especially when empowered by Platonic anagogy (a figure alluding to heaven, or the afterlife) – provided a sanctioned position from which to validate the discourse on and dramatization of what clerics might otherwise consider to be corrupting topics: this took the form of allegorizing or 'medievalizing' Plato, Ovid and Homer.[9] For romance writers in these medieval cultures, it was evidently problematic to write about romantic love unless such passion could be shown to be in part an anagogic 'path to divine love'.[10] Whether in medieval Persia, Europe or Japan, allegory was a favoured, at times almost necessary, literary strategy, largely, it seems, because of pressures from the dominant faiths. In effect, allegory was a key tool in the validation of medieval love literature and its romances. *The Tale of Genji* has been seen as, in some respects, a lightly veiled Buddhist allegory which ironizes the relation of *monogatari* (old tales) to truth, and provides gentle reminders of current religious canons.[11] While the *Genji* is not truly an instructive 'mirror for princes',[12] the extensive use of pervasive mists and metaphors of illusion in the final 'Uji' chapters highlights the polarizing of blindness and illusion as against vision and truth. This trope, effectively the antithetical 'symbol' codes, is presented still more dramatically in the painted *Genji Illustration Scrolls* (Tokugawa and Gotoh collections), which were themselves a significant form of reception a century or so on.[13]

The ready adoption of the vernacular as the language of love, the heart and its lyrics is widely found in the medieval in many cultures. That romance was often written 'for a woman', or an audience of 'good women', as Wolfram claims of his *Parzival*, is perhaps of more general significance.[14] In Heian Japan, we witness both the emergence into literary prominence of the vernacular in love poems (no longer confined by the clumsy Manyo script), and its somewhat subversive role as the vehicle of the new women's romance literature. A related development is that of the easy and fluid ambiguity of gender and genre in Heian narrative and poetry, as men and women write in the 'feminine' mode, or 'feminine hand' of *kana* calligraphy, which has been the subject of recent gender studies.[15]

The ironizing of vision, found in the perception of self and other, is a further significant trope in medieval romance, which invites cross-cultural, global enquiry across disparate literatures and cultures. The playful problematizing of 'truth' in twelfth century medieval French romance is most typically shown in the multiple interpretations of truth in the re-narration of the Tristan story in diverse editions.[16]

The *Roman de la Rose* opens with a light-hearted debate on the value of dreams as a source of truth (*songe et mensonge*: dream and lies):

> *Maintes genz cuident qu'en songe N'ait se fable non et mensonge. Mais on puet tel songe songier Qui ne sont mie mençongier, Ainz sont apré bien aparant.*
>
> (Many are those who say that there is nothing in dreams but fables and lies, but one may have dreams which are not deceitful, whose import becomes quite clear afterward.)[17]

This resonates with the ironies found in the 'Fireflies' chapter where Genji ruminates on *monogatari* (old tales):

> To conclude that they [*monogatari*] are all empty lies (*soragoto*) gainsays the heart of the matter (*koto no kokoro*).[18]

Genji, in tones worthy of Macrobius, continues to point out that 'tales' have meaning just as some Buddhist teachings provide 'parables', containing hidden meanings:

> Put in its best light, it turns out that all things, no matter what they are, do not amount to nothing.[19]

This is a nicely Buddhistic mediation, similar to that found in European thought where veils (*integument*a) and allegorizing were a core trope in medieval tradition.

The twelfth century Persian poet Nizami highlighted themes of romantic love in many of his great poetic romances; first, its virtues in his *Khusraw and Shîrîn*; later in an ill-starred romance in *Laylî and Majnūn*; and further in the philosophy of a world conqueror in his *Iskandarnâma* (Book of Alexander). In his greatest work, the *Haft Paykar*, love stories provide 'a complex allegory of spiritual and moral growth'.[20] All his five great poems are seen to be redolent with the theme of human perfectibility, and the concept of the Perfect Man; the Prophet Muhammed was so envisaged by Sufi mystics such as 'Abd al Qâdir al-Jîlânî (d. 1166), founder of the Qâdiriyya Sufi order. Nizami's romance has seven main allegorical figures, the Seven Domes, each representing a story told by the princess of that realm, and each contributing to the spiritual progress of the listening prince, Bahrâm. The rich and erotic imagery of the gardens in these realms plays an important role in the allegory, with frequent, mildly ironizing reference to the perfections and sensual pleasures of the Quranic Paradise. The allegorical gardens here are of particular interest for comparative studies, whether literary or art historical.

A patronage and audience composed largely of high-ranking women and their confidantes is a feature of the privileged salons that is shared alike in medieval France, and Japan, when it comes to 'old tales'. In Persia, Nizami's tales, like those of Scheherazade in which wisdom and delight are alike conveyed, are told by women, and against a background of canonical authorities' condemnation of 'fanciful tales', traditionally considered as 'misleading falsehoods and of no moral value'.[21] Further, the authorial interventions in the *Genji* and their denials of full knowledge of their own fictions, this the very stuff of performed narrative, are among the diverse ways in which these romance traditions share a new and often subtle ambivalence with regard to subject and self.

Another form of 'medievalism' in romance narrative is found in the distancing of identity in Heian narratives, their resistance to being irrevocably pinned to a particular speaker, which is achieved by constant manipulation of particles, suffixes and relativizing stratagems; this serves to undermine modernizing readings and translations (like that of Edward Seidensticker, and translations into modern Japanese), all of which assert a will to 'novelize' the text with a clear sense of who is speaking or thinking at any one point in the novel; this despite the fact that modernist Western writing has familiarized us with the concept of 'free indirect discourse' and the subject dissolved in dialogism. Tomiko Yoda says of Bakhtin, very relevantly, that in rejecting the grammatically defined unity of the 'sentence' he also 'staunchly refused to reduce the utterance to an act of an individual subject'.[22] Modernist texts of the West, like Western medieval texts, may be said to operate in some interesting ways like Heian texts, in their erasing the possibility of saying who speaks, and of attributing a subject within the sentence. Intertextuality is but another way of putting the same point: we do not know who is speaking, because the text is full of other texts, which destroy the imagined unity of the single text and the single speaker.[23]

Genji's gardens of love are here compared to that of the *Roman de la Rose* and its genre; in both traditions romance narrative strategies, which subvert stability of vision or perception and ironize notions of 'truth' and 'tales', are common concerns: this is perhaps nowhere more strikingly illustrated than in the *Roman*'s enigmatic Fountain of Narcissus, discussed below.

Deferral of closure is found to be central to the romances of Chrétien de Troyes; in Wolfram's *Parzival*; and in Guillaume de Lorris' first *Roman de la Rose*, as proposed by David Hult.[24] The *Genji* also invites comparison in these terms as regards the loose ending of the tale,[25] where Ukifune appears to have drowned but reappears in the last chapter – protected, however, by monks from further transgressive attention or tragic infatuation on the part of the two male contenders, Kaoru and Niou. As David Hult has argued, with regard to Guillaume's first part of the *Roman de la Rose*, deferral was integral to the narration of love's story in early medieval texts. Guillaume de Lorris gives a hint of how the hidden truth of the *Roman's* dream legend will eventually be apparent:

> *La verité, qui est couverte,*
> *Vos en sera lores toute aperte,*
> *Quant espondre m'orroiz le songe,*
> *Car il n'i a mot de mençonge.* Roman: 2071–74.

[The truth, which is hidden, will be quite open to you when you hear me explain the dream, for it doesn't contain a lying word.]

These commandments of the God of Love to the Lover assert that revelation will only be apparent to those who are prepared to wait for the end of the story:

> I tell you that he who will hear the end of the dream can learn a great deal more about the games of Love, provided that he wishes to wait while I tell the tale in French and explain the dream's significance. Roman: 2063–70[26]

Lee Paterson has remarked that Guillaume's *politesse* 'in not presuming to project the end of the story', is a condition of the author's reliance on a personification allegory which promises, but does not in fact culminate in, clarified vision; the vision propounded makes of revealed essences mere shadows, a vision like that of the dark mirror of St Paul. The image of vision presented in the *Roman*'s Narcissus fountain implies that the first *Roman* seems to hope for historic rather than poetic fulfilment; namely, Guillaume hopes against hope for erotic fulfilment with his patroness; hence, his garden is a *prison amoureuse*, not unlike the garden in the White Dome story of Nizami's romance.[27] This tends to suggest that deferral and reluctance to impose closure in love lyrics, as also found in *Genji*'s embedded *waka* poetry and its often refractive character, is integral to the genre.

HISTORIC GARDENS AND ROMANCE'S *DIFFÉRENCE*

In Japan, there is a vast volume of valid documentary data, which together with well preserved sites, which together closely inform our notions of Japan's medieval historic gardens. Such gardens are invaluable markers throwing light on the cultural codes so deftly woven into romance narratives. In both Europe and Persia, by contrast, there is an extreme paucity of reliable and relevant data on the layout and contents of medieval gardens. Europe offers a few exceptions, mainly those of the Islamic gardens of al-Andalus, such as those at the

Alhambra in Granada, or Seville. In Kyoto today, there are remnants at the Kajūji imperial villa garden (Fig. 6-2) of a musicians' island, which would formerly have had an access bridge and other large islands not dissimilar to the layout of mansions like the historic, now lost, Tōsanjō Mansion, or the Hōjūji mansion (Fig. 6-3).[28] With the aid of such sites and their data, it is possible in the case of Japan to perform relatively close readings of the *différence* between the historic and the romance text layouts, and thereby examine more closely romance strategies; these reveal much regarding ideology, myth, allegory, poetics and the loading of the semic codes, as seen associated with rocks, islands, streams, flowering trees and flowers. This is not truly feasible in the case of Europe, Persia or related regions, where one is left with little other than an already transformed, ideologically thematized and schematic image in manuscript paintings and miniatures. Orhan Pamuk, in his novel *My Name is Red*, has painted a compelling image of the cultural and religious issues faced by Islamic illustrators of the sixteenth century, at a point when the 'Frankish' Western style was considered blasphemous.[29] We would be foolish to rely too heavily on paintings such as that of Babur directing the design of his Garden of Fidelity at Kabul in 1504; however, with the aid of the *Memoirs of Babur* (*Babur-Nama*), which are specific about the locale, size and layout, a clearer idea of such *différence* emerges.[30]

The Tale of Genji, and the twelfth century *Illustrations Scrolls* which inform its later reception, invite close study of the *différence* between historic gardens, the gardens of the romance text and those presented in the *Illustrations*. This fortunate circumstance allows the comparative literary and art historian to formulate notions of strategies in romance texts, their reception (in paintings), and the manner in which both continuously adapt and transform the material from the historic loci to which both refer. Murasaki herself offers some quasi-historic evidence in her diary about the Tsuchimikado mansion of Fujiwara Michinaga (966–1028), where she lived for some time, and the role of the garden scene, and setting in which formal and more informal social rituals took place.[31]

The literary gardens of *Genji*, are often metaphors, or synechdoches, of the beauty or anguish of the women they contain, and the bewildering experiences of lovers therein; they offer a cornucopia of poetic material adaptable to stories of romantic love. The literary gardens of *Genji*, in this regard not unlike their counterparts in the Persian tradition, most notably the *Haft Paykar* (1197), provide metaphors for a subtle blend of sensory and sensual pleasure, combined with a Scheherezade-like, courtly deferral of closure. A further trope of present sensory satisfaction, associated in the European tradition with the *locus amoenus* or earthly paradise, is also found quite frequently in the romance strategies of the *Genji*. The *Tale* at times evokes a sense of idyll, and 'mythic' time, a trope comparable to that found in late Latin literature and medieval European romance. The physical framing of the romance narrative, which in the *Tale* consists of relatively frail fences, which shield and enclose the female from her or her lover's transgressive desire, provides an ever-present, often enigmatic metaphor of the dilemma of the lover, or the target of love.

Literary gardens of love in these medieval cultures, despite the wide divergence in their cultural heritage and religious canons, may thus be seen to have shared common cause in the construction of desire and its fulfilment. Medieval romance literature in these cultures seems to have favoured literary strategies ironizing and problematizing 'truth', often in delicate, subtle and contraptuntal tension with the religious canons of their time and region. The prime points of comparison are here taken from the eleventh century (*Genji*), its twelfth century reception in the form of *The Tale of Genji Illustrations Scrolls*, and twelfth century romance in Persia (*Haft Paykar*) and France, in the romances of Chrétien de Troyes and related re-tellings (*remaniements*), and in other European medieval romances.

THE GARDENS OF *GENJI*

The gardens of Heian love poetry and romance literature, emerging from eighth-century love literature, such as the short poems (*tanka*) of Ōtomo Yakamochi, feature in hosts of Heian *waka* poems. Their flowery realms, often metaphors of desire on the part of lovers, fenced in the women whose image they enhance; the frailty of their defences was easily breached by roguish heroes like Ariwara no Narihira (*Tales of Ise*), or the fictional Genji, and his rivals or progeny, usually in the shades of night. On verandas overlooking gardens, young men would demonstrate their superior cultural achievements in poetry, calligraphy or music; their skills proclaimed and promoted their right to romance, sexual affairs, and even procreation, with the enclosed but nonetheless relatively independent ladies of rank.

Although associated with feminine enclosure, what I here term the 'enclosed garden' of Heian romance was commonly associated with aristocratic sexual adventure for those of appropriate social rank. In Japan, as in Europe, what this medieval game required was evidence of noble birth, noble character, high rank and respectable cultural accomplishments: in a word, eligibility. The medieval Japanese enclosed garden was – in fiction and in fact – a region associated with privileged sexual adventure. Further, as a form of feminine enclosure, the garden provided a wealth of lyric metaphors of the beauty, elegance and desirability of the ladies veiled by its shades: the garden became one of the cultural codes of its time.[32]

In the 'The Broom Tree' chapter, Genji and his young friends discuss various escapades. The guard officer tells how one bright moonlit autumn night he, and his fellow adventurer, went out and, on the way, caught sight of an opportunity to indulge their sportive natures:

> One beautifully moonlit night in the tenth month ... You could see the lake through a break in the garden wall, and it seemed a shame to go straight past a house favoured even by the moon [reflecting in the lake], so I got out as well. He must have arranged it all with her beforehand, because he was excited when he sat down on the veranda, I suppose it was, of the gallery near the gate. For some time he watched the moon. The chrysanthemums had all turned very nicely, and the

autumn leaves flitting by on the wind were really very pretty. Taking a flute from
the fold of his robe, he began to play and to sing snatches of 'You will have shade',
and so on, while she accompanied him expertly on a fine-toned *wagon* [Japanese
koto] that she had all ready and tuned.[33]

And so things progressed.

Such scenes lend themselves to comparison with the 'gardens of love' of
medieval European romance, usually found as an enclosed garden, or *hortus
conclusus*. In *Cligés*, Chrétien de Troyes describes the orchard of young Fénice:

> In the early summer, when flowers blossom and trees leaf out and when little birds
> make merry, gaily singing their songs, it happened that Fénice heard the nightin-
> gale sing one morning ...
>
> She stepped through the door into the pleasant and delightful orchard. In the
> middle of the orchard stood a grafted tree, covered with leaves and flowers, with a
> wide-spreading top. The branches were trained into a sort of bower, hanging down
> and nearly touching the ground, except that the upper trunk from which they
> sprang grew straight and tall. It was all that Fénice could want!

The imagery ironizes the Garden of Eden and the Tree of Knowledge.

> Beneath the green grass grew fair and soft, and even when the sun was at its hottest
> at noon, no ray could penetrate the bower, so skilfully had John trained and
> arranged the branches. Fénice went there for her repose, and by day they set up her
> bed beneath the tree where the lovers had their joy and pleasure.

The bliss of Adam and Eve in Eden is evoked:

> The orchard was surrounded by high walls connected to the tower and no one
> could enter there without first passing through the tower. Fénice was very
> contented, with nothing to disrupt her pleasure and all desires fulfilled now that
> she could embrace her lover whenever she wished beneath the leaves and flowers.[34]

It is an enclosed, earthly paradise, a latter day *locus amoenus*, in which all the
senses were completely satisfied.[35] In *Cligés*, the narrative rapidly proceeds to
the erotic and voyeuristic discovery by Bertrand of the couple 'side by side,
completely nude'.[36]

Genji's gardens, suggestive of seduction and romance, are a venue for the
promotion of romance, though sexual adventure is pursued indoors. The
gardens are nonetheless powerful metaphors of sexual freshness and allure,
which incite desire on the part of the lovers and their voyeuristic audience
alike.

Enclosure itself is ironized, in 'The Green Branch' ('Sakaki') chapter of the
Genji, where Genji visits Lady Rokujō in her temporary Shintō shrine:

> Within a low, frail, brushwood fence stood a scattering of board-roofed buildings,
> very lightly built. [T. 194]

This sacred enclosure, not properly a garden, but a haven intended to protect
the incumbent against evil and demons, and keep adventurers like Genji out, is
directly symbolic of the vulnerability of the lady located in a rustic context on
the moor, protected only lightly by priests. The passage gently ironizes the
social 'enclosures', normally mansions, in which ladies of her rank were

contained. The evergreen branch, *sakaki* (*cleyera ochnacea*), used in Shintō ritual, highlights the cultural codes of ritual purity, the virginity of shrine maidens and the holy. Lady Rokujō, though no virgin, here enjoys a metonymic (virtual) virginity as mother of the new shrine maiden at Ise. Once Genji is on the veranda, he slips a fragrant branch of *sakaki* to her under the blinds, versifying in sexual metaphors which reinforce the semic codes of sacral virginity:

> This is the constant colour that led me to penetrate the sacred paling ... [T. 194]

Genji is at first rebuked but, as the lady's resistance weakens, there is mention again of the setting moon, symbolic of her weakness, or inability to resist him. At length, she is seduced.

Medieval romance, globally, makes extensive use of various forms of voyeuristic manipulation of its readers or audiences. In *The Tale of Genji*, peeping (*kaimami*) through blinds and fences, primarily by male protagonists on the activities of the ladies, a common prelude to romance, encourages readers to share the adventurer's 'view' of events. Kaoru, hearing of the two daughters of Prince Hachi tucked away in the remote mansion at Uji, decides to investigate in 'The Lady at the Bridge' ('Hashihime') chapter (Fig. 6-4). Hearing a *koto* playing, Kaoru bribes a guard to let him in:

> The Captain [Kaoru] cracked open the door that seemed to lead through the fence and peered in through prettily moonlit mist to where the women sat, beyond the rolled-up blinds ... One of the women within, partially hidden behind a pillar, had a *biwa* [lute] before her and was toying with the plectrum. Just then the moon, which had been clouded, burst forth brilliantly. 'You can call out the moon with this, too,' she said, 'though it is not a fan.'[37] Her face as she peered outside was wonderfully fresh and appealing.
>
> ... their casual, bantering exchange struck him as more engagingly attractive than anything he had imagined. When he heard young gentlewomen read old tales (*monogatari*) with scenes like this, he always assumed disappointedly that nothing of the kind could actually happen, but there were after all such corners in real life! He was already losing his heart to them. [T. 837]

Playing on the *soragoto* (falsity) of 'old tales', we find vision again in question, as so often in these medieval romances. *Genji*'s voyeuristic manipulations of subject and self and their inherent 'gaze' issues have been extensively studied, with regard to the image of the female as surveyed object, and surveyor of herself;[38] others have stressed the trope of transgressive appropriation in the furtive glimpse (*nozokimi*).[39] Edith Sarra has observed that it can happen that both the male hero figure, and the women being viewed 'are mediated and enclosed by the ironic perspective of the narrating voice who reveals all of them to ... [Murasaki Shikibu's] by now self-consciously voyeuristic readers'. Further, there are numerous issues highlighting the gendering of the gaze and narrator: here, as Edith Sarra puts it, there is 'a tradition in which women are situated on both sides of the keyhole'.[40]

This tradition resonates closely with the voyeurism of European medieval romance narratives, where manipulation of viewpoint and subject through a voyeuristic framing of forbidden sexual activities in the garden, or inner household, is a very familiar trope. 'Looking' and 'listening' constructed by the narrative, or narrator, with regard to 'secret' watchers and listeners, places the audience in a privileged position, hybridizes viewpoint, and ironizes the relationship of 'story' to truth, introducing a wealth of critical problematics.[41] In *The Romance of Tristan*, King Mark of Cornwall, the lawful husband of Queen Iseut (the ill-fated lover of Tristan), takes a vantage point overlooking the garden in Tintagel Castle so that he can spy on Tristan and his queen:

> The King remained at the entrance of a large garden ... for without a doubt this garden stretched all the way as far as the Queen's chambers ...[42]

The narrator walks his audience into the adventure of passing 'unseen' and 'unheard' through the spring scenery until with the King we reach a point in one of the rooms from which both enjoy a view over a large part of the garden; the King affirms that he had found the best possible position and that the Queen could do nothing that he would not see.

Later in the romance, King Mark, consumed by mortal hatred of Tristan, hides himself up a tree in the garden in Tintagel Castle, the better to catch the lovers in the act. Here again the narrator shares a voyeuristic perspective with his audience:

> And if anyone should ask me where they [the lovers] used to meet, since the tower was so well guarded that Tristan would not have got in without the greatest difficulty, I would say that they saw each other in a garden which was at the foot of the tower. It was a large and beautiful garden with many different kinds of trees; but amongst all the others there was a laurel, so splendid and so tall a tree that in the whole of Cornwall one could not find such a lovely tree. Beneath this tree it was very pleasant, and the two lovers often came there at night time when everyone was resting, and there they would talk together and do much of what they wished to do. [C. 305]

The laurel tree, analogous to the Tree of Knowledge in Genesis, is here eroticized by Chrétien, as did Chaucer and other medieval English writers. King Mark climbed up this tree and, since 'the moon was bright and beautiful, and lit up the whole garden', he could see everything, or thinks he has total knowledge. The readership is told, however, that he was spotted by the lovers individually as they came under the tree (of false Knowledge, for Mark), with the result that all King Mark hears is their plaintive speeches protesting their innocence.[43] The occasionally omniscient perspective of the narrative voice intervenes to provide a still more voyeuristic viewpoint.[44] These narrative strategies of twelfth century French romance provide interesting points of comparison with the plays on voice and distance that characterize the *Genji*.

In Murasaki Shikibu's romance, a fictive, authorial voice establishes a separate presence within the text, which both augments the figural strategy of 'peeping from behind the scenes' and provides a 'view' that further pluralizes the text, a feature which is subject to further narrative manipulation in the illustrations of *The Tale of Genji*.[45] These tropes play an important role in ironizing narrative truth and fiction, and are even used to defer closure, as we shall see below.

The European garden of love is nowhere more richly celebrated than in the allegories and ironies of the *Roman de la Rose* by Guillaume de Lorris and Jean de Meun.[46] Here the garden in which romance develops is soon presented, as an earthly paradise: A. C. Spearing has called this 'a place of the mind, a universal psychic archetype'.[47] The visionary imagery of this demi-paradise derives from a mélange of scriptural sources, including The Garden of Eden, the Apocalypse, Solomon's *Song of Songs* and literary traditions of Late Antiquity, where the enclosed garden (*hortus conclusus*) is celebrated in distinctly sexual allegory:

> 4:12 A garden inclosed is my sister, my spouse; a spring shut up, a fountain sealed
> ...
> 4:15 A fountain of gardens, a well of living waters, and streams from Lebanon.
> 4:16 ... Let my beloved come into his garden, and eat his pleasant fruits.[48]

This lyric tradition was a rich topos mixed with reference to classical sources, among them, Homer, Theocritus and Virgil, in which the image of an earthly paradise (*locus amoenus*) is identifiable as a garden largely Mediterranean in character, bearing fruit all year long.[49] The most classic topoi appear early in Greek and Latin epics. The gardens of Alcinous, in *Odyssey* V, are probably the earliest of this kind:

> Outside the courtyard, near the entrance, is a garden of four acres, with a fence running round, this way and that. Here are planted tall thriving trees – pears, pomegranates, apples with glistening fruit, sweet figs, rich olives. The fruit of all these never fails or flags all the year round, winter or summer; here the west wind is always breathing – some fruits it brings to birth, some to ripeness.[50]

In the Greek tradition, the garden of happiness and pleasure was frequently presented as close to the abodes of gods such as Zeus, Phoebus, or Aphrodite. In the *Aeneid* [VI, 638 ff.], Virgil presents a vision of Elysium:

> *Devenere locos laetos et amoena virecta*
> *Fortunatorum nemorum sedesque beatas.*
>
> To joyous sites they came and lovely lawns,
> Blest seats, in woods which no misfortune scathes. [Cu. 192]

A poem of Petronius [*carm.* 131] presents a similar image, as an ideal locus for romantic love:

> *Dignus amore locus; testis silvestris aedon*
> *Atque urbana Procne, quae circum gramina fusae*
> *Et mollae violas cantu sua rura colebant.*

> The place was fit for love: Witness the wood-haunting nightingale and the town-haunting swallow both, who, flitting over the grass and tender violets, beautified the place with their singing. [Cu. 195–6]

Ironizing these traditions, Guillaume de Lorris opens the *Roman de la Rose*, with a dream evoking Macrobius, the famed authority on dreams, then soon afterwards describes the garden into which the Lover is introduced as an earthly paradise (Fig. 6-1):

Then I entered into the garden ... and, when I was inside, I was happy and gay and full of joy. Believe me, I thought that I was truly in the earthly paradise. So delightful was the place that it seemed to belong to the world of spirit, for, as it seemed to me then, there was no paradise where existence was so good as it was in that garden which so pleased me ...

[It was a] ... completely straight, regular square, as long as it was wide. Along the brooks and banks of the clear, lively fountains, sprang the thick, short grass. There one could couch his mistress as though on a feather bed, for the earth was sweet and moist on account, since as much grass as possible grew there.[51]

While the square format suggests a lineage related to the pre-Islamic *chahar bagh* format of Persia, and to the Old Persian word *paradaēza* (in Greek, *paradeisos* from which we get 'paradise'), it may be worth observing, for the sake of *différence*, that designs like the one described in the *Roman*, existed in historic medieval gardens in parts of France, as seen in the excavations at Plessis-Grimoult in Calvados, and that this scheme is often pictured in medieval manuscript illustrations.[52] The excavated, fortified garden of this French site covered an area of about 10 metres by 12.7 metres. Further, the format of a turreted, enclosed garden suggests affinity with the enclosed, fortified gardens of the Roman era, an example of which survives complete with its turrets at the villa of Settefinestre (first century AD).[53] The element of fortification doubtless satisfied practical needs not unlike those suggested by the evidence of moated gardens found in medieval England (like that at St Cross in Winchester) where defence against intrusion by wild animals, no less than casual intruders and thieves, would have been a consideration.[54]

A common feature of the European model, seen in manuscript illustrations of the Biblical Garden of Eden such as the *Très Riches Heures du Duc de Berry*, was a Gothic fountain, evoking the *fons clausa* of *The Song of Songs*. Such fountains were frequently a feature of historic European medieval enclosed pleasure gardens, and were clearly derived from their Arab ancestors in al-Andalus, to say nothing of earlier Islamic and pre-Islamic traditions. Here, the blend of classical and medieval themes appears to have been as important a feature of the real life *horti conclusi* as those of their literary heritage. Physical sources of this imagery have been traced back through medieval examples in Islamic architecture in Seville and the Alhambra at Granada, and to records of ancient Persian palace gardens like that of Xenophon.[55]

Le Roman de la Rose features its own variant on Ovid in the enigmatic Fountain of Narcissus. The text has an account of what are at times a pair of crystals, and at others singular, by which device Guillaume de Lorris allows the Lover to perceive the entire garden at a glance, and pursue his headlong course towards the chosen 'rose' of his passion: this, as Hult has observed, provides a finely problematized, and ironized locus of uncertainty with regard to vision, truth and subjectivity, and presents challenges to its readers on presumed assumptions regarding self and other. This trope of doubt with regard to the perception of truth and delusion, is widely found in the love stories of the European medieval, and, of course, in the *Genji*: witness the moments of self-reflective 'understanding' or appropriation of responsibility on the part of the

Shining Prince, as the consequences of his amours are foregrounded in refractive manners. Most famous among them is the love affair of Kashiwagi and the Third Princess, which reminds Genji of the unfortunate consequences of his romance with his own father's consort, which gave birth to Emperor Reizei; the *Illustrations* stress this irony, as Genji looks at the face of the illegitimate baby Kaoru, whose face he fears may resemble its true father, Kashiwagi (see *Suzumushi II*). Genji sees what is both not his child, yet as 'his' child reflects directly his moral errors. As Hult has put it, with regard to Narcissus's vision in the *Roman*:

> The Lover sees both the reflective surface and the revealing profundity, the image and shadow, and it is perhaps this dual projection that brings out the truth of his being, the soul.[56]

The mystery of the Fountain of Narcissus highlights the ambiguity, perhaps above all, the instability of the Lover's perception of either self, or other. It is by no means a *speculum*, or mirror that tells the truth of the world, but rather an instrument which places in jeopardy such a notion, and raises issues proper to fiction itself, and to the illusionary perceptions of one who falls in love. So too, the mind of Genji, as his world is revealed to him, is drawn into speculations on truth and reality.

By contrast, the literary gardens of Nizami's medieval Persian romance provide directly allegorical veils, which by turns hide and reveal truth, highlighting the blind lust of the lover who finds himself engrossed in passion in these gardens. The rich and fragrantly erotic gardens of Nizami's *Haft Paykar* (completed 1197), which are surrounded by high walls, include rose gardens, fountains, mirror-like pools, and the constant sense of an earthly and sensual paradise, to Western eyes more exotic by far than those of European romances.[57] In the final 'White Dome' story of this cycle, the garden, here belonging to a wise and chaste man, is an Iranian paradise garden:

> He had a garden like Iram,
> that gardens circled, like a shrine ...
> Its four walls, carefully designed,
> were smooth and solid all around.
> Its buildings to the moon rose high;
> no way therein for Evil Eye.[58]

The master, finding the garden closed one day at the time of noonday prayer, and hearing the sound of music and song from within, breaks in,

> ... so that he might watch,
> and dance among them, Sufi-like;
> That he might to this music listen
> (pretending to inspect the garden),
> See who was making this uproar,
> how fared the garden and the gardener. [M. 219]

However, the 'jasmine-breasted maids' who are keeping watch on the garden proceed to beat him thoroughly as a 'garden-violator', but finally recognize him as the owner, and make amends. Later, through a hole in the wall:

> ... the master spied
> rosy-faced maids with narrow eyes.
> On every side were roses strewn:
> sweet-pomegranate-breasts, and limbs
> Of silver had those maids, who lit
> the eyes' lamps; sweeter than ripe fruit ...
> Amid that garden's verdure was
> a grassy mead by a cypress grove. [M. 221–222]

He spies on the maidens who come to the pool and there swim naked (Fig. 6-5), and becomes infatuated with one of them named Bakht (Fortune); in the course of trying to take her, several incidents wreak disappointment on his passion; finally, as he submits to moral law and makes her his lawful wife, he wins his prize. The allegory of love in Nizami's poetic masterpiece, though far more direct and pointed than that found in *Genji*, nonetheless highlights the common dilemmas of these adventurers and the risks and disappointments they encounter.

In Europe, Chaucer (circa 1340–1400) made extensive and satirical use of the French tradition of romance, and the bawdy *fabliau* stories; these account for much of the raucous and delightful humour in the *Canterbury Tales*.[59] Among them, the *Merchant's Tale* is a hilarious satire of the Garden of Love of the *Roman de la Rose*, which Chaucer had himself rendered into English. Here, the rich but ugly old man, Januarie, has married his choice lady May; 'he kisseth hire ful ofte; with thikke brustles of his berd [beard] unsofte, Lyk to the skyn of houndfissh, sharp as brere [briar] ...' and for his '... fresshe May,'

he made a gardyn, walled al with stoon;	[stone]
So fair a gardyn woot I nowher noon.	[know]
For out of doute, I verraily suppose	
That he that wrote the Romance of the Rose	
Ne koude of it the beautee well devyse	[could not imagine its beauty]
Ne Priapus ne mighte nat suffise,	
Though he be god of gardyns, for to telle	
The beautee of the gardyn and the welle	[well]
That stood under a laurer alwey grene.	[laurel tree]
And whan he wolde paye his wyf her dette	[marital debt]
In sumer seson, thider wolde he go,	[thither]
And May his wife, and no wight but they two;	
And thinges which that were nat doon abedde,	
He in the garden parfourmed hem and spedde.	[speedily]
And in this wyse, many a murye day,	[merry]
Lyved this Januarie and fresshe May.	
[R. 163–164; ll. 2029–37, ll. 2047–54]	

Later, while her lover, Damyan, is up a fruit tree, she and her now blind husband, Januarie, come into the garden, and she expresses her burning desire to eat the 'peres' on the pear tree:

'Now sire', quod she, 'for aughte that may betyde,	
I moste han of the peres that I see,	[have, pears]

>   Or I moot dye, so soore longeth me
>   To eten of the smale peres greene.'
>   [ll. 2330–33; R. 167]

This imagery, based loosely on *The Song of Songs* ('As an apple tree among the trees, so is my lover among men')[60] is mirrored in Middle English lyrics, which lightly play on the sexual metaphor:

>   I have a newe garden,
>   and newe is begunne;
>   Swych another garden
>   know I not under sunne.
>   In the middes of my garden
>   is a perer set,   [pear-tree][61]

In Chaucer's *fabliau*, the wanton merchant's wife then climbs up on the back of her husband Januarie into the tree, and makes love with her Damyan in the tree, at which point Pluto gives her husband back his sight. Undone, yet quite undaunted, she regales him with the story, that she did it only in order to help her Januarie regain his sight and, 'God woote, I dide it with ful good entente.'

Chaucer's literary contestation of sexual morality was not limited to garden or otherwise 'natural' settings. His roster of characters includes the devout and courtly 'cok, highte Chauntecleer', who was a valiant servant of Venus, the 'goddesse of plesaunce', and that, 'More for delyt than world to multiply' [R. 253]. Chaucer seems constantly to be mediating the contested territory of love and its stories, much of which was based in the raucous, free-wheeling bawdiness of the Ovidian tradition, while at the same time validating the ecclesiastics on sexuality and romantic love.[62]

Another aspect of this philosophical, and one might add, highly medieval, literary contest over the domains of love is found in the meticulous courtliness exhibited by the Gawain poet, in *Gawain and the Green Knight*, where Gawain, as 'nobility' and 'virtue', triumphs over the seductive behaviour of his host's lady: the story, a lurid and tangible metaphor for courtly love. Gawain triumphs, but only just, and with a clear acknowledgement of human vulnerability on the part of the noble hero.[63]

ENCHANTMENT AND DANGER IN THE GARDEN

Genji has many gardens of infatuation, as seen in the chapters 'Bamboo River' and 'Lady at the Bridge'. There are no gardens of magical enchantment, however, as in the European tradition where we find the theme of a magic, or enchanted, garden with walls of air. A magic horn, called 'Joy of the Court' (*Joie de la Cour*) and possibly related to Celtic traditions of the Horn of Bran, was hidden in just such an enchanted garden in *Érec et Énide* by Chrétien de Troyes (circa 1170):

> Around the garden the only wall or palisade was one of air; yet by black magic the garden was enclosed on all sides with air as though it were ringed with iron, so that nothing could enter except at one single place.[64]

The antecedents for such an idea were quite ancient; the garden of the enchantress, first found in gardens such as that of Calypso in Homer, re-emerges in the enchanted gardens of the *Orlando* romances of Boiardo and Ariosto, where passion and the madness of infatuation are associated with powers beyond human control.[65]

Genji's gardens, however, are mainly loci of a sanctioned social order, of care and maintenance, or the lack of it. They are set in contrast to the 'wild', or that which lies outside the capital city, where fearful or strange things were to be found.[66]

THE ENCLOSED GARDEN OF JAPANESE ROMANCE

The enclosed, or courtyard, gardens in the *Genji* match in many respects the literary functions of their European counterpart, the *hortus conclusus*. Like the locus of the *Roman*, they are walled off realms of the feminine, of adventure, risk and privileged cultural performance, which offer routes to courtship, romance and erotic consummation.

A garden of amorous temptation is presented in 'Evening Mist', where the young Yūgiri courts the widow of Kashiwagi. The enclosure here is light, elegant, and a metaphor for what may be easily breached by transgressive amorous adventure. The locale is a rustic and remote mountain villa.

> Sunset was approaching, mist beautifully veiled the sky, and the mountain shadows seemed to dim, while everywhere cicadas sang and pinks gracefully nodded their pretty colours along the fence.[67] The flowers in the near garden bloomed in bright profusion to cooling water sounds, while the pines sighed like a forest in the mournful mountain wind; and when the bell rang in new monks to take up the perpetual scripture reading for the old, the voices of both blended a moment to awesome effect. [T. 721]

The scene described is a front garden, usually set in Heian mansions on the southern side, complete with blooming flowers and a babbling brook (*yarimizu*). The author sets the scene for romance with the evocative sounds of an autumn night:

> The night had grown late, and a mournful wind was blowing. Cricket songs, a stag's belling, the noise of the waterfall – all blended to such wild and stirring effect that the dullest simpleton would have lain sleepless under these skies, for the shutters were still up, and the setting moon that hung above the rim of the mountains gave the scene a quality too poignant not to call forth tears. [T. 723]

Yūgiri applies all his charms but, despite the overwhelming atmosphere of romance, the lady resists, so eventually he leaves under cover of the morning mists.

In the 'Bamboo River' ('Takekawa') chapter, we find the young lieutenant, Kurōdo no Shōshō, peeking through blinds on the scene of the daughters of Tamakazura at his residence. Here is a *Genji* garden of infatuation: the setting is a courtyard garden, set adjacent to one of the wings of the main building:

The third month came. Once the cherries were in bloom, falling petals clouded the sky;[68] at such a glorious time of year, for young ladies who lived a secluded life,[69] there would be nothing wrong with sitting out near the veranda.

  Her daughters must then have been eighteen or nineteen. Both were delightful in person and looks. The elder was so vivid, stylish and proud that one felt she would indeed be wasted on a commoner. She fairly exuded charm in her timely choice of a cherry blossom long dress and a *kerria* rose layering, and her deportment suggested dignity and intelligence, and all the grace of spring willow fronds. Yet despite the tall, slender poise of her figure and her air of graver depth, many felt it was the elder who conveyed the most exquisite appeal.

  The forehead line and sweep of their hair presented a lovely picture as they faced each other at Go, and the Fujiwara Adviser sat beside them to referee. [T. 811, adapted]

The *Genji Illustration Scrolls* present this scene as a view of a gallery garden (*Bamboo River II*: Fig. 6-6); here, as fellow voyeurs, we are accorded a peeping Tom view (*sukimi*) into this charming scene. The veranda looks out on a courtyard garden completely enclosed by *watadono* galleries.[70] In the centre of the scene is the ebulliently flowering cherry tree, a metaphor for the collective charms and sexual allure of the young women. Gallery gardens of this kind were common in historic Heian mansions, and *Genji* features a good number since the women of the household were often to be found there.[71]

In 'The Eastern Cottage' ('Azumaya'), Ukifune moves into the Nijō mansion where Nakanokimi lives with Niou; she is found located in rooms overlooking an enclosed gallery garden, with a flowery *yarimizu* brook running through it:

> She was leaning on an armrest near the veranda, gazing out at the lovely little garden before her, enclosed by the gallery, with its profusion of flowers in many colours and its tall rocks all along the brook. [T. 990]

The enclosed garden imagery here augments, metonymically, the beauty, sexuality and eligibility (as a target of romantic love) of the young woman. While such 'enclosed gardens' have no life-giving fountain or central, paradisal tree, as in the European tradition, occasionally a flowering tree plays a significant part as a metaphor for the desired, the topos of love, as in the scene pictured in *Bamboo River II* (Fig. 6-6): 'a particularly lovely cherry tree that grew among others in the garden nearby', which becomes the prize for the winner of a game of *go* played between the two sisters, Oigimi and Nakanokimi. This scene focalizes the erotic elegance and desirability of the two sisters, about to become the targets of love of both Prince Niou and Kaoru.

Standard features of the Heian mansion garden are often used to great effect: the *yarimizu* garden brook found in Ukifune's garden at Nijō above, evokes a sense of natural music, which augments the semic codes of purity, innocence and beauty. Purity, even an ironic innocence, is evoked by the babbling brook motif in the *Genji Scrolls* rendering of Genji's visit to the Third Princess, when already in seclusion as a nun. This scene, painted in *The Bell Cricket I* (*Suzumushi I*; Fig. 6-7), shows the Princess overlooking the garden, listening to the sonorous cricket song. The Third Princess here plays the part of the bell cricket, closely encompassed both by fate and the encircling garden of a self-imposed seclusion.

> That autumn he turned the garden before the western bridgeway, up to the east side of the median fence,[72] into a wild moor, and he decorated that part of the house with a holy-water shelf and so on. [T. 711]

The Third Princess's garden at Rokujō is located 'in front of the western bridgeway' (*nishi watadono no mae*), meaning at the west side of the main hall of the southwest quarter, whose features were best appreciated in autumn:

> At dusk on the night of the fifteenth, before the [full moon] had risen, Her Highness [The Third Princess] sat before her altar, looking out at the [garden] scenery near the veranda, meditatively chanting the holy Name [of Amida]. Two or three young nuns were offering flowers. With the sounds of the holy water vessel ringing, and the sounds of [holy] water [being poured], and with all this bustling over unfamiliar matters, she was feeling doleful and sad ... [T. 712]

The Genji Illustrations Scrolls (T/G) rendering has amplified the Princess' low voiced Buddhist chant, the sounds of holy water vessels clinking and holy water being poured (codes of purity and paradise), by adding in the painting the stream and its implied musical babble, and depicts the crickets of the chapter's title. All this augments and ironizes the tropes of purity and paradise, interposing an element of sadness, even misery. The not yet risen full moon is a further Buddhist code, obliquely implying that the fullness of the truth is not yet visible:

> Just then, as so often, Genji entered ... 'Pine crickets probably do not live long, despite what their name suggests. They really and truly sing only in the mountains, where no one can hear them, or among the pine forests below, which suggests that they prefer solitude. The bell cricket's gentle freshness is what makes it so appealing.'
> *'I have long since learned how very cruel a time autumn often brings, yet I would not wish to lose the bell cricket's lovely song,'*
> she said very low, and with a wonderful air of grace and artless distinction.
> 'What do you mean?' Genji replied. 'I never thought to hear you say that!'
> *'You may, for yourself, have no wish but to be free of this poor abode, yet your sweet bell cricket song for me never will grow old.'* [T. 712]

Although inscribing this loving exchange, excerpted *text* of *The Genji Illustrations Scrolls* focuses its audience on the virtual despair embodied in the enclosed, demi-monastic state of the young Princess. Her autumn garden, and its crickets' song provide unrelenting reminders of imminent frosts and death. The *Illustrations* painting, by contrast, presents her as a gorgeous young heroine, admired by Genji.

In the *Genji*, there are many gardens of longing, infatuation or ill-starred love, and those that speak of a lover's neglect, like the overgrown wasteland of the Suetsumuhana garden in 'A Waste of Weeds', a metaphor for Genji's neglect of his red-nosed lady, and her sense of despair. This trope too, the garden of absence or longing, has antecedents that reach back to the eighth century Yakamochi, and the *Tales of Ise*.[73]

THE ROKUJŌ GARDENS FOR ALL SEASONS:
A TROPE OF IMPERIAL SAGE-RULERSHIP

In 'The Maidens' ('Otome') chapter, we find Genji's overall design of the Rokujō mansion gardens which he has arranged so that each of the four leading ladies of the household has a wing and a season to herself.[74]

The southeast (spring) garden was for Lady Murasaki, and himself. Here:

> The hills were high in the southeast quarter, where spring-blossoming trees and bushes were planted in large numbers. The lake was most ingeniously designed. Among the plantings in the forward parts of the garden were cinquefoil pines, maples, cherries, wisteria, *yamabuki* (*kerria japonica*) and rock azalea, most of them trees and shrubs whose season was spring. Touches of autumn were scattered through the groves. [T. 402, adapted.]

The southwestern wing was given to Lady Akikonomu, who loved autumn:

> In Her Majesty [Akikonomu]'s quarter, he planted the hill already there with trees certain to glow in rich autumn colours, turned springs into clear streams, added rocks to the brook to enhance its voice, and contrived a waterfall, so the whole expanse was like an autumn moor and flowers bloomed in all the profusion of the season. The result was an autumn to put to shame the moors and mountains of Saga and Ōi ... [T. 402]

This sector is reminiscent of Fujitsubo's southwestern quarter in *The Tale of the Cavern*, where:

> A brook flowed through the garden, and made a cascade falling from some rocks. Beside the cascade there were *kerria* flowers in full bloom, and beside the lake there was a pine tree from whose branches beautiful clusters of wisteria hung in rich profusion.[75]

Genji's summer garden for the lady of the orange blossoms was in the northeast quarter:

> The northeast quarter, with its cool spring, favoured summer shade. Chinese bamboo grew in the near garden, to freshen the breeze; tall groves offered welcoming depths of shade, as in a mountain village; the hedge was of flowering deutzia; and among the plantings of orange, fragrant with the past, of pinks and roses and peonies, there also grew spring and autumn flowers. The east edge of this quarter was divided off into a riding ground with a pavilion and surrounded by a woven fence. Sweet flag had been induced to grow thickly beside the water, for the games [the Sweet Flag Festival] of the fifth month, and the nearby stables housed the most superb horses. [T. 402]

Murasaki displays remarkable clarity with regard to the layout of her fictive domains. The architectural historian Ōta Seiroku, in his 'reconstruction' of the fictional Rokujō gardens, places a large pond here.[76] The irises, grown for the Sweet Flag Festival of the fifth month, which was associated with equestrian events, were presumably envisioned by the writer as planted close to the racecourse, which was usually aligned north to south. The racecourse in historic mansions, as seen in the evidence of the historic Kayanoin mansion built by Fujiwara Yorimichi in 1019–21, was normally located close to the edge of the eastern walls of the compound.[77]

The winter garden, in the northwest quarter, was for the lady from Akashi. Here:

> In the northwest quarter [of the Lady of Akashi], beyond the artificial hills on the north side, there were rows of storehouses. As a dividing fence he planted a dense stand of pines intended to show off the beauty of snow. There was a fence entwined with chrysanthemums to gather the morning frosts of early winter, a grove of deep-hued oaks,[78] and a scattering of nameless trees transplanted from the fastnesses of mountains ... [T. 403, adapted.]

Genji had run small earthen walls and wooden galleries between naturally secluding features, such as pines and artificial hills, so that privacy was maintained, yet access between them easy and relaxed. It is clear that the whole complex envisaged by Murasaki Shikibu covers an area of four blocks, or *chō* (each about 2.45 acres), the same area as that of the Tsuchimikado mansion of her patron, Fujiwara Michinaga, in which Murasaki Shikibu had lived. The estate, then, is essentially a single entity, with its riding grounds and stables in the northeast, and storehouses in the northwest. A *yarimizu* brook ran on through to the southwest, Akikonomu's quarters, where 'he added rocks to the brook to deepen its voice, and contrived a waterfall' as it approached the pond.[79]

The large pond is here envisioned as occupying the southern sectors, as in all historic mansions of this time, and fed by the same stream as it meandered from its entry point in the northeast past the waterflags near the racecourse towards the southeast quarter (Genji's residence) and on towards Her Majesty's southwest garden, where it poured into the extensive miniature lake. The pond need not have been of a symmetrical shape, but graced with curves as it enveloped the hills that were already in place.[80]

The overall layout of these gardens establishes Genji as a magnanimous and princely patron and paramour, and has strong undertones of geomancy suggesting he is the master of the four directions, hence a kind of private universe: once seen as a unified residential complex, the universality of the whole becomes apparent. While, as Norma Field has shown, there are numerous Japanese antecedents for this notion associated with the practices of the emperor, one may also observe that notion of a 'four seasons' garden, with a special sector for each season, invites comparison with the geomantic principles seen in tenth century Chinese paintings of flowers, birds and animals of the four seasons; a prime example is that of the Hall of the Eight Trigrams (*Baguadian*) made in 953 for the Southern Tang ruler Li Yu, decorated with screen paintings by Huang Quan and his son.[81] These principles resonate closely with those of imperial Chinese palaces dating back to the first imperial parks of Han, and may be seen to assert rulership over both visible and invisible domains.[82] Japanese emperors were almost certainly drawing on these very ancient templates of universal rulership.

An example of Buddhist geomantic principles, closer to the world of Murasaki Shikibu, is the four seasons layout of the Amida *raigō* (paradise rebirth) paintings on the interior doors of the famous Phoenix Hall of the

Byōdō-in at Uji (1053). These effectively proclaim the right of this Buddha to universal rulership (as Sage-Ruler, or *Râjâ Cakravartin* (*Denrin-shō'ō*), in Buddhist and Tantric traditions). This notion is expressed in numerous *sutras*, including the *Wu-liang-shou jing* (J. *Muryōjukyō*) which describes the vows and paradise of the Buddha Amitābha (J. Amida) and was well known in Murasaki Shikibu's time. While Fujiwara Yorimichi's Phoenix Hall is the only surviving temple of this kind, the descriptions in the *Tale of Flowering Fortunes* (*Eiga monogatari*) of the 'Buddha worlds' at Fujiwara Michinaga's Hōjōji temple are further evidence of this tradition.[83] Another contemporary example, associated with rulership over the four seasons, was the Kayanoin, built in 1019 by Fujiwara Yorimichi, which was likened to the Dragon King's undersea dwelling.[84] Like Genji, Yorimichi is reported to have taken a direct part in garden design. He was also interested in the acquisition of fine rocks, reminding one of the contemporaneous fashion for exotic rocks dramatically headed by the aesthete-ruler Emperor Huizong, whose extravagant Genyue park in the Song capital of Kaifeng was built between 1117 and 1122.[85] Genji seems here constructed as a demi-emperor who establishes a form of symbolic sage-rulership over a more or less private domain, that of the high-ranking women of his household. The loaded symbolism of the ideal princely ruler would not have been lost on Murasaki Shikibu's readership. Genji's gardens might be said, therefore, to highlight his construct as a prince fully deserving of the right to rule, as emperor-sage.

THE GARDENS OF 'MYTHIC' SPRING[86]

In the 'Butterflies' ('Kochō') chapter, there is an archetypal imaging of spring, already a direct metaphor for Murasaki herself:

> The twentieth day of the third month had passed, and the garden of the lady of the spring [Murasaki], was so remarkable with flowers and birdsong that were lovelier than ever, that people began to wonder how they could possibly have lasted so long ... [T. 441, adapted.]

Murasaki's spring garden at Genji's Rokujō mansion invites comparison with the European tradition of the *locus amoenus* (earthly paradise), and its metonymies. Medievals in Europe were familiar with Ovid's *Metamorphoses*, and the image of Proserpina, in her garden of eternal spring:

> *silva coronat aquas cinguens latus omne suisque*
> *frondibus ut velo Phoebeos submovet ictus;*
> *frigora dant rami, Tyrios humida flores:*
> *perpetuum ver est. quo Proserpina luco*
> *ludit et aut violas aut candida lilia carpit,*

> [A wood crowns the heights around its waters on every side, and with its foliage as with an awning keeps off the sun's hot rays. The branches afford a pleasing coolness, and the well-watered ground bears brightly coloured flowers. There spring is everlasting. Within this grove Proserpina was playing, and gathering violets or white lilies.][87]

Dante evokes this scene in *Purgatorio* XXVIII, where:

> *Tu mi fai rimembrar dove e qual era*
> *Proserpina nel tempo che perdette*
> *la madre lei, ed ella primavera.*
>
> [You make me recall where and what
> Proserpina was at the time her mother lost her,
> and she the spring.]⁸⁸

Here Dante, in Canto XXVIII, brings his explorer into a garden of endless spring, redolent of the tradition of the *paradisus voluptatis*, the secular paradise of the senses, whose fragrance is all pervasive, '*lo suol che d'ogne parte aulive*' (l. 6), whose breeze is soft and steady, and where little birds sing in harmony. He paints a spring garden, with 'the great variation of fresh flowers of May' ('*la gran variazion d'i freschi mai*' l. 36). The solitary lady he finds in the garden evokes the legend of Proserpina, who was taken off by Pluto to the underworld (Hades), leaving her mother Ceres without either her daughter, or Spring. The themes of innocence, virginity and a sense of a mythic, spring garden at the dawn of history, are central to the image.⁸⁹

Ovid had presented Flora in similar guise in his *Fasti*, which was the inspiration for the haunting beauty of the image in Botticelli's *Primavera*:

> *vere fruor semper: semper nitidissimus annus,*
> *arbor habet frondes, pabula semper humus.*
>
> [I (Flora) enjoy perpetual spring; most buxom is the year ever; ever the tree is clothed with leaves; the ground with pasture.]⁹⁰

A mythic dimension of Murasaki's spring garden is presented in Chapter 23, 'The Warbler's First Song' ('Hatsune'), reinforced with lightly, and soon ironozed paradisial imagery:

> ... how poorly mere words convey the exquisite beauty of the gardens of his ladies! The one before the spring quarter (Murasaki's southeast sector), where the scent of the plum blossoms mingled with the fragrance within the blinds, especially recalled the land of a living Buddha (生ける佛の御國とおぼゆ), although actually the mistress of the place lived there in peace and quite at her ease. [T. 431]

After the death of Murasaki, the intensity of Genji's feelings of loss reinforce her status as the virtual goddess of spring, a season which becomes unbearable without her. In 'The Seer', Genji returns to the Rokujō mansion to face the thought of life without her:

> In the second month, when mist prettily veiled the trees in flower and others yet to bloom, a warbler appeared in that favourite red plum tree, singing splendidly, and Genji went to watch it.
>
> '*How the warbler sings, just as though nothing had changed, there among the flowers, in the tree she planted then, even when she is no more,*'

Later:

> Genji leaned against a railing outside the corner room [her quarters, it seems] and gazed now out into the garden, now back through the blinds.

'Now the time has come, must I consign to ruin what she who is gone specially loved with all her heart, her hedge bright with spring flowers?' [T. 769–70]

Murasaki has become synonymous with the spring garden, a virtual Persephone (Prosperina); when it blooms without her, this brings an intolerable sense of *aware* (pathos) to those viewing all her favourite spring plants. The author has gone a long way towards mythologizing Murasaki, as a symbol of spring. Not that this trope is itself new in Japan. The *Tales of Ise* had passed this into the canon,[91] and still earlier Ōtomo Yakamochi's mourning for his deceased lover (circa 739) was a memorable icon of love lost.[92] The loss of Murasaki brings to the fore a sense of the loss of spring, and the extraordinary sadness associated with this trope. In European tradition a similar image became a metaphor for paradise lost, the loss of the mythic Golden Age, and the fall of mankind from grace.[93]

THE 'EARTHLY PARADISE' AND SPIRITUAL PERFECTIBILITY

The European 'earthly paradise' is known in probably its most influential form in the cosmological epic poem, *Anticlaudianus*, by the twelfth century Alan of Lille, also among the sources of inspiration for Dante:

> There is a spot set far off from our clime,
> mocking the turmoil of our dwellings.
> Alone, this spot can be whatever all can be;
> the rest's deficiency is made full in the one …
> Here, growing up with tender down of flowers,
> studded with her own stars, flushed with the tinge of roses, earth vies to paint
>   another heaven.
> Here the grace of the newborn flower does not die; dying in being born;
> the girl-rose of the morning does not languish, old-woman-rose, at night;
> no, joyful at her unchanging face, she's young with an eternal spring.
> Winter does not blast the flower, nor summer scorch it.[94]

Dante, in *Purgatorio* XXVIII, presents us with a vision of celestial joy whose rapture is its own end.[95] Here we find Dante's hymn to what *Genesis*, in the Vulgate text, called *paradisus voluptatis*. With the already archetypal elements of the soft breeze, the birdsong and the translucent stream, we are seduced by a hypnotic image of a locus in time, where the stream is purer than any other and *'che si mova bruna bruna sotto l'ombra perpetüa'* (which moves darkly, darkly under perpetual shadow). The poet is transfixed by the sight of a lovely woman walking all alone who reminds him of the fragile beauty of the young goddess Persephone (Proserpina), embodiment of the bliss of spring, and of the earthly paradise itself, yet a poignant image of something about to be lost.[96] In this view, the earthly paradise is the gateway to its counterpart, the celestial paradise, here located in time, but barely.

The trope of the perfect garden, and a distinct paradisial realm of perfection was a strong trope in the literary culture of Europe's neighbouring cultures, including those of Persia and Arab countries. In Persia it is found rooted in Sufi gnostic traditions, which travelled with Islam and Arab culture to al-Andalus and other regions. The Sufi martyr, Sarmad, clarifies the wholly gnostic nature of the garden of love in this tradition:

> Come you into my garden, then
>   will you see
> The white blaze of the light of unity.
>   Look closely –
> Beloved and lover, rose and thorn,
>   are One!⁹⁷

Here the ancient tradition of the garden of love has been transformed into a vision of unity in which the lovers are no longer two; they have merged into unity, which includes the entire garden too, itself also seen as a manifestation of Truth.

The vision of the heart as a garden, like that found in the vision of Sufi Abū'-Husayn an-Nūrî (d. 907),⁹⁸ is integral to the Persian tradition of garden lyrics, and their rose and nightingale allegories of love, which are frequently found in eleventh and twelfth century Persian poetry. Rûzbihân Baqlî (d. 1209) writes:

> Look well, for the heart is the marketplace of His love, and there the rose of Adam on the branch of Love is from the colour of manifestation of His Rose. When the nightingale 'spirit' becomes intoxicated by this rose, he will hear with the ear of the soul the song of the bird of *Alast* ['Am I not your Lord?'] in the fountain place of pre-eternity.⁹⁹

This accords with the vision of Sufi such as Maulânâ Jelâluddîn Rūmî, the thirteenth century poet and Sufi saint, who says in the *Mathnawî* collection:

> The Beloved is all, the lover just a veil.
> The Beloved is living, the lover a dead thing.¹⁰⁰

In the Sufi mystic garden of the heart, every rose is a sign, and more. It tells of the ineffable secrets of the final union of the Lover and the Beloved once the mystic path has been trodden to the end – and the rose of union grasped for what it is: the Self unveiled, that One who cannot be seen except with the eyes of the Beloved. It might be said of this literature that it presents, in indisputably gnostic terms, the completion of the quest for perfection.

This contrasts quite dramatically with the trope of a quest for perfection in medieval Europe manifesting as the pursuit of Saint Graal. The latter provided so elusive and haunting an image to European medievals that many long continuations were added to its enigmatic and unfinished symbolism. However, in Europe, as in other regions, orthodoxy would not validate such deviations, hence the quest for perfection became qualified by a concomitant, inevitable deferral of closure, itself a powerful instrument for the writer of romance.¹⁰¹

The Roman church had long shunned the mystic currents in medieval literature.¹⁰² Nonetheless, with the onset of the cult of Mary, starting from at least the Council of Nicaea in 325, the mother of Jesus came to be seen as a secret inner garden (*hortus conclusus*) in imagery drawn from the *Song of Songs*. Her purity was associated with the closed fountain (*fons clausa*), and she herself came to be symbolized by the rose, a trend already deeply entrenched by the twelfth century.[103]

We find, nonetheless, the famed mystic, Hildegard of Bingen (1098–1179), writing:

> I am that living and fiery essence of the divine substance that glows in the beauty of the fields. I shine in the water, I burn in the sun and the moon and the stars.[104]

Hildegard, however, makes a very stark distinction between divine love and human or carnal love, allowing no mix of *courtoisie* and the divine.[105] Her distinctly gnostic vision seems to prefigure the Beatrice of Dante, both his muse and, as sanctifying grace, his own perfectibility,[106] '*quella che 'mparadisa la mia mente*' (she who imparadises my mind),[107] ennobling him and raising him to her state.

In *Paradiso* XXXI, Dante speaks in similar visionary terms of the snow-white rose (Mary/the church/ or in Sufi terms, the Lover) whom Christ himself had made his bride (*che nel suo sangue Cristo fece sposa*):

> *ché la luce divina è penetrante*
> *per l'universo secondo ch'è degno,*
> *sì che nulla le puote essere ostante.*
>
> [For the light divine so penetrates
> The universe, according to its merit,
> That naught can be an obstacle against it.][108]

The poetic view of human perfectibility, powerfully expressed in Dante, was a central feature of Persian allegorical romance. Hence, we may propose that belief in the final perfectibility of man was, overall, a key feature of allegory in medieval romance, globally. It was strongly present in Eastern cultural codes, in the form of mainstream Mahayana Buddhism, most notably in the Kegon, and Tendai and Shingon sects of Japan. And in Zen tradition too. Allegory in many medieval cultures depended for its impact on widespread acceptance of these ontologies. In the Mahayana Buddhist canon, the manifest universe itself, and all its natural features, are seen to be the 'voice'; the 'music'; the very 'body' of the Buddha.

Besides this, a more dualist and approachable doctrine is found in the Pure Land Buddhist *sutras*, such as the popular *Amida Sutra*, which provide highly sensuous descriptions of the Western Paradise of Amida as a direct, and thus imaginatively tangible experience.[109] *Genji* featured elements of Buddhist paradise codes, as noted above. Further, the *Tale of Flowering Fortunes* (*Eiga monogatari*) idealizes Fujiwara Michinaga's Hōjōji temple as a palace 'resembling' paradise, a form of anagogy, which ironizes 'truth'.[110] A concern with an invisible perfect world, and the accompanying anagogy of uplifting the mind beyond the mundane to a higher almost paradisial reality, is found in the numerous figures of metaphor, art and explication in Christian medieval Europe, most notably in the Gothic cathedrals inspired by the idealism of clerics such as Abbot Suger of Saint-Denis.[111]

Non-dual mysticism, while suppressed, was not absent from European theology, which had long remained deeply steeped in Pseudo-Dionysius who wrote, on beauty:

> That, beautiful beyond being, is said to be Beauty – for it gives beauty from itself in a manner to each, it causes the consonance and splendour of all, it flashes forth upon all, after the manner of light, the beauty producing gifts of its flowing ray, it calls all to itself, when it is called beauty.[112]

St Bernard of Clairvaux spoke of beauty in metaphors of light, and Thomas Aquinas expounded at length on '*claritas*'; as Umberto Eco has put it, 'a mysticism of light, a love of light, and a poetics of light were constants in medieval culture'.[113] And Dante is seen by some as a mediator between orthodoxy and the mystic elements in the medieval tradition, such as St Bernard's notion of deification by grace.[114]

Likewise, the varied cultural codes that animate the imagery of the narrative in *The Tale of Genji* include both anagogical, partly dualistic, Pure Land codes, and those of firm belief in the non-dual doctrines treating of the ultimate perfectibility of man.

EXCURSIONS AND IDYLL ON THE POND

The larger gardens in *Genji*, like that of the Suzaku Emperor's Palace, normally incorporated a large pond. Murasaki clearly based her images on the numerous historic gardens of this kind in Heian Kyoto of which almost none survive in any recognizable form. But Saga-no-in (Ōsawa Pond) northwest of Kyoto, and Kajūji temple just southeast of Kyoto (Figs 6-2, 6-3) illustrate early trends. The layout of these historic pond-gardens provides keys to the ways in which Murasaki's literary gardens functioned and their 'horizons of expectation' which can here be identified in terms of poetic response.[115]

A familiar feature of the typical pond-garden was the babbling brook, or *yarimizu*, which led water into the main pond. As shown in a mansion depicted in the *Annual Ceremonies Scrolls*, the *yarimizu* brook usually ran between the east wing and the central main hall, and then southward towards the lake (Fig. 6-8).[116] In these scrolls, we have a particularly graphic image of the musical quality of the *yarimizu* stream, inlaid and bound with rocks against which the brook can be almost heard to gurgle.

In the 'Butterflies' ('Kochō') chapter, the writer makes skilful use of the tropes of allegory and myth in descriptions of excursions on the pond. The scene is set late in the third lunar month, when the spring garden of Murasaki was coming into full bloom:

> As the sights of the groves on the hills, the [distant] view of the [central] island, and the expanses of richly glowing moss, all seemed to make the younger women a little restless,[117] Genji had Chinese-style barges made and outfitted, and on the very day they were launched, he summoned people from the Office of Music to perform aboard them.[118]
>
> ... The mistress of the southeast quarter [Murasaki] thought it time to answer Her Majesty [Akikonomu]'s challenge to one 'whose garden waits to welcome spring,' ... but since she could not visit without sufficient reason, merely for the

pleasure of the blossoms, he [Genji] had young gentlemen of hers – ones apt to enjoy the adventure – board a boat and row towards them along the southern lake. The small hillock he had built [in the pond] which looked like a boundary [dividing the gardens] did not keep them from coming straight round its little promontory and up to the east fishing pavilion, where he had assembled other women from his side. [T. 441, adapted.][119]

Here, the garden of Akikonomu in the southwest quarter, and that of Genji and Murasaki in the southeast, are envisioned as sharing one large central pond in the southern part of the large garden. It was possible to negotiate a passage round a small boundary hillock, devised as a kind of minor barrier between them, and proceed eastwards towards the fishing pavilion (*tsuridono*) which lay at the border of Genji's sector of the pond in the southeast.[120] This contrasts with designs that place a fishing pavilion on the central island, as in Masayori's residence pictured in *The Tale of the Cavern*. Further, as in *The Tale of the Cavern*, there was no bridge to the central island.[121] It is evident here that Murasaki Shikibu had in mind an allegorical excursion by boat, and a resultant form of self-defining discovery on the pond. This must have been a deliberate choice on Murasaki Shikibu's part, since most of the historic mansions of her time, such as Tōsanjō, and Michinaga's Tsuchimikado mansion, had a fine bridge by which to approach the central island, which functioned in many as a locus for musicians.[122] Murasaki Shikibu continues:

> The dragon-prow and roc-prow barges[123] were adorned magnificently in continental style, and the boys wielding the steering oars wore twin tresses as in China. The astonished women were thrilled and delighted to find themselves launched on so broad a lake, and they felt as though transported to an unknown land.[124] When they came under the great rocks of the island's little cove, they marvelled to find the least stone standing as though in a painting (中島の入江の岩蔭にさし寄せて見れば、はかなき石のたたずまひも、ただ絵に描いたらむやうなり). [T. 441.][125]
>
> ...The cherries that were gone elsewhere smiled here in all their beauty, and the wisteria twined around the galleries opened into deep-hued clusters, flower by flower.[126] How marvellously the *kerria* roses (*yamabuki*) were mirrored in the water and spilled in superb profusion from the bank! Waterbirds, sporting in loyal pairs, flitted about with twigs in their bills, while mandarin ducks made a brilliant pattern on the ground weave of the waves, until one longed only to turn it all into a painted design. That day one's axe handle could well have rotted away. [T. 441–2, adapted.]

Here, in *Genji*'s Rokujō garden, the cultural codes reveal a sense of 'mythic' idyll: the affinity for allegory is transparent. The deracinated quality of this dream world shares much with the trope of the *locus amoenus* in European tradition; it is replete with flavours reminiscent of Georgic idyll, the earthly paradise, and the notion of a 'Golden Age'. *Genji* plays on Chinese legend, namely Wang Zhi's forester, who became so absorbed in watching two hermits playing chess in a cave that at the close of the game, which had seemed to him only minutes long, his axe had sprouted leaves. Murasaki Shikibu invokes a mythic past, a Daoistic golden age. The mandarin ducks are symbolic of marital harmony, so too the 'loyal pairs' of waterbirds. One wished to paint it, she says, because in effect it stands for idyll, a scene of virtually everlasting spring.

Intertexts are provided in the accounts in *Murasaki Shikibu, Her Diary and Poetic Memoirs* of historic events in Michinaga's mansion, just following the celebration on the fifth day after the birth of an imperial prince to Michinaga's daughter Shōshi in 1008:

> The next evening there was a beautiful moon, and some of the younger women went out in a boat.[127]

Informal excursions on the ponds of such gardens were frequent historical events, in which the theme of Daoistic immortality is repeatedly evoked in what one might term pond-top idyll. On the occasion of an imperial visit to the Saionji mansion garden (now Kinkakuji) found in *The Clear Mirror* (*Masukagami*) which covers the years 1277–87, the poetic narrative reads:

> When the imperial boat halted at the [central] island, the scene was indescribably pleasant; nameless little birds flitted to and fro, and the tranquil waters of the lake rippled in the deep shadows cast by ancient pines among the rocks, their intertwined boughs laden with hoary moss. It seemed a spot remote from human habitation: as the guests looked out towards misty distant rocks, which cradled the outflow from a waterfall in the surrounding hills, they asked themselves whether an immortal's grotto might not look much the same.[128]

In the poems composed during the fictional excursion in Murasaki Shikibu's 'Butterflies' chapter, the author makes very clear the transition to mythic idyll:

> No, I shall not seek the mountain the turtle bears [Penglai]! It shall be my fame that I chose immortality here aboard this very boat![129]

Such exchanges were close to the events, and socio-poetic customs of Murasaki Shikibu's day, as we find in the *Diary*. One evening (circa 1009 – early 1010):

> A hazy moon emerged. It was refreshing and pleasant to hear His Excellency's sons all in one boat singing songs in the modern style, but it was amusing to see Masamitsu, Minister of the Treasury, who had got in with them in all seriousness, now sitting there meekly with his back to us, not unnaturally loath to take part. The women behind the screens laughed softly. 'And in the boat he seems to feel his age,' I said.[130]
> 'Xu Fu and Wen Cheng [seekers of the immortal isles] were empty braggarts,' he murmured. I was most impressed.

In both this historic exchange, and the light-hearted poetic responses ('the mountain the turtle bears') of *Genji*'s 'Butterflies' chapter, there is unambiguous reference to Bai Juyi's playful treatment in his 'Ocean Wide' poem of the legend of the five isles of the immortals, Penglai and others, where the inhabitants were, or became, immortal.

The pond-top excursion in the *Tale of Genji* transports the women with delight into an allegorical world of virtual eternity. The excursion is a prime example of allegory in an Asian medieval romance. The playful use of the mythic quest for eternal life is itself a vibrant example of a generically medieval trope: fiction here weaves together its story in terms that elaborate, embellish and mythologize historical fact. The *Diary* proves invaluable as a means of monitoring the creation of romance, and its idylls. Further, the poet chosen for evoking a sense of garden idyll is not the sometimes bombastic Li Bai (701–762), who writes flamboyantly of immortals and Penglai, but Bai Juyi, famous for his numerous contemplative 'pond-top' poems written aboard a boat in his own pond garden near Loyang.[131]

Murasaki Shikibu may be seen to have designed with great care this garden in the 'The Pink' ('Tokonatsu') chapter, where the angling pavilion is shown to be in the southeast quarter [T. 467]. The central island (*nakajima*) in the pond is clearly unapproachable by land, that is it has no bridges connecting it to the shoreline; this sets it apart from the usually bridged islands seen in most historic mansions. She has designed the layout in such a way that the rock arrangements must be 'discovered', like 'an uncharted land', when parties approach it by boat. It has an invisible *irie* or cove-like bay, in which such boats can moor for a period, while they appreciate the design of the rocks. An important design feature that could only be appreciated by discovering it by boat. The design thus incorporates an intended allegorical journey of adventure – and one richly referenced in the *Tale* with poems referring to the Penglai myth. The Rokujō garden lake idyll in *The Tale of Genji* blends classic idyll, and Bai Juyi's reflective irony, with a sense of being transported to a demi-paradise.

Murasaki Shikibu was not inventing such design features, since many of the contemporary gardens of her time were equipped with just such islands; a fine island in the pond garden of the twelfth century Mōtsuji, in Hiraizumi (Fig. 6-9) seems to indicate that pond-top journeying was a fundamental part of the design; the choice of rocks and their arrangement highlights their changing aspects when passed by in boats. Some exquisite examples of such rockwork can be found among the twelfth century small islands in the Saihōji, Kyoto.

Later in the 'Butterflies' chapter, the topos of Murasaki Shikibu's garden as a garden of mythic, and virtually eternal, spring is sounded yet again:

> ... Despite the spring light that forever shone in the southeast quarter [いつも、春の光をこめ給へるおほ殿なれど], some regretted that the lady there had no one to receive her deepest love; ... [T. 443][132]

Here, idyll in the garden and the sense of a mythic, almost endless spring, now semic codes for Murasaki herself, are inextricably blended together.

CONCLUSION

The gardens of *Genji* provide material for comparison with several major tropes in medieval literature worldwide: these include the 'gardens of love', the 'earthly paradise'; allegory and other forms of veiling 'truth'; the ironizing of clerical dogma, often against gnostic ontologies or belief in human perfectibility; anagogy and the erotic; the role of the vernacular in the new literature of love; the *mise en abyme* of concepts of self and other, and self and objective truth; the manipulation of viewpoint and voyeurism; the linguistic distancing of identity; the wisdom of 'tales', and the role of women in the telling or validation of tales; the quasi-deification of the feminine; the tropes of demi-paradise, mythic time, and the quest for the eternal, and adventure in unknown realms; and the construction of the prince and his amours at the centre of a mandala of world rule, as marked in *Genji* as that of Nizami. Finally, it is clearly apparent that these tropes fall out of favour when these cultures become more humanist, as rationalism begins to displace faith in the divine, and the mainstay of romance irony is weakened.[133]

NOTES

1. The term 'gnostic' is here used in the sense indicated by scholars of Islamic literature. *Ma'rifa* (gnosis) is said to mean union with the divine; Annemarie Schimmel, *Mystical Dimensions of Islam* (Chapel Hill, N.C.: University of North Carolina Press, 1975), p. 130.
2. Establishing an ironic position *vis-à-vis* a spiritual ideal is as much the project of the authors of *Le Roman de la Rose* as it is of the Sufis whose metaphors for divine love include that of the thirst for wine. See the 'Wine Ode' of Ibn al-Fârid (d. 1235), Schimmel, op. cit., pp. 275–6. For the ambiguities and ironies of Persian lyrics, see Schimmel, ibid., Chapter 7: 'The Rose and the Nightingale: Persian and Turkish Mystical Poetry'. There has been debate over whether the *ghazals* of Hâfiz should be seen as mystic or erotic; ibid., pp. 287–8. The writers of the *Roman de la Rose*, ironizing Platonic anagogy, validate Eros as the instigator of the will to perfect love. By contrast, Sufis like Hâfiz, speaking from divine union, picture desire as an analogue for the soul's aspirations for union. These two positions are not the same, but meet in their establishing a locus of irony.
3. C. S. Lewis, *The Allegory of Love* (Oxford: Oxford University Press, 1936); Ernst Robert Curtius, *European Literature and the Latin Middle Ages*, translated by Willard R. Trask (London: Routledge and Kegan Paul, 1953); Peter Dronke, *The Medieval Poet and His World* (Roma: Edizioni di Storia e Letteratura, 1984) and *Intellectuals and Poets in Medieval Europe*, Raccolta di studi e testi, vol. 183 (Roma: Edizioni di Storia e Letteratura, 1992); John Fleming, *The 'Roman de la Rose': A Study in Allegory and Iconography* (Princeton: Princeton University Press, 1969), and *Reason and the Lover* (Princeton: Princeton University Press, 1984); A. C. Spearing, *Medieval Dream-Poetry* (Cambridge: Cambridge University Press, 1976); David F. Hult, *Self-Fulfilling Prophecies: Readership and Authority in the First 'Roman de la Rose'* (Cambridge: Cambridge University Press, 1986); Maria Rosa Menocal, *The Arabic Role in Medieval Literary History: A Forgotten Heritage* (Philadelphia: University of Pennsylvania Press, 1990) and *The Literature of Al-Andalus*, edited by Maria Rosa Menocal, Raymond P. Scheindlin and Michael Sells (Cambridge: Cambridge University Press, 2000); Julie Scott Meisami, 'Allegorical Gardens in the Persian Poetic Tradition: Nezami, Rumi, Hafez,' *International Journal of Middle Eastern Studies*, vol. 17 (1985). See also a variety of approaches in *Rethinking the Romance of the Rose: Text, Image, Reception*, edited by Kevin Brownlee and Sylvia Huot (Philadephia: University of Pennsylvania Press, 1992): this contains essays on reading the texts of *Roman de la Rose*, and on reading 'The Illuminated *Rose*', which are pertinent to our present study of *The Tale of Genji*, and its illustrations. See also Daniel Heller-Roazen, *Fortune's faces: the Roman de la Rose and the poetics of contingency* (Baltimore: Johns Hopkins University Press, c2003).
4. *The Literature of Al-Andalus*, op. cit.; see especially Michael Sells, 'Love', pp. 126–58; Tova Rosen, 'The muwashshah', 165–89; and ibid., Part III Andalusians, pp. 237–374; Michael A. Sells, *Mystical Languages of Unsaying* (Chicago and London: University of Chicago Press, 1994), Chapters 3 and 4, 'Ibn 'Arabi's Polished Mirror: Identity Shift and Meaning Event', and 'Ibn 'Arabi's Garden among the Flames: The Heart Receptive of Every Form', pp. 63–115; and Michael A. Sells, *Stations of Desire: Love Elegies from Ibn 'Arabi and New Poems* (Jerusalem: Ibis Editions, 2000).
5. Dante Alighieri, *Vita Nuova: Italian Text with Facing English Translation*, by Dino S.

Cervigni and Edward Vasta (Notre Dame, Indiana and London: University of Notre Dame Press, 1995), Section 25, l. 6, pp. 108–109. See also A. J. Minnis, A. B. Scott, and David Wallace, *Medieval Literary Theory and Criticism c1100–1375: The Commentary Tradition* (Oxford: Clarendon Press, 1988), p. 377.
6. *Kokinshū: A Collection of Poems Ancient and Modern* translated and annotated by Laurel Rasplica Rodd with Mary Catherine Henkenius (Tokyo: University of Tokyo Press, 1984); Helen Craig McCullough, *Tales of Ise* (Stanford: Stanford University Press, 1968).
7. Chun-fan Yu, *Kuan-yin: The Chinese Transformation of Avalokitesvara* (New York: Columbia University Press, 2001); Yu discusses the transformation of the bodhisattva from a male image to female, and enlarges on the Mahayana concept of *upaya* (convenient means).
8. Minnis, Scott and Wallace, op. cit., pp. 396–8.
9. Peter Dronke, *Fabula: Explorations into the Uses of Myth in Medieval Platonism* (Leiden: E. J. Brill, 1974).
10. Paul Friedlander, 'Beyond Being', *Plato: An Introduction* (Princeton: Princeton University Press, 1969), pp. 59–84.
11. Jinichi Konishi, *A History of Japanese Literature*; translated by Aileen Gatten and Nicholas Teele; edited by Earl Miner (Princeton: Princeton University Press, 1984).
12. Compare Andreas Capellanus, *The Art of Courtly Love*, translated with Introduction by John Jap Parry (New York: Ungar, 1970).
13. What Roland Barthes terms the 'symbol' codes in narrative, highlighting antithesis and contrasting values, are much used in the twelfth century paintings of the *Genji*, demonstrating that this aspect of ironizing the scene, as in *Yomogiu*, *Suzumushi II* and many others, was fundamental to the twelfth century 'reception' of *Genji*; see *S/Z* (Oxford: Blackwell, 1990), translated by Richard Miller. Mitani Kuniaki and Mitamura Masako have further argued that the veils and mists prominently visible in *The Tale of Genji Scrolls* re-reading may have had a contemporary, problematic political motivation; Mitani and Mitamura 1998.
14. Wolfram says in closing: 'And since it was done for a woman, she should speak [or concede] sweet words to me.' Arthur Groos, *Romancing the Grail: Genre, Science, and Quest in Wolfram's Parzival* (Ithaca: Cornell University Press, 1995), p. 14.
15. Tomiko Yoda, 'Reading Literary History Against the National Frame, or Gender and the Emergence of Heian Kana Writing', *Positions* 8, vol. 2 (Fall 2000), pp. 629–68; and *Gender and National Literature: Heian Texts and Constructions of Japanese Modernity* (Durham, North Carolina and London: Duke University Press, 2004).
16. Matilda Tomaryn Bruckner has pointed to 'the intertextual nature of medieval writing, ... the problem of signs and their multiple interpretations from multiple points of view, the role of language, and the transposition from action to discourse, from oral tale to written romance, the *mise en question* of categories as they play through gender and genres, ending up more often than not as non-disjunctive oppositions, the linking of truth and fiction, history and romance'; *Shaping Romance: Interpretation, Truth, and Closure in 12th Century French Fictions* (Philadelphia: University of Pennsylvania Press, 1993), p. 2. The terms 'disjunctive and non-disjunctive oppositions' refer to a distinction made by Kristeva in analysing a semiotic shift from symbol to sign; Julia Kristeva, *Sēmiōtikē; Recherches Pour une Sémanalyse (Extraits)* (Paris: Editions du Seuil, 1969), pp. 55–62.
17. Guillaume de Lorris et Jean de Meun, *Le Roman de la Rose*, ll. 1–4 (Paris: Le Livre de Poche, 1992), p. 42. The poet then proceeds to discuss the medieval dream theory classic by Macrobius. See *Macrobius: Commentary on the Dream of Scipio*, translated by William Harris Stahl (New York: Columbia University Press, 1952).
18. Richard Okada, *Figures of Resistance*, op. cit., p. 226.
19. Ibid.
20. *The Haft Paykar*, translated, with an Introduction and Notes by Julie Scott Meisami (Oxford: Oxford University Press, 1995), p. xi.

21. Ibid., p. xxiii.
22. See Tomiko Yoda, *Gender and National Literature*, op. cit. She cleverly faults the idea of seeing Heian literature as essentially more open to the feminine, and draws attention instead to certain essentializing tendencies within Japanese criticism which – by leaving out the thought of agency, and rather arguing for a 'multiplicity and fluidity of spatial, temporal, modal, and other orientations of narratorial perspective' (p. 159) – avoid questions of relations of power with their own force fields (the sphere of Foucault's work). In that sense, the privileged status of the femininity of Heian discourse may be questioned, justly.
23. See Murakami Fuminobu, Chapter 4 in this volume.
24. Guillaume de Lorris et Jean de Meun, *Le Roman de la Rose*, op. cit; Arthur Groos, *Romancing the Grail*, op. cit.; David F. Hult, *Self-Fulfilling Prophecies*, op. cit.
25. See Aileen Gatten, *The Secluded Forest: Textual Problems in the Genji Monogatari* (Ann Arbor, Michigan: University Microfilms, 1981), Chap. 5.
26. Hult, op. cit., p. 165. Armand Strubel, in *Le Roman de la Rose*, op. cit., points out that the trope of the quest is here invoked, which reminds us of the endlessness of the Grail cycles and their continuations in this romance tradition.
27. See Hult, op. cit., 'The allegory of incompletion', pp. 160–74, and Lee Paterson, 'Feminine Rhetoric and the Politics of Subjectivity: La Vieille and the Wife of Bath', *Rethinking the Romance of the Rose: Text, Image, Reception*, op. cit., p. 325.
28. For Kajūji's history and design, see Shigemori Mirei and Shigemori Kantō (1971–1976), vol. 2; Ōta Seiroku 1987: pp. 311–96.
29. Orhan Pamuk, *My Name is Red*; translated by Erdag Goknar (New York: Alfred A. Knopf, 2001).
30. *Babur Giving Instruction for the Layout of the Bagh-I-Vafa*, Victoria and Albert Museum, ms. 1.M.1913–276A, 276 (c.1594); see Donald Newton Wilbner, *Persian Gardens and Garden Pavilions* (Washington, D.C.: Dumbarton Oaks, 1979), pl. 18; Elizabeth B. Moynihan, 'The Lotus Garden Palace of Zabir al-Din Mohammed Babur', *Muqarnas* Vol. 5 (1988), pp. 135–52.
31. Richard Bowring, *Murasaki Shikibu: Her Diary and Poetic Memoirs* (Princeton: Princeton University Press, 1982). See also his *The Diary of Lady Murasaki* (Harmondsworth: Penguin, 1996).
32. See n. 13, above.
33. *The Tale of Genji*, translated by Royall Tyler, 2 volumes (Harmondsworth, Middlesex: Penguin, 2001) [Hereafter 'T.'], p. 30. The *saibara* song suggests that the singer wants to spend the night.
34. *Chrétien de Troyes: Arthurian Romances*, translated and with Introduction by William W. Kibler (Harmondsworth: Penguin, 1991), pp. 200–201 [hereafter, K]. See Old French edition [hereafter OF], *Chrétien de Troyes, Œvres complotes*, edited by Daniel Poirion (Paris. nrf, Gallimard, 1994), pp. 326–7, ll. 6332 ff., and ll. 6375 ff. See also discussion of this and related themes in Derek Pearsall, 'Gardens as Symbol and Setting,' *Medieval Gardens*, edited by Elizabeth B. MacDougall, *Dumbarton Oaks Colloquium on the History of Landscape Architecture IX* (Washington, D.C.: Dumbarton Oaks, 1986).
35. See John H. Harvey on the 'pleasaunce' in Europe and its connections with Arab culture, in *The Oxford Companion to Gardens* edited by Geoffrey and Susan Jellicoe, Patrick Goode and Michael Lancaster (Oxford: Oxford University Press, 1986), pp. 388–441.
36. OF, p. 328, ll. 6432–6433.
37. The girl here is considered to be Nakanokimi, the younger of the two sisters; NKBT, vol. 4, p. 314.
38. Norma Field, *The Splendor of Longing in the Tale of Genji* (Princeton, N.J.: Princeton University Press, 1987).
39. Shinohara 1973: 56–67. For a critique of Shinohara, see Edith Sarra, 'The Poetics

of Voyeurism in 'The Pillow Book',' *Fictions of Femininity: Literary Inventions of Gender in Japanese Court Women's Diaries* (Stanford: Stanford University Press, 1999), pp. 232 ff. For further discourse arguing for disempowerment of the looker by the act of looking, that 'to see is to be possessed,' as opposed to the configuration of looking and power, see Takahashi Tōru (1991b): 262–5.

40. Sarra, op. cit., p. 29.

41. A. C. Spearing, *The Medieval Poet as Voyeur* (Cambridge: Cambridge University Press, 1993), makes good companion reading to the *Genji*; Kathryn Starkey has further highlighted the hybridity of illustrations and narrative voice in medieval narrative, in her *Reading the Medieval Book: Word, Image and Performance in Wolfram von Eschenbach's Willehalm* (Notre Dame, Indiana: University of Notre Dame Press, 2005).

42. *The Romance of Tristan, the Thirteenth-Century Old French 'Prose Tristan'*, translated by Reneé L. Curtis, World's Classics (Oxford: Oxford University Press, 1994; hereafter Cu], p. 256.

43. On the *fabliau* elements in this scene see Friedrich Ranke, 'Die Allegorie der Minnegrotte' (The Allegorical Significance of the Love-Grotto), *Schriften der Königsberger Gelehrten Gesellschaft, Geisteswissenschaftliche Klasse*, vol. 2/2 (München, publisher unnamed, 1925), pp. 21–39; Peter Dronke, 'The Rise of the Medieval Fabliau: Latin and Vernacular Evidence,' *The Medieval Poet and His World*, op. cit., Chapter 6; Gottfried von Strassburg, *Tristan*, translated (German) by Rüdiger Krohn, 3 volumes (Stuttgart: Reclam, 1984), translated by A. T. Hatto (New York: Penguin Books, 1975); John Hines, *The Fabliau in English* (London and New York: Longman, 1993).

44. Bruckner, *Shaping Romance*, op. cit., Chapter 1: 'Truth in Disguise: The Voice of Renarration in the *Folie Tristan d'Oxford*'.

45. See Sano Midori, Chapter 2 in this volume.

46. See John Fleming, *The 'Roman de la Rose'*, op. cit., and his *Reason and the Lover*, op cit.; *Rethinking the Romance of the Rose*, edited by Kevin Brownlee and Sylvia Huot, op. cit.; on the rewriting of the *Rose* romance, its *remaniements* (retellings) and glosses, which throw extensive light on its reception, see Sylvia Huot, *The Romance of the Rose and its Medieval Readers: Interpretation, Reception, Manuscript Transmission* (Cambridge: Cambridge University Press, 1993).

47. A. C. Spearing, *Medieval Dream-Poetry*, op. cit., p. 17. For dream in allegorical literature, see David F. Hult, 'The Narration of Allegory,' in *Self-Fulfilling Prophecies*, op. cit., Chapter 2.

48. *Song of Songs*, Chapter 4.

49. See Ernst Robert Curtius, op. cit., Chapter 10 [hereafter, Cu]; C. S. Lewis, 'Allegory,' in *The Allegory of Love*, op. cit., Chapter 2; Terry Comito, *The Idea of the Garden in the Renaissance* (New Brunswick: Rutgers University Press, 1978); and A. Bartlett Giamatti, *The Earthly Paradise and the Renaissance Epic* (Princeton: Princeton University Press, 1966).

50. 'Homer's Garden', translated by Massimo Venturi Ferriolo, *Journal of Garden History*, vol. 9 (1989), pp. 84–94. See also *Homer: Odyssey*, with English translation by A. T. Murray (1919), revised by George E. Dimock (Cambridge, Mass.: Harvard University Press, 3rd edition 1998), pp. 255–6.

51. *The Romance of the Rose*, translated by Charles Dahlberg (Princeton: Princeton University Press, 1971), pp. 39–40, 48–9. For the OF original, see Guillaume de Lorris et Jean de Meun, *Le Roman de la Rose*, op. cit., ll. 631–90, pp. 76–8; ll. 1320–1343, pp. 112–16.

52. Elizabeth Zadoura-Rio, 'Hortus conclusus: un jardin médiéval au Plessis-Grimoult (Calvados)', *Mélanges d'Archéologie et d'Histoire Médiévales: en Honneur du Doyen Michel de Boüard, Mémoires et Documents publiés par la Société de l' École des Chartres XXVII* (Genève: Librairie Droz, 1982), pp. 393–404.

53. The walled and turreted enclosed garden occupies an area of about 37 metres by 45

metres. See *Esclaves et Maîtres en Étrurie Romaine; les Fouilles de la Villa de Settefinestre* (Pisa and Siena: Centre National de la Recherche Scientifique, 1981).
54. 'Medieval Britain and Ireland in 1992', *Medieval Archaeology*, vol. 37 (1993), pp. 83, 265; *Hampshire Gardens Trust Journal*, vol. 11 (1992), pp. 19–22.
55. D. Fairchild Ruggles, *Garden, Landscape, and Vision in the Palaces of Islamic Spain* (University Park, Pennsylvania: Pennsylvania State University Press, 2000).
56. Hult, op. cit.
57. See D. Pearsall and E. Salter, 'The Enclosed Garden', *Landscapes and Seasons in the Medieval World* (London: Paul Elek, 1973), Chapter 4; Julie Scott Meisami, 'Allegorical Gardens in the Persian Poetic Tradition', op. cit., pp. 229–60; *Nizami Ganjavi, The* Haft Paykar: *A Medieval Persian Romance*, translated with Introduction by J. S. Meisami (Oxford: Oxford University Press, 1995).
58. Ibid., Section 38: 'How Bahrâm Sat in the White Dome: The Tale of the Princess of the Seventh Clime,' ll. 27 ff. p. 218 [hereafter M].
59. Chaucer presents many versions of the *locus amoenus*: notably in the *Book of the Duchess* (ll. 397–415; p. 335); the *Parliament of Fowls* (ll. 183–210; pp. 387–8); and the *Prologue to the Legend of Good Women* (ll. 89–103; p. 591); *The Riverside Chaucer*, edited by Larry D. Benson (Oxford: Oxford University Press, 1988) [hereafter R]. On the *fabliau* and its consequences in fourteenth century French lyrics, see Leonard W. Johnson, *Poets as Players: Theme and Variation in Late Medieval French Poetry* (Stanford: Stanford University Press, 1990); also Per Nykrog, *Les Fabliaux: Etude d' 'Histoire Littéraire et de Stylistique Médiévale* (Genève: Librairie Droz, 1973), who claimed these works were a kind of courtly genre; R. Howard Bloch, *The Scandal of the Fabliaux* (Chicago: University of Chicago Press, 1986).
60. *The Song of Songs*, Chapter 2: v. 3.
61. Sloane ms. 2593, British Library, London; *Medieval English Lyrics 1200–1400*, edited by Thomas G. Duncan (Harmondsworth: Penguin, 1995), p. 125.
62. On the tensions between the clerical and anti-clerical, the bawdy and the spiritual, the romantic and the cynical, see especially Peter Dronke on Nigel of Longchamps' *Speculum Stultorum* (translated by Chaucer as 'Daun Burnel the Asse'), 'Peter of Blois and Poetry at the Court of Henry II', *The Medieval Poet and His World*, op. cit., Chapter 11, p. 285 ff. Chaucer's aping of devotional attitudes to romantic or courtly love by romantic heroes speaks perhaps less (than say Jean de Meun) of directly sexual discourse than a playful and comical exploration of the private realms of human feeling. Thomist orthodoxy, and even freer thinkers like those in Chartres, were less forgiving on such matters.
63. R. Spearing, *The Gawain-Poet: A Critical Study* (Cambridge: Cambridge University Press, 1970).
64. *Œuvres complètes* (Paris: Gallimard nrf, 1994), pp. 140–1; E. Newstead, 'The "Joie de la Cort" Episode in Erec and the Horn of Bran', *Publications of the Modern Language Association of America*, vol. 51 (New York, 1936), pp. 13–25.
65. See *Matteo Maria Boiardo, Orlando Innamorato*, translated with Introduction by Charles Stanley Ross (Oxford and New York: Oxford University Press, 1995), and *Orlando Furioso: A Romantic Epic by Ludovico Ariosto*, translated with Introduction by Barbara Reynolds (London and New York: Penguin Books, 1973).
66. On polysemy and ambivalence with regard to the wild in Chrétien de Troyes, see Eugene Vance, 'Si est homo, est animal', *From Topos to Tale Logic and Narrativity in the Middle Ages*, Foreword by Wlad Godzich (Minneapolis: University of Minnesota Press, 1987), Chapter 5.
67. NKBT, vol. 4 (addit. Notes 332), p. 484, observes the reference to *Kokinshū* 204: 'A cicada sang, and I thought the sun had set, but I had just come under the shadow of the mountain' [T. 721]. Another *Kokinshū* poem, no. 685 ('Love Poems', vol. 4), reads: 'Ah, I miss them so, and how I long to see them, the pinks abloom in that rustic fence' [T. 721].

68. A reference to *Kokinshū* 349 by Ariwara no Narihira: 'O cherry blossoms, cover me with clouds of falling petals, that no one may know how age is coming for me' [T. 811].
69. This phrase obliquely suggests virginity, a nature unspoiled by social exposure to eligible men.
70. Here these galleries may be interpreted as those linking the main building with either the east or west wing.
71. See Ōta 1987, who illustrates a reconstruction of the Tōsanjō mansion, Figs. 71, 72 and pp. 314–52.
72. Tyler observes: 'The bridgeway connects the main house to the west wing. The fence (*naka no hei*) appears to stand between the house and the wing and to screen the two from each other.' [T. 711, note 12].
73. For unfulfilled yearning, see *Man'yōshū* (vol. 8, no. 1602), a poem by Ōtomo Yakamochi (circa 743) which reads: *Yamabiko no aitoyomu made tsumagoi ni ka naku yamabe ni hitori nomi shitei* (In the hills a deer /Cries in longing for his mate/And his echo sounds reply — alone) (Tokyo: Iwanami NKBT *Man'yōshū* vol. 2, p. 335). See Paula Doe, *A Warbler's Song in the Dusk: The Life and Work of Ōtomo Yakamochi 718–785* (Berkeley: University of California Press, 1982), p. 109. In the *Tales of Ise*, *dan* 4 highlights the lover's loss of his lady, appropriated by the Emperor: 'Is not the moon the same, the spring the same as that of old..(*tsuki ya aranu, haru ya mukashi no haru naranu..*; *Tales of Ise*, translated by Helen McCullough, op cit., p. 71.
74. Murasaki Shikibu likely derived inspiration for this plan from the fictional mansion of Masayori, found in *The Tale of the Cavern* (*Utsuho monogatari*), translated by Uraki Ziro (Tokyo: Shinozaki shorin, 1984), p. 350. See Ōta 1987: Chapter 2: Section 5 and Chapter 3: Section 6. Other theories, including those related to the palace of a dragon king built along such lines are discussed in Norma Field in *The Splendor of Longing*, op. cit., Chapter 2, (especially p. 111 ff.). Field emphasizes the mimicry of the imperial palace's inner female household, the Kōkyū, and the parallels with the structuring of the natural world as seen in the imperial poetry anthologies, and suggests that *The Tale* likens Genji to the emperor in his sexual journeying through the various women's quarters, and further, to seigneurial surveys of the land by Japanese emperors.
75. *Utsuho monogatari* (Tokyo: Iwanami NKBT, 1983), vol. 3, p. 100. Intertexts here include early tenth century poems like Lady Ise, *Ise shū* [flor. ?877 – ?940] *ike no tsuranaru matsu ni fuji sakeru tokoro* 池のつらなる松に藤さける所 (Where wisteria blooms on pines ranged by the pond), Ienaga Saburō 1966: item 217 (circa 913), p. 36.
76. Ōta 1987, pp. 228–34. Arguably, however, this would have been small and connected to the great southern pond.
77. Compare the layout of Kayanoin, ibid., Fig. 44, p. 247.
78. *Hahaso*; possibly the *nara* oak, famed for deep red late autumn foliage in poetry, or the *kashiwa*.
79. Some historic mansions may have had a brook flowing in from the southwest; see Ōta 1987, Fig. 40, p. 216; however this was not the normative manner, as is clear from evidence of Michinaga's mansions, and in Tōsanjō, Hōjūji, etc.; ibid., Figs. 33, 38, 71 and 132.
80. Murasaki Shikibu's text shows remarkable clarity with regard to locating buildings, and their adjacent gardens. This is highlighted by the fact that the only chapter in which less clarity is apparent in this regard is 'The Bamboo River' chapter, which has been critiqued as possibly not the work of Murasaki Shikibu; see Haruo Shirane, *The Bridge of Dreams: A Poetics of 'The Tale of Genji'* (Stanford: Stanford University Press, 1987), p. 224.
81. Ogawa 1992, pp. 7–22; see *Yizhou minghua lu* account in *Song, Liao, Jin huajia shiliao* (Materials on Painters of the Song, Liao and Jin Dynasties), edited by Chen Kaohua (Peking: Wenwu chubanshe, 1984), pp. 106–108; Ogawa 1987.
82. Lothar Ledderose, 'P'eng-lai and Jōdo: Some Paradise Compounds in China and Japan', *Interregional Influences in Art History: International Symposium on the Conservation*

and Preservation of Cultural Property (Tokyo: Tokyo National Research Institute of Cultural Properties, 1982), pp. 105–22.

83. For further exploration of this idea see Kawazoe 1992: Chapter 4: Section 2, pp. 222–5, where she refers to a commentary on the Lotus Sutra, *Hokke giso*, found in *Dainihon bukkyō zensho* (Tokyo: Kodansha, 1970–1973).

84. See 'Komakurabe no gyōkō' (An imperial visit to the horse races), *A Tale of Flowering Fortunes*, translated and annotated by William H. and Helen Craig McCullough (Stanford: Stanford University Press, 1980), Chapter 23 p. 631 ff.: '... the Kayanoin seemed to belong to another realm – to be quite equal, in fact, to the Dragon King's dwelling, where one can see a different season in each of the four directions'. The idea here seems to have been based on *sutras* such as *Kisen inpon kyō*; *Taishō shinshū Daizōkyō* 1924–1932: vol. 1, p. 387. See also Ōta Seiroku (1987) 244–8. Chinese *zaju* popular theatre, a tradition dating back to the Tang dynasty, features many stories related to the eight great Dragon Kings, their daughters, and their underwater domain; see *Liu Yi and the Dragon Princess*; *A Thirteenth Century* Zaju *Play by Shang Zhongxian*, translated and adapted by David Hawkes (Hong Kong: The Chinese University Press, 2003). In the Huayen (J. Kegon) sect Buddhist tradition, the Dragon King is seen as preserving sutras under the sea from the corruption of the world above; *Kegon sōshi eden* (Illustrations Legends of Patriarchs of the Kegon Sect), Komatsu Shigemi 1977–94: *Nihon emaki taisei*, vol. 18, p. 85.

85. See *Sakuteiki: Visions of the Japanese Garden*, translated by Takei Jirō and Marc P. Keane (Boston, Rutland and Tokyo: Tuttle, 2001), pp. 195–6. On Huizong's Genyue park, see Zhang Hao, *Genyue ji* (Record of the Genyue); *Zhongguo lidai mingyuanji xuanju* (Selected and Annotated Records of Famous Gardens throughout China's History), edited by Chen Zhi et al. (Anhui: Kexue Zhimu Chubanshe, 1983), pp. 56–64.

86. Foucault has stressed the political dimensions of tropes suggesting a golden mythic world and the diversionary function of such paradisal themes; see Michel Foucault, *Language, Counter-Memory, Practice: Selected Essays and Interviews*; edited with an introduction by Donald F. Bouchard; translated from the French by Donald F. Bouchard and Sherry Simon (Oxford: Blackwell, 1977). Nonetheless, where societies – in diverse cultures – are seen to favour 'yearning' for paradise, and tend to endorse the perfectibility of man in religious terms, then these notions are bound to be felt as widely shared cultural codes, despite their deracinating of locus with regard to immediate power.

87. Frank Justice Miller, *Ovid in Six Volumes, III, Metamorphoses, with English Translation* (Cambridge, Mass.: Harvard University Press, 1934), vol. 5, ll. 388–392, pp. 264–5.

88. Dante Alighieri, *The Divine Comedy*, translated with a commentary by Charles S. Singleton (Princeton: Princeton University Press, 1989–91), *Purgatorio*; pp. 306–307.

89. As Peter Armour has shown, Dante's exquisite reflexive verse here implies that there was here, not a double, but a quadruple loss: 'the daughter has lost her mother and the mother a daughter; and the daughter has lost her spring, her flowers, her virginity, and the mother too, in losing her daughter has lost spring'. The whole passage compresses the legend of Eve's fall from grace and paradise, and man's loss of his earthly paradise; see Peter Armour, '*Purgatorio XXVIII*', *Dante Commentaries: Eight Studies of the Divine Comedy*, edited by David Nolan (Dublin: Irish Academic Press, 1977), pp. 115–41.

90. *Ovid's Fasti*, translated by Sir James George Frazer (London and New York: Heinemann, 1931), vol. 5, ll. 207–208, pp. 274–5.

91. Se *Ise monogatari*, Item 4: 'Is not the moon the same?/ The spring/ The spring of old?/ Only this body of mine/ Is the same body'; *Tales of Ise*, op. cit., translated by Helen McCullough, p. 71.

92. See *Man'yōshū*, vol. 3, no. 469 (Iwanami NKBT, volume 1, p. 221): 'The flowers bloom in the garden/ She once looked out upon, /As time slips past, /Though my tears have yet to dry'; translated by Paula Doe, *A Warbler's Song in the Dusk*, op. cit., p. 89.

93. On the Greek tradition regarding *muthos* (myth) and *logos* (the word), and nostalgia

for a mythologized phase of '*muthos* as the conveyor of a stabilized universe', see Gregory Nagy, 'Can Myth Be Saved?', *Myth: A New Symposium* edited by Gregory Shremp and William Hansen (Boulder, Col.: Netlibrary, 2002), pp. 240–9.

94. Alain de Lille, *Anticlaudianus, texte critique avec une introduction et des tables*, Textes philosophiques du mōyen âge 1, edited by R. Bossuat (Paris: Librairie Philosophique J. Vrin, 1955) vol. 1, pp. 55 ff.; translated by Peter Dronke in 'Dante's Earthly Paradise', *Intellectuals and Poets in Medieval Europe*, op. cit., pp. 392–3.

95. Ibid., p. 390.

96. Ibid., pp. 403 ff. and Note 25; see *Livre de l'eschiele Mahomet*, vol. 96, *Il 'Libro della Scala'*, edited by E. Cerulli (Rome: Città del Vaticano, 1949); Leonardo Olschki, 'Mohammedan Eschatology and Dante's Other World', *Comparative Literature*, vol. 3, no. 1. (Winter, 1951), pp. 1–17; Mahmoud Manzalaoui, 'English Analogues to the "Liber Scalae",' *Medium Ævum XXXIV* (1965), vol. 1, pp. 21–35.

97. *Darshan: In the Company of Saints /Bursting with Joy*, vol. 124 (New York: Syda Foundation, 1997), p. 13. Sarmad was martyred on the orders of the Mogul ruler, Aurangazeb, in 1660.

98. For Abu Husayn An-Nuri (d. 907), see Schimmel, op. cit., pp. 59–62.

99. Ibid., p. 298.

100. *Rumi: Daylight, A Daybook of Spiritual Guidance, Three Hundred and Sixty-Five Selections from Jelaluddin Rūmī's 'Mathnawi'*, translated by Camille and Kabir Helminski (Boston and London: Shambala, 1999), p. 17.

101. See 'The Story of the Grail (Perceval)', *Chrétien de Troyes: Arthurian Romances*, translated and with Introduction by William W. Kibler, op. cit.; OF edition, 'Perceval ou Le Conte du Graal,' *Chrétien de Troyes: Œvres complètes* (Paris: Gallimard nrf, 1994); Arthur Groos, *Romancing the Grail*, op. cit.

102. For medieval poetics, reception of Aristotle, the contribution of Arab scholarship, and its flavours, see discussion about Averroes (Ibn Rushd) of Cordoba, and his translation by Hermann the German in Minnis, Scott and Wallace, 'Placing the Poetic: Hermann the German: An Anonymous Question on the Nature of Poetry', *Medieval Literary Theory and Criticism*, op. cit. For a strong critique of orientalizing of Arab culture in medieval studies, see Maria Rosa Menocal, *The Arabic Role in Medieval Literary History: A Forgotten Heritage* (Philadelphia: University of Pennsylvania Press, 1990), and *The Literature of Al-Andalus*, op. cit.; Peter Dronke, raising the issue of Ibn al-'Arabi's book of love lyrics, the *Futuhat* (1215) and its possible influence on Dante, finally settles for 'analogies' over 'imitations' in this instance. The case is of interest to comparative studies, since Ibn al-'Arabi presents a young woman, beautiful as she was holy, as the inspiration for his works: P. Dronke, *Dante's Second Love: The Originality and Contexts of the Convivio* (Exeter: The Society for Italian Studies, 1997).

103. See Albertus Magnus, '*Et nota, quod Christus rosa, Maria rosa, Ecclesia rosa, fidelis anima rosa*' (And note that Christ is a rose, Mary is a rose, the Church is a rose, and the faithful soul is a rose), *De laudibus B Mariae Virginis* XII, in *Opera omnia* edited by Auguste and Emile Borgnet (Paris: Vivé, 1890–1899), vol. iv, p. 33; Singleton, *Paradiso*, op. cit., vol. 1, Canto XXIII, ll. 73–4: 'Here is the Rose wherein the Divine Word became flesh', Singleton, ibid., pp. 260–1; ibid., Canto XXXI, ll. 1–3, pp. 346–7: 'In form then of a pure white rose the saintly host was shown to me'; ibid., vol. 2, *Commentary*, pp. 511 ff. See also Peter Dronke, 'Symbolism and Structure in *Paradiso 30*', *Romance Philology*, vol. XLIII, no. 1 (August 1980), reprinted in *Dante: The Critical Complex*, edited with introduction by Richard Lansing (New York and London: Routledge, 2003), pp. 381–400.

104. *Studies in the History and Method of Science*, edited by Charles Singer (Oxford: Oxford University Press, 1917), p. 33. Hildegard had found favour with Pope Eugene and St Bernard at the Synod of Trier (1147–1148); hence her visions were published, and she did not suffer the condemnation faced by Abelard, William of Conches and others. See Peter Dronke, 'Hildegard of Bingen', *Women Writers of the Middle Ages* (Cambridge: Cambridge University Press, 1984), Chapter 6, pp. 144–201.

105. She presents an image of Caritas, or Divine Love, who is seen as: 'a girl of surpassingly radiant beauty, with such dazzling brightness streaming from her face that I could not behold fully. She wore a cloak whiter than snow, brighter than stars, her shoes were of pure Gold. In her right hand she held sun and moon, and caressed them lovingly.' Dronke, *The Medieval Poet and His World*, op. cit., p. 67.
106. See Charles S. Singleton, *Journey to Beatrice* (Baltimore and London: Johns Hopkins University Press, 1958).
107. Dante, *Paradiso*, XXVIII, vol. 1, l. 3, translation by Singleton, op. cit., *Paradiso 1: Text*, pp. 312–13.
108. Dante, ibid., Canto XXXI, ll. 22–24; Singleton, ibid., p. 348.
109. *Amidakyō* [Sanskrit: *Sukhâvatî-vyūha*], the most popular and shortest of the three central Amida Paradise *sutras*.
110. Here, the fundamental doctrine, well known to the author, holds that the world – as it 'seems' to be – is illusory in 'seeming' other than the body of bliss constituting the realized Tathâgata (Buddha).
111. See Peter Dronke, *Fabula*, op cit; Edwin Panofsky, *Abbot Suger on the Abbey Church of Saint-Denis and its Art Treasures* (Princeton: Princeton University Press, 1979), p. 65; Otto Simson, *The Gothic Cathedral: Origins of Gothic Architecture and the Medieval Concept of Order* (New York: Pantheon Books, c. 1962).
112. *The Divine Names*, IV, translated from the Latin text (*De Divinis Nominibus*) of the Saracenus translation in Philippe Chevalier, *Dionysaca*, 2 volumes (Paris and Bruges: Brower, 1937–1950), p. 7. John Scotus Eriugena and Hugh of St Victor drew extensively on Pseudo-Dionysius; the former wrote about the 'one God, one Goodness, one Light, diffused in all things'; Umberto Eco, *The Aesthetics of Thomas Aquinas* (1956), translated by Hugh Bredin (Cambridge: Harvard University Press, 1988), pp. 56–7. On the relation to Platonism, see Paul Friedlander, *Plato*, op. cit., pp. 59–84.
113. Umberto Eco, op. cit., pp. 106–107.
114. St Bernard's '*Sic affici, deificari est*' (To enjoy this feeling, is to be deified) becomes in Dante '*trasumanar*' (to become – mysteriously – 'transhumanised'), Dante (*Paradiso*, Canto 1, l. 70), 'Trasumanar significar *per verba/* non si poria; però l'essempio basti/ a cui esperïenza grazia serba' (The passing beyond humanity may not be set forth in words: therefore let the example suffice for whom grace reserves that experience); Singleton, op. cit., *Paradiso I: Text*, l. 70, pp. 6–7. On Dante's 'coining' the ineffable, see Brenda Deen Schildgen, 'Dante's Neologisms in the *Paradiso* and the Latin Rhetorical Tradition', *Dante Studies*, CVII (Albany, New York: State University of New York Press, 1989), pp. 101–19.
115. Hans Robert Jauss, *Toward an Aesthetic of Reception*, translated by Timothy Bahti (German), with introduction by Paul de Man (Minneapolis: University of Minnesota Press, 1981). The vast body of poetry composed in gardens is well documented; see Shigemori Mirei and Shigemori Kantō 1971–1976.
116. For data on the Tōsanjōden, see Ōta 1987: Chapter 4: Section 4, pp. 364–86.
117. Adapted from T. 441, whose rendering does not highlight the fact that the central island could not have featured a bridge by which to approach it. The high-ranking women were not socially permitted to go to visit one another by boat; see Shōgakukan: *Genji monogatari*, NKBZ, vol. 3, p. 158.
118. The entertaining of imperial guests commonly featured the launching of music boats on the pond; see Chapter 7: 'Beneath the Autumn Leaves' where 'the musicians' barges rowed around the lake, as always, and there were all sorts of dances from Koma and Cathay' [T. 136].
119. Commentators (NKBT, vol. 2, p. 395) take the view that this hillock was 'in the pond', which seems quite consistent with the allegorical flavour of the overall design (see below). Ōta Seiroku's 'reconstruction' of this literary garden is unsatisfactory, however, having streams supplying *two* lakes, both from the southwest, thus inappropriately contravening the *Sakuteiki* rules for streams (see below); Ōta 1987: pp. 223–34. Ōta's diagram, however, makes the two southern ponds link.

120. We read of Genji's retiring to the east fishing pavilion (*tsuridono*) to cool off on a hot summer's day, at the outset of Chapter 26: 'The Pink' [T. 467].

121. The account of General Masayori's residence recounts how boats were tied together to make a floating bridge: see *The Tale of the Cavern*, op. cit., Chapter 7: Section 3, p. 148. Reconstruction by Ōta 1987, Fig. 27, p. 103.

122. Ōta 1987, pp. 153–78, 316–51, and Fig. 72 for a reconstructed plan of the Tōsanjō mansion.

123. Music barges usually featured the head of a dragon, or a roc (*geki*: a fabulous mythic bird able to survive storms and fly at great heights), as décor on the prow.

124. Adapted from Tyler. A key phrase here: 'さる大きなる池の中にさし出でたすれば、まことの知らぬ国に来たらむ心地して' (as they set forth on so large a pond, they felt as though transported to an unknown land) was omitted for no apparent reason by Seidensticker, op. cit., depriving this passage entirely of its allegorical intertext.

125. SNKBZ, vol. 3, p. 158.

126. This passage directly evokes a line from Bai Juyi's 'Mourning a Home' (*Shang zhai*); see *Bai Juyi ji* (Collected works of Bai Juyi) edited and annotated by Gu Xuejie (Peking: Zhonghua shuju:, 1999), vol. 1, *juan* 2, pp. 31–2. Kondō 1990: pp. 311–14; for an annotated bibliography on this field, see Ōta Tsugio: 1998: vol. 7, pp. 384–421.

127. Bowring, *The Diary of Lady Murasaki*, op. cit., p. 19; see *Murasaki Shikibu nikki*, NKBT, vol. 19, p. 458.

128. *The Clear Mirror: A Chronicle of the Japanese Court During the Kamakura Period (1185–1333)*, translated by George W. Perkins (Stanford: Stanford University Press, 1998), Chapter 10, 'Waves of Longevity', pp. 133–4.

129. The legends of the Immortal Isles, found in the *Liezi* (Book of Liezi), the *Shiji* (Book of History), and the *Hanshu* (History of the Han Dynasty), were already well known in Japan, also by way of the famous 'Hai manman' ('Ocean Wide'). In her diary account, Murasaki refers directly to the line which reads: 'Not finding Penglai they dare not return, the young men and women grow old in their boats'; see *Bai Juyi ji*, op. cit., vol. 1, pp. 56–7. See Bowring, op. cit., pp. 141–2. SNKBZ 3: 159. Kondō 1990, pp. 52–68.

130. Here, as in the response by Michinaga ('Xu Fu and Wen Cheng were empty braggarts'), direct reference is made to 'Ocean Wide'; Bowring, op. cit., p. 143.

131. Bai Juyi, famous for his satirical vision of the infamous Yang Guifei in a Penglai paradise found in 'Long Lament' ('Changhen ge'), composed numerous 'pond-top' poems, capped by a 'Pondtop Essay' ('Chishang pian'), *Bai Juyi ji*, op. cit., vol. 4, pp. 1450–1). Sugimura 1966: Chapter 5, pp. 46–8; Kondō 1981, pp. 64–91.

132. NKBT, vol. 2, p. 398.

133. In Japan, even within Buddhist traditions, the down-to-earth realism of the Kei school sculpture displaces, by the early thirteenth century, the idyllic and feminine manner of the previously dominant school of Jōchō, the master sculptor of the Phoenix Hall of 1052.

Appendix

ଚ

Key to *Genji* original chapter titles; translation references; and attributions to the five teams of calligraphers and painters I–V; page references to text excerpts (*kotobagaki*) in the *Genji Scrolls* as translated by Edward Seidensticker [S.] and Royall Tyler [T.].

	Japanese chap. titles	Tyler chap. titles (pages)	Seid chap. title (pages)	Calligraphers and painters I–V	Text excerpts (*Kotobagaki*) in the *Genji Scrolls* (pages)
1	Kiritsubo	The Paulownia Pavilion (1)	The Paulownia Court (3)		
2	Hahakigi	The Broom Tree (19)	The Broom Tree (20)		
3	Utsusemi	The Cicada Shell (45)	The Shell of the Locust (49)		
4	Yūgao	The Twilight Beauty (53)	Evening Faces (57)		
5	Waka Murasaki	Young Murasaki (80)	Lavender (84)	Call. III	
6	Suetsumu hana	The Safflower (111)	The Safflower (112)		
7	Momiji no ga	Beneath the Autumn Leaves (133)	An Autumn Excursion (132)		
8	Hana no en	Under the Cherry Blossoms (153)	The Festival of the Cherry Blossoms (150)		
9	Aoi	Heart-to-Heart (163)	Heartvine (158)		
10	Sakaki	The Green Branch (191)	The Sacred Tree (185)		
11	Hanachiru sato	Falling Flowers (221)	The Orange Blossoms (215)		
12	Suma	Suma (227)	Suma (219)		
13	Akashi	Akashi (255)	Akashi (247)		
14	Miotsukushi	The Pilgrimage to Sumiyoshi (279)	Channel Buoys (271)		

172 APPENDIX

	Japanese chap. titles	Tyler chap. titles (pages)	Seid chap. title (pages)	Calligraphers and painters I–V	Text excerpts (*Kotobagaki*) in the *Genji Scrolls* (pages)
15	Yomogiu	A Waste of Weeds (299)	The Wormwood Patch (290)	Call. II	*Illustration Text* T. 308; S. 298–9
16	Sekiya	At the Pass (313)	The Gatehouse (303)	Call. II	*Illustration Text* T. 316–17; S. 303–304
17	Eawase	The Picture Contest (319)	A Picture Contest (307)		
18	Matsukaze	Wind in the Pines (331)	The Wind in the Pines (318)		
19	Usugumo	Wisps of Cloud (345)	A Rack of Cloud (331)	Call. V	
20	Asagao	The Bluebell (363)	The Morning Glory (348)		
21	Otome	The Maidens (377)	The Maiden (360)	Call. V	
22	Tamakazura	The Tendril Wreath (404)	The Jewelled Chaplet (387)		
23	Hatsune	The Warbler's First Song (429)	The First Warbler (409)		
24	Kochō	Butterflies (438)	Butterflies (418)		
25	Hotaru	The Fireflies (453)	Fireflies (430)	Call. V	
26	Tokonatsu	The Pink (465)	Wild Carnations (441)	Call. V	
27	Kagaribi	The Cressets (479)	Flares (454)		
28	Nowaki	The Typhoon (485)	The Typhoon (457)		
29	Miyuki	The Imperial Progress (497)	The Royal Outing (467)		
30	Fujibakama	Thoroughwort Flowers (513)	Purple Trousers (482)		
31	Makibashira	The Handsome Pillar (523)	The Cypress Pillar (491)		
32	Umegae	The Plum Tree Branch (545)	A Branch of Plum (511)		
33	Fuji no uraba	New Wisteria Leaves (559)	Wisteria Leaves (523)		
34	Wakana: Jō	Spring Shoots I (575)	New Herbs: Part One (537)		
35	Wakana: Ge	Spring Shoots II (625)	New Herbs: Part Two (587)		
36	Kashiwagi	The Oak Tree (673)	The Oak Tree (636)	Call. I	*Illustration Texts* I: T. 680; S. 642 II: T. 683–4; S. 645–7 III: T. 687; S. 650

APPENDIX 173

	Japanese chap. titles	Tyler chap. titles (pages)	Seid chap. title (pages)	Calligraphers and painters I–V	Text excerpts (*Kotobagaki*) in the *Genji Scrolls* (pages)
37	Yokobue	The Flute (695)	The Flute (657)	Call. I	*Illustration Text* T. 702–703; S. 663–4
38	Suzumushi	The Bell Cricket (707)	The Bell Cricket (668)	Call. I	*Illustration Texts* T. 712; S. 671–2 I: T. 712 S. 671–2 II: T. 713–4 S. 673–4
39	Yūgiri	Evening Mist (717)	Evening Mist (676)	Call. I	*Illustration Text* T. 730–1; S. 687–8
40	Minori	The Law (753)	The Rites (712)	Call. I	*Illustration Text* T. 759–60; S. 717–18
41	Maboroshi	The Seer (765)	The Wizard (723)		
42	Niō miya	The Perfumed Prince (783)	His Perfumed Highness (735)		
43	Kōbai	Red Plum Blossoms (793)	The Rose Plum (743)		
44	Takekawa	Bamboo River (803)	Bamboo River (751)	Call. IV	*Illustration Texts* I: T. 807–808; S. 754–5 II: T. 811–13; S. 758–61
45	Hashihime	The Maiden of the Bridge (827)	The Lady at the Bridge (775)	Call. IV	*Illustration Text* T. 837; S. 785
46	Shii ga moto	Beneath the Oak (847)	Beneath the Oak (799)		
47	Agemaki	Trefoil Knots (869)	Trefoil Knots (821)		
48	Sawarabi	Bracken Shoots (915)	Early Ferns (872)	Call. III	*Illustration Text* T. 922–3, S. 879–80
49	Yadorigi	The Ivy (927)	The Ivy (885)	Call. III	*Illustration Texts* I: T. 930–1; S. 887–8 II: T. 945; S. 900 III: T. 960; S. 922–3
50	Azumaya	The Eastern Cottage (973)	The Eastern Cottage (936)	Call. III	*Illustration Texts* I: T. 993–4; S. 957–9 II: T. 1000–1001; S. 965–7

174 APPENDIX

Japanese chap. titles	Tyler chap. titles (pages)	Seid chap. title (pages)	Calligraphers and painters I–V	Text excerpts (*Kotobagaki*) in the *Genji Scrolls* (pages)
51 Ukifune	A Drifting Boat (1007)	A Boat upon the Waters (972)		
52 Kagerō	The Mayfly (1044)	The Drake Fly (1012)		
53 Tenarai	Writing Practice (1075)	At Writing Practice (1043)		
54 Yume no ukihashi	The Floating Bridge of Dreams (1111)	The Floating Bridge of Dreams (1081)		

Bibliography of Japanese Sources

☙

Akita Sadaki 秋田定樹, 1969,「源氏物語の内話」(Monologue in the *The Tale of Genji*), *Shinwa kokubun*『親和国文』, no. 2, (December).
Akita Sadaki, 1976,『中古中世の敬語の研究』(Study of Honorifics in the Heian and Medieval Periods), Tokyo: Seibundō.
Akiyama Ken 秋山虔, 1984,『王朝の文学空間』(The Literary Space of the Heian Period), Tokyo: Tokyo daigaku shuppan kai.
Akiyama Ken 秋山虔 and Taguchi Eiichi 田口栄一 eds, 1988,『豪華「源氏絵」の世界 源氏物語』(*The Luxurious World of Genji Pictures: The Tale of Genji*), Tokyo: Gakushūkenkyūsha.
Akiyama Terukazu 秋山光和, 1964,『平安時代世俗画の研究』(*Studies in Heian-period Secular Painting*), Tokyo: Yoshikawa kōbunkan.
Akiyama Terukazu, 1978,「源氏物語絵巻若紫図断簡の原形確認」(Verifying the Original Format of the 'Waka Murasaki' Fragment of the *Genji Scrolls*),『國華』*Kokka* no. 1011 (May).
Akiyama Terukazu, 2000,『日本絵巻物の研究』(*Studies in Japanese Picture Scrolls*), 2 volumes, Tokyo: Chūōkōron bijutsushuppan.
Arikawa Haruo 有川治男, unpublished manuscript,『西洋絵画全解』(Interpreting Western Painting).
Aristotle, 1997,『詩学』(*Artistotle's Poetics*), Matsumoto Nisuke 松本仁助 and Oka Michio 岡道男 eds, Tokyo: Iwanami bunko.
Chino Kaori 千野香織, 1988,「日本の絵画を読む – 単一固定視点をめぐって」(Reading Japanese Paintings: Concerning Single Fixed Viewpoints),『物語研究』(Research on Narrative), vol. 2, Special Edition, 視線 (*Lines of Sight*), Tokyo: Shinjidaisha, pp. 8–25.
Egami Yasushi 江上綏, 1989,「装飾経」(*Decorated Sutras*), volume 278 of the series『日本の美術』*Nihon no bijutsu* (Japanese Art), Tokyo: Shibundō.
Egami Yasushi, 1992,「扇面画 古代編」(Fan Paintings of the Ancient Period), volume 319,『日本の美術』*Nihon no bijutsu* (Japanese Art), op. cit.
Egami Yasushi, 1999,「料紙装飾 箔散らし」(*Paper Decoration, Sprinkled Foil*), volume 397 of the series『日本の美術』*Nihon no bijutsu* (Japanese Art), op. cit.
Enomoto Masazumi 榎本正純, 1976,「源氏物語における語りの諸問題」(Problems of narrative modes in 'The Tale of Genji'),『国語と国文学』, November issue.
Enomoto Masazumi, 1990,「源氏物語の時間性に関する一二の問題」(One or Two Issues Regarding the Nature of Time in *The Tale of Genji*),『和歌山大学教育学部紀要人文科学』(*The Bulletin of the Education Faculty of Wakayama University, Humanities*), vol. 39 (February).
Enomoto Masazumi, 1992,「絵画と文学−源氏物語絵巻と源氏物語との間−」(Painting and Literature – Between *The Tale of Genji Scrolls* and *The Tale of Genji*), 平安文学論究会

(Discourse on Heian Literature Association) eds, 『講座平安文学論究第八輯』 (*Lectures on Discourse on Heian Literature*), Tokyo: Kazama shobō.

Fujii Sadakazu 藤井貞和, 1980, 『源氏物語の始原と現在』 (*The Origin and Present State of* The Tale of Genji), Tokyo: Tōjusha.

Fujikoge Toshiaki 藤河家利昭, 1981, 「流離物語の史実と伝承」, Akiyama Ken 秋山虔, Kimura Masanori 木村正中 and Shimizu Yoshiko 清水好子 eds, 『講座源氏物語の世界』, 9 volumes, Tokyo: Yūhikaku, vol. 3, pp. 226–240.

Gotō Museum 五島美術館, 1990, 『国宝源氏物語絵巻 - 隆能源氏のすべて』 (The National Treasure Genji Scrolls – All About the Takayoshi Genji Scrolls), Tokyo: The Gotō Museum.

Haruna Yoshishige 春名好重, 1993, 『平安時代書道史』 (History of Heian Period Calligraphy), Kyoto: Shibunkaku.

Higashihara Nobuaki 東原伸明, 2004, 『源氏物語の語り・言説・テクスト』 (*Narrative, discourse, text of The Tale of Genji*), Tokyo: Ōfū.

Ienaga Saburō 家永三郎, 1966, 『上代大和絵年表』, Tokyo: Bokusui shobō

Imai Gen'e 今井源衛, 1976, 「紫式部の父系」, Yamagishi Tokuhei 山岸徳平 and Oka Kazuo 岡一男 eds, 『源氏物語講座』, 8 vols., Tokyo: Yūseido, vol. 6, pp. 77–78.

Inamoto Mariko 稲本万里子, 1999, 「『源氏物語絵巻』の詞書と絵をめぐって‐雲居雁、女三宮、紫の上の表象」 (Concerning the Textual Excerpts of the *Genji Scrolls* – Representations of Kumoinokari, the Third Princess, and Murasaki), in 『交渉することば (*Words that Negotiate*)』, 『叢書 想像する平安文学』 (Series: Imagining Heian Literature), vol. 4 (Tokyo: Bensei shuppan), pp. 219–40.

Ishida Jōji 石田穣二, 1971, 「源氏物語の情景描写」 (Description of scene in *The Tale of Genji*), Yamagishi Tokuhei 山岸徳平 and Oka Kazuo 岡一男, eds, 『源氏物語講座』 (Collection of Papers on *The Tale of Genji*), Tokyo: Yūseidō, vol. 7, pp. 26–7.

Ishihara Shōhei 石原昭平, 1981, 「宇治の伝承」, Akiyama Ken, Kimura Masanori and Shimizu Yoshiko eds, 『講座源氏物語の世界』, 9 volumes, Tokyo: Yūhikaku, vol. 8, pp. 14–32.

Itoi Michihiro 糸井通浩, 1981, 「源氏物語と助動詞『き』」 (*The Tale of Genji* and the auxiliary-verb 'き'), in Genji monogatari tankyūkai ed., 『源氏物語の探究』 (Research on *The Tale of Genji*), vol. 6, Tokyo: Kazama, pp. 107–39.

Itoi Michihiro, 1986, 「物語・小説の表現と視点」 (Expression and perspective in *monogatari*/ novel) in 『表現学論考 第二』 (Study of Hyōgengaku, no. 2), Nagakute, Aichi: Imai Fumio sensei koki kinen ronshū kankō iinkai, pp. 65–72.

Itoi Michihiro, 1992, 「物語言語の法 - 表現主体としての『語り手』-」 (Grammar of the *monogatari* language: 'narrator' as the subject of expression), Itoi Michihiro and Takahashi Tōru 高橋亨 eds, 『物語の方法』 (*Method of Monogatari*), Kyoto: Sekai shisō sha, pp. 21–34.

Itoi Michihiro, 1993, 「視点と語り」 (Perspective and narrative) in 『表現学論考 第三』 (Study of Hyōgengaku, no. 3), Nagakute, Aichi: Imai Fumio sensei kiju kinen ronshū kankō iinkai, pp. 41–50.

Itoi Michihiro, 1995, 「源氏物語と視点」 (*The Tale of Genji* and perspective), in Takahashi Tōru 高橋亨 and Kubo Tomotaka 久保朝孝 eds, 『新講源氏物語を学ぶ人のために』 (New Lecture: For People Who Study *The Tale of Genji*), Kyoto: Sekai shisō sha.

Kaneoka Takashi 金岡孝, 1962, 「源氏物語の表現主体」 (Subject of expression in *The Tale of Genji*), 『清泉女子大学紀要』, vol. 9.

Katayama Tetsu 片山哲, 2001, 『大衆詩人白楽天』, Tokyo: Iwanami shoten.

Kawazoe Fusae 河添房江, 1992, 『源氏物語の喩と王権』, Tokyo: Yūseidō.

Kitahara Yasuo 北原保雄, ed., 1978, 『論集日本語研究9』 (Collection of Papers on Japanese Language, no. 9: Honorifics), Tokyo: Yūseidō.

Kohitsugaku kenkyūjo 古筆学研究所, ed., 1994, 『古筆と絵巻』 (*Ancient Script and Narrative Handscrolls*), Tokyo: Yagi shoten.

Komai Gasei 駒井鵞静, 1988, 『源氏物語とかな書道』 (*The Tale of Genji and Kana Calligraphy*), Tokyo: Yūsankaku.

Komatsu Shigemi 小松茂美, 1970, 『日本書流全史』, Tokyo: Kōdansha.

Komatsu Shigemi ed., 1972, 『源氏物語絵巻、寝覚物語絵巻』 (The Genji Scrolls, The Tale of Nezame Scrolls), volume one of the series 『日本絵巻大成』 (Compendium of Japanese Painted Handscrolls), Tokyo: Chūōkōronsha.

Komatsu Shigemi ed., 1977–1994. 『日本絵巻物大成』 (Compendium of Japanese Painted Handscrolls), Tokyo: Chūōkōronsha.

Komatsu Shigemi, 1987, 『源氏物語絵巻、寝覚物語絵巻』 (The Genji Scrolls, The Tale of Nezame Scrolls), volume one of the series 『日本の絵巻』 (Handscroll Paintings of Japan), Tokyo: Chūōkōronsha.

Komatsu Shigemi, 2005, 『平家納経：平清盛とその成立』, Tokyo: Chūōkōron bijutsushuppan.

Kondō Haruo 近藤春雄, 1981, 『長恨歌・琵琶行の研究』 (Studies of *Changhenge* and *Pibaxing*), Tokyo: Meiji shoin.

Kondo Haruo, 1990, 『白氏文集と国文学： 新楽府、秦中吟の研究』, Tokyo: Meiji shoin.

Kumakura Chiyuki 熊倉千之, 1990, 『日本人の表現力と個性』 (Japanese People's Ability to Express and Individuality), Tokyo: Chūkō shinsho.

Kuroda Hideo 黒田日出男, 1986, 『姿としぐさの中世史』 (Medieval History of Physical Appearance and Gesture), Tokyo: Heibonsha.

Matsumoto Nisuke 松本仁助, Oka Michio 岡道男 (eds) 『アリストテレース 詩学 ホラーティウス詩論』 (Aristotle's Poetics, Horatius' Poetics) *Iwanami bunkô*, Tokyo: Iwanami Shoten, 1997.

Mitani Kuniaki 三谷邦明, 1978 (1969–1982), 「源氏物語における＜語り＞の構造」 (Structure of 'narrative' in *The Tale of Genji*), 『日本文学』, vol. 27, (November 1978), p. 43, compiled in Nihon bungaku kenkyū shiryō kankō kai ed., 『日本文学研究資料叢書 源氏物語』, 4 volumes, Tokyo: Yūseidō, 1969–1982, vol. IV, pp. 182–97.

Mitani Kuniaki, 1989, 『物語文学の方法』 (*Method of Monogatari Literature*), 2 volumes, Tokyo: Yūseidō.

Mitani Kuniaki 三谷邦明 and Mitamura Masako 三田村雅子, 1998, 『源氏物語絵巻の謎を読み解く』 (*Reading the riddle of The Tale of Genji Scrolls*), Tokyo: Kadokawa shoten.

Mori Ichirō 森一郎, 1985, 「源氏物語の表現構造としての敬語法」 (Grammar of Honorifics as the Structure of Expression of *The Tale of Genji*), 『学大国文』, no. 28, Ōsaka: Ōsaka kyōiku daigaku, pp. 65–79.

Mori Ichirō, 1986, 「源氏物語の表現構造としての敬語法（続）」 (Grammar of Honorifics as the Structure of Expression of *The Tale of Genji* [Continued]), 『学大国文』, no. 29, Ōsaka. Ōsaka kyōiku daigaku, pp. 43–59.

Mori Osamu 森蘊 1969, 『庭園とその建物』 (Gardens and their Buildings) *Nihon no bijutsu* (Arts of Japan), Tokyo: Shibundo, no. 34.

Morino Muneaki 森野宗明, 1966, 「源氏物語における敬語」 (Honorifics in *The Tale of Genji*), 『国文学解釈と教材の研究』, July issue, Tokyo: Gakutōsha, pp. 66–71.

Morino Muneaki, 1972, 「源氏物語の敬語」 (Honorifics in *The Tale of Genji*), 『国文学解釈と教材の研究』, December issue, Tokyo: Gakutōsha, pp. 51–8.

Morino Muneaki, 1975, 『王朝貴族社会の女性と言語』 (*Women and Language in Heian Aristocratic Society*), Tokyo: Yūseidō.

Murakami Fuminobu 村上史展, 1994, 「小説の日本語」 (Japanese in the novel), *Nihongo kyōiku nyūsu* 『日本語教育ニュース』, no. 6, Hong Kong: Society of Japanese Language Education, Hong Kong.

Mushanokōji Minoru 武者小路穣, 1990, 『絵巻の歴史』 (*History of Narrative Handscrolls*), Tokyo: Yoshikawa kōbunkan.

Nagoya Akira 名児耶明, 1999, 『日本書道史年表』 (*Chronolgy of Japanese Calligraphy*), Tokyo: Nigensha.

Nakayama Masahiko 中山真彦, 1995, 『物語構造論』 (*On Narrative Composition*), Tokyo: Iwanami Shoten.

Negoro Tsukasa 根来司, 1977, 「源氏物語の表現と語る文」 (Expression and Narrative Sentence in *The Tale of Genji*), 『国文学解釈と教材の研究』, vol. 22, no. 1, January issue, pp. 17–22.

Negoro Tsukasa, 1983, 「源氏物語の敬語法」 (Grammar of honorifics in *The Tale of Genji*), 『中古文学』, no. 31, May issue, Chūko bungakkai, pp. 41–50.

Negoro Tsukasa, 1991, 『源氏物語の敬語法』 (Grammar of Honorifics in *The Tale of Genji*), Tokyo: Meiji shoin.

Ogawa Hiromitsu 小川裕充, 1987, 「壁画における<時間>とその方向性 – 慶陵壁画と平等院鳳凰堂壁画扉画」, *Bijutsu shigaku* 『美術史学』 9.

Ogawa Hiromitsu, 1992, 「黄筌六鶴圖壁畫とその系譜（上）」 (Wall painting of six cranes by Huang Quan and its genealogy: Part I), 『國華』 *Kokka*, no. 1165 (December), pp. 7–24.

Okudaira Hideo 奥平英雄, 1987, 『絵巻物再見』 (Re-examining Illustrated Handscrolls), Tokyo: Kadokawa.

Orikuchi, Shinobu 折口信夫, 1965, 『折口信夫全集』 (*The Collected Works of Orikuchi Shinobu*), volume 1, Tokyo: Chūōkōronsha.

Ōta Seiroku 太田静六, 1987, 『寝殿造の研究』 (*Studies on Shinden Style Mansions*), Tokyo: Yoshikawa kōbunkan.

Ōta Tsugio 太田次男 et al. eds, 1998, 『日本における白居易の研究』 (Studies on Bai Juyi in Japan), 『白居易の研究講座』 (Discussion of Bai Juyi), Tokyo: Benseisha, vol. 7.

Oyama Atsuko 小山敦子, 1991, 「光源氏の原像」 (The Original Form of Hikaru Genji), 『源氏物語とは何か』 (What is *The Tale of Genji*?), Imai Takuji 今井卓爾, et al. eds, 『源氏物語講座』 (Discussion of *The Tale of Genji*), 10 volumes, Tokyo: Benseisha, vol. 1, pp. 163–85.

Sano Midori 佐野みどり, 1989, 「説話画の文法 - 信貴山縁起絵巻にみる叙述の論理」 (The Grammar of Buddhist Narrative Painting: The Logic of Description Seen in the *Illustrated Handscroll of The Miraculous Origins of Mt. Shigi*), 『山根有三先生古希記念論集 日本絵画史の研究』 (*A Collection of Essays Presented on the 70th Birthday of Professor Yamane Yūzō: Research on the History of Japanese Art*), Tokyo: Yoshikawa kōbunkan.

Sano Midori, 1991, 「王朝の美意識 8」 (The Aesthetic Consciousness of the Imperial Court, 8), 『書苑案内』 (Guide to the Garden of Writing), no. 70 (August).

Sano Midori, 1994a, 「近世における源氏物語享受の一側面」 (One View of the Reception of *The Tale of Genji* in the Premodern Era), 『画像と言語 平成四年、五年、科学研究費補助金研究成果報告書』 (*Pictures and Language: Report on Research Results of the Science Research Assistance Fund, 1992 and 1993*), Tokyo: Tokyo Cultural Research Institute.

Sano Midori, 1994b, 「女房の視線」 (The Viewpoints of Ladies-in-waiting), in 『新編日本古典文学全集』 (New Compendium of Classical Japanese Literature) (SNKBZ), vol. 20, 月報 (*Monthly Report*) no. 1, Tokyo: Shōgakukan.

Sano Midori, 1994c, 「『紫式部日記』と『紫式部日記絵巻』の間」 (Between *The Diary of Murasaki Shikibu* and *The Illustrated Handscroll of the Diary of Murasaki Shikibu*), in SNKBZ, volume 26, 月報 (*Monthly Report*) no. 7, Tokyo: Shōgakukan.

Sano Midori, 1994d, 『人の<かたち>人の<からだ>』 (*The Human Form, The Human Body*), Tokyo: Heibonsha Image Reading.

Sano Midori, 1996, 「枕草子絵巻の視点・構図」 (The Viewpoint and Composition of *The Illustrated Scroll of The Pillow Book*), 『国文学』 (National Literature), Tokyo: Gakutōsha.

Sano Midori, 1997, 『風流・造型・物語』 (*Elegance, Formation, and Narrative*), Tokyo: Skydoor.

Sano Midori, 2000, 『じっくり見たい源氏物語絵巻』 (A Close Look at the Genji Scrolls), Tokyo: Shōgakukan.

Sano Midori, 2004, 『中世日本の物語と絵画』 (*Medieval Japanese Narrative and Painting*), Tokyo: Hōsō daigaku kyōiku shinkō kai.

Shigemori Mirei 重森三玲 and Shigemori Kantō 重森完途, 1971–1976, 『日本庭園史大系』, 20 volumes, Tokyo: Shakai shisōsha.

Shimazu Hisamoto 島津久基, 1947, 『日本文学考論』 (Research on Japanese Literature), Tokyo: Kawade shobō.

Shimizu Yoshiko 清水好子, 1966, 「場面と時間」 (Scene and Time) in Shimizu Yoshiko, 1980. First published, 『国文学』, 「解釈と鑑賞」 (December).

Shimizu Yoshiko, 1980, 『源氏物語の文体と方法』 (*Text and Method in The Tale of Genji*), Tokyo: Tokyo University Press.

Shinohara Yoshihiko 篠原義彦, 1973, 「源氏物語に至る覗見の系譜」 (The tradition of surreptitious peeping in the *Tale of Genji*), 『季刊文学・語学』, vol. 68 (August), pp. 56–67.

Sugimura Yūzō 杉村勇造, 1966, 『中国の庭』, Tokyo: Kyūryūdō.

Sugiyama Yasuhiko 杉山康彦, 1973, 「源氏物語の語りの主体（上）」 (The subject of narrative in *The Tale of Genji*, vol. 1), 『文学』, vol. 41, no. 4.

Takahashi Bunji 高橋文二, 1985, 『風景と共感覚』 (*Scene and the Sympathetic View*), Tokyo: Shunjūsha.

Takahashi Tōru 高橋亨, 1982, 『源氏物語の対位法』 (*The Polyphony of The Tale of Genji*), Tokyo: Tokyo daigaku shuppan kai.

Takahashi Tōru, 1987, 『物語文芸の表現史』, Nagoya: Nagoya daigaku shuppan kai.

Takahashi Tōru, 1991a, 「初期物語の遠近法」 (The Perspective of Early Narrative), in 『日本文学史を読む - 古代後期』 (*Reading Japanese Literature History: The Latter Part of the Classical Period*), Tokyo: Yūseidō.

Takahashi Tōru, 1991b, 『物語と絵の遠近法』, Tokyo: Perikansha.

Takehara Hiroshi 武原弘, 1977, 「源氏物語における敬語の特殊相と物語叙法」 (A special aspect of honorifics and the method of expression in *The Tale of Genji*), 『私学研修』, no. 74, March issue.

Takeoka Masao 竹岡正夫, 1963, 「助動詞『けり』の本義と機能」 (The meaning and function of auxillary verb "keri"), 『言語と文芸』, no. 31, November issue, cited from (Umehara ed., 1979).

Tamagami Takuya 玉上琢弥, 1964–1969, 『源氏物語評釈』 (*Commentary Notes on the Tale of Genji*), 14 volumes, Tokyo: Kadokawa.

Yokoyama Hide 横山英, 1941, 「太平記の敬語」 (Honorifics in the *Record of Great Peace*), 『国語国文』, vol. 11, no. 7, July issue, pp. 48–80.

Yoshida Kōichi 吉田幸一, 1984; 1985, 「慶安三年山本春正跋『絵入源氏物語』六十巻の存在価値と絵入本としての意義（上）（下）」 (The Value of the 60 Extant Volumes of Yamamoto Shunshō's Keian 3 (1650) Edition of *The Illustrated Tale of Genji* and Its Significance as an Illustrated Text), 『平安文学研究』 (*Heian Literature Studies*) vol. 72 (December), pp. 131–46; vol. 73 (June), pp. 160–73.

Yoshioka Hiroshi 吉岡曠, 1976, 「源氏物語における『けり』の用法 一」 (The uses of 'keri' in *The Tale of Genji*, no. 1), 『研究年報』, vol. 23, pp. 149–93.

Yoshioka Hiroshi, 1977a, 「源氏物語の語り手と書き手と朗読者と」 (Narrator, Writer and Reciter of *The Tale of Genji*), 『国語国文』, vol. 46, no. 3, March issue, pp. 1–22.

Yoshioka Hiroshi, 1977b, 『源氏物語を中心とした論攷』 (Study Focusing on *The Tale of Genji*), Tokyo: Kasama.

Yoshizawa Yoshinori 吉沢義則, 1940, 「源氏つれづれの三」 (Essay on *The Tale of Genji*, no. 3), 『国語国文』, vol. 10, no. 6, May issue, pp. 86–90.

Yotsutsuji Yoshinari 四辻善成, 1978, 「河海抄」 (*Kakaishō*), in 『紫明抄』, Tamagami Takuya 玉上琢弥 ed., Tokyo: Kadokawa shoten.

General Index

☙

aesthetic, the, 64–7, 71, 73, 77 n3 & n7 & n17
   skill on *koto*, 71
Akashi (place), 70, 95
Al-Andalus, 102, 136, 143, 15143, 155, 161 n3, 168 n102
allegory, 133–7, 142, 145, 155–60, 161 n3, 163 n27, 164 n43 & n47 & n49, 169 n119, 170 n124
An Lushan (leader of rebellion of 755–763), 109
Ariwara no Narihira, 138, 165 n68
Ariwara no Yukihira, 70
ato (tracks/stains/pain), 6, 23 (scar), 31 n17
Auspicious Event Reporter, 49
authorial narrative situation, 84–6, 88, 90, 92
aware ('the pathos of things'), 108, 110

Bai Juyi (Tang poet) (774–846), *Changheng ge* (Song of Everlasting Sorrow), 50–2, 59 n45, 60 n48, 109–10
Balzac, Honoré de, *Sarrasine*, 103
Ban Dainagon, Chancellor, The Story of, 伴大納 言絵巻, 41
Barthes, Roland, *S/Z*, 103, 109, 112, 131
   Action codes, 103
   Cultural codes, 104, 111, 112, 136, 138, 140, 149, 156–8, 167 n86
   Hermeneutic codes, 103, 111
   Semic codes, 104, 110, 112, 137, 140, 148, 160
   Symbol codes, 103–105, 112, 133, 162 n13
Beatrice (Dante's *Divine Comedy*), 156, 169 n106
boundary-like animals (境界的動物), 22

calligraphic distension, 4
calligraphic 'interruption' (yami 止み), 18
chahar bagh, 143
chivalry and learning, 107
cognition, 89–90, 93, 98 n13
cognitive activity, 85–90, 93
cognitive distance, 94
cognitive narrative modality, 93
Cold War, 64
consciousness, 81, 83–92, 95, 97, 98–9 n13
consorts – junior or senior (*kōi* or *nyōgo*), 69

Damyan (Chaucer, *The Merchant's Tale*), 145–6
didacticism, 107
différence (between historic and romance layouts), 148
discourse **Now,** 94–7
displacements, 66–9, 71, 73–7
   (aesthetic), 64–5
   (masculinist), 66
   (patriarchal gender), 66
duplicated cognition, 89
duplicated psychological description, 85
duplicated *telling* mode, 85

earthly paradise, 137, 139, 142–43, 152, 158, 154, 160, 164 n49, 167 n88, 168 n94
eavesdropping, 48
emperor manqué, i.e. Genji, 70
Empress Shōshi, 106
enchanted gardens, 147
enclosed garden (hortus conclusus), 138–9, 142–3, 147–8, 164, 165 n57
epistemic modal suffix, 98 n1
epistemic modality, 98 n2
eshi (head artist), 7

evergreen branch, *sakaki* (*cleyera ochnacea*), 140

fabliau, 145–6, 164 n43, 165 n59
false frame of the *The Tale of Genji*, 49
falsity of old tales (*soragoto*), 137
feminine enclosure, 138
feminized exile, 67
Fénice, 139, 142
fictional language, 82, 84, 89, 90, 96, 99 n27
Flora (Ovid's *Fasti*), 153
Fountain of Narcissus, 135, 138, 144
fountains, 143–4
    fons clausa (sealed fountain), 143, 155
Fujitsubo (*Tale of the Cavern*), 150
Fujiwara Korechika (974–1010), 67, 70
Fujiwara marriage strategy, 68
Fujiwara Michinaga (966–1028), 76, 79 n20, 137, 151–2, 156
Fujiwara Yukinari 藤原行成 (972–1027), 8
Fujiwara Sadanaga 藤原定長 (later known as Jakuren 寂蓮) (1139?–1202), 8
Fujiwara Takaie (914–82), 67
Fujiwara Yorimichi, 152

Garden of Eden, 139, 142–3
garden of infatuation, 147
gardens of perpetual spring, 152–4, 158, 160, 167 n87
Gawain (*Gawain and the Green Knight*), 146, 165 n63
Genji's 'exile', 70
Geoffrey of Monmouth (1136–37), 106
geomancy, 151
gin noge (silver hairs), 15
gnostic traditions, 131, 155, 156, 160, 161 n1
Gothic space, 106
hakanaki ('evanescent/fragile/short-lived'), 27

Heike Nōkyō 平家納経 (1164) (Fig. 1–2: *Heike Nokyo Jobon*), 8
Historic mansions
    Hōjūji, 137
    Kayanoin, 150, 152, 166 n77, 167 n84
    Tōsanjō Mansion, 137
    watadono galleries, 148–9
    yarimizu (brook), 147–48, 151, 157
Hogen and Heiji Insurrections, 7

Hōjūji, 137
Honganji-bon sanjurokunin kashu 本願寺本三十六人歌集 (ca. 1112; Fig. 1–1), 8
honorific, 80–9, 91–8, 98 ns2–3 & n5, 99 ns20–21
humbleness, 84

illness, 4–7, 11, 13–15, 18–26, 28, 30–1, 33, 35
'illness' ('yami' 病み, 14 (Fig. 1–13: The Oak Tree I, sheet two), 14
Illustrated Tale of Wakeful Sleep, The, 53–4
inner thinking, 85, 88–9
Ise monogatari, 167 n91
Izumi Shikibu, Diary of, 65

Januarie (Chaucer, *The Merchant's Tale*), 145, 146
'Joy of the Court', a magic horn, 146

Kagerō nikki (The Gossamer Diary), 68, 78 n11 & n14
Kaguya-hime, heaven-sent princess of *Tale of Bamboo Cutter*, 72, 75, 79
Kashiwagi, 1–17, 19–26, 29–36
Kawachi-bon, 99 n21
Kayanoin, 152
kazome scented dye, 15
King Mark of Cornwall, 141
kirihakū 切り箔 (cut gold or silver foil), 8, 13, 34 n59
Kokinshû Imperial anthology (905), 113, 133, 162 n6, 165 n67 & n68
kokubungaku 'national literature', 63,
Kōrōden, 111
kotobagaki (narrative calligraphic prefaces), 7, 31 n8
Koya gire 2 style, and Minamoto Kaneyuki 源兼行 (1023?–74?), 33 n37
Kōzei style calligraphy, 32 n34
Kyoto, 95

ladies-in-waiting, 98 n2
literary language, 88, 99 n16
locus amoenus, 137, 139, 152, 158, 165 n59
Lover, The, 136–7, 138, 144, 15–6, 161 n3, 164 n46, 166 n73
Lovers, The, 139

Mansions of *The Tale of Genji*
    Nijō mansion, 148

Rokujō mansion gardens, 108
Rokujō palace, 50
Sanjō mansion, 97
Marie de Champagne, 106
Ma'rifa (gnosis), 161 n1
Medieval History of Physical Appearance and Gesture by Kuroda Hideo, 22
mental activity, 84–5, 89
midare-gaki 乱れ書き (tangled script), 8, 9, 11, 16, 18–19, 23–7, 29–30, 31 n19, 35 n87 & n88, 36 n96,
mijin 微塵 (silver dust, pulverized dust), 8, 13, 17, 30 n6, 34 n51 & n59
Minamoto no Takaakira (914–82), 67–9, 74, 78–9
Minamoto no Tôru (822–895), 67, 74
Miraculous Origins of Mt Shigi, The (信貴山縁起絵巻), 41
modal marker, 89, 93, 99 n13
modal suffix, 80, 98 n1
Molt bel conjointure (fine composition), 107
monogatari (tales), 67
monologue, 84, 88, 89, 90, 92
mourning and melancholia, 111
Murasaki Shikibu, 49, 66–9, 71, 73, 76–9, 141, 151–2, 158–60, 163 n31, 166 n74 & n80, 170 n127
mythic worlds, mythic time, mythic idyll, 137, 153–4, 157–60, 167 n86, 170 n133

narration, 84, 88–90, 97, 98, 98 n2
   narrated monologue, 92
   narrated time, 94
   narrating moment, 94
   narrating **Now,** 96
   narrating present, 100 n36
   narrating time, 94, 96
   narrative description, 89
   narrative distance, 80, 85–6, 88, 91, 93, 98 ns1–2 & n13
   narrative modal marker, 89, 93, 99 n13
   narrative perspective, 82–3, 88, 94
   narrative point of view, 83
   narrator, 80, 82–98, 98 n2, n13
   narratorial standpoint, 80, 97, 98 n9
narrative
   as manipulation, 38
   content and form, 39
   floating narrators, 49
   Genette's *histoire*, *recit* (narrating), & 'narration', 55 n10
   'I did not see all the details' (authorial intervention), 49
   ladies in waiting, (transparent narrators), 44, 48
   locus of narration, 37–8
   narrating, 3–8
   narrator as 'inadequate observer', 49
   omniscient narrator, 43
   perspective of narrating, 42
   plot (Aristotle's *mythos*), 54 n1
   plurality of perspective, 42 (in painting), 47
   presence and presentness of the locus of narration, 37, 38, 40, 55 n2
   scene and viewpoint, 42
   voiced narrator, 43
narrative scroll formats
   punctuated format (senbyô shugi 線描主義) *renzoku-shiki* (continuous format) narrative scrolls, 41
Nijō mansion, 148
noge 野毛 (wild hairs), 8–9, 13, 15–16, 34 n 59
noyama (野山: fields and mountains), 16–17

Occidental individualism, 107
'Ogre causing fear of darkness, The', 5
'Ogre causing paralysis and constipation, The', 6
old tales (*monogatari*), 133–4, 140
Orlando (romances of Boiardo & Ariosto), 147, 165 n65
otoko-e 男絵 style, 26
Ōtomo Yakamochi, 138, 166 n73

painting
   as a frame, 40
   as an all-at-once experience, 40
   birds's eye view, 43
   focalization, 43
   high angle view, 43
   interior perspective, 43
   its comprehensive gaze, 40
   its parameters, 39–40
   onna-e 女絵 (feminine painting), 26, 43
   view of the entire scene, 53
   viewpoint, 57 n24
   zero-focalization, 43
paradisus voluptatis, 153
peeping (*kaimami* or *sukimi*), 141, 158
perception verb, 93, 98 n9
perspective, 82–3, 85, 88, 93–5, 97–8, 98 n2
Platonic anagogy, 133, 156, 160, 161 n2

Plessis-Grimoult, 143, 164 n52
prolonged illness (ながやみ・長病み), 19
Proserpina, 152–3
psychological attitude, 98
psychological description, 84–5
psychology, 84
public/private distinction, 112

Reading the Medieval Text, 105
respect, 80–5, 88, 99 n21
respect form, 80
Rokujō gardens, 149, 150–3, 158, 160
Rokujō mansion gardens, 108
Rokujō palace, 50

sacred enclosure, 139
sakaki (cleyera ochnacea), 139–40
Sanjō mansion, 97
Sarashina nikki (The Sarashina Diary), 68
Sei Shōnagon, *The Pillow Book* (*Makura no sôshi*), 65, 68, 77 n8, 78 n11
self, 81–2, 85, 88–92, 96–8
  semantic overlap, 14
sententiae, 112
'serving at the palace' (*miyazuka*i), 69
Sessonji 世尊寺 school lineage, 8
setsuwa 説話 (narratives), 41
Settefinestre (first century AD), 143
Shigisan-engi 信貴山縁起 (ca. 1176; *Legends of Mt Shigi*), 26
shita-gaki (undersketch), 7
shōji 障子 screen, 48
sickness ('wazurai' 患ひ), 14
silence, 76
single-folded mode, 99 n13
slander theme, 111
songe et mensonge: dream and lies, 134
Song of Songs, The, 142–3, 146, 155, 160 n60
sonic theory (Egami) and *luminosity*, 15
sōshiji, 97
speaker, 82, 89–90
spirit possession (mono no ke 物の怪), 30
story, 93–8, 99 n4, 10 n36
  story **Now**, 93–8
  story **Past**, 94–7
  story time, 14
suffix, 80, 85, 88, 91–2, 96–8, 98 n1
Sufi gnosticism, 135, 144, 154–6, 161 n2
Suma (place), 89, 95
synchronic narrative, 93

Takayoshi Genji, 7
Tale of Genji, chapters
  'Akashi', 70
  'Bamboo River', 96, 146–8, 150, 166 n80
  'Beneath the Oak', 82 ff.
  'Broom Tree, The', 138
  'Eastern Cottage, The', 148
  'Evening Faces', 94
  'Evening Mist', 48, 50, 147
  'Festival of the Cherry Blossoms', 86
  'Gatehouse', 95
  'Green Branch, The', 139
  'Ivy, The', 48, 97
  'Kashiwagi', 4, 6, 9, 13–14, 16–17, 19, 23, 30, 31, 31 n9
  'Lady at the Bridge, The', 140, 146
  'Law, The', 42, 47, 56
  'Maidens, The', 108, 150
  'New Herbs' (Part 2), 88, 91
  'Oak Tree, The', 49
  'Paulownia Court, The' (Kiritsubo), 93, 105, 111
  'Sacred Tree', 97
  'Suma', 70
  'Typhoon, The', 86
  'Waste of Weeds, A', 149
  'Wisteria Leaves', 81
  'Wormwood Patch', 94–5
Tale of Genji, Illustration Scrolls
  Bamboo River I, (Fig. 2-6), 53
  Bamboo River II, (Fig. 6-6), 56 n18, 148
  Bell Cricket I, The, (Fig. 6-7), 148–9
  Bell Cricket II, The, (Fig. 2-5), 50
  Evening Mist (Fig. 2-2), 48, 56 n18
  Ivy I, The (Fig. 2-3), 48, 56 n18
  Kashiwagi (Fig. 1-3: *The Oak Tree*, painting), 22
  Kashiwagi I, kotobagaki, 8
  Kashiwagi II (Fig. 1-15, sheet five), 8
  Lady at the Bridge, The (Fig. 6-4), 140
  Law, The (Fig. 1-22) painting, 23
  Law, The, sheet five (Fig. 1-26), 29
  Minori (御法・みのり) (Fig. 1-25, *The Law*, sheet three), 8, 24
  Oak Tree I, The, 'yami' (Figs. 1-13, 1-6), 18
  Oak Tree I, The, sheets one and two (Figs 1-8a, 1-8b), 10
  Oak Tree I, The, sheet two (Fig. 1-6), 9–10,
  Oak Tree I, The, sheet one (Fig. 1-11), 12

Oak Tree I, The, sheet two (Fig. 1-12; willow branches), 12
Oak Tree I, The, sheet two, columns 4–8 (Fig. 1-9), 10
Oak Tree I, The, sheet two, detail columns five to nine (Fig. 1-12), 13
Oak Tree I, The, sheet two: 'ya-mi' (Fig. 1-13), 13
Oak Tree I, The, sheet three (Fig. 1-10), 11
Oak Tree I, The, sheet three (Fig. 1-7), 10
Oak Tree II, The, sheet three; (Fig. 1-16), 15
Tale of Genji Picture Scrolls, The, 4
  T/G (Tokugawa/Gotoh collections), 41–2, 47, 50 56 ns18–19, 59 n37
  adapted or edited text *(shôshutsubon* 抄出本), 42
  'four hands' of painters, 56 n19
  total surviving scenes, and text excerpts, 56 n18
Tale of Genji, protagonists
  Akashi Lady (daughter of ex-governor of Akashi, wooed by Genji), 70–1, 75–6, 81–2, 98 n5, 151
  Akashi priest (father of Akashi lady), 71
  Akashi princess, 81
  Akikonomu (daughter of Lady Rokujō, later empress to Reizei) , 70–2, 75–6, 112, 139, 149
  Aoi lady, Yūgiri's mother, 73
  Eighth Prince, 70, 74–5
  Fujitsubo (consort of Genji's father), 71–2, 105
  Genji, 50, 82, 86–9, 95, 134, 140, 148–53, 157–8, 169 n20
  Hotaru (Prince, and half-brother of Genji), 50
  Kaoru (son of Kashiwagi and Third Princess liaison), 48, 74–7, 82–3, 97, 140, 144, 148
  Kashiwagi (Tō no Chūjō's eldest son), 50, 73–5, 88, 90–2, 144, 147
  Kiritsubo Lady (consort of 'old emperor'), 93, 105, 113
  Kiritsubo's mother, 93
  Kokiden (original consort of 'old emperor'), 110, 112
  Kumoinokari (Tō no Chūjō's second daughter and wife of Yūgiri), 48, 73
  Locust Shell Lady (Utsusemi, wife of Vice-Governor of Iyo), 95
  Masakonokimi (character), 53
  Murasaki (Genji's second wife), 66, 76, 81, 82, 85–7, 96, 98 n5, 150, 152–4, 157
  Nakanokimi (younger daughter of Prince Hachi), 148, 163 n37
  Niou (Prince, son of Emperor Kinjō and Akashi empress), 136, 148
  Oborozukiyo (sister of Lady Kokiden), 86
  Oigimi (elder daughter of Prince Hachi), 82–3, 148
  Onna San no Miya (The Third Princess), 5, 31 n17 & n19, 35 n83, 88, 91, 148
  Princess Ochiba (the Second Princess, daughter of Emperor Suzaku), 50, 97
  Reizei Emperor, 72–4, 96
  Retired Emperor Reizei, 50
  Rokujō lady, 70–6, 79 n24 & n29, 113, 139
  Suetsumuhana (the lady with the red nose; subject of chapter 6), 149
  Suzaku Emperor , 70, 73–5, 96
  Tamakazura, Tō no Chūjō's daughter, 72–3, 75–6, 95, 95
  Tō no Chūjō (brother of Lady Aoi), 88
  Tō no Chūjō's daughters, 71
  Ukifune (unrecognized daughter of Prince Hachi and a consort), 75–8, 136, 148
  Vice-Governor of Hitachi (stepfather of Ukifune), 95
  Vice-Governor of Iyo, 95
  Yūgao (lady wooed in chapter 4), 94
  Yūgiri (Genji's first son by his first wife, Lady Aoi), 48, 50, 72–3, 87, 89, 94, 99, 147
Tale of the Bamboo Cutter, The, 73
temporal distance, 94–6
temporal suffix, 80, 96–7, 98
time
  aporia of time, 39
  conceptualizing time, 37
  giving form to time, 37
  giving physicality to time, 56 n16
  imaging and re-imaging of time, 39
  intratextual time, 40
  localized present time, 38
  logos and *chronos*, 39
  manifestation of time, 38
  presence and presentness of the locus of narration, 37, 38, 40, 44, 55 n2

time in *The Tale of the Bamboo Cutter* (*Taketori monogatari*), 55 n8
time negotiated between narrative and reader, 39
vague ticking away of time, the, 37–8
Tōsanjō Mansion, 137
'tracks of strange birds, the' (*ayashiki tori no ato*), 5, 22–3, 30 n1, 53 n83
transgression, 64, 67, 72–6
Tree of Knowledge, The, 139, 141
Tristan, 134, 141, 164 n42 & n44
Troyes, Chrétien de, 106, 107, 117, 126, 128, 131
Troyes, Chrétien de, *The Knight of the Cart*, 105, 106, 108, 114, 119, 121, 124
  Calogrenant, 107, 112
  Cligés, 109, 112
  Erec and Enide, 106, 112
  'molt bel conjointure', 105, 107
  Yvain, 107, 108
tsukuri-e 作り絵 ('built picture'), 26
Tsukushi, 67, 72, 75

Uji chapters, 74, 76, 78–9
unmo 雲母 (mica powder), 8

voice convention, 38
  narrating viewpoint, 57 n28
  narrating voice, 44
  narrating constructing time, 55 n6
  narrating manifests 'now' and 'here', 38
volitional conjugated form of verb, 89–90
volitional suffix, 88, 91–2
voyeurism, 139–40

watadono galleries, 148–9
women and literature, 104, 106

Xuanzong (Tang Emperor, 685–762), 109

Yamamoto Shunshō's 山本春正 *The Illustrated Tale of Genji*, (*E-iri Genji monogatari* 絵入源氏物語), 42, 56 n22
Yamato Waki's comic (*manga*) adaptation of *The Tale of Genji*, *Asaki yume mishi* (Passing Dreams), 43–4, 58 n34
Yang Guifei (Tang Xuancong's favourite consort, 719–756), 109
yarimizu (brook), 147–8, 150–51, 157, 160 n79
yase-sarahohi, to slim severely, 20
yowari, (to 'exhaust', 'enfeeble', 'break down' and 'weaken'), 14

Author Index

∞

NOTE: This index is provided in lieu of a full bibliography and is intended to ensure ease of access to full reference and context.

'Abd al Qâdir al-Jîlânî (d. 1166), 135
Akita, Sadaki, 98 n3, 99 n14, 175
Akiyama, Ken, 57 n23, 98 n6, 175
Akiyama, Terukazu, 8, 26, 31 n22, 32 n25 & 28, 36 n93, 36 n94, 56 n18, 175
Alain of Lille (*Anticlaudianus*), 154, 168 n94
Arikawa, Haruo, 55 n13, 175
Aristotle, 51–2, 54, 54 n1
Ariwara no Narihira, 138, 165 n68
Aston, W. G., 78 n11
Auerbach, Erich, 130

Babur, 137, 163 n30, 136
Bai, Juyi (Tang poet) (774–846), 50–3, 59 n45, 60 n46, 118
Bakhtin, Mikhail, 99 n24, 103, 129, 135
Bargen, Doris, 130
Barthes, Roland, 103, 109, 112, 131
Bernard of Clairvaux, 133, 168, 169 n114
Booth, Wayne C., 99 n23
Bowring, Richard, 108
Brownlee, Kevin, 161, 164
Bruckner, Matilda Tomaryn, 162 n16, 164 n44

Chatman, Seymour, 94, 99 n24 & n28 & n33
Chaucer, Geoffrey, 129
Chino, Kaori, 57 n24, 175
Cohn, Dorrit, 99 n24
Curtius, Ernst, 132

Dante, 132, 133, 135, 153, 154, 156, 157, 161 n5, 167 n87,168 n94 & n96 & n102 & n103, 169 n107 & n108 & n114

Decoker, Gary, 32 n34
Derrida, Jacques, 99 n16, 130, 131
Dronke, Peter, 132, 161 n3 & n9, 164 n43, 165 n61, 168 n94 & n102 & n104, 165 n105, 169 n111

Eco, Umberto, 54, 60 n51
Egami, Yasushi, 15–16, 32 n29, 34 n47 & n49 & n57 & n61, 175
Enomoto, Masazumi, 37–8, 42, 55 n2 & n7, 57 n25 & n28, 99 n27, 175

Field, Norma, 126, 131, 151, n.38, n74
Fleming, John, 132, 161, n3
Frawley, William, 100 n35
Freud, Sigmund, 115, 120, 126, 130, 131
Fujikoge, Toshiaki, 79, 176
Fujiwara, Tetsu, 60 n45, 176,

Genette, Gerard, 55 n10, 57 n27, 58 n28, 130
Graybill, Marybeth, 32 n25

Haruna, Hiroshige, 32 n36
Hauser, Arnold, 106
Heller-Roazen, Daniel, 161, n3
Higashihara, Nobuaki, 99 n21 & n27, 176
Homer, 133, 142, 147, 164 n50
Hult, David, 132, 136, 143–4, 161 n3, 163 n24 & n26 & n27, 165 n56
Huot, Sylvia, 161, 164

Imai, Gen'e, 79, 176
Ishida, Jōji, 99 n20, 176
Ishihara, Shôhei, 79, 176
Itoi, Michihiro, 98 n2, 99 n1 & n27, 100 n36, 176

Jackson, Reginald, 42

Kawabata, Yasunari, 66, 77 n7
Keene, Donald, 65–66, 77 n6
Komai, Gasei, 31, 35 n87 & n88, 177
Komatsu, Shigemi, 32 n29 & n34
Kumakura, Chiyuki, 99 n27, 177
Kuroda, Hideo, 22, 35 n81, 177

Lacan, Jacques, 119, 130, 131
Lessing, Gotthold, 40, 56 n15
Lewis, C. S., 132, 163, 164 n49
Lorris, Guillaume de, 136, 142–3, 162
  17, 163 n24, 164 n51
Lot, Ferdinand, 107
Lyotard, Jean Francois, 56 n17

Macrobius, 134, 142, 162 n17
Martin, Wallace, 99 n24
Matsumoto, Nisuke, 55
McCullough, Helen, 105, 108, 115, 116,
  121, 124, 126
Meech-Pekarik, Julia, 32 n29
Meisami, Julie Scott, 132, 161, n3, 162,
  n20, 165, n57
Menocal, Maria Rose, 132, 161, n3
Mitani, Kuniaki, 99 n1 & n34, 177
Mori, Ichirō, 98 n3 & n8, 99 n17, 99
  n19, 177
Morino, Muneaki, 98 n3, 177
Morris, Ivan, 57 n28, 65–66, 77 n8, 78
  ns10–14, 106, 115
Murakami, Fuminobu, 59 n38, 98 n1, 177
Murasaki, Shikibu, Diary of, 49

Nagoya, Akira, 31 n23, 179
Nakayama, Masahiko, 38, 55 n5, 98 n1,
  177
Negoro, Tsukasa, 98 n3, 178
Nizami, 134–6, 144–5, 161, 165 n57
Nykrog, Per, 107

Oka, Michio, 55
Okada, Richard, 33 n39, 35 n66, 79 n25,
  99 n27 & n30
Ōkagami (Anon: The Great Mirror 大鏡),
  59 n41
Okudaira, Hideo, n18, 33 n39,
Orikuchi, Shinobu, 59 n40, 178
Ovid, 133–4, 136–8, 141, 143–6, 152–3,
  155–7, 159–60, 167 n90

Pamuk, Orhan, 136
Patterson, Lee, 136, 163, n. 27

Pekarik, Andrew, 78 n17
Petronius, 142
Plato, 133, 161, n2, 162 n9 & n10, 169
  n112
Prince, Gerald, 98 n11
Proust, Marcel, 106, 129

Ranke, Friedrich, 164 n43
Rosen, Towa, 161 n4
Rosenfield, John, 31 n14, 32 n35 n88, 34

Said, Edward, 63
Sano, Midori, 7, 11 n24, 31 n23, 32 n28,
  36 n95, 60 n46 & ns52–53 &
  ns57–58, 178
Sansom, Sir George B., 63–7 n1 & n4 &
  n5
Sarra, Edith, 140, 163 n39, 164 n40
Scarry, Elaine, 6, 7, 24, 28, 30, 31 n19 &
  n21, 35 n76 & n86, 36 n101
Scheherazade, 137
Schimmel, Annemarie, 132, 161 n1, 168
  n98
Seidensticker, Edward G., 42, 58 n28, 78
  n16, 79 n28 & n31, 88, 90, 98 n5,
  105, 108, 114, 119, 121, 124, 135,
  170 n124
Sells, Michael, 161, n4
Shimazu, Hisamoto, 99 n20, 179
Shimizu, Yoshiaki, 32 n32, 32 n34, 35
  n88, 36 n105
Shimizu, Yoshiko, 37–8, 55 n3, 99 n20,
  179
Shirane, Haruo, 78 n19, 93, 93, 106, 113
Spearing, A. C., 132, 143, 144, 161 n3,
  164 n47, 165 n63
Spivak, Gayatri, 66, 78 n15
Stanzel, Franz, 98 n12
Stinchecum, Amanda, 82, 93
Suleiman, Susan Rabin, 63

Taguchi, Eiichi, 57 n23
Takahashi, Tōru, 79, 99 n27, 179
Takehara, Hiroshi, 99 n25, 179
Takeoka, Masao, 99 n27, 179
Tamagami, Takuya, 98 n3, 99 n20, 179
Theocritus, 142
Tokugawa, Yoshinobu, 59 n35
Troyes, Chrétien de, 106, 107, 117, 126,
  128, 131, 136, 138–9, 146, 163 n34,
  165 n66, 168 n101
Tyler, Royall, 30 n1, 57 n28, 88, 90, 91,
  92, 105, 163 n33, 166 n72, 170
  n124

Virgil, 142

Waley, Arthur, 105
Weidner, Marsha, 32 n25
William of Conches, 133
Wolf, Virginia, 78 n12
Wolfram, 134, 136, 162 n14, 164 n41

Yamato, Waki, 44
Yao, Kambei (1660), 56 n22
Yoda, Tomiko, 135, 162 n15, 163 n22
Yokoyama, Hide, 99 n20, 179
Yoshida, Kōichi (1650), 56–7 n22, 179
Yoshizawa, Yoshinori, 99 n20, 179